Toward Decentering the New Testament

"This is the book I wish had been assigned in my days as a young Christian college undergraduate student. The authors go beyond pointing out the hubris of those who think a New Testament introduction can somehow be politically objective or ideologically neutral. Instead, they show us how a 'de-centering' of Scripture—in all its messiness—can serve as a form of 'resistance literature' which opens up ways of thinking *otherwise* and of imagining new worlds altogether."

—**Roberto Sirvent**, Hope International University

"This exemplary volume represents refreshingly unchartered terrain in New Testament introductions, with conceptual and theoretical analyses that will help the reader understand why apprehending the noetic complexities of the politics of empire and power, gender, race, intersectionality, migration, postcolonial theory, and questions of hybridity, and subaltern agency, are thoroughly indispensable in interrogating early Christian origins, and in adjudicating the ever-evolving iterations and often contested implications of what this history means for critical pedagogies and practices of resistance, hope, and justice in our times."

—**Clarice J. Martin**, Colgate University, Hamilton, New York

"The authors bring to the literary surface voices often relegated to the margins. The margin does not replace the center, but through historical, racial, ethnic, class, and gender analyses the book provides tools on how to dismantle its metes and bounds. This work renders a less hegemonic and more inclusive hermeneutical lens for studying the New Testament and the context that produced its content."

—**Stephanie Buckhanon Crowder**, Chicago Theological Seminary

"This book establishes so many firsts. The most important may be that it marks a liminal moment in NT studies. In foregrounding what has been in the background it will open up new worlds of learning for students and teachers alike."

—**Michael Joseph Brown**, President of Payne Theological Seminary

"Mitzi Smith and Yung Suk Kim offer a refreshing orientation to the New Testament that privileges marginalized perspectives, and deftly challenges many traditional assumptions about texts. Impressive in its scope and depth, the book masterfully explicates both historical-cultural contexts such as slavery and contemporary issues like migration. Anyone who reads this book will see the New Testament in a very different light. A much needed addition to biblical scholarship."

—**Raj Nadella**, Columbia Theological Seminary

Toward Decentering the New Testament

— *A Reintroduction* —

Mitzi J. Smith

Yung Suk Kim

FOREWORD BY

Michael Willett Newheart

CASCADE *Books* • Eugene, Oregon

TOWARD DECENTERING THE NEW TESTAMENT
A Reintroduction

Copyright © 2018 Mitzi J. Smith and Yung Suk Kim. All rights reserved. Except for brief quotations in critical publications or reviews, no part of this book may be reproduced in any manner without prior written permission from the publisher. Write: Permissions, Wipf and Stock Publishers, 199 W. 8th Ave., Suite 3, Eugene, OR 97401.

Cascade Books
An Imprint of Wipf and Stock Publishers
199 W. 8th Ave., Suite 3
Eugene, OR 97401

www.wipfandstock.com

PAPERBACK ISBN: 978-1-5326-0465-2
HARDCOVER ISBN: 978-1-5326-0467-6
EBOOK ISBN: 978-1-5326-0466-9

Cataloguing-in-Publication data:

Names: Smith, Mitzi J. | Kim, Yung Suk.

Title: Toward decentering the New Testament : a reintroduction / by Mitzi J. Smith and Yung Suk Kim

Description: Eugene, OR: Cascade Books, 2018 | Includes bibliographical references.

Identifiers: ISBN 978-1-5326-0465-2 (paperback) | ISBN 978-1-5326-0467-6 (hardcover) | ISBN 978-1-5326-0466-9 (ebook)

Subjects: LCSH: Bible. New Testament—Introductions. | Bible. New Testament—Criticism, interpretation, etc. | Marginality, Social—Biblical teaching.

Classification: LCC BS2330 T6 2018 (print) | LCC BS2330 (ebook)

Manufactured in the U.S.A.   08/17/18

Contents

Foreword by Michael Willett Newheart | vii

Chapter 1: Introduction | 1

Section I: Interpretation and Contexts

Chapter 2: Biblical Interpretation: An Invitation to Dialogue | 11

Chapter 3: Greco-Roman and Jewish Influences on the New Testament | 31

Chapter 4: Refugees, Immigrants, and Foreigners in the New Testament | 39

Chapter 5: Roman Slavery and the New Testament | 45

Chapter 6: Intersectionality and Reading Complexity in the New Testament | 52

Chapter 7: The Privatization of Water, Ancient Rome, and the New Testament | 61

Chapter 8: Some Matters of Translation and the New Testament | 67

Section II: The Gospels and Acts

Chapter 9: The Danger of a Single Story: The Synoptic Gospels | 75

Chapter 10: Gospel of Mark | 84

Chapter 11: Gospel of Matthew | 105

Chapter 12: Gospel of Luke | 139

Chapter 13: Gospel of John | 161

Chapter 14: The Acts of the Apostles | 176

Section III: Pauline Epistles

Chapter 15: Significance of Paul as a Jewish Man in Diaspora | 195

Chapter 16: The Body of Christ | 201

Chapter 17: Romans | 205

Chapter 18: 1 Corinthians | 221

Chapter 19: 2 Corinthians | 236

Chapter 20: Galatians | 246

Chapter 21: Ephesians | 254

Chapter 22: Colossians | 262

Chapter 23: Philippians | 266

Chapter 24: Philemon | 272

Chapter 25: 1–2 Thessalonians | 279

Chapter 26: 1–2 Timothy and Titus | 285

Section IV: Catholic Texts

Chapter 27: Letter of James | 295

Chapter 28: Jude | 302

Chapter 29: 1–3 John | 307

Chapter 30: 1 Peter | 311

Chapter 31: 2 Peter | 315

Chapter 32: Hebrews | 319

Section V: The Apocalypse of John/The Book of Revelation

Chapter 33: Contemporary and Ancient Apocalyptic Texts and Their Significance | 329

Chapter 34: Apocalypse of John/Book of Revelation | 334

Bibliography | 353

Foreword

It is a pleasure for me to write this foreword to this very forward-thinking book, with the provocative title *Toward Decentering the New Testament: A Reintroduction*. What does it mean to "decenter" the New Testament (NT)? Why does it need to be "decentered"? And once the NT is decentered, why does it need to be reintroduced? The academic study of the NT has historically been "centered"—and introduced—in white, elite male discourse. Mitzi Smith and Yung Suk Kim wish to decenter—and recenter and reintroduce—the NT in the concerns of "minoritized communities and scholarship." The authors themselves are minoritized scholars teaching in minoritized communities. (Smith is an African American woman teaching predominantly African American seminary students; Kim is a Korean American man teaching in a historically African American seminary.) As they say in chapter 1,

> [T]his [book] is our attempt to move in the direction of a decentered introduction to the NT that privileges many voices, concerns and scholarship of minoritized communities.

And again,

> This text attempts to honor and give space to the voices of minoritized scholars; as an aggregate, we *majoritize* our work and perspectives as authoritative voices and resources for understanding the NT and for further study. [Emphasis theirs]

And finally,

> *Toward Decentering the New Testament* is overtly interested in contemporary social and justice issues.

A NT text that's "overtly interested in contemporary social and justice issues"? Now, that's different, refreshing—and necessary. Most NT introductory texts are interested in the ancient past—the first century and early second, when Jesus and Paul lived and the NT documents were written. But to focus exclusively on the past is to reify the present. And Smith and Kim want to change the present—with all of its violence and injustice—in keeping with Jesus's vision of the kingdom of God. And such is an academic and moral task!

Furthermore, the authors say that this text "privileges many voices." Minoritized scholars do not speak in one voice. This textbook does not do so either. Thus, we read of the richness that is NT study. Finally, these writers "majoritize" minoritized scholarship. And that's a "major" accomplishment. It's forward-thinking! Decentering can be disorienting, but it can be orienting as well because it leads to centering and recentering—and reintroducing. After decentering, then, the reintroduction is so much deeper and fulfilling.

It is amazing that in 2018 we do not have a textbook such as this, a NT introductory textbook that "foregrounds" (rather than marginalizes) minoritized scholars. Indeed, some of the most creative scholarship is coming from such scholars, yet we hear little about it from textbooks that come from the "mainstream" ("male-stream") publishers. This book seeks to redress this error, coming from two such "racialized" scholars who have themselves contributed much to changing the conversation in contemporary NT studies.

As I read the book, I felt excited. This material is not the "same-old, same-old" that most textbooks contain. It includes the material that all introductory textbooks cover (author, date, provenance, themes), but it goes beyond. This book contains fresh perspectives that will make the student—and teacher—sit up and read, ponder, question, and perhaps even act. They might say, "Wow! I have never thought about the NT in this way before. I have never thought about how important issues of race, gender, and class are to the reading of the NT. It is important to get an array of perspectives, and the perspectives of these two—Smith and Kim—speak so pointedly, profoundly, and powerfully. I don't think I'll read the New Testament in the same way again."

This text is "for such a time as this," in which issues of race, power, and social justice are on everybody's—well, maybe not everybody's—mind. I envision this textbook being widely adopted in seminaries and divinity schools, as it fills a gap in contemporary biblical studies. I also see it being studied in church groups because the book seeks to span the gap between the ancient world and our own. Church folks resonate with the authors' approach to the NT as a resource for social justice. This book, then, could serve as an important resource for the church as well as the academy.

FOREWORD

I must admit that most NT introductions are boring. This one is not! It contains some nice turns of phrases, such as "Matthew's Mulatto Messiah" in chapter 12. The authors shared this chapter with me early in the writing stage, and I had students in my own NT Intro read it so as to "test-drive" the chapter (and thus the book). Students found the phrase "Mulatto Messiah" provocative, as they did a number of points in the chapter. Along with my students, I was particularly struck with this line about Jesus's teaching in Matthew: "Revolutionary, liberating teaching breaks open the student and perhaps challenges the teacher too." That statement is true of this textbook too: It is revolutionary and liberating, and it will break open the student and challenge the teacher. I invite you to be liberated, broke open, and challenged.

I am also struck with the physical appearance of the book, which is written with the student in mind. Many chapters begin with a quotation from authors as diverse as Nat Turner, Cornel West, Martin Luther King, Jr., James Baldwin, Dietrich Bonhoeffer, Ahn Byung-Mu, Nelson Mandela, Mahatma Gandhi, Zilpha Elaw, Desmond Tutu, Frederick Douglass, Albert Schweitzer, and Fannie Lou Hamer. Chapters also begin and end with "at a glance" boxes to facilitate learning. And to facilitate reflection, there are "Consider and discuss" boxes, in which the contemporary significance of the NT texts is probed.

Of particular note is chapter 2 when the authors take a dialogical approach to biblical interpretation. It is interpretation as conversation, often personal, allowing us to know who the authors are and what "makes them tick." I have known Smith for over twenty years. She was a student of mine at Howard University School of Divinity, and I have known Kim for over ten years, and we hit it off because we both have concerns about transformation and we both teach NT at historically black theological schools. In this dialogical chapter 2, I learned things about them I did not know. Again, how forward thinking of them!

And this forward thinking is shown in the headings of the book: "Home as Public Contested Space and Fluid Fictive Kinship Boundaries" (Mark), "Faith, Discipleship, and Transformation" (John), "Violence and Unjust Incarceration in Acts," and "Anti-Imperial Reading and 1 Thessalonians." Furthermore, the authors help set up the interpretation of the NT by including important chapters on such diverse topics as translation, water, slavery, and migration. And the following words appear frequently in the text: hybridity, empire, race, gender, class, othering, power, privilege, colonized, minoritized, oppressed. Certainly these words are popular in academic discourse these days, but Smith and Kim demonstrate how using these words can help us develop a transformative view of the NT. Decentering, as well as reintroducing, is transforming!

In the chapter on Matthew, the authors speak about "most traditional readings of Matthew," and then say, "We address . . . " It reminded me of Jesus's own words in the Sermon on the Mount: "You have heard it said of old . . . But I say to you . . . " (Matt 5:21–48). It is that spirit in which this book is written. It acknowledges the "great tradition" of NT interpretation, but it goes beyond it, to something new and transformative.

I do not want to delay you from reading the book itself. I want this foreword to send you forward into the book. You are in for a treat. Your reading of the NT will not be the same after you have read this book. YOU will not be the same. I congratulate the authors for their work. I congratulate you for taking up their work and reading this book. May it take you to levels deeper and wider in the NT than you ever thought possible.

As Jesus says in the middle of his Farewell Discourse in the Gospel of John, "Rise, let us go forward" (John 14:31).

Michael Willett Newheart

Professor Emeritus of New Testament Language and Literature
Howard University School of Divinity

CHAPTER 1

Introduction

Ad astra per aspera! [To the stars through difficulties!]

—Cain Hope Felder[1]

The Bible is too important to be left solely in the hands of the ignorant and the powerful, and after Auschwitz we should know better than to do so.

—Peter J. Gomes[2]

A FEW YEARS AGO, sitting in an Association of Theological Schools (ATS) working group of mid-career scholars in religion, I (Mitzi) shared with my colleagues that I no longer use an introductory text for teaching core New Testament and Old Testament courses (although I am a NT scholar, I teach both testaments at a satellite campus). I am an African American woman and NT scholar/professor whose students are primarily (but not exclusively) African American women and men. I am frustrated when opening an introductory text of the Testaments that either excludes or trivializes the voices of minoritized, nonwhite biblical scholars. I am annoyed and weary of texts on biblical interpretation that misrepresent African American biblical interpretation and ignore and marginalize womanist scholarship. As African American NT scholar Vincent Wimbush aptly states, "In the latter-day empire that is the United States . . . the views, sentiments, passions,

---

1. These were the first words that Cain Hope Felder wrote in my copy of his book *Stony the Road We Trod* on April 27, 1999. I had no idea how difficult and rewarding this road would be, and I almost did not arrive on this road. Sometimes a stop sign is followed by a U-turn.

2. Gomes, *Good Book*, 119. Gomes (1942–2011) was a scholar and professor at Harvard University and Senior Pastor of the Harvard Memorial Church.

testimonies, and interpretations of nonwhites, especially black peoples, are devalued. Their 'readings' within this racialized society are always necessarily understood by the 'white' mind/ear/eyes—in the complex effects of empire, attached to any color of body!—as a 'lack,' a '*mis*reading' of a different kind."[3] I remember feeling violated (not unlike how I felt when I arrived home one night from church to find my front door cracked and that I had been burglarized) as I peeled open a textbook that the majority of my department colleagues voted to use as a common primary text for a core course in biblical interpretation only to find a brief section on African American biblical interpretation that did not mention a single work by an African American biblical scholar but instead peddled Henry Louis Gates's *Signifying Monkey* as the foundation and paradigm for doing African American interpretation. And the chapter was not even written by an African American biblical scholar! One black body was as good as the next, I suppose; we are all equally substitutable to some. As postcolonial biblical scholar R. S. Sugirtharajah has correctly observed, the hermeneutical work of minoritized scholars has, in many cases, been systematically edited out, constituting a "hermeneutical strategy of negation."[4] In introductory texts our words are too often whited-out (I first learned to type on a manual Underwood typewriter when the only method for correcting mistakes or deleting text was a solution or tape called "white out"). As biblical scholar Renita Weems states, "It is not just a matter of whose reading is 'accurate,' but whose reading is legitimated and enforced by the dominant culture."[5] I would never again allow my freedom in the classroom to be usurped, especially not in the matter of textbook selection. A white female colleague in the aforementioned ATS mid-career group said to me, "If you want to write a text, just do it." I never forgot her words. I apologize for not remembering her name, but if she should read this introduction and remember that moment, thank you! Three or four years later I am just doing it, in collaboration with my colleague Dr. Yung Suk Kim who also realizes the need for such a textbook. We both currently teach in spaces where the student body is primarily African American; however, this text is not just for nonwhite minoritized students.

We find that nonwhite students are also socialized and indoctrinated to view texts that are not introductory texts as less authoritative. And sometimes they shun their own voices or the voices of scholars from their own communities. Sometimes minoritized students passively and silently accept

---

3. Wimbush, "Knowing Ex-centrics," 2.
4. Sugirtharajah, "Critics, Tools, and the Global Arena," 57.
5. Weems, "Reading *Her Way* through the Struggle," 63.

the silencing of their voices and concerns out of fear of authority and/or being accused or perceived as introducing race and racism into the classroom or space. They have been taught in too many churches and seminaries that all they need is Jesus, and Jesus is supposedly color-blind. But often race, ethnicity, and gender are not just the elephant in the room; it built the room. Minoritized students are conditioned to view the white male voice as the authoritative voice and the white male body as the most legitimate presence in the classroom, which are also presented as the norm through textbook selections and the lack of real representative diversity among faculties. But as postcolonial biblical scholar Fernando F. Segovia asserts, "Ethnic and racial minorities [scholars] insist on reading with their own eyes [and in their own skin] and making their own voices heard, while challenging their colleagues in the West to do the same, in an explicit and public fashion."[6]

It is necessary that minoritized scholars produce authoritative texts too, not as *the* authoritative or legitimate voice, but as one among other introductory texts. This text, *Toward Decentering the New Testament: A Reintroduction*, is a step in the direction of creating an introductory text that focuses on and prioritizes diverse and nonwhite readers and contemporary issues that affect real flesh-and-blood minoritized readers and our sisters and brothers as allies. It is presumed that what impacts and concerns the least of these among us and/or oppressed communities, effects all of us. This text attempts to honor and give space to the voices of minoritized scholars; as an aggregate, we *majoritize* our work and perspectives as authoritative voices and resources for understanding the New Testament and for further study. Of course, we do not exclude the expertise and foundational work of majority or dominant scholarship, but in this text such contributions are presented alongside perspectives of the authors (an African American woman and an Asian male, both NT biblical scholars) and other minoritized scholars as equally legitimate and authoritative. At times, we may unknowingly slip into a dominant mode of reading or we may oscillate (like a newborn taking her first steps), but this is our attempt to move in the direction of a decentered introduction to the New Testament that privileges many voices, concerns, and scholarship of minoritized communities. We acknowledge the difficulty and the struggle of constructing this text as a decentering project, given that we have been trained in the academy predominated by white males with scholarship produced mainly by white males from the perspective of white males. A white male perspective is presented as objective, value-free, and culturally and ideologically neutral, but it is not. As feminist biblical scholar

---

6. Segovia, *Decolonizing Biblical Studies*, 167

Elisabeth Schüssler Fiorenza asserts, "Interpretation is intrinsically interested and value-laden . . . [but an] *ethics of communication* assesses interpretive practices as to whether they do justice not only to the text and its interpretations but also to contemporary readers."[7]

Toward Decentering the New Testament constitutes our attempt to do justice and our due diligence to students of the biblical text and to produce the work that our souls call us to do. This book is both speaking out and talking back; it is about agency and creativity and resistance to a status quo that systematically or routinely silences the concerns of nonwhite communities and the scholarship they produce. This introductory text constitutes a cultural, spiritual, and political endeavor. The act of raising one's voice in the public sphere, to exercise one's freedoms for or against a cause and the production and dissemination of resources and knowledge, are political acts. It is political to attempt to assist in the cause of freedom in education and to ultimately impact not just individuals and religious institutions, but society at large; we are connected to each other, to the wider world. As Paulo Freire has asserted, "[E]ducation as the practice of freedom—as opposed to education as the practice of domination—denies that [humanity] is abstract, isolated, independent, and unattached to the world; it also denies that the world exists as a reality apart from people."[8] It is a political act to say nothing to address a problem or issue that adversely impacts people's lives, or to teach and write under the guise that only what "dead (or living) white men" have to say is most significant; it goes to who are viewed and treated as the legitimate producers of knowledge and what knowledge can be disseminated as authoritative. A decision to exclude certain contemporary issues or to altogether refuse to address policies, practices, and abuses that impact nonwhite minoritized communities is a subjective choice that reflects individual, communal, cultural, and ideological interests of the dominating group. But an *ethics of accountability* requires that we act responsibly in choosing theoretical interpretive paradigms and addressing and illuminating "the ethical consequences and political functions of biblical texts in their historical as well as in their contemporary sociopolitical contexts."[9] This contemporary sociopolitical context includes the classroom and religious institutions. *Toward Decentering the New Testament* is overtly interested in contemporary social and justice issues; like all human-produced texts, it is ideological and cultural (all people have cultural contexts). We have attempted to make *Toward Decentering the New Testament* accessible to a broad audience. We

---

7. Schüssler Fiorenza, "Defending the Center," 46.
8. Freire, *Pedagogy of the Oppressed*, 62.
9. Schüssler Fiorenza, "Ethics of Biblical Interpretation," 120.

have written it with seminary and divinity school students in mind, but we also hope that undergraduate schools and other religious institutions like churches will find the text useful and accessible for their students, parishioners, or congregants. And we write this text for people who are interested in reading the biblical text but who choose not to occupy a pew in a church. I have not been able to spend much time on Twitter recently, but I have a Twitter follower, a young African American female, who shared that she found her people, her church on Twitter!

This introductory text is cultural, theological, and thematic, and in it we raise critical questions and issues that are relevant to minoritized communities and their allies. We have strategically inserted questions throughout each chapter that introduce a biblical book in order to focus readers' attentions on contemporary concerns and interests in dialogue with biblical texts. We have also placed epigraphs or quotations at the beginning of most chapters, primarily from nonwhite, minoritized peoples. This project is intentionally designed to encourage and center an interpretative agenda that prioritizes contemporary issues and critical engagement with minoritized voices and the biblical texts as read by minoritized scholars—an African American female and an Asian-American male. We solicit critical engagement with contemporary contexts and the relationship between interpretation, lived faith, and communal and global issues like justice, enslavement, neighbor love, poverty, incarceration, suicide, violence, forced and voluntary migration, war, and more. In section 1 (chapters 2–8), beginning with chapter 2 we prioritize the reader as interpreter addressing matters of interpretation in the format of a dialogue between the authors and invite our readers into this space to engage also in critical reflection. In chapter 3, Kim discusses first-century CE Greco-Roman and Jewish historical influences and background for the NT. In chapter 4, "Refugees, Immigrants, and Foreigners in the New Testament," Smith relates contemporary issues concerning the treatment of "others" and/or foreigners and the constructed perpetual foreign other in relation to the study of the New Testament. In chapter 5, "Roman Slavery and the New Testament," Smith provides a brief introduction to ancient Rome as a slave society and its significance for reading biblical texts. In chapter 6, "Intersectionality and Reading Complexity in the New Testament," Smith gives a brief history of the development of the term, how it has traveled across disciplines and is used by biblical scholars as a research tool that raises one's consciousness, and how it can address contemporary social justice issues and hopefully impact our thinking, choices, and behaviors in society for justice. In chapter 7, "The Privatization of Water, Ancient Rome, and the New Testament," Smith discusses the privatization of water in our contemporary context and the problems it causes, especially for the poor, with regard to access to clean and affordable water, Rome's solution to the problem of access to water, and the use and significance of water in the NT. In chapter 8, "Some Matters of Translation and the New Testament," Kim and Smith discuss particular Greek words, phrases, clauses, or verses, such as *pistis Christou* (faith of/in Christ), *dikaiosunē* (righteousness/justice), 1 Cor 7:21, and *doulos* (slave), in order to demonstrate the complexity of NT translation from Greek into English and how context matters.

In section 2, chapter 9, "The Danger of a Single Story: The Synoptic Gospels," Smith introduces students to source criticism and the Synoptic Problem through the lens of internationally known and award-winning Nigerian novelist Chimamanda Ngozi Adichie's TED talk entitled "The Danger of a Single Story." A single story of a people, event, and place creates stereotypes and robs readers of a kind of paradise. In chapters 10–14, we introduce students to the canonical gospels of Mark, Matthew, Luke, and John as well as the Acts of the Apostles. As Smith reads the Gospels of Matthew, Mark, Luke, and the Acts of the Apostles, she sees Jesus as a colonized mulatto revolutionary; God as one who visits the oppressed and downtrodden with hospitality served up with the impossible; Jesus as an unconventional Messiah constantly assailed by border patrols; and an inclusive and empowering God that never relinquishes God's agency, not even to Jesus. In his reading of the Gospel of John, Kim challenges traditional incarnational theology and high Christology in favor of Jesus as the Jewish Messiah who embodies the logos (word) of God. We hope that student-teachers and teacher-students, to use Freire's concept of dialogical education for freedom, will take time, at the beginning and end of each chapter, to ruminate on the epigraphs that head the chapters. After the quotations, each chapter begins with an "at a glance" list of historical, literary, and thematic information about each biblical book or text. The authors approach the chapters from their particular context, raising questions that, we believe, would be of significance to minoritized and non-minoritized peoples and their allies. We use and name resources published by minoritized scholars, as well as malestream or mainstream scholarship. María del Carmen Salazar asserts that one principle and practice of humanizing pedagogy is teaching "students mainstream or dominant knowledge and discourse styles," for doing so, as an additive to "student's prior knowledge and discourse patterns . . . provides students with 'insider' knowledge that is needed to successfully navigate the educational system."[10] However, we hope to leave readers with the realization of that which minoritized

---

10. Salazar, "Humanizing Pedagogy," 140.

scholars already putatively know, which is that our scholarship is significant, impactful, and should/will not be marginalized.

In section 3 (chapters 15–26), we introduce the Pauline epistles, those considered authentically written by him and those that were likely written by his disciples and/or coworkers in ministry. In chapter 15, "Significance of Paul as a Jewish Man in Diaspora," Kim discusses the significance of Paul as a Jewish Pharisee, whom God called to preach the Gospel to the Gentiles and who developed an unwavering passion for the Gentiles and embraced the world as his Diaspora. In chapter 16, "The Body of Christ," Kim investigates the significance of *the body of Christ* as one of the most complex metaphors that the Apostle Paul employs, which means to embody Christ. In chapters 17–31 (sections 3 and 4), we introduce students to Paul's letters, including the catholic or general letters. Kim authored the following chapters: "Romans," "1–2 Corinthians," "Galatians," "Colossians," "Philippians," "1–2 Thessalonians," "1–2 Timothy and Titus," and "1–3 John." And Smith authored "Ephesians," "Philemon," "James," "Jude," "1–2 Peter," and "Hebrews." In chapter 33, "Contemporary and Ancient Apocalyptic Texts and Their Significance," Smith discusses ancient apocalyptic literature through the framework of contemporary apocalyptic film and the apocalyptic vision of the enslaved African Nat Turner who led a slave revolt in Virginia in 1831 as a result of his visions and his reading of the biblical text. In chapter 34, Smith provides an introduction to The Apocalypse of John/Book of Revelation, the only book of its kind in the New Testament, that we might read as the resistance literature of a community that is either under siege or perceives of itself in those terms. Throughout the chapters, we continue the pattern of strategically inserting query boxes containing questions for consideration and discussion. These questions focus students on contemporary issues. At the end of each book chapter, we have inserted lists of summary points that the authors consider significant for recall. Finally, most chapters include suggested further readings, prioritizing the works of nonwhite, minoritized scholars. We hope that this textbook will stimulate readers to engage critically with biblical texts and to initiate dialogue with more and other diverse voices.

Toward Decentering the New Testament is a collaborative project—one in which we worked in partnership primarily by email. We sometimes disagreed about particular matters of interpretation and eventually arrived at a middle ground. This is a give-and-take project that reflects our unique voices and our common goal to provide a decentering text that we would be proud to use in our classrooms and that we hope other teacher-students and student-teachers will as well.

Mitzi J. Smith and Yung Suk Kim

Section I

Interpretation and Contexts

CHAPTER 2

Biblical Interpretation: Invitation to Dialogue

A text has no meaning and history has no path without an interpreter. . . . All reading strategies and theoretical models as well as all recuperations of meaning and reconstructions of history were constructs on the part of such real readers.

—Fernando F. Segovia[1]

Unless we confuse ourselves—as tradition-bearing individuals and communities—with God, we will acknowledge a double relativity: our interpretations are relative to (conditioned by) the presuppositions we bring with us, and those presuppositions, as human, all too human, are themselves relative (penultimate, revisable, even replaceable) and not absolute.

—Merold Westphal[2]

IN THIS CHAPTER, OUR goal is to encourage critical reflection and dialogue regarding matters of biblical interpretation. We list and respond to some questions about biblical interpretation that we (and our students) have raised, consider significant, and that require critical engagement. Of course, we do not consider our responses to be exhaustive in terms of our own thinking or in any way definitive for understanding biblical interpretation. Answers can be less instructive and helpful in developing one's

1. Segovia, *Decolonizing Biblical Studies*, 151.
2. Westphal, *Whose Community? Which Interpretation? Philosophical Hermeneutics for the Church*, 14–15.

interpretive skills than constructing questions. The questions that we raise are sometimes more important than the answers we tend to idolize. We encourage readers to enter the conversation with us and to raise their own questions. Our first question is about how we might define interpretation, and we end with the relationship between interpretation, freedom, and transformation. In between we address the significance of the reader's context and share information about our own personal contexts and our approaches to reading biblical texts, among other subjects. Developing one's own voice and interpretative lens often comes with and through personal experience and reflection and in conversation with our own locatedness as well as in dialogue with other voices.

How Do You Define Interpretation?

SMITH: Interpretation is a dialogical (listening and questioning) process between readers and texts, and it is initiated by readers trying to understand something about the potential meaning(s) of the events, situations, texts, and contexts. Interpretation involves negotiation (give and take) between the reader and texts in the process of meaning-making. Interpretation is an attempt to discern the sense of a text and its possible application or relevance for contemporary life, for one's own life and the life of or within communities. Exegesis (literally meaning to lead or draw out) as a method of interpretation employs historical critical tools (criticisms or interrogation relating to historical context, sources, literary forms, text traditions, text as narrative, and so on). The concept of exegesis superficially demands that readers separate the process of interpretation from their own identities as subjective readers, in my view. I have arrived at the understanding that all exegesis (reading meaning out of a text) is eisegesis (reading meaning into a text); we are always reading into texts, whether we admit it or not, regardless of race/ethnicity, gender, class, or any other social identity markers. Reading does not take place otherwise. As NT postcolonial biblical scholar Fernando Segovia asserts, "All exegesis [is] ultimately eisegesis. . . . There is no objective and impartial reader; all views of the past are contemporary constructions; all interpretation is contextual and ideological."[3] Of course, the language of the text itself and its historical context generally determine some parameters or boundaries in terms of range of meanings that readers can construct.

---

3. Segovia, *Decolonizing Biblical Studies*, 152.

KIM: Interpretation is about explaining biblical texts from various critical perspectives. It involves at least three things: text, reader, and reading lens. A text can be read in many different ways. Namely, meaning can be located "behind the text," "within the text," and "in front of the text." For this diversity of meaning, we need a variety of critical methods, ranging from historical-critical to literary to postcolonial methods. But various textual methods do not guarantee sound interpretation because it is readers who must decide topics to focus. Moreover, we can bring to the text our critical perspectives and experiences. We can embrace certain voices in the text and yet reject other abusive voices. A reading lens or framework deals with hermeneutical (interpretative) choices in terms of, for example, which sense of atonement should be applied to the cause and significance of Jesus's death. Since not all reading lenses are equally preferable, we must critically engage reading lenses, including our own, in conversation with others. Also, biblical interpretation is very complex because there are at least three layers of difficulties concerning interpretation: matters of text, matters of translation, and matters of interpretation. Since we do not have copies of the original Greek text, we must seek a secure or reliable text by deliberate textual study. Even if we have a secure or reliable Greek text, we must have a translation, which is not an easy task. Even if we have a good translation, the meaning of a text is not crystal-clear since explanation is necessary.

Is the Bible a Self-Interpreting Text? Why or Why Not?

SMITH: No, the Bible is not a self-interpreting text. At a minimum it requires the ability to read. In some African slave narratives, we find a literary trope (a technique) called the *talking book*. Enslaved Africans in the American South were forbidden to learn to read or write. Of course, there are a few exceptions; some of the enslaved learned to read and write without their enslavers' consent, but they had to do so secretly or clandestinely. Nevertheless, enslaved Africans saw white preachers and others reading books, particularly the Bible, but also catechisms and prayer books. Some of the enslaved assumed the book was talking to the white person. They did not understand the concept of reading. Thus, when the person stopped reading and left the book unattended, the enslaved African would secretly approach the book and place his or her ear on it, expecting it to speak to him or her. To their great disappointment, the book did not speak to them and some concluded that even God, if the text was a Bible, despised them because of their black skin. This is a poignant example of how at the very least reading any book, including the Bible, requires a level of literacy. The temporal, historical, and cultural (includes language) distance between contemporary readers and the biblical text requires access to information that can help bridge the interpretative gaps. Some gaps we will never be able to bridge; we will never know with certainty an ancient author's intent. The Apostle Paul is not hanging around for me to ask him what he meant, for example, when he wrote 1 Cor 7:21. Even contemporary authors, like myself, cannot always remember what they wrote, let alone why they wrote what they wrote. Yet, we do our best and should remain humble in the face of efforts to interpret the biblical text.

KIM: Strictly speaking, the Bible does not say or speak, but we discover what it means through careful interpretation. Even a single verse can be interpreted from multiple perspectives. For example, John 14:6 ("I am the way, and the truth, and the life. No one comes to the Father except through me") can mean several things. Traditional interpretation looks at the high Christology (divinity of Jesus) and exclusive salvation through Jesus. Jesus is God incarnate and leads people to God. But one alternative interpretation looks at the importance of Jesus's embodiment of God; that is, Jesus as the Son of God shows the way of God through his life. Anyone who follows Jesus may dwell in God. Still other interpreters may see Jesus's saying at 14:6 as his comforting words to the Johannine community, which is in crisis due to separation from the Jewish community.

How Significant Is the Identity and Context of the Reader?

KIM: Biblical texts do not mean anything without the reader. But biblical interpretation is not decided solely by the reader. The reader determines which interpretations are more solid or better than another. Indeed, some readings may be harmful or dangerous for some readers and not for others. Therefore, what is needed is a candid, critical evaluation of interpretations, including one's own interpretation. The positive side of the reader's role in interpretation is that we can discern what is good in the text and what is not acceptable. However, one interpretation cannot apply to all readers or all situations. Since any interpretation is contextual and limited, no one can say his or her interpretation is permanent or universal.

SMITH: Yes, reading or interpreting is very subjective; I read or should read as a subject. I should see myself as a reading subject with agency. The reader and her or his context impacts interpretation throughout the interpretation process, beginning with the selection of a text to read or interpret. Even if I as a reader decide not to interpret for myself but to surrender my agency to commentators, my pastor, or Sunday or Sabbath School teacher as the interpretative authority, this does not negate the fact that their readings are subjective too. Nobody's reading or interpretation is objective or scientific. Sometimes the dominant voices silence and marginalize other voices in their determination of what is good, legitimate, and truthful interpretations. Interpretations that are viewed as liberating interpretations for some women and/or marginalized and oppressed peoples may not be for other readers, especially if it means, for example, loss of privilege or dominance. An interpretation of Gal 3:27–28 as supporting the erasure of hierarchy and subordination and promoting parity and equity, in public, private, and liminal spaces regardless of gender, race, and class is not regarded as a good, legitimate, or truthful translation for some readers. The reader's context is extremely significant. We bring all of who we are to the task of reading or interpreting. We come to the task with biases and experiences of which we may or may not be conscious: our literacy level; our prior knowledge about the text; our individual or personal experiences—the good, bad, and ugly; our theological commitments and beliefs; the doctrines and beliefs of the faith communities that we have joined; and more. For example, one reader's faith community and its leaders may believe that God does not call women to pastoral ministry, and one's commitment to them will impact how one reads the Apostle Paul's exhortation that women are to remain silent. On the other hand, a woman who feels that she has experienced the call of God might read that Pauline injunction silencing women differently or she might feel conflicted depending on other influences that make up her context. If I am a woman that a man has sexually violated, I may gravitate toward certain texts and refrain from others, depending upon where I am in my healing journey.

Describe Yourself as a Reader and How Your Context Impacts the Way You Read

SMITH: I read texts as an educated African American woman who was raised in a loving household with three sisters and one brother. My upbringing significantly impacts how I read and what I choose to read. My African American mother raised us as a single parent. My father developed alcoholism after returning from serving in World War II, and my mother chose to separate from him when I was a baby. I met my father as an adult just before he died from cirrhosis of the liver. I often say I am the first in my immediate family to earn a four-year college degree (I have a first cousin who earned a BS degree in civil engineering). I am the first in my immediate and extended family (and so far, the only one) to earn graduate degrees. My mother attended nursing school in the South for as long as she could financially afford college (after two years). She worked as a nursing assistant and a salad girl in restaurants in Columbus, Ohio, until her legs gave out. My mother raised us from her wheelchair through half of my childhood. Because she did not want her children removed from her home, my mother taught us how to clean house meticulously and to pay attention to details. She was a woman of faith and it was from her that I learned perseverance, faith, compassion, and love for self and others. My mother modeled what it meant to love people unconditionally. I watched her struggle with health issues without proper or any access to medical care most of her life. My interest in social justice and poverty stems from my childhood experiences. I also read biblical texts from womanist and African American reading perspectives, but this comes from my introduction to womanist (and feminist) ways of reading as a master's student at Howard University School of Divinity and then at Harvard. I privilege the experiences, knowledge production, and historical and contemporary artifacts of African American women and our communities. My reading perspective is also informed by my experience as a sexual abuse survivor. I am also interested in engaging with global voices on issues of interpretation and social justice. These are just some of the experiences and contexts that inform my contextual reading of texts. I currently teach and live in the Detroit metro area, and most of my students are African American and female. It is not unusual for my students to have experienced the murder of a child or to write or share their personal experiences as survivors of sexual violence that men have committed against them. All of the above, and more, impact how and what I choose to read.

KIM: I am an Asian-American biblical scholar that grew up in South Korea. I bring my former experience in international business to my study of theology. I was trained as a biblical scholar in the United States, where I teach at a predominantly African American school in the South (Richmond, Virginia). I have a passion for human transformation when I read biblical texts. In light of my hybrid identity living in the US as an American citizen, I focus on issues of identity, transformation, and justice not only in America but in the global village when I read the Bible. This means I often challenge Western interpretations that are based on the imperialistic Christian gospel. On the one hand, as a voluntary immigrant, living and teaching in the Diaspora, I celebrate the diversity of culture and freedom for the pursuit of truth.

On the other hand, I find myself powerless and confused about my cultural academic identity due to racism. With this puzzling context of my life in America, while celebrating the diversity of biblical interpretation, I must challenge the Western interpretation of triumphalism that subjugates the non-Western world and its interpretation in a search for justice and equality. I also consider myself as a global citizen who has solidarity with the powerless and vulnerable in the world. I try to be more than where I am and who I am, attempting to communicate with the world at large.

What Is Unique About the Bible? How Is It Different from Other Texts?

KIM: The Bible contains some unique stories and covenants: the Noachite covenant, the Abrahamic covenant, and the Davidic covenant (Gen 9:1–19; 11:26—17:27; 2 Sam 7:8–17). We also find various stories about ancient Israel ranging from the Davidic monarchy to the Babylonian exile to post-exilic Second-Temple Judaism. But this does not mean that the contents of the Hebre Bible (HB) were not influenced by surrounding cultures such as Egypt or Babylon. The idea of covenant derives from the suzerain treaties in ancient kingdoms. Creation accounts in Genesis are also influenced by various creation myths in the ancient Near East. Various sets of biblical laws in the HB/OT are also borrowed from other cultures in the same region. But biblical writers and Jewish communities do not simply copy and paste various sources/stories of other cultures but use them to recreate the meaning of their time and history. In the NT, Jesus's story is unique, and the significance of his life is reflected upon by his followers. In it, Jesus is declared the Son of God, who does the work of God, risking his life. He is crucified because of his work as God's son, but God raises him. Christians spread the good news of God and of Jesus, testifying to the truth of God, and continuing Jesus's work. But all this does not mean that Christians (or the Bible) possess exclusive truths about God or the salvation of humanity. Indeed, other religious traditions or sacred texts also deal with these topics in their own way. For example, to both Jews and Muslims, Abraham is important in their own ways, and they embrace their sacred traditions. Buddhists and other religionists do not share Abrahamic stories; yet, they discuss truth in regard to their sacred teachings about humanity and the world. Ultimately, what is important is not who owns truth(s) but how different religious traditions can work together, focusing on the work of truth, which is none other than respect for life.

SMITH: Yes, it is important that we do not forget the commonalities we share with our sisters and brothers in other religious traditions. The Jewish Scriptures or the Hebrew Bible compose more than half of our Bible. The Bible consists of many different literary genres or types of literature, including Torah (narratives, instructions, and law codes), prophetic literature, poetry, hymns, myths, or stories about origins or how things came to be or started, genealogies, ancient historical biographies/Gospels, Apocalypse/Revelation, prophetic oracles, miracle stories, exorcism stories, sermons, prayers, parables, letters (and letters within letters), and so on. These diverse literary forms were written by many different authors, known and unknown, and the contents of which covers thousands of years. The Bible is like a collection of documents, like a mini library that has been combined to form an authoritative corpus. The Bible can be purchased in many different English translations as well as in many other languages; it is the most purchased and popular book in the world. Despite this, biblical illiteracy in the US among the churched is increasing. Christians are more illiterate than ever when it comes to their sacred text. Yet, Christians believe that God can speak to humans through the biblical text. It is a sacred text.

What Makes a Text Authoritative? Sacred? What Is the Difference?

SMITH: I think that a community or an individual decides whether or not a text is considered authoritative for individual life and for a community. By authoritative, I am understanding that one allows it to have some power over how one lives one's life, and how and what one believes about God and faith. I know that some Christians regard, at least confessionally, the entire Bible as authoritative, even though they do not consider some texts or teachings as applicable to their lives. For example, the Levitical dietary or culinary laws do not permit the consumption of pork, but many Christians love and eat pork. Or, when Jesus states that if somebody steals your coat, give them your shirt (Luke 6:29); instead we press charges and build a prison nation. Or we treat thieves more harshly rather than with compassion regardless of the reason for the theft (e.g., cold, homeless, mentally ill). It is possible to regard something as sacred and yet not authoritative or only influential over certain aspects of our behaviors and at particular seasons. The Levitical dietary codes can be considered sacred as part of the biblical text that we regard as sacred, but not authoritative for the way we eat, if that is how we relate to them. Belief in God is sacred, but we continually seek to understand God—faith is seeking understanding.

KIM: I agree with my colleague. Authority is not encoded in the text. Rather, it is constructed by a reader's faithful, critical engagement with texts. Readers can choose certain texts and embrace certain interpretations, while rejecting certain texts and interpretations.

What Is the Most Significant Advice You Would Offer to Someone Who Desires to Read the Bible Responsibly?

SMITH: Learn to (re)read for yourself; do not relinquish your agency! Engage with many other perspectives, but develop your own strategies and confidence for reading the biblical text. And do not assume the final word has been said about any given text. Read for a liberating love for God, for yourself, others, and the world.

KIM: I would say, "You need critical interpretive skills to appreciate the full power of a text." I want to add this: "Know yourself, your community, and the world at large" because reading must begin with the self and his/her social location.

What Basic Tools Do You Think Readers Need to Read the Bible Responsibly?

KIM: It is not easy to talk about basic tools that readers need to read the Bible because so many things are involved in reading the Bible responsibly. I believe the most fundamental thing required is a sense of one's identity as a reader. I mean they must know where they are from, what they look for, and why they want to read the Bible. Often, biblical interpretation can be one remote thing that does not connect or communicate to our lives. Or, even if one is helped by the text, one's reading may be naïve. Also, even before one reads the Bible, he or she must be an informed reader, knowing what is happening in society and the world at large. With this self-understanding of the reader, one can read the text closely, in conversation with his/her life situations. Before reaching for a commentary, one must read the text several times and forge something out to further discuss or reflect upon. After this, one can study resources such as a Bible dictionary and related commentaries, articles, or books.

SMITH: Readers should be willing to devote time to reading the biblical text. Too often students express a desire to study the biblical text, and yet they do not invest the time to read it. Some people will watch a movie several times and each time they notice something they missed in previous viewings. The same attitude and enthusiasm should be brought to a reading of the biblical text. So, the first tool is a willingness to do the necessary work and to spend time with the text. Other tools include histories, dictionaries, lexicons, theological word studies, monographs (book length treatments of particular subjects pertinent to the biblical text and its context), journal articles, and commentaries. A word about commentaries: I always advise students to become familiar with the biblical texts they are studying so that they can have an informed conversation with a commentator. Also, students should engage diverse voices and read commentaries, monographs, and essays that reflect many different contexts and perspectives. Absent human diversity (which we should seek as conversation partners), literature can function as a kind of diversity of dialogue partners. And, of course, it can always be helpful to learn a biblical language. But again, it requires an investment in time and energy in and outside of the classroom and beyond in order to learn to use the language at a level that enhances one's reading of biblical texts.

If I Use the Right Tools, Will I Arrive at the Right Interpretation? Why or Why Not?

KIM: Biblical interpretation uses a variety of critical methods, but there is no guarantee that one can get a right interpretation because of the same methods used. This is because interpreters have choices about their research topics, theological perspectives, and ethical considerations. Therefore, what is needed is to read in dialogue with others.

SMITH: The answer to this question lies partly in the plethora of scholarly works on any one biblical book, text, or subject. Even scholars can use, for example, historical critical methods (historical, source, form, textual criticisms), biblical language skills, and so on, and still find considerable disagreement as to the meaning of texts. The answer is a resounding "no!" Again, I think this is because we do bring our own cultural contexts (white and nonwhite peoples), experiences, and methods of interpretation to the task of interpretation. I think perhaps a "right" interpretation is one that liberates, demonstrates love and compassion, and attempts to reincarnate the justice, love, and peace of God.

Is It Acceptable to Critique or Interrogate the Biblical Text, Its Stories, Its Language and Characterizations, Even of God and Jesus?

KIM: Everything in the Bible can be studied, discussed, and evaluated in terms of its validity and value. If there are oppressive, abusive, sexist texts or theologies and ideologies present in the Bible, we can expose them and vehemently reject them. For example, if God appears as a colonialist as in the HB/OT book of Joshua, we need not embrace such a construct of God as cruel and destructive of other peoples. Often, God-talk (theological reflection) emerges out of the human need to understand and be in relationship with God. Since Jesus is variously portrayed and understood in the NT, we need a critical reevaluation of his life, work, and death; he is not exempt.

SMITH: Exactly. It is important to remember that the biblical text is both a human text and a sacred text. Inspiration does not extract or eliminate the messiness of what it means to be human. For me, the miracle is that we can find God in the midst of human fallibility and our mess. Despite that Moses murdered a man and was not held accountable, we hold him up as an example of how God can use a human being to deliver a people from human bondage. We need not overlook Moses's faults. Perhaps, to remember the Exodus is to remember the good, the bad, and the ugly, and to progress in the direction of the good and learn from the bad and ugly. So as the enslaved Africans did, without labeling it as such, we employ a hermeneutics of suspicion, so as not to repeat, imitate, and promote the evil and the ugly—the misogyny (bias, hatred, and violence against women), xenophobia (bias, hatred, and violence against foreigners), slavery, race, and ethnic biases, androcentrism (focus on male interests and concerns at the expense of others), patriarchy (hierarchical subordination of everyone under men), kyriarchy (other forms of hierarchical oppression), holy war, victim blaming, and so on. We have to remember that most texts in the Bible, if not all, were written from elite male perspectives.

Is the Language of the Bible God's Language? Why or Why Not?

KIM: The Bible as a written text must be distinguished from the word of God, which is impossible to hear unimpeded. The Bible is a human medium, although it was inspired to various degrees. Through our reading of the language of the Bible, we can learn things about God and ourselves. But there are also limits to our God-knowledge because the Bible is a human medium that cannot contain all that is God.

SMITH: Yes, we cannot forget that the Bible is a medium—one medium through which God can and does speak to us. Some students think that if they learn biblical koinē Greek or biblical Hebrew, then they can know exactly what God meant to say through the biblical text. This is not the case. Greek and Hebrew are human languages. God was neither Greek nor Hebrew, Jewish nor Aramaic; God is God and God does not need language to communicate, but humans do. The problem of historical and cultural distance and the human medium remain both a channel or medium and an obstacle.

What Role Does Intuition and the Spirit Play in Interpretation?

KIM: The Spirit may work in biblical interpretation. But it must work together with reason. So to speak, what we need is both prayer and critical study.

SMITH: God made us as whole, organic human beings. I believe that intuition is God-given, but it must be sharpened through use, just like our brain power or intellect must be honed by exercise or engagement. God's Spirit works with us and through us. It matters what we give the Spirit to work with. Also, I think the Spirit invites us to engage in critical dialogue with others different from ourselves.

Should We Expect or Desire a Single Authoritative Interpretation of Biblical Texts?

SMITH: Throughout my over twelve years of teaching, invariably every year at least one student asks me if I think that all Christians should think alike or believe in one truth. There are, of course, some things that we agree on, I think: God is creator of all things. God sent Jesus; Jesus lived, ministered, was crucified, and resurrected. There is a lot of stuff in between that we differ on in minute and more extensive ways. I think the only way to ensure that all Christians or religious people in general think alike would be by force. It has happened in Christian history when so-called heretics were burned at the stake, for example. God forbid such evil tactics should ever be instituted again. I believe God values diversity of interpretation; the Bible is a testimony to that, if we believe God inspired it (and this is a concept we all should critically process). Human beings are more threatened by diverse interpretations, than God ever will be. If we choose a single interpretation, whose interpretation would we choose? Many interpretations are valid and legitimate. We should seek interpretations, in my view, that are liberating (engender freedom) and relevant to the real lived experiences and circumstances of human beings in their various contexts.

KIM: One single authoritative interpretation is impossible because the Bible contains divergent voices in different writings, written in different times. Instead, we must celebrate the diversity of biblical interpretation. Meaning should not be controlled by one person or one special group of Christians or scholars. But at the same time, not all interpretations are equally valid or good. Therefore, we must evaluate other readings, including our own.

The Bible Is Invoked in the Public Square by Politicians and Others. What Does the Bible Have to Do with Politics?

KIM: The Bible has political implications for our contemporary world. For example, our thoughts and actions about and in our world depend on how we perceive of Jesus and his work. Is he a Jewish prophet who challenged Rome and Jerusalem because of lack of justice? Is he a mere spiritual savior who paves the way to heaven? How can we interpret his proclamation of the kingdom of God? Is God's kingdom established here or only in another place in the future? Our political involvement in the world may be impacted, depending on how we answer these questions.

SMITH: True. It is also important to know that the biblical text itself is full of political intrigue and the mingling of politics and religion. Despite its metaphorical use in the NT, a kingdom is a political entity; the construction of and desire for a nation and nationalism are political ideas and movements. Politics and religion merge when characters in a sacred text assert that God instructed them to take another people's land and to kill all the inhabitants in the process or even when God is that chartacter. Biblical interpretation is a political act; in a sense it is a meta-political act. It is political when biblical interpretations are used to support the enslavement of entire peoples. It is political when our biblical interpretations impact the social positions we take for or against the poor/poverty, war, foreigners/

immigration, gun violence, women's rights, police brutality, education, and so on. It is political to say which interpretations are more legitimate and which are not or who can produce legitimate knowledge. These types of decisions create a hierarchy of knowledge and knowledge production, and hierarchy is necessarily political.

What Does It Mean to Read the Biblical Text Closely?

SMITH: In order to read the biblical text closely, I encourage students to try to be aware of the presuppositions they have about the meaning of the text and try to be open to the text and the Spirit of God saying or showing them something new or different. If we understand the God of the text as a living God, then God continues to speak. The text itself may be static as literature, but the God about which it purports to bear testimony is not. We should also keep in mind that God transcends the biblical text. And by this statement I mean that God is not synonymous with the Bible itself. To think otherwise would be to reduce God to a piece of literature, even if it is considered sacred; God becomes an idol, a human made one and one who only fairly recently appeared on the scene with the invention or improvement of writing mediums and tools or the printing machine. This brings me to a second point: The Bible is literature, and it is a tangible medium of communication. It is also an artistic form: portions of it are poetic or poetry; most of the prophetic literature, for example, is poetry. The biblical text contains literary forms that include hymns or songs, historical narratives, parables, metaphors, miracle stories, exorcism stories, and so on.

Similarly, to read the Bible closely is to be open to reading it again and again and again. Do not assume you know everything in the text and there is nothing more to see or to know. The same rings true for God; we cannot know everything there is to know about God either through the biblical text or through personal encounters with God. As the Apostle Paul says, we see through a glass darkly. But we continue to peer through that glass hoping the image will become a little clearer and more focused each time, perhaps adjusting our lens to see it from different angles and perspectives. God is a multidimensional God, I like to believe. God is accessible and yet inaccessible. God is God; we are human beings created by God.

As we re-read or revisit the biblical text, we should pay attention to the smallest literary units (words) and the larger units like stories/narratives and letters or books and how they interconnect and mutually impact one another. Pay attention to how characters are described and how they interact with each other. We should ask questions as we read and note our questions and observations. For example, who is speaking and acting? Who is silenced and rendered invisible? What difference does it make? Of course, close reading also involves a search for historical contexts and how they help us understand our text.

KIM: I agree with my colleague. Reading the biblical text closely means various things and requires an informed, critical reading. In my case, for example, the occurrence of the word *faith* requires a close, critical reading of the NT. Faith is diversely—often divergently and complexly—understood in various writings of the NT; it is never a mono sound. First, we can see God is the most faithful character in the Bible. God calls Abraham out of nowhere and gives him hope. Second, the Messiah Jesus is faithful to God and embodies God's love and justice in a chaotic world. The result is his crucifixion, because the dominant classes oppose his message and ministry. A Christian Gospel that does not emphasize Jesus's faith is hollow and naïve. Third, we see the faith of Christians who trust God and the Messiah Jesus. Fourth, there is another concept of faith; that is, faith can refer to specific knowledge or teaching about God and Jesus. This aspect of faith appears mostly in the Deutero-Pauline and Pastoral Letters where one of the major issues is false teaching. Fifth, in Hebrews, faith is understood as assurance or conviction. Here, faith signifies that God is with his people under any circumstances. Lastly, in James, we see the work of faith. Faith without works is dead: "a person is justified by works and not by faith alone" (Jas 2:24). Of course, the above aspects of faith are not exhaustive, but the point is that a close reading should recognize the diverse ways that the word *faith* is used in the NT. Otherwise, readers should not absolutize one understanding or one aspect of faith.

How Do You Understand Ideas Like *Freedom* and *Transformation* in Relation to Reading the NT?

KIM: Freedom and transformation are very important to me as a NT scholar. The Messiah Jesus worked to liberate the oppressed and marginalized from the grips of the Roman Empire and elites. He proclaimed "the good news of God," not the good news of Caesar or of the High Priest in Jerusalem. He healed the sick, fed the hungry, ate with the "sinners," motivated them to rise against all restraints, and wept for the daughters of Jerusalem. All that Jesus did was to help the oppressed live a life of freedom. Jesus's followers should base their action on Jesus's teaching. Then, they will know the truth, and the truth will make them free (John 8:32). Notice here the future tense of "the truth will make them free," which means freedom is yet to be realized; it comes after one follows the footsteps of Jesus. Freedom is not completed even though Jesus died for freedom.

For me, transformation means a change of self, community, and the world. John's water baptism was a means of entering a world of transformation, based on God's justice and peace. The Greek word *metanoia* means a change of mind, not a repentance as most of us understand it. *Metanoia* is not like a penitential prayer of confession of one's sins. The Hebrew equivalent is *shub*, which means "to turn back" or "return." That is, a return to God is important. John was committed to renewing a Jewish society by calling for a change of mind toward God. Now after John was arrested, Jesus continued his transformative work, proclaiming God's good news, starting with Galilee. He declares that God's time or God's rule has come or is present now; in the present, people are asked to change their minds toward God. Jesus said that now is the time that they must embrace a new rule of God by seeking God's mercy and justice. The Apostle Paul also asks for a renewing of mind to seek the will of God (Rom 12:1–2). Likewise, we need to transform ourselves, moving away from sectarianism, triumphalism, individualism, exclusivism, and any ideological constructs that hegemonize or oppress others.

SMITH: For me, at this moment, as an African American woman who stands in solidarity with the most vulnerable among us—"the least of these" as Matthew's Gospel puts it—I read for freedom. Freedom and transformation are interconnected. The Apostle Paul says, "For freedom Christ has set us free. Stand firm, therefore, and do not submit again to a yoke of slavery" (Gal 5:1). Slavery in our contemporary contexts may be understood historically and metaphorically. As a metaphor it signifies various systems of oppression, including racism, sexism, heterosexism, classism, and so on. The Galatian believers had experienced a change or revolution from enslavement to freedom. Freedom is not just freedom to do something, but freedom from oppression, hatred, violence, poverty, and so on. A function of truth, according to John's Jesus, is to set people free or to liberate. I think the closer we come to the Truth as a full revelation of God, the freer we become. I also think that faith as seeking understanding, the pursuit of the Truth about God is for human beings a perennial search—the search of a lifetime that remains incomplete when we die. The more freedom-loving and free we become the more we recover the image of God in us that has been tainted by sin. And the more we understand or discover about God, the more we experience and encourage freedom. The more freedom-loving and free we become the more justice-loving and justice-doing we become and the less oppressive and violent we will be toward ourselves, other human beings, and the earth over which God has given us guardianship for our benefit. Just as the Sabbath was made for human beings and not human beings for the Sabbath, it is the same with the earth, I believe. We are, if we choose, forever becoming more human and will act more responsibly. God created us to be human and humane. So as we learn and practice reading Scripture with transparency, with vulnerability toward God, our own insecurities as individuals, groups, and communities, we discover truths and Truth. Again, God is not synonymous with the biblical text. As human beings created in the image of God, we are sacred texts that God pronounced as very good and set apart for good and redeemed for good. I think most religious people, Christians and otherwise, would acknowledge that it is not by reading our sacred texts alone that we came to believe in God but by personal experiences or encounters with the divine. The biblical text was not the first to tell me that God calls women, calls me to ministry; it was God speaking to me, beyond the text. Some people do not like the word "transformation," but I have not heard a better suggestion (this does not mean none exists). Our language is limited, but God's action is not; God is not limited by our words—those that we speak or that we read printed in text, even sacred texts. God in various ways engenders transformation or change toward freedom in our lives and in the world. I think the more we allow God to transform us the more vulnerable we become in the direction of freedom, justice, love, and peace. This does not mean we become more certain about our interpretations and constructions of God, but we become more humble about them and therefore more open to freedom, not just for myself but for others different from me. God took a chance when God created humans with free will and this earth; we are the product of God's vulnerability and humility. This same vulnerability and humility should be brought to our reading of sacred texts in order to engender freedom and transformation.

Further Reading

An, Choi Hee, and Katheryn Pfisterer Darr, eds. *Engaging the Bible: Critical Readings from Contemporary Women*. Minneapolis: Augsburg Fortress, 2006.

Bailey, Randall C., Tat-Siong Benny Liew, and Fernando F. Segovia, eds. *They Were All Together in One Place? Toward Minority Biblical Criticism*. Semeia Studies 57. Atlanta: Society of Biblical Literature, 2009.

Bailey, Randall, et al. "African and African Diasporan Hermeneutics." In *The Africana Bible*, edited by Hugh R. Page Jr., 19–24. Minneapolis: Fortress, 2010.

Bird, Jennifer G. *Permission Granted: Take the Bible Into Your Own Hands*. Louisville: Westminster John Knox, 2015.

Blount, Brian K. *Cultural Interpretation: Reorienting the New Testament*. Minneapolis: Fortress, 1995.

Brettler, Marc Zvi. "Biblical Authority: A Jewish Pluralistic View." In *Engaging Biblical Authority: Perspectives on the Bible as Scripture*, edited by William P. Brown, 1–9. Louisville: Westminster John Knox, 2007.

Brock, Rita Nakashima. "Dusting the Bible on the Floor: A Hermeneutics of Wisdom." In *Searching the Scriptures*. Vol. 1, *A Feminist Introduction*, edited by Elisabeth Schüssler Fiorenza, 64–75. New York: Crossroad, 1997.

Brown, Michael Joseph. "Hearing the Master's Voice." In *Engaging Biblical Authority: Perspectives on the Bible as Scripture*, edited by William P. Brown, 10–17. Louisville: Westminster John Knox, 2007.

Brueggemann, Walter, William C. Placher, and Brian K. Blount. *Struggling with Scripture*. Louisville: Westminster John Knox, 2002.

Byron, Gay L., and Vanessa Lovelace. *Womanist Interpretations of the Bible: Expanding the Discourse*. Atlanta: Society of Biblical Literature, 2016.

Callahan, Allen Dwight. *The Talking Book: African Americans and the Bible*. New Haven: Yale University Press, 2006.

Cannon, Katie. "The Biblical Mainstay of Liberation." In *Engaging Biblical Authority: Perspectives on the Bible as Scripture*, edited by William P. Brown, 18–28. Louisville: Westminster John Knox, 2007.

Cardoza-Orlandi, Carlos F. "'Lámpara es a mis pies tu palabra': Biblical Authority at the Crossroads." In *Engaging Biblical Authority: Perspectives on the Bible as Scripture*, edited by William P. Brown, 27–35. Louisville: Westminster John Knox, 2007.

Countryman, William. "Reading Scripture—and Rereading It." *Anglican Theological Review* 86 (2004) 573–84.

Day, Linda, and Carolyn Pressler. *Engaging the Bible in a Gendered World: An Introduction to Feminist Biblical Interpretation in Honor of Katharine Doob Sakenfeld*. Louisville: Westminster John Knox, 2006.

De la Torre, Miguel. *Reading the Bible from the Margins*. Maryknoll, NY: Orbis, 2006.

Felder, Cain Hope, ed. *Stony the Road We Trod: African American Biblical Interpretation*. Minneapolis: Fortress, 1991.

Fiensy, David A. *Insights from Archaeology. Reading the Bible in the 21st Century.* Minneapolis, Fortress, 2017.

Gafney, Wil. "Reading the Hebrew Bible Responsibly." In *The Africana Bible*, edited by Hugh R. Page Jr., 45–51. Minneapolis: Fortress, 2010.

Green, Joel B., ed. *Hearing the New Testament: Strategies for Interpretation.* 2nd ed. Grand Rapids, MI: Eerdmans, 2010.

Heinrichs, Steve, ed. *Unsettling the Word. Biblical Experiments in Decolonization.* Manitoba, CN: CommonWord, 2018.

Isasi-Díaz, Ada María. "La Palabra de Dios en Nosotras—The Word of God in Us." In *Searching the Scriptures.* Vol. 1, *A Feminist Introduction*, edited by Elisabeth Schüssler Fiorenza, 64–75. New York: Crossroad, 1997.

Kim, Yung Suk. *Biblical Interpretation: Theory, Process, and Criteria.* Eugene, OR: Pickwick, 2013.

———. *Resurrecting Jesus: The Renewal of New Testament Theology.* Eugene, OR: Cascade, 2015.

Patte, Daniel. *Ethics of Biblical Interpretation: A Reevaluation.* Louisville: Westminster John Knox, 1995.

Perry, Peter S. *Insights from Performance Criticism.* Minneapolis: Fortress, 2016.

Richards, E. Randolph, and Brandon J. O'Brien. *Misreading Scripture with Western Eyes: Removing Cultural Blinders to Better Understand the Bible.* Downers Grove, IL: Intervarsity, 2012.

Schüssler Fiorenza, Elisabeth. *Jesus and the Politics of Interpretation.* New York: Continuum, 2000.

———. *Rhetoric and Ethic: The Politics of Biblical Studies.* Minneapolis: Augsburg Fortress, 1999.

Segovia, Fernando F., and Stephen D. Moore. *Postcolonial Biblical Criticism: Interdisciplinary Intersections.* New York: T. & T. Clark, 2007.

Segovia, Fernando F., and Mary Ann Tolbert, eds. *Teaching the Bible: The Discourses and Politics of Biblical Pedagogy.* Minneapolis: Fortress, 2009.

Sharp, Carolyn J. *Wrestling the Word: The Hebrew Scriptures and the Christian Believer.* Louisville: Westminster John Knox, 2010.

Slater, Thomas. *Afrocentric Interpretations of Jesus and the Gospel Tradition: Things Black Scholars See that White Scholars Overlook.* New York: Edwin Mellen, 2015.

Smith, Mitzi J. *Insights from African American Interpretation*. Minneapolis: Fortress, 2017.

———, ed. *I Found God in Me: A Womanist Biblical Interpretation Reader*. Eugene, OR: Cascade, 2015.

Soulen, Richard N. *Sacred Scripture: A Short History of Interpretation*. Louisville: Westminster John Knox, 2009.

Sugirtharajah, R. S. *The Postcolonial Bible*. Sheffield: Sheffield, 1998.

———. *The Postcolonial Biblical Reader*. Malden, MA: Blackwell, 2006.

———. *Voices from the Margin: Interpreting the Bible in the Third World*. Maryknoll, NY: Orbis, 1997.

Tiffany, Frederick C., and Sharon H. Ringe. *Biblical Interpretation: A Roadmap*. Nashville: Abingdon, 1996.

Trible, Phyllis. "Authority of the Bible." In *The New Interpreter's Study Bible*, edited by Walter Harrelson, 2248–54. Nashville: Abingdon, 2003.

Wimbush, Vincent L., ed. *African Americans and the Bible: Sacred Texts and Social Textures*. New York: Continuum, 2003.

———, ed. *MisReading America: Scriptures and Difference*. New York: Oxford University Press, 2013.

Wright, *The Last Word: Beyond the Bible Wars to a New Understanding of the Authority of Scripture*. New York: HarperSanFrancisco, 2005.

Yamasaki, Gary. *Insights from Filmmaking for Analyzing Biblical Narrative*. Minneapolis: Fortress, 2016.

Yang, Seung Ai. "The Word of Creative Love, Peace, and Justice." In *Engaging Biblical Authority: Perspectives on the Bible as Scripture*, edited by William P. Brown, 132–40. Louisville: Westminster John Knox, 2007.

CHAPTER 3

Greco-Roman and Jewish Influences on the New Testament

THE NEW TESTAMENT WAS written in Greek and composed in Roman cities outside the Jewish land. But it is about Jesus the Jew who proclaimed the good news of God in Galilee and elsewhere in Palestine. After he died, the significance of his life and work was widely circulated among his followers. Stories about him reached big cities throughout the Roman Empire such as Syrian Antioch, Alexandria, and Rome. The Jesus tradition continued to be told and retold throughout the first century CE and beyond. At some point, just before or during the First Jewish War (66–70 CE), Mark was written down. Some scholars believe that Jesus's sayings gospel (the hypothetical gospel called Q, which is from the German word *Quelle* meaning "source") existed before Mark. In 85–90 CE, Matthew and Luke were composed with the use of Mark and Q as common sources (see chapter 9). John was composed a little later than Matthew or Luke. Outside of these canonical Gospels, the Coptic version of the *Gospel of Thomas* (dated to the fourth century CE) was discovered in Nag Hammadi, an Egyptian monastery, in 1945. Thomas is composed of 114 sayings attributed to Jesus. But the early fragmentary Greek version is dated to about the early second century CE. Thomas was heavily influenced by Gnosticism, which features a dualism between the body and soul, knowledge of divine secrets, and so on. As more time passed, during the second to fourth centuries CE, a good number of Christian apocryphal gospels were written to fill in the gap regarding Jesus's childhood or marriage, for example. The Gospel spread quickly throughout the major Roman cities. An overall picture of the NT against its cultural and religious background follows in this order: (1) Hellenization and the New Testament; (2) First-century Judaism, Jesus, Paul, and the New Testament.

Hellenization and the New Testament

Hellenization has to do with the spread or promotion of Greek culture, language, religion, and philosophy that Alexander the Great (356–323 BCE) brought to his conquered regions. He died in 323 BCE and his kingdom was divided into four kingdoms ruled by his generals. But his legacy of Hellenization continued throughout the Roman Empire. For Greek-speaking Jews living outside Palestine, the Hebrew Bible was translated into Greek, which is known as the Septuagint (LXX). Under this cultural environment, it is not surprising that the NT was written in *koine* (common) Greek. With the openly shared Greek language and the development of convenient travel routes throughout the Roman Empire, the Gospel spread quickly. In what follows, we see further a range of cultural influences upon the formation of the NT and the early Jesus movement.

First, polytheism is the religious view of the Roman Empire where people are free to worship any gods but are asked to participate in emperor veneration (worship) and other state cults. Mystery religions such as Isis (Egyptian goddess) worship and Mithraism (cult of Persian deity Mithras) were very prominent in this time because people wanted peace and security in their chaotic lives. The Gospel is introduced to this polytheistic world. On the one hand, early believers, as in Thessalonica where Paul established his first diaspora *ekklēsia* (often anachronistically translated "church"), experienced hardships and persecution because of their commitment to the God of Jews. On the other hand, the Gospel was viewed with suspicion by the Roman populace because it was deemed a new and mysterious cult. In fact, in ancient times, anything new was considered suspicious. By contrast, Judaism was highly regarded given its long history and traditions.

Nevertheless, the *ekklēsiai* or Jesus movements grew fast and their message was accepted and worked in ways that the Gentiles felt secure and peaceful amidst the chaos and insecurity of the empire. Jesus was presented as the Son of God and the Messiah who exemplified God's way and his righteousness or justice. His teaching about "the *basileia* of God" (*kin*dom/kin-dom or Divine rule*) is different from that of Rome. Whereas the Gospel has an appeal to the poor, the enslaved, and other marginalized persons through tangible compassion, equality, and love in Christ, the imperial gospel compels people to follow a rigid system of hierarchy that serves the upper classes only. The early Christian groups were very much like voluntary associations in society and showed God's love to people in need, distinguishing themselves from the pagans.

Second, Stoicism is the most influential philosophy or ruling ideology in the first-century Roman Empire, which has implications for the NT and the early *ekklēsiai*. Stoicism originated with Zeno (ca. 336-265 BCE) in Athens, who emphasized the importance of universal reason and the goodness of ethical life based on virtue. His influence is seen in many philosophers throughout the period of the Roman Empire, including Epictetus (ca. 55-135 CE). During the first century CE, we see some common characteristics of Stoicism: the idea of one world, unity or concord (*homonoia*), and virtue ethics based on self-control. This idea of "one world" was adopted by Paul and Luke, both of whom carried the Gospel to the global stage, with a resulting widespread impact. Paul calls himself the apostle to the Gentiles, and Luke makes Jesus the savior of the world. But the details of their vision for one world, as shown in their writings, are not the same. While Paul's vision sometimes opposes the Roman Empire's program, Luke does not challenge it politically. Paul's view of "one world" is very different from that of Stoicism, and his body politics is basically egalitarian as he says in Gal 3:28: "There is no longer Jew or Greek, there is no longer slave or free, there is no longer male and female; for all of you are one in Christ Jesus."[1] By contrast, the body politics of Rome is hierarchical and exploitive. Stoicism emphasizes unity and not equality of people. In that view, society is one not because all are treated equally but because it is viewed as an organism. Stoics view society as an unequal, hierarchical system. Likewise, the human body is also understood hierarchically, as the Menenius fable demonstrates. According to the fable, one day hands and feet rebelled against the belly because it did not work and ate all the time. They complained that life is unfair and that they were not going to work any longer. The belly then said, "That is fine with me. If you go on strike, I will be starving to death, and then you will also die." The rhetorical point of this fable is obvious in that the enslaved must work hard without complaints.

Paul refutes the body politics of Rome and the Stoics, as he suggests in 1 Cor 12:12-27. In 1 Cor 12:12, he says that the body is one, but has many members. This sounds like Stoic philosophy. But his body politics is egalitarian, and for him, the body is not a hierarchical organism but a system of care and support. All different parts, wherever or whatever they are, are united to the same body, rejoicing and suffering together.

Third, there is also a difference between Stoicism's virtue ethics based on self-control and a Christian understanding of it. In Stoicism, self-control touches on inner peace alone without dealing with social justice in

---

1. While Gal 3:28 confirms Paul's view of the egalitarian community, 1 Cor is a bit ambiguous about his view of the community. On the one hand, women in the Corinthian *ekklēsia* are free to participate in worship and receive the gift of the Spirit equally with men (cf. 1 Cor 11:5; 12:4-11). On the other hand, Paul seems to affirm gender hierarchy in 1 Cor 11:2-16. We address this further in chapter 18.

society. Stoic philosophy ignores the prophetic voices that challenge the unjust society. But in the Gospel, it applies to a broad range of life, including personal and communal matters, seeking peace and justice for all in the community.

First-Century Judaism, Jesus, Paul, and the New Testament

From cradle to grave, Jesus and Saul/Paul (the former being his Jewish name, the latter his Roman name) were first-century Jewish men who practiced Judaism. First-century Judaism can be characterized variously. First, apocalyptic Judaism is one popular trend during this period because Jews yearn for a better place to live away from foreign domination. Jews look for the Davidic Messiah who will deliver them from the hegemony of the Roman Empire. For example, Essenes in the Qumran community expect two kinds of Messiahs: a Teacher and a Priest. Other Jews believe that the Son of Man figure, like the one in the Book of Daniel, will appear in the last day to judge the world and restore God's *basileia* on earth.

Second, first-century Judaism is hardly a unified religion, contrary to what is commonly thought. According to Josephus, there are four different sects within Judaism that rival one another: Pharisees, Sadducees, Essenes, and the Fourth Philosophy. The Pharisees are among the most learned and emphasize the strict observance of the law. They believe in the resurrection and keep the oral Torah as well. Their zeal for God and the law is well-known among the populace. The Sadducees are wealthy aristocrats who run the Temple. They consider only the five books of Moses (the Pentateuch or Torah) to be authoritative and do not believe in the resurrection. The Essenes are an apocalyptic, sectarian group that withdraws to the desert (Qumran), forming their own ascetic community, interpreting their scriptures, and waiting for their own messiahs. They dislike the leadership of the Jerusalem Temple and claim that they alone are the children of light. The Jerusalem priests are the sons of darkness. The Fourth Philosophy (Zealots) is a group of people who wage an armed resistance against Roman domination. These people are close to the spirit of the Maccabean revolt that broke out against the Seleucid Empire in the second century BCE (167–160 BCE), resulting in the Hasmonean rule. Additoinally the Acts of the Apostles refers to the Jesus movement is also referred to as a new sect within Judaism (28:22)

Third, we also must see first-century Judaism through the lens of economic exploitation. Many people, especially the Galilean peasants, suffered considerably because of the various forms of oppression and evil. Heavy taxation by Rome and Jerusalem, coupled with abuses perpetrated by local elites, proved unbearable at times. Jesus's teaching about the *basileia* of God, including many of his parables, can be understood within this socioeconomic and political context.

Fourth, we also must consider the First Jewish War (66–70 CE) seriously because Jews struggled to define their identity in a time when the Temple had been destroyed. The period 70 CE was a time of (re)formation for both Jews and Jewish and Gentile Christians because they had to resettle their lives without the Temple. Mainline Judaism shifted its focus to the study of scripture and worship in any place. Christian communities, as seen especially in the Gospels, also deal with the absence of the Temple by reinterpreting it through the significance of Jesus.

Jesus and the New Testament

Against the backdrop of first-century Judaism, Jesus the Jew must be placed somewhere in the spectrum of the Jewish world under the Roman Empire. His teaching is similar to that of the Pharisees in some respects because Jesus also emphasizes the God of Jews and Jewish Scriptures. Jesus, like the Pharisees, believes in the resurrection. But the difference between Jesus and some of the Pharisees is also distinct. Jesus interprets the law flexibly and sometimes very radically, but not in every respect. For example, a radical Jesus can be seen when he breaks the law to promote human welfare over the objections of some Pharisees and heals the sick on the sabbath. Jesus says, "The sabbath was made for humankind, and not humankind for the sabbath" (Mark 2:27). He also reinterprets the law, as he does in the Sermon on the Mount (Matt 5:17–48). That is, even hate is deemed the same as murder. Jesus's teaching is also distinct because his parabolic teaching about God's reign challenges the power center of society. He challenges a culture of self-seeking and greatness and teaches the importance of humility and the rule of God in the present. Yet, it is a mistake to think that Jesus was the only Jewish Rabbi to share such views.

One pivotal question about Jesus in history concerns his view of the end-time (apocalyptic eschatology). Did he expect that the end would come during his lifetime, as Mark 9:1 states? "Truly I tell you, there are some standing here who will not taste death until they see that the kingdom of God has come with power." The issue is whether Mark 9:1 comes from the mouth of the historical Jesus. Scholars are divided over this issue. Given the urgent apocalyptic atmosphere in Mark, some suggest that Mark 9:1 is a redaction by the author. But it is also plausible that Jesus must have shared a core belief about apocalypticism with other Jews, since in the first century CE most Jews believed that the messianic age would come in the end. But it is highly questionable that Jesus was confident in predicting such an end during his lifetime. There are several reasons. In Mark and elsewhere, Jesus says that God alone knows the end time (Mark 13:32; Matt 24:36; cf Acts 1:6–7). Also, he thinks of himself as a human being who cannot replace God (Mark 10:18). His point is not when the end would come but how much of God's rule can be implemented among people in the present. Mark 1:15 signals such an idea very well: "The time is fulfilled, and the kingdom of God has come near; repent, and believe in the good news." *Kairos* (time) has come (the perfect tense), and the *basileia* of God (God's rule) has come near (the perfect tense). He does not say that God's rule will come in the future. Rather, it has already come and will be fulfilled day by day. His logic is because God's rule came to the world, now they have to change their mind toward God. Even though the end did not come completely, the end began with his teaching and work. Jesus's real focus is not how soon the end will come but how much God's reign will be realized in the present. This view of time or the *basileia* of God is called a tensive symbol, as opposed to a steno symbol.[2] While the latter points to a particular time of God's rule, the former emphasizes God's activities (which are God's rule) on earth.

Jesus's teaching and work focused on changes in real life in the present, and as a result, he was crucified on the cross because his deeds posed a threat to the Roman authorities, including the Jerusalem leaders. After he died, his teaching and life were remembered by his followers and spread all the way to Rome and elsewhere in the Roman Empire and beyond. But strictly speaking, the historical Jesus is different from portrayals of him in the Gospels because the gospel communities understood him in their own ways. For example, in my view, the Markan Jesus comes not to be served but to serve, and to give his life a ransom for many (Mark 10:45). The Matthean Jesus comes to fulfill the law and the prophets because the Matthean community takes up the issue of the law (Matt 5:17). The Lukan Jesus comes to seek out and to save the lost because Luke emphasizes the need of salvation for the Gentiles (Luke 19:10). The Johannine Jesus comes to testify to the truth because it is his primary mission (John 18:37).

Paul and the New Testament

Besides Jesus, Paul is of paramount importance to the NT not only because he wrote many letters, but because his apostolic work is distinguished from

---

2. Perrin, *Jesus and the Language*, 71–80.

his former life in the Jewish Diaspora (outside of Palestine). He was a Pharisee who was raised by Jewish parents within their Jewish culture. He believed that the God of the Jews is for Jews only and all the laws must be kept strictly based on the Pharisaic tradition. Thus, he could not stay at home when he saw those who believed in Jesus as God's Messiah preaching about the Jewish God, as Gal 1:13 hints: "You have heard, no doubt, of my earlier life in Judaism. I was violently persecuting the *ekklēsia* of God and was trying to destroy it." He also thought that the true Messiah was unlike Jesus who was crucified. But at a certain point in time, God revealed his Son to him (Gal 1:16). Most probably, his call is close to that of the Hebrew prophets. When Paul was called, he was given a special mission to the Gentiles.

Because of this revelatory experience with Jesus, Paul changes his view of God, God's Messiah, and the Law. Rom 3:29–31 indicates his changed view of God: "Or is God the God of Jews only? Is he not the God of Gentiles also? Yes, of Gentiles also, since God is one; and he will justify the circumcised on the ground of faith and the uncircumcised through that same faith. Do we then overthrow the law by this faith? By no means! On the contrary, we uphold the law." Paul's view of the Messiah also radically changes. Formerly, the true Messiah was thought to be someone like David, who could liberate the Jews from Rome. But now he believes that Jesus, the crucified one, is the true Messiah who demonstrated God's righteousness to the world through faith (cf. Rom 3:21–22). Paul's view of the law also changes. While the law is holy and good, it cannot be absolutized because what comes first is God's grace or promise. Then faith comes and accepts God's grace. Children of God must live by faith (Hab 2:4; cf. Rom 1:17). The law was given through Moses to guide Israelites into a peaceful, just community and it should be kept through the eyes of faith. He also makes it clear that faith cannot overthrow the law. The issue is not a choice between faith and the law but a life of faith that seeks the way of God, as he says in Rom 3:30–31.

Otherwise, Paul neither founded a new religion nor established a new doctrine called "justification by faith." In his view, the issue was not about Judaism or the law per se but the Jews' zeal for the law or their rejection of the Messiah. But after Paul died, his legacy became one of passive faith and social conservatism. For example, faith means a set of teachings about Jesus in the Deutero-Pauline and Pastoral Letters (e.g., Eph 2:8–9; Col 2:5–7; 1 Tim 1:3–5; 2 Tim 3:15). Post-Pauline churches are ruled by the household codes that regulate social relationships between a master and slaves, between spouses, between parents and children, and between genders (Col 3:18–4:1; Eph 5:21–6:9; Titus 2:1–10. cf. 1 Pet 2:18–3:7).

Further Reading

Barrett, C. K. *The New Testament Background: Selected Documents.* New York: HarperOne, 1995.

Collins, A. J., and John Collins. *King and Messiah as Son of God: Divine, Human, and Angelic Messianic Figures in Biblical and Related Literature.* Grand Rapids, MI: Eerdmans, 2008.

Fiorenza, Elisabeth Schüssler. *In Memory of Her: A Feminist Theological Reconstruction of Christian Origins.* New York: Crossroad, 1994.

Hendricks, Obery M., Jr. *The Politics of Jesus: Rediscovering the True Revolutionary Nature of Jesus's Teachings and How They Have Been Corrupted.* New York: Three Leaves, 2006.

Hengel, Martin. *Judaism and Hellenism: Studies in Their Encounter in Palestine during the Early Hellenistic Period.* Eugene, OR: Wipf and Stock, 2003.

Kim, Yung Suk. *Resurrecting Jesus: The Renewal of New Testament Theology.* Eugene, OR: Cascade, 2015.

King, Karen L. *What Is Gnosticism?* Cambridge: Harvard University Press, 2005.

Klauck, Hans. *The Religious Context of Early Christianity: A Guide to Graeco-Roman Religions.* Minneapolis, MN: Fortress, 2003.

Koester, Helmut. *History, Culture and Religion of the Hellenistic Age.* 2nd ed. Berlin: Gruyter, 1995.

Lefkowitz, Mary, and Maureen Fant, eds. *Women's Life in Greece and Rome: A Source Book in Translation.* Baltimore: Johns Hopkins University Press, 2016.

Levine, Amy-Jill. *The Misunderstood Jew. The Church and the Scandal of the Jewish Jesus.* New York: HarperOne, 2006.

Long, A. A. *Hellenistic Philosophy: Stoics, Epicureans, Sceptics.* Los Angeles: University of California Press, 1986.

Meyer, Marvin, ed. *The Ancient Mysteries: A Sourcebook of Sacred Texts.* Philadelphia: University of Pennsylvania Press, 1999.

Sanders, E. P. *Judaism: Practice and Belief, 63 BCE–66 CE.* Minneapolis, MN: Fortress, 2016.

Vanderkam, James. *An Introduction to Early Judaism.* Grand Rapids, MI: Eerdmans, 2000.

CHAPTER 4

Refugees, Immigrants, and Foreigners in the New Testament

> Our image of God has been one of power, domination, and omniscience....I propose the image of Spirit as a way of overcoming some of the traditional images of God that have contributed to the Othering of many groups of people.
>
> —Grace Ji-Sun Kim[1]

> Identifying Christianity with a particular cultural pattern and religiosity is a betrayal of the Christian gospel that is expressed in Peter's confession—"I truly understand that God shows no partiality, but in every nation, anyone who fears him and does what is right is acceptable for him" (Acts 10:34–35).
>
> —Chan-Hie Kim[2]

ENSLAVED PEOPLES ARE NOT immigrants. Some people in our contemporary societies seem confused on this point. In 2015 the immigrant population in the United States numbered over 45 million people or about 13.5 percent (the African American population is 14.3 percent). In 2015 India was the primary country of origin for recent immigrants, with 179,800; from China, 143,200; from Mexico, 139,400; 47,500 arrived from the Philippines; and 46,800 came from Canada. In 2013, India and China surpassed Mexico as the primary countries of origin for recent arrivals.[3]

---

1. Kim, *Embracing the Other*, 33.
2. Kim, "Reading the Cornelius Story," 174.
3. Zong and Batalova, "Frequently Requested Statistics."

In our contemporary contexts, hostilities and violence toward immigrant populations (primarily and ostensibly toward nonwhite peoples that some people may regard as easily identifiable as foreigners) have increased exponentially, particularly by nonwhite persons having lost sight of their own immigrant histories and/or who view immigrant populations as obstacles to their own socioeconomic mobility, and perhaps have a burning desire to return to a romanticized past (when America was great for enslavers and the beneficiaries of Jim/Jane Crow and disenfranchisement).

Most American politicians, even former President Barack Obama, yielded to the pressure from some segments of the American public to crack down on illegal immigration. President Obama signed DACA (Deferred Action for Childhood Arrivals), which offers administrative relief from deportation. Under DACA eligible immigrant youth who came to the United States when they were children are protected from deportation. DACA gives young undocumented immigrants protection from deportation and a permit to work. However, President Donald Trump rescinded the DACA Act and placed a ban on the entry of certain ostensibly nonwhite persons (from mostly, if not only, ostensibly nonwhite countries) that attempt to enter or return after leaving the USA. In 2017 thousands of fathers, mothers, sisters, brothers, grandmothers, and children impacted by the Trump Administration's rescinding of DACA have been deported, imprisoned, and/or are awaiting deportation, with no compassionate regard for the impact on their families or the individual. Prior to the rescinding of DACA hundreds of millions of people globally were already displaced. In 2018 the government has separated children from their parents as they cross the border seeking refuge in the USA. As of this writing, thousands of children taken from their parents cannot be located.

Of course, European (neo)colonization dispossessed indigenous peoples of their lands and displaced them, forcing them onto less fertile and arable lands and onto reservations or government missions. Such dislocation results in the fracturing of familial, social, and cultural bonds. Such displacement has the major effect of pathology among indigenous peoples. Additionally, large numbers of internally displaced peoples (IDPs) are forced or obliged to relocate when faced with natural disasters (California wildfires, hurricanes, flooding) and/or the effects of global warming, human created environmental hazards such as oil spills, and by gentrification and/or infrastructural and agricultural projects or failures. IDPs often do not migrate across internationally recognized state borders but must leave their homes or habitual residences.

Although many immigrants choose to relocate and to make their home in another country outside of their native land, they often do so in search of better opportunities and perhaps a life free from the constant threat of violence. Even when immigrants choose to leave their homelands, it can be precipitated by poverty, the threat of or actual violence, lack of educational opportunities, and so on.

The HB provides a crucial historical and literary context for understanding the NT. The HB was the Jewish Scriptures for Jesus, his Jewish disciples, the Apostle Paul, as well as God-fearers and proselytes to Judaism (Acts 8–11; 6:5). The Hebrew Scriptures were a source of sacred information and a guide for Gentile God-fearers like the Ethiopian eunuch who read and sought to understand them. One of the most significant Israelite patriarchs was Abraham who was told to leave his homeland and to become an immigrant in a promised land that Yahweh would show him. Consequently, he and his family migrated from Ur and became immigrants (Gen 12). The covenant that God made with Abraham serves as a perpetual reminder to Israel and readers of the biblical text that Israel's descendants are immigrants. Even much later after the children of Israel (Jacob) were liberated from Egyptian slavery, they became immigrants in the land of Canaan, a fertile land of milk and honey, between Syria to the north and Egypt to the south. The process by which Israel became immigrants in the Promised Land is not dissimilar from the colonists and settlers who waged war in order to take by violence the land they desired from the indigenous populations in North America and other places. Both should be critiqued and condemned. The practice of immigrating in search of a better life is at least as old as Abraham.

The Patriarchs Abraham, Joseph, Jacob, and others are mentioned often in NT (e.g., Mark 12:26; Luke 3:34, 20:37; Acts 3:13; 7:12, 32; Heb 11:9, 20–21). Jacob and his sons and their families and livestock immigrated to Egypt during a famine and remained there as immigrants for over seventeen years (Gen 47). The children of Jacob flourished during that period. When a Pharaoh (King of Egypt) ascends to the throne in Egypt and is unfamiliar with the Israelites, he submits to his fears, based on ignorance, that they would become the dominant population; consequently he enslaves them. Fear of the immigrant provokes hostilities and violence against them. Immigrants and refugees are memorialized in the hall of faith in chapter 11 of the NT book of Hebrews.

Jesus and his family were of course refugees that fled to Egypt for a period to escape the deadly violence initiated by King Herod in order to annihilate a baby said to be the Jewish Messiah, his competition (and Rome's). Fortunately, Mary and Joseph and their child are graciously received into Egypt (Africa), until God calls God's son out of Egypt (Matt 2). But few readers stop long to consider or mourn with Rachel over the many babies who did not escape Herod's genocide. The Apostle Apollos in the

Acts of the Apostles and 1 Cor (Acts 18:24; 19:1; 1 Cor 1:12; 3:4–6, 22; 4:6; 16:12) may have been a Diaspora immigrant from Alexandria, Egypt, who preached and lived in Corinth. Africa functions in the NT narrative as a hospitable place for refugees and as a place from which eloquent, educated immigrants migrate. The Ethiopia eunuch, of course, is not an immigrant, but a literate well-connected Gentile visitor in Jerusalem who worships the God of Israel; in other words, he is a God-fearer like Cornelius (Acts 8–10). The Ethiopian eunuch is just passing through; his country has not been conquered or colonized by the Roman Empire, yet he is portrayed as a liminal figure by Luke; it is unclear how Luke would have known about his sexuality and not his name. The Ethiopian like Apollos enjoys free movement. Ethiopia functions in Acts as one of the ends of the earth as it was known by the ancients. "'Blacks' or Ethiopians were used to represent polluted doctrines and developments in early Christianity that needed to be avoided. But Ethiopians and Blacks were used not only as models of 'heresy.' They also appeared in many sources as models of virtue."[4]

Africa emerges again at Jesus's crucifixion in Matthew as a symbol of relief, albeit forced this time. Africa functions as a source of assistance or relief twice in Jesus's life; at the beginning and at the end. The African Simon of Cyrene seems to be a Diaspora immigrant living in the countryside around Jerusalem, according to Mark's Gospel (Mark 15:21; Matt 27:32; Luke 23:26). Mark humanizes this African immigrant, informing his readers that Simon is a father and his children's names are Alexander and Rufus. If he should not make it home or is injured while carrying the cross, his family will suffer too. As an African immigrant, Simon is compelled to carry Jesus's cross when Jesus buckles under the weight of the lynching tree. We can side with the oppressed or the oppressor.

In the Acts of the Apostles, it is possible that a number of immigrants attended the Pentecost celebration. People, we are told, living in Jerusalem from "every nation under heaven" attended (2:5). Luke and the Spirit celebrate and respect the various cultures. Language is a crucial aspect of one's culture. Perhaps we might learn from Pentecost to respect the culture and language of the nonwhite minoritized immigrants, as well as white citizens with immigrant histories, that reside among us. In contemporary society, we tend to insist that nonwhite minoritized immigrants speak English and only English; that they speak and speak well the language of the dominant white population. Yet, the majoritized white populations (and some nonwhites as well) refuse to learn the cultural languages of minoritized peoples. Majoritized white populations are the descendants of immigrants and they

---

4. Byron, *Symbolic Blackness*, 108.

impose burdens upon more recent nonwhite immigrants and minoritized citizens that they would not impose upon themselves. Foreigners are usually not accepted into religious groups without a willingness to assimilate to the values and culture of the dominant group and are consequently compelled to relinquish their own culture. We can see this phenomena at work in the NT in attempts to force Gentiles who want to join the Jesus Movement in Acts to be circumcised and to practice the same culinary and/or food restrictions of the dominant group; the Jerusalem Council reaches a compromise, rejecting the possibly fatal requirement of adult circumcision (chapter 15; Gal 2:11–14). Many majoritized white populations and many nonwhites who have assimilated to a certain negative attitude toward the immigrant foreigner and the indigenous other and their cultures were themselves, or their ancestors, immigrants.

As noted, people emigrate for various reasons. Some emigrate and become immigrants because they believe God told them to move and establish a home for themselves and their families in another country. Peoples from developing countries often flee their own countries due to the violence of war, human rights abuses, violence-associated poverty, corrupt governments, or because of famine and/or lack of adequate, affordable, or healthy water and food sources, educational opportunities to improve quality of life, or lack of freedom to practice their faith. The crowds that follow Jesus most likely include immigrants and enslaved peoples whom Jesus heals and feeds, freely and free of cost. Matthew's Jesus boldly and unequivocally claims that when we meet the needs of others (without judgment), we show hospitality to Jesus, God's son (25:31–46).

Further Reading

Brown, Michael Joseph. *The Lord's Prayer Through North African Eyes: A Window into Early Christianity*. New York: T. & T. Clark, 2004.

Byron, Gay L. *Symbolic Blackness and Ethnic Difference in Early Christian Literature*. New York: Routledge, 2002.

Carroll, M. Daniel. *Christians at the Border: Immigration, the Church and the Bible*. 2nd ed. Grand Rapids, MI: Brazos, 2013.

Ekblad, Eugene Robert, Jr. *Reading the Bible with the Damned*. Louisville: Westminster John Knox, 2005.

Hawk, L. Daniel. *Joshua in 3-D: A Commentary on Biblical Conquest and Manifest Destiny*. Eugene, OR: Cascade, 2010.

Kim, Chan-Hie. "Reading the Cornelius Story from an Asian Immigrant Perspective." In *Reading from This Place: Social Location and Biblical Interpretation in the United States*, edited by Fernando F. Segovia and Mary Ann Tolbert, 165–74. Minneapolis: Fortress, 1995.

Kim, Grace Ji-Sun. *Embracing the Other: Transformative Spirit of Love*. Grand Rapids, MI: Eerdmans, 2015.

Rivera-Rodríguez, Luis. "Toward a Diaspora Hermeneutics (Hispanic North America)." In *Character Ethics and the Old Testament: Moral Dimensions of Scripture*, edited by M. Daniel Carroll R. and Jacqueline Laosley, 169–89. Louisville: Westminster John Knox, 2007.

Smith, Mitzi J. *The Literary Construction of the Other in the Acts of the Apostles: Charismatics, the Jews, and Women*. Princeton Theological Monograph Series 154. Eugene, OR: Pickwick, 2011.

Wingeier-Rayo, Philip. "Jesus as Migrant: A Biblical Understanding of Immigration as a Cross-Cultural Model for Ministry." *Apuntes* 35 (2015) 19–32.

CHAPTER 5

Roman Slavery and the New Testament

> Let me put it this way: that from a very literal point of view, the harbors and the ports and the railroads of the country; the economy, especially of the Southern states, could not conceivably be what it has become if they had not had, and do not still have, indeed, and for so long—so many generations—cheap labor.
>
> —JAMES BALDWIN (1924–87), NOVELIST,
> PLAYWRIGHT, SOCIAL CRITIC[1]

THE ROMAN EMPIRE, a significant historical context for the authors, writings, and events of the NT, was a slave society like Greece and the American South. The enslaved, as human speaking tools, labored and lived in every part of the Empire. No kingdom or empire in history has been built and maintained without slave labor.[2] Where did the Roman Empire retrieve their slaves? Most of the slave population constituted the spoils of war. Rome conquered peoples and enslaved some of them. According to Roman law, slaves (Latin *servi*) were so named because of the practice of army commanders to order that captives be sold and thus saved rather than killed. A less used Latin word for slave was *mancipia* derived from the phrase *manu capiuntur* (captured by the enemy). Wealthy relatives of captured persons could ransom them from slavery or death. Of course, as with slaves in the American South, enslaved women only birthed slave children (*vernae*). Enslaved women could be offered incentives for birthing

---

1. Baldwin, *I Am Not Your Negro*, 75.
2. Perhaps the only exception is the Persian Empire under King Cyrus, the only Gentile to have been called God's Messiah.

four children. The enslaved population was primarily maintained from a combination of war captives and breeding.

Thus, the enslaved population consisted of many nationalities. Among them were Phrygians, Numidians, Cappadocians, Syrians, Jews, Egyptians, Ethiopians, Spaniards, Gauls, Germans, Thracians, and Greeks. Roman citizens could not be enslaved; slaves were outsiders. A Roman could be enslaved as a form of legal punishment, but he could only be sold abroad.

Despite the *Pax Romana* (Roman peace) instituted under the first Roman Emperor Augustus (Octavian) (27 BCE–180 CE) in 27 BCE (lasting until 180 CE), war remained a significant and major source of slave supply. According to the first century CE Jewish historian Josephus, when Vespasian (17–79 CE) conquered Japha, 2,130 captives were enslaved. After another war, Vespasian sent 6,000 enslaved Jewish captives to tunnel through the Isthmus.[3]

Slavery was a cruel and peculiar institution that forced social isolation or death upon dominated peoples. Orlando Patterson defines slavery as "the . . . violent domination of naturally alienated and generally dishonored persons."[4] Slaves possessed no honor in Roman society; no socially recognized honor was attributed to slaves. The enslaved were forcefully uprooted from their family, homeland, and culture, and had no rights. Enslavers possessed total access to the bodies, sexuality, and labor of the slaves they owned.

Although the enslaved were a ubiquitous presence throughout the Empire, including in the imperial household of Caesar, slaves/slavery, and references to slaves/slavery are not always rendered visible in the pages of the NT. For example, slaves melt into the crowds that follow Jesus from the time he performed his first miracle or exorcism to the moment he breathed his last on the cross. Sometimes references to slaves/slavery are lost in translation. Even when the Greek word for slave, *doulos/doulē* (masculine and feminine respectively; sometimes *paidiskē* for female slave, Matt 26:69; Mark 14:66, 69) is found in the Greek text of the NT, translators often choose the more euphemistic or innocuous translation of *servant*. For example, in some of the earliest documents of the NT, the authentic letters of Paul, the Apostle Paul identifies himself as a metaphorical slave (*doulos*) of Jesus Christ, but some translators prefer *servant* (Phil 1:1; Rom 1:1; cf. Rev. 1:1).

Most scholars agree that the Apostle Paul did not condemn slavery and was indifferent regarding the possibility that enslaved believers might have the opportunity to gain their freedom (1 Cor 7:21–22). No evidence

---

3. Josephus, *JW*, 3.305, 3.540.
4. Patterson, *Slavery and Social Death*, 13.

exists to support the assertion that members of the Jesus movement freed their slaves when the households to which they belonged converted. It is possible that some communities of faith manumitted (emancipated) slaves later in the second century CE, but this is not certain. We find the metaphorical use of *doulos* elsewhere in Paul's writings with reference to Jesus's incarnation. The hymn of Christ that Paul inserted in his letter to the Philippians states that Jesus voluntarily relinquished equality with God and assumed the form of a *doulos* (Phil 2:6–7).

In the NT, high religious, military, and government officials owned slaves who performed various tasks and to whose bodies and labor they had unrestricted access (Luke 7:2–3; John 10:26; Acts 10:3–7). Slave jobs or occupations included agent (Chloe's people, 1 Cor 1:11), messenger, overseer (*vilicus*), cook, server, prostitute, doorkeeper (Mark 13:35; Rhoda, Acts 12:13–15), fuller, ploughman, hunter, tracker, poultry fattener, pig breeder, planter, maidservant, pruner, silversmith, doctor, secretary, wet nurse, footman, clothes mender, masseuse, slave in charge of pictures, food-taster, singer, waiter, tailor, architect, prophetess/seer/diviner (Pythian slave girl, Acts 16:16–19), and more. Slaves could not serve in the military. Slave owners would demote or promote a slave. A master could permit a slave to earn monies (*peculium*) for her or his labor, but such monies belonged to the master who would determine if or how much a slave might retain or use. Some slaves either possessed useful and lucrative skills or trades when captured and enslaved or slave masters invested in the training of worthy/obedient slaves to increase their potential for producing revenue for the master's household. Petronius's first century CE fictional work *Satyricon* contains a chapter titled "Cena Trimalchionis" (dinner with Trimalchio) about a wealthy and ridiculed freedman named Trimalchio. The freedperson could become wealthy but remained socially stigmatized as a former slave, as noted in more detail below.

According to the Roman household codes, slaves were the most inferior members of the household (see Col 3:22–4:1; Eph 6:5–9; 1 Pet 2:18–21; 1 Tim 6:1–2; Titus 2:9–10). The master was the *paterfamilias* or the father of the family. Slaves were expected to obey their masters, and masters were not to treat their slaves with cruelty. Of course, in practice the (mis)treatment of one's slaves was left to the master's discretion and perception. Seneca recounted the story of a male slave that served wine and was forced to dress in women's clothing and stay alert throughout the night, alternating between his master's drinking needs and sexual desires.[5] Everyone in the household was subordinate to the husband/father/master (Greek *kyrios*).

---

5. Seneca, *Epistulae Morales*, 47.7, 8.

The household codes exhorted wives to respect and submit to their husbands; fathers to refrain from provoking their children to anger; and of course for slaves to obey their earthly masters as unto Christ or God who is their heavenly father. The enslaved were subordinated to master and other free born members of the household.

Subordination is reflected in the power of naming. *Onesimus* and *Chloe* seem to have been typical slave names in Roman slave society and in the American South. One could not determine a slave's ethnicity or nationality based on the name given to him or her when enslaved. Slave names were Greco-Romanized; they were Greek or Roman. If any slave retained his or her native name, it was Latinized or Graecized. Slave masters could arbitrarily rename their slaves. Home born slaves (*vernae*) received names reflecting the master's identity and their names sometimes indicated the physical and moral qualities of the ideal slave. Philemon is the one NT text that arguably depicts the return of a slave named Onesimus to his slave master.

A number of parables in the Gospels demonstrate the stereotypical master-slave relationship. A good and wise slave is faithful, awake or alert, productive (in the master's presence and absence), obedient and loyal, and is rewarded with increased labor or responsibilities for servile behavior; a slave that fails to be a good slave is considered wicked, unfaithful, useless, and lazy and is severely punished (Matt 24:24—25:30). In slave parables, God is represented as the slave master, and the characteristic dynamics of the cruel master-slave relationship are put forth as a model for participation in the Kingdom of God/heaven. It is possible that the ten virgins in Matthew's parable of the bridegroom are also slaves (Matt 25:1–13). Regardless of a slave's behavior, a slave was not considered a person of honor like a freeborn man. A slave had no honor or shame that a freeborn citizen was bound to recognize. Slaves could not bring litigation proceedings against their slave masters. But slaves could be forced to testify in legal cases involving disputes between slave masters. However, slave testimony was only admissible under torture. It was believed that a slave would only deliver truthful testimony while being tortured.

Any incentives offered to the enslaved, including manumission (emancipation), served the institution of slavery, which meant the creation of obedient, loyal, and productive slaves. Enslavers attempted to obtain the optimum usefulness or productivity from their enslaved by offering positive benefits (*beneficium*) for slave loyalty (*fides*) and obedience (*obsequium*). The benefits included permission to enter into *de facto* marriage (*contubernium*) and the promise of manumission. *Contubernium* denoted the cohabitation of soldiers or animals but also a quasi-marital and illegal union of two slaves or a slave and a free person with the permission of the slave owner. *Contubernium* was valid according to natural law but not civic law.

Enslavers could legally manumit their slaves in two ways that concurrently conferred Roman citizenship on the freedperson: (a) a slave master could manumit through his Last Will and Testament. The *Lex Fufia Caninia* (2 BCE) required that the Will names the slaves to be freed and limited the number of slaves that could be manumitted at one time. An enslaver with 3–10 slaves could free up to one half of them; 11–30, one third; 31–100, one-fourth; 101–500, one fifth; and no one could manumit over 100 slaves at once; and (b) the slave master could declare his intent to manumit his slaves before the appropriate magistrate by rod (*vindicta*). Informally, enslavers could manumit slaves by letter of *inter amicos* (among friends or witnesses), but this manner conferred the inferior Junian Latin status and not Roman citizenship. Some enslavers might prefer the informal method of manumission because it meant greater succession rights for the former master or patron. For example, if a freedperson died testate (with a will) with full Roman citizenship and at least three surviving freeborn children, the patron/former master was prohibited from access to the freedman's inheritance. But the inheritance of a freedman with Junian Latin status passed to his patron's heirs, since the freedman Latin's heirs were excluded from succession. The *Lex Aelia Sentia* (4 CE) limited the age for manumission. A slave under the age of thirty could only be manumitted by *vindicta* for good cause shown before a council (*consilium*). The slave master was required to be at least twenty years of age to manumit a slave, except by *vindicta* for good cause shown. A freed slave was likely never under thirty years old.

A slave master could allow a slave to purchase his or her freedom. If a slave were offered his freedom in exchange for a sum of money (*statuliber*), the enslaved could be allowed to use his or her peculium to pay the fee. All powers of manumission rested with the slave master and was generally for his benefit. Primarily, if not only, loyal, productive, well-trained, educated, and obedient slaves might be manumitted. Slaves were not guaranteed manumission; it was dangled before them to encourage obedience.

Slaves that were manumitted remained stigmatized, forever known as freedmen or freedwomen. Also, many freedmen were required to maintain a patron-client relationship with their former master, which meant the freedperson continued to have financial obligations (*obsequium*) toward the patron and/or was required to perform services (*operae*) for the patron. The freedperson entered a higher social category when manumitted, but with no severe economic loss to the slave master. The new relationship formed between the former enslaved and patron (former slave master) was in theory characterized by mutual respect but the latter remained the social superior of the former. If a freedperson's patron experienced economic poverty, the freedperson was expected to support his patron. Delinquency in performing services due to the patron could result in punishment or even a return to slavery. Manumission was subject to restrictions and could be revoked. It is possible that both Lydia (Acts 16:14–15) and Chloe (1 Cor 1:10) were freed women and independent heads of their own households who became slave owners themselves, as well as members of the Jesus movement. Among African slaves in the American South, Christian slave owners had a reputation as the most cruel. The technical term for a freedperson occurs once in the NT in Paul's first letter to the Corinthians where he argues that a person who was a slave (*doulos*) when called to the Lord (*kurios*, also translated master) is the Lord's freedman (*apeleutheros*) (1 Cor 7:22).

We have no extant ancient slave narratives like those that survive about American slavery (e.g., Linda Brent/Harriet Jacobs, Frederick Douglass, Nat Turner, Sojourner Truth, et al.) or any abolitionist literature or narratives. The knowledge we have of slavery comes from elite males and/or slave owners. The slave narratives of Africans enslaved in the American South might help to imaginatively fill in some gaps. Slave resistance ranged from lying, cheating, stealing, feigning sickness, working at a slow pace, petty sabotage, running away, and acts of violence like infanticide, suicide, or homicide. Dio Chrysostom claimed that slave women either aborted their fetuses or committed infanticide (sometimes in collusion with the fathers) so that they were not compelled to raise their children in slavery.[6] Perhaps some ancient writers and laws encouraged and supported some level of relatively humane treatment of the enslaved is indicative of a moral consciousness regarding the evils of slavery despite the participation and/or complicity of those same voices in the peculiar and cruel institution.

Further Reading

Andrews, William L., and Henry Louis Gates, eds. *Slave Narratives*. New York: Library of America, 2000.

Bradley, Keith R. *Slavery and Rebellion in the Roman World, 140 B.C.–70 B.C.* Bloomington: Indiana University Press, 1989.

———. *Slavery and Society at Rome*. Cambridge: Cambridge University Press, 1994.

---

6. Chrysostom, "The Fifteenth Discourse: On Slavery and Freedom I," Sec. 8.

Columella, Lucius Junius Moderatus. *De Re Rustica: IV on Agriculture*. Translated by Harrison Boyd Ash. Loeb Classical Library 361. Cambridge: Harvard University Press, 1977.

DuBois, Page. *Slavery, Antiquity and its Legacy*. New York: Oxford University Press, 2009.

———. *Torture and Truth*. New York: Routledge, 1991.

Garnsey, Peter. *Ideas of Slavery from Aristotle to Augustine*. Cambridge: Cambridge University Press, 1996.

Glancy, Jennifer A. *Slavery in Early Christianity*. Minneapolis: Fortress, 2006.

Harrill, Albert J. *Manumission of Slaves in Early Christianity*. Tübingen: Mohr Siebeck, 1998.

———. *Slaves in the New Testament: Literary, Social and Moral Dimensions*. Minneapolis: Fortress, 2009.

Joshel, Sandra R., and Lauren Hackworth Petersen. *The Material Life of Roman Slaves*. New York: Cambridge University Press, 2016.

Martin, Clarice J. "The Eyes Have It: Slaves in the Communities of Christ Believers." In *Christian Origins*, edited by Richard Horsley, 221–39. Minneapolis: Fortress, 2010.

———. "The *Haustafeln* (Household Codes) in African American Biblical Interpretation: 'Free Slaves' and 'Subordinate Women.'" In *Stony the Road We Trod: African American Biblical Interpretation*, edited by Cain Hope Felder, 206–31. Minneapolis: Fortress, 1991.

Patterson, Orlando. *Slavery and Social Death: A Comparative Study*. Cambridge: Harvard University Press, 1982.

Shaner, Katherine A. *Enslaved Leadership in Early Christianity*. New York: Oxford University Press, 2018.

Smith, Mitzi J. "Chloe, a Freedwoman in Corinth (1 Cor 1:10): A Womanist Reconstruction." In *After the Corinthian Women Prophets: Rhetoric, Power, and Possibilities*, edited by Joseph Marchal. Semeia Studies. Forthcoming.

———. "Roman Slavery in Antiquity." In *The African American Jubilee Bible*, 157–85. New York: American Bible Society, 1999.

———. "Slavery in the Early Church." In *True to Our Native Land: An African American Commentary of the New Testament*, edited by Brian Blount et al., 11–22. Minneapolis: Fortress, 2007.

CHAPTER 6

Intersectionality and Reading Complexity in the New Testament

THE BIBLICAL TEXT IS full of binary opposites like good/evil, light/dark, slave/free, Gentile/Jew, male/female, rich/poor, child of God/pagan, which gives the impression that there is nothing in between. And even when these binaries and dualities are not present in a particular story or text, we impose them upon characters and ideas that are more complex and multi-dimensional. *Intersectional-type* reading or *intersectionality* encourages us to interrogate such simplistic constructions and to think about human existence and ideas in more complex ways. Life is complex; human beings are complex. In this chapter, we shall define intersectionality, provide a brief history of the theory and its use, and discuss some of the ways that it is already being used in the study of ancient texts and of the NT specifically.

Patricia Hill Collins and Sirma Bilge provide the following formal definition of intersectionality. They describe it as:

> A way of understanding and analyzing the complexity in the world, in people, and in human experiences. The events and conditions of social and political life and the self can seldom be understood as shaped by one factor. They are generally shaped by many factors in diverse and mutually influencing ways. When it comes to social inequality, people's lives and the organization of power in a given society are better understood as being shaped not by a single axis of social division, be it race or gender or class, but by many axes that work together and influence each other. Intersectionality as an analytic tool gives people better access to the complexity of the world and of themselves.[1]

Intersectionality or *intersectional-type* analysis is increasingly being used in the social and political sciences, as well as in the field of religion

---

1. Collins and Bilge, *Intersectionality*, 7.

and more specifically in biblical studies. As a research tool, intersectionality invites or permits one to critically reflect on what and how social categories such as gender, race/ethnicity, class, sexuality, religious affiliation, dis/ability, and nationality, co-constitute in human experience. For example, my gender, race, and class, mutually and simultaneously impact how I experience the world. It is not that my gender impacts me one way and my class another, as discreet social categories, but my race, gender, and class interconnect, overlap, and conjointly influence my experience. I do not experience life as an African American or as a female separately. This does not mean that every highly educated African American woman will experience life in the exact same way and in every context; experience is always contextual and contexts impact us differently even when we belong to the same social categories. Nevertheless, African American women, for example, will share some historical and contemporary experiences in common, as will Latina, African, Native Indian, Asian and other nonwhite women, but we also have experiences unique to us as individuals.

Intersectionality has also been employed to examine social processes such as classism, nativism, (neo)colonialism, postcolonialism, ageism, heterosexism, ableism, as well as racism and sexism. Intersectionality or intersectional-type analysis raises our consciousness regarding oppressive systems and processes and about the complexity of human existence and experiences, the construction of social categories and their impact in real life and in literature. How we read impacts how we exist and behave in the world, as well as what policies we vote for and enact and the systems we support or attempt to dismantle. A focus on systems of oppression avoids the trap of entering into discussions about who is most oppressed, but focuses on eliminating oppressive systems. Intersectional-type analysis prompts us to ask other questions, questions we might not otherwise ask, and to engage intricate social identities, processes, and experiences that mutually impact, overlap, or cohere in the lives of individuals and groups.

Before legal expert Kimberlé Crenshaw coined the term *intersectionality*, black feminist scholars articulated theories about the impact of the intersection of race, gender, and class in black women's lives. The term *intersectionality* was first used in the field of law and critical race theory in 1989, but in the early 1980s black feminists theorized about the interconnected and simultaneous impact of the social categories of race, gender, and class on black women's lives and experiences and the interlocking forms of oppression to which they are subjected. In her 1984 book *Feminist Theory from Margin to Center*, black feminist bell hooks states that in Betty Friedan's seminal text *The Feminine Mystique*, she wrote as if black and other nonwhite oppressed women did not exist or matter. Hooks wrote, "She ignored the existence of all non-white women and poor white women. She did not tell readers whether it was more fulfilling to be a maid, a babysitter, a factory worker, a clerk, or a prostitute, than to be a leisure class housewife ... She made her plight and the plight of white women like herself synonymous with a condition affecting all American women. In so doing, she deflected attention away from her classism, her racism, her sexist attitudes towards the masses of American women."[2] Freidan voiced a one-dimensional perspective that ignored the impact of race/racism, class/classism, and capitalist patriarchy in women's lives. "Women who were not opposed to patriarchy, capitalism, classism, or racism labeled themselves 'feminist.'"[3] According to hooks, "Feminism as a movement to end sexist oppression directs attention to systems of domination and the inter-relatedness of sex, race, and class oppression."[4] We can understand the social status of women as a collective, hooks argues, by understanding the experiences of women most impacted by sexism because of the inter-related experience of class and race. Most women share the experience of sexism, but not all are oppressed because of their race and/or class. Feminism should be a movement to eradicate all forms of oppression and not just sexism. In her 1981 book *Ain't I a Woman: Black Women and Feminism*, bell hooks described the impact of sexism and racism on black women's lives as simultaneous rather than independent.[5]

In a 1982 essay Barbara Smith argued that few pure oppressors or victims can be found in a system of interlocking race, gender, class, and sexual oppression.[6] Black feminist Patricia Hill Collins employs this same term *interlocking* to refer to systems of oppression.[7] In 1990, Collins theorized about black women's intersectional identities; she does not appear to be yet aware of Crenshaw's coining of the term *intersectionality*. At the micro level, Collins used terms like interconnected, interdependence, and multi-dimensional identities focusing on how mutually impacting categories of race, class, and gender effect black women's lives. At the macro level or at the level of dominant systems of oppression and power, Collins invoked interlocking systems of oppression or a matrix of domination to refer to the overlapping impact of racism, sexism, and classism on black women's lives. Intersectional-type analysis first disrupted the race/gender binary and the silencing and marginalization of black women's experiences and subjectivity

2. Hooks, *Feminist Theory*, 1–2.
3. Hooks, *Feminist Theory*, 7.
4. Hooks, *Feminist Theory*, 31.
5. Hooks, *Ain't I a Woman*, 7.
6. Smith, "Racism and Women's Studies."
7. Collins, *Black Feminist Thought*.

in the context of the priority placed on white women's feminism and black male experiences with racism. In other words, gender analysis referred to white women, and theories about race generally signified black men. Black women's experiences were obscured, ignored, and silenced.

The genesis of intersectionality in black feminist theory should not limit its potential as an analytical tool in other domains or fail to acknowledge that it is already at work in other places or disciplines; it has traveled quite a bit. More recent intersectional-type analysis disrupts binaries such as black/white, heterosexual/homosexual, poor/wealthy, and so on. Following black feminist theory, womanist and/or Africana ethicists, theologians and biblical scholars have increasingly employed intersectional analysis when analyzing and theorizing about religion, religious (con)texts and experience, biblical texts, Africana communities, and systems of oppression.

As noted above, the term *intersectionality* was birthed by legal scholar Kimberlé Crenshaw in her 1989 essay "Demarginalizing the Intersection of Race and Sex," where she addresses the multidimensionality of black women's lived realities. Focusing on the most privileged class of white women marginalizes poor minoritized women. Crenshaw argues that both feminist and anti-racist politics assisted in marginalizing the problem of violence against women of color. Feminists focused on white women's experience of violence as universal for all women, and black men prioritized their experience with racial violence as primary or universal for black people. The law courts would not permit black women to serve as a representative class for women in general or for black people, but white women were allowed to represent all other women as a class, and black men were permitted to represent all black people.

In her 1991 essay, Crenshaw states that her "focus on the intersections of race and gender only highlight the need to account for multiple grounds of identity when considering how the social world is constructed."[8] Crenshaw's intersectionality has always been about legal reforms, social activism, and policy change. She argued that intervention strategies for battered women that focus solely on women's experiences without regard for the convergence of race, gender, class, and violence in nonwhite women's lived realities, were of little assistance to poor women of color.[9] "Intersectional subordination need not be intentionally produced; in fact, it is frequently the consequence of the imposition of one burden that interacts with preexisting

---

8. Crenshaw, "Mapping the Margins," 1245.
9. Crenshaw, "Mapping the Margins," 1246.

vulnerabilities to create yet another dimension of disempowerment."[10] "Different needs demand different priorities."[11] "Political intersectionality" underscores the reality that nonwhite women are located within two or more "subordinated groups that frequently pursue conflicting political agendas. The need to split one's political energies between two sometimes opposing groups is a dimension of intersectional disempowerment that men of color and white women seldom confront."[12] For reasons already discussed, anti-racism strategies that fail to consider the intersection of gender often reproduce women's subordination; feminist strategies that ignore the intersectional impact of race tend to duplicate and reinforce subordination of nonwhite people. Thus, anti-racist and feminist discourses fail to adequately articulate the full dimensionality of racism and sexism, and "one analysis often implicitly denies the validity of the other."[13]

Intersectionality has traveled across disciplines and in unmapped territory; the categories of race, gender, and class are not essential for doing intersectional analysis. Although necessary for addressing the experiences of nonwhite women, intersectionality is not limited to black women or poor black women's experiences as legitimate subjects of analysis. Additionally, intersectionality should not indulge contests over which social group is worse off than another group. Not every nonwhite woman will be disadvantaged or advantaged in the same way as every other nonwhite woman or women in general. Not every white woman will be disadvantaged or advantaged in the same way as every other white woman. "Intersectionality does not lock the double-jeopardy claim onto particular social categories." Double-jeopardy argues that the more subordinated social categories one belongs to, the more disadvantaged one will be. Black lesbians are not in every context more disadvantaged than black heterosexual men. "Mapping fixed hierarchies onto particular identities obscures that both power and social categories are contextually constituted."[14]

Intersectionality is also a response to essentialism; scholars employing intersectional-type analysis must be careful not to fall victim to what it seeks to avoid. Not all African American and/or nonwhite minoritized women experience racism, classism, and sexism in the same way or to the same degree. We must be careful not to limit minoritized women's identities to race and gender, or race, class, and gender. The impact of race, gender, and class may change throughout history and/or from one context to another. Minoritized women's experience is multiplicative; they are indivisible beings with

---

10. Crenshaw, "Mapping the Margins," 1249.
11. Crenshaw, "Mapping the Margins, 1250.
12. Crenshaw, "Mapping the Margins, 1252.
13. Crenshaw, "Mapping the Margins, 1252.
14. Carbado, "Colorblind Intersectionality," 813–14.

multilayered experiences that include racism x sexism x classism, and love x joy x creativity x perseverance x strength x weakness x pain and so on. It is important to remember that black women, for example, are not a monolithic or unitary group. Black women, like other human beings, also have unique individual experiences and experiences with systems of oppression. Gender, class, and race can be complicated by dis/ability, nationality, language, ethnicity, sexuality, etc. We can ask how privilege and oppression co-constituted or intersect to inform minoritized women's experiences. How do privilege and oppression intersect to inform the experiences of minoritized women raised in poverty or in a middle-class family? How are some minoritized nonwhite women victims of oppression *and* privileged in relation to other nonwhite minoritized women (and men)? Some have suggested that black NFL players drawing multi-million dollar checks have no right to protest racism, as if they do not experience racism. They fail to see that some are exercising the privilege of their public platform to combat racism. Individual wealth and social position do not immunize minoritized or nonwhite women (and men) from systemic racism or individual acts of racism; they too are subjected to police misconduct or profiling and brutality. A wealthy nonwhite (or white) person who is a victim of police brutality, wrongful imprisonment, and survives, will have the financial means to obtain a competent lawyer to launch a defense and the monies to post bail. Theorist and practitioners of intersectionality should also consider intra-categorical complexity. For example, among African American women, some darker skinned and lighter skinned women may experience racism and sexism differently. This intra-categorical complexity is also a reality among African, Latina/o, Asian, and Native women and men as well.

The use of intersectional analysis among biblical scholars has increased. In her 1988 seminal text, *Just a Sister Away,* Hebrew Bible scholar Renita Weems offers an intersectional-type reading of women in both the Hebrew Bible and the NT, as well as the apocryphal Gospel of Mary. Weems states that she wrote *Just a Sister Away* with African American women in mind, as a *womanist* concerned with how race, gender, and class intersect in women's lives. But her goal is not simply to focus on differences but on similarities and the ways that white and nonwhite sisters can develop more positive relationships. NT biblical scholar Clarice Martin has employed intersectional-type analysis in her reading of the household codes. Martin argues that in reading the household codes in the Deutero-Pauline texts, the African American church and others reject the admonition for slaves to obey masters but fail to critique the submission of women and she notes the implications of this failure on the African American women's lives and experiences.[15] More recently, white feminists and/or scholars of early

---

15. Martin, "The *Haustafeln* (Household Codes) in African American Biblical

Christianity have begun to employ intersectional analysis to analyze cultural complexity.[16] For example, NT scholar Marianne Kartzow uses Gal 3:28 (there is no longer male or female, slave or free, Jew or Gentile) to examine the Colossian household codes in order to ask how social categories interact and mutually construct each other.[17] By looking beyond nationality/ethnicity, class and gender as separate categories to see how they interact and simultaneously impact lives, we can demonstrate a more complex social structure. Kartzow notes eight hypothetical combinations: Jewish slave male, Jewish slave female, Jewish free male, Jewish free female, Greek slave male, Greek slave female, Greek free male, and Greek free female. These additional categories make the household codes and their impact more complex.[18] With such analysis, Kartzow can raise the question of who functions as the parent of a slave child when the Colossian household codes require obedience to parents.[19] In her essay "Enslaved Women in Basil of Caesarea's Canonical Letters," Bernadette Brooten, a scholar of Christianity, gender, classical, and religious studies employs intersectional analysis to examine the distinction in the construction and condemnation of enslaved women and virginal women in Basil's letters. Basil had greater condemnation for virgins who broke their chastity or marriage vows by engaging in sexual immorality than for enslaved women. Enslaved women were not seen as capable of sexual immorality. NT biblical scholar Mitzi Smith's 2017 essay "*Dis*-membering, Sexual Violence, and Confinement" examines the intersection of race, gender, class, violence, and incarceration. Smith argues that the Levite's secondary wife (Jdg 19–20) experienced gradual dis-membering from the moment she was relegated to second class status and subjected to violence that results from membership in several interconnected subordinated social categories; her mutilation is the ultimate result of interlocking systems of oppression that engender annihilation.

Of course, other social complexities have been and can be examined in extracanonical texts and in the NT, like biracial/bi-ethnic identities represented by persons like Timothy whose father was Jewish and mother was Greek (Acts 16:1), or even Jesus who, according to Luke, was conceived of a Jewish mother and God's Spirit. Intersectionality as a tool of analysis has found a place in religious studies and will continue to travel as a field of study in its own right and across disciplines.

Interpretation."

16. For example, Nash, "Re-Thinking Intersectionality"; Davis, "Intersectionality as Buzzword"; and Nasrallah and Schüssler Fiorenza, *Prejudice and Christian Beginnings*.

17. Kartzow, "Asking the Other Question."

18. Kartzow, "Asking the Other Question," 377.

19. Kartzow, "Asking the Other Question," 380.

Further Reading

Bailey, Randall C. "That's Why They Didn't Call the Book Hadassah! The Interse(ct)/(x)ionality of Race/Ethnicity, Gender, and Sexuality in the Book of Esther." In *They Were All Together in One Place? Toward Minority Biblical Criticism*, edited by Randall C. Bailey, Tat-Siong Benny Liew, and Fernando F. Segovia, 227–50. Semeia Studies 57. Atlanta: Society of Biblical Literature, 2009.

Bose, Christianity E. "Intersectionality and Global Gender Inequality." *Gender and Society* 26 (2012) 67–72.

Brooten, Bernadette J. "Enslaved Women in Basil of Caesarea's Canonical Letters: An Intersectional Analysis." In *Doing Gender—Doing Religion: Fallstudien zur Intersektionalität im frühen Judentum, Christentum und Islam*, edited by Ute E. Eisen et al., 325–55. Tübingen: Mohr Siebeck, 2013.

Carbado, Devon W. "Colorblind Intersectionality." *Signs* 38 (2013) 811–45.

Chun, Jennifer Jihye, George Lipsitz, and Young Shin. "Intersectionality as a Social Movement Strategy: Asian Immigrant Women Advocates." *Signs* 38 (2013) 917–40.

Collins, Patricia Hill. *Black Feminist Thought: Knowledge, Consciousness, and the Politics of Empowerment*. 2nd ed. New York: Routledge, 1991.

———. "It's All in the Family: Intersections of Gender, Race, and Nation." *Hypatia* 13 (1998) 62–82.

Collins, Patricia Hill, and Sirma Bilge. *Intersectionality*. Malden, MA: Polity, 2016.

Crenshaw, Kimberlé. "Demarginalizing the Intersection of Race and Sex: A Black Feminist Critique of Antidiscrimination Doctrine, Feminist Theory, and Antiracist Politics." *University of Chicago Legal Forum* 140 (1989) 139–67.

———. "Mapping the Margins: Intersectionality, Identity Politics, and Violence against Women of Color." *Stanford Law Review* 43 (1991) 1241–99.

Crenshaw, Sumi Cho, and Leslie McCall. "Toward a Field of Intersectionality Studies: Theory, Applications, and Praxis." *Signs: Journal of Women in Culture and Society* 38 (2013) 785–810.

Dhamoon, Rita Kaur. "Considerations on Mainstreaming Intersectionality." *Political Research Quarterly* 64 (2011) 230–43.

Fiorenza, Elisabeth Schüssler. "Introduction: Exploring the Intersections of Race, Gender, Status and Ethnicity in Early Christian Studies." In *Prejudice and Christian Beginnings: Investigating Race, Gender, and*

Ethnicity in Early Christian Studies, edited by Laura Nasrallah and Elisabeth Schüssler Fiorenza, 1–23. Minneapolis: Fortress, 2009.

hooks, bell. *Ain't I a Woman: Black Women and Feminism*. Boston: South End, 1981.

———. *Feminist Theory from Martin to Center*. Boston: South End, 1984.

Hudson-Weems, Clenora. *Africana Womanism: Reclaiming Ourselves*. Troy, MI: Bedford, 1993.

Kartzow, Marianne Bjelland. "'Asking the Other Question': An Intersectional Approach to Galatians 3:28 and the Colossian Household Codes." *Biblical Interpretation* 18 (2010) 364–89.

Liew, Benny Tat-Siong. "Margins and (Cutting-) Edges: On the (Il)Legitimacy and Intersections of Race, Ethnicity, and (Post)Colonialism." In *Postcolonial Biblical Criticism. Interdisciplinary Intersections*, edited by Stephen D. Moore and Fernando F. Segovia, 114–65. New York: T. & T. Clark, 2007.

Marchal, Joseph A. "Difficult Intersections and Messy Coalitions (But in a Good Way)." *Journal of Feminist Studies in Religion* 30 (2014) 158–61.

Moxnes, Halvor. "Identity in Jesus's Galilee—From Ethnicity to Locative Intersectionality." *Biblical Interpretation* 18 (2010) 390–416.

Nash, Jennifer C. "Rethinking Intersectionality." *Feminist Review* 89 (2008) 1–15.

Smith, Barbara. "Racism and Women's Studies." In *But Some of Us Are Brave*, edited by Gloria T. Hull et al., 48–51. Old Westbury, NY; Feminist, 1982.

Smith, Mitzi J. "*Dis*-membering, Sexual Violence, and Confinement: A Womanist Intersectional Reading of the Story of the Levite's Wife (Judges 19)." In *Insights from African American Interpretation*, edited by Mark Alan Powell, 99–122. Minneapolis: Fortress, 2017.

———. *Womanist Sass and Talk Back: Social (In)Justice, Intersectionality, and Biblical Interpretation*. Eugene, OR: Cascade, 2018.

Smith, Shanell T. *The Woman Babylon and the Marks of Empire: Reading Revelation with a Postcolonial Womanist Hermeneutics of Ambiveilance*. Minneapolis: Fortress, 2014.

Weems, Renita. *Just a Sister Away*. West Bloomfield, MI: Warner, 2005.

Williams, Demetrius K. "'Upon All Flesh': Acts 2, African Americans, and Intersectional Realities." In *They Were All Together in One Place? Toward Minority Biblical Criticism*, edited by Randall C. Bailey, Tat-Siong Benny Liew, and Fernando F. Segovia, 289–310. Semeia Studies 57. Atlanta: Society of Biblical Literature, 2009.

CHAPTER 7

The Privatization of Water, Ancient Rome, and the New Testament

IN OUR CONTEMPORARY CONTEXTS, the privatization of water has presented a particular challenge for the poor in developing or underdeveloped nations, as well as in developed nations like the USA. Contaminated and/or unaffordable water caused major problems for the poor and vulnerable in US cities like Flint and Detroit, Michigan, and Baltimore, Maryland, to name only a few of the many cities and towns impacted. In 2018 in the United States, people are living without water and/or without clean, uncontaminated drinkable water. The privatization of water is a form of neocolonialism whereby interest in steep revenues overrides sustainable solutions and human need. When private companies privilege profits and stock/stakeholder satisfaction, there is very little, if any, concern for the public good and customer satisfaction. Rather than protect existing supplies, enhance conservation efforts, help vulnerable populations, curtail pollution, and raise public consciousness, government officials prefer privatization. Private companies pressure customers to either pay the higher prices resulting from privatization of water or go without access to clean water and sanitation. Detroit residents saw their water costs rise 300 percent within nine months; this is a significant increase for people living in poverty and/or on limited incomes. In most cases, children are suffering.

People cannot live long without water, yet profits over people persist with little public outcry and resistance. The privatization of water is a prerequisite that some formerly colonized countries must meet in order to qualify for loans (for water and other needs) from the World Bank (WB).[1] The WB has been pushing the commodification of water for over a decade, leaving millions of people without water. In 2004 ten major corporations were delivering water and wastewater services to over 300 million custom-

---

1. Water for All Campaign, "Top 10 Reasons"; Barlow and Clarke, "Water Privatization."

ers in 100 countries; those corporations continue to grow exponentially. By 2014 the top three providers will likely control 70 percent of the market in Europe and North America. During the Flint, Michigan, water crises, the only winners were big corporations like Nestle from whom compassionate donors were forced to purchase water for Flint residents. This was also the case with the first water shutoffs in Detroit. Countries like Senegal and South Africa have turned off water to tens of millions of people, many of whom are forced to use untreated water. A politics of disgust constructs and promotes a stereotype of those residents that are unable to meet the rising water costs as deadbeats who just do not want to pay their water bills. Nothing could be further from the truth for the overwhelming majority of the people impacted.

In a historic move, on July 28, 2010, the UN General Assembly "recognized" water and sanitation as a human right. Bolivia's Ambassador to the UN, Pablo Solon, verbally amended that UN resolution substituting the word "recognized" for "declared" as an acknowledgement of the preexisting understanding of water as a human right. It was not the case that access to water *became* a human right with the UN Declaration; it was already presumed to be a human right. The UN Declaration fully recognizes water and sanitation as an independent right, rather than an element or component "of other rights such as 'the right to an adequate standard of living'" or the "right to life."[2] Individuals can survive for weeks without food but only a few days without water, Solon reminded the Assembly. About sixty-five percentage of our bodies, including our blood and brains, is water; more deaths result from illnesses caused by lack of drinking water and sanitation than by war; and worldwide approximately one in eight people still lack potable water.[3]

The "second operative paragraph" of the UN resolution calls for "states and international organizations to provide financial resources; capacity-building and technology transfer through international assistance and cooperation, in particular to developing countries, in order to scale up efforts to provide safe, clean, accessible and affordable drinking water and sanitation for all."[4] For individuals who do not make a living wage, "affordable drinking water" will have to be free drinking water. "It is necessary," Solon argued, "to call on states to promote and protect the human right to drinking water and sanitation."[5]

---

2. Solon, "UN Declares Water as Human Right," 4.
3. Solon, "UN Declares Water as Human Right," 1.
4. Solon, "UN Declares Water as Human Right," 2.
5. Solon, "UN Declares Water as Human Right," 3.

People living in the first century CE, including Jesus, his disciples, the crowds that followed him, residents in and around the region of Galilee and Judea, the Apostle Paul, members of the *ekklēsia*, children, the enslaved, those without homes, the diseased, and others all needed access to clean, uncontaminated water for many of the same reasons that we need and use water in this twenty-first century. People used and needed water for drinking, food preparation, to fish for their livelihood, bathing, for religious and temple services and offerings, and for religious rituals that required water such as baptism and cleansing of utensils. People needed water for planting and watering their crops and for their animals or livestock.

Jesus did not baptize anyone, but John the Baptist performed water baptisms in the Jordan River, as did the apostles and disciples that continued to preach the Gospel and baptize after Jesus's death. In Luke's Gospel, Jesus chastised the judgmental Simon for his failure to offer Jesus the proper hospitality when he entered Simon's house (7:36–50). Yet, Simon viewed the unnamed woman who demonstrated hospitality toward Jesus as a sinner. But the woman, whom Simon considered a sinner, washed Jesus's feet with her tears of gratitude and dried them with her hair. It is not impossible that Simon had not drawn enough water that day to wash Jesus's feet, or he was being thrifty with his water given the effort it might take to draw it. Men evidently (collected and) carried water too, although women might have been the primary members of the household drawing water from wells, unless one had slaves tasked with doing so (Mark 14:12–14; Luke 22:10–13, this man could have been a slave). When Jesus transforms water into wine at the wedding in Cana in John's Gospel, the (male?) servants (*diakonoi*) draw and fill a number of water pots that were used for Jewish rites of purification, and they carry them to Jesus (2:1–11). Poor people and people generally living in rural areas had to draw their water from wells, like the Samaritan woman Jesus met at Jacob's well in John's Gospel (4:1–42). It is also possible that when the Pharisees and their scribes complained about Jesus's disciples not washing their hands before eating, they did not do so because they had no water readily accessible (Mark 7:1–23; Matt 15:1–20). Water is mentioned almost 100 times in the NT in reference to water baptism, hand washing, fishing, rites of purification (cleansing hands, utensils, and food), feet washing, and as a metaphor for spreading the gospel and its impact distinguishing the work of Paul from that of Apollos (e.g., Mark 9:41; 14:13; Luke 5:4; John 5:7; 13:5; 1 Cor 3:6). The act of providing water and food to the thirsty and hungry is equivalent to doing the same for Jesus (Matt 25:35). Jesus walks on water, demonstrating his command of nature (Matt 14:28; 17:15), and he offers living water to the nameless Samaritan woman he meets at the well (John 4:1–42). Jesus's offer of living water to the Samaritan woman may function subversively as a political statement challenging the power of the Roman Empire. Living water is running, free flowing, and clean.

The ancient Roman Empire recognized the importance of access to clean running, accessible water for drinking, food preparation, and health and leisure activities. Roman urban centers, like Greek cities, relied on a continuous flow of water. The Romans excelled in channeling water through rough terrain and across broad plains, which often surrounded their cities. Much of the water from Roman aqueducts, about seventeen percent, was consumed for public baths. It was the emperor's responsibility to provide water, but sometimes the wealthy paid for and constructed their own aqueducts. In 19 BCE Marcus Vispanius Agrippa, a prominent statesman, constructed the Aqua Virgo for his own private baths.[6] Rome was the first vast city characterized by its management of drinking water. The Romans relied upon the ideas of many of their foreign predecessors, but they were famous for their aqueducts that carried water via natural gravity and nonstop, massive amounts of water daily to Roman cities. The first Roman aqueduct, the Appia, was constructed in 312 BCE and ten others were added within five centuries. The aqueducts ensured a steady, continuous flow of water to public baths and lavish fountains, and for private homes that could afford to pay taxes on the spigot. "To the average Roman resident ... water in the city was available by right, as free for the taking as water from the Tiber River."[7] Archaeological evidence from the ruins of the Roman city of Pompeii dated around 79 CE shows that piped water was a luxury and access to piped water was potentially a status symbol of wealth and influence. Prior to the introduction of piped water via aqueducts, water was used moderately. Access to a private water supply piped directly into one's household was expensive and served as an ostensible symbol of high social status.

Still the urban population had access to public water supply through huge, elaborately decorated water basins. *Lacus* or public water basins were placed in Roman cities for the benefit of the public who would gather, as at a well, and draw water freely. But the amount of water a person could draw was limited, of course, by the effort and time it took to carry the water from the *lacus* to one's home. The Emperor Augustus made an indelible political statement when he increased public access to water through the *lacus*. As the first Emperor after the murder of Julius Caesar, Augustus's imperial gesture quite possibly served as a reminder to "the common people that they received their water from imperial beneficence in the name of their ruler. . . . The Roman's right to water was acknowledged, ensured, and enhanced as

---

6. Fagan, *Elixir*, 184, 194.
7. Salzman, *Drinking Water*, 54–56.

Aqua Nomine Caesaris—water in the name of Caesar."[8] The construction of the aqueducts by Rome's leaders achieved for them a prestige that "defined political relationships between the rulers and the ruled."[9] When the Roman Empire collapsed, the aqueducts would eventually cease to flow and what remained was traditional sources of water, e.g., wells and cisterns, which did not require an abundance of prisoners and slave labor.[10]

The control and allocation of water is political and always privileges the wealthiest consumers. Inga Winkler, a legal advisor to the UN Special Rapporteur on the Human Right to Safe Drinking Water and Sanitation, argues that "addressing the crisis in the lack of access to water requires, of course, water resources. . . . Yet above all, it requires the political will to use these resources in a way to prioritise [sic] basic human needs"; it is both a management and a political issue.[11] Sufficient water exists to meet the basic need of every household, but the broader demand beyond household needs exceeds availability, so that competing interests necessitate the setting of priorities in the allocation of water that privilege basic human needs.

Further Reading

Fagan, Brian. *Elixir: A History of Water and Humankind.* New York: Bloomsbury, 2011.

Horsley, Richard. *Jesus and the Powers: Conflict, Covenant and the Hope of the Poor.* Minneapolis: Fortress, 2011.

Jones, Rich, and Damian Robinson. "Water, Wealth, and Social Status at Pompeii: The House of the Vestals in the First Century." *American Journal of Archaeology* 109 (2005) 695–710.

Salzman, James. *Drinking Water: A History.* New York: Overlook Duckworth, 2012.

Smith, Mitzi J. "Water is a Human Right, but It *Ain't* Free: A Womanist Reading of John 4:1–42." In *Womanist Sass and Talk Back: Social Injustice, Intersectionality and Biblical Interpretation.* Eugene, OR: Cascade, 2018.

Solon, Pablo. "UN Declares Water as Human Right." *ClimateandCapitalism*, July 28, 2010. http://climateandcapitalism.com/2010/07/28/un-declares-water-a-human-right/.

---

8. Salzman, *Drinking Water*, 56–57.
9. Fagan, *Elixir*, 197.
10. Fagan, *Elixir*, 197.
11. Winkler, *Human Right to Water*, 7.

Sultana, Farhana, and Alex Loftus. *Right to Water: Politics, Governance, and Social Struggles.* New York: Routledge, 2012.

Winkler, Inga T. *The Human Right to Water: Significance, Legal Status and Implications for Water Allocation.* Oxford: Hart, 2014.

CHAPTER 8

Some Matters of Translation and the New Testament

STUDENTS OF THE NT should remember that every translation is an interpretation. New Testament interpretation is complex because it involves the historical context, original language, translation, methods of interpretation, and, of course, the interpreter and his or her context. Since we do not have copies of the original Greek New Testament, scholars arrive at one established (or secure) Greek text based on variant readings. There are about 5,000 New Testament manuscripts including fragments and lectionaries, and they are primarily in the common (*koinē*) Greek language. Even if we have an established text of the Greek New Testament, we must translate it into English. By and large, there are two kinds of translations: literal translations (word-for-word) and dynamic equivalent or paraphrase translations. The New Revised Standard Version (NRSV) and the King James Version (KJV) purport to be literal translations, and the latter is found in some other modern English Bibles such as the New International Version. Of course, the NRSV and the KJV read quite differently in many places, therefore, literal does not mean only one translation is possible for each Greek word, and the NRSV intentionally uses inclusive language. For example, when the Greek noun *adelphos* occurs in the greetings of Paul's letters, it is translated as "brothers and sisters," but a literal translation in the KJV is "brethren" (e.g. 1 Cor 12:1 in NRSV and KJV). For a critical academic study of the NT, a literal translation like the NRSV or the Oxford Annotated Bible is preferred. Then, even when we use a good translation, the meaning of the text is not as obvious as it may seem. And more than one legitimate meaning is possible. The method(s) of interpretation that readers choose to employ and/or the interpreter's context matter. And knowledge of the koinē (common) or biblical Greek can be very helpful; otherwise, readers must rely on translations, which are themselves interpretations. In the absence of knowledge of the Greek language, readers would do well to consult a number of English translations.

Since translation of the NT involves a number of issues, we cannot cover them all here. However, we will discuss a few important examples where translation matters. First, a significant translation issue for some concerns the Greek phrase *pistis christou*, which is often translated as "faith (*pistis*) of Christ (*christou*)," for example at Gal 2:16 and in Rom 3:21–22. *Pistis christou* involves a genitive case (like the English possessive meaning, as in the phrase "the children *of* the woman," which can be expressed as "the woman's children"). The phrase "faith of Christ" is the most literal translation of *pistis christou*. Some readers ask, "What does 'faith of Christ' mean?" Technically, there are two options for interpretation: a subjective genitive case or an objective genitive case. If Paul means to express a subjective genitive sense, *pistis christou* might be translated as "Christ's faith." That is, Christ is the one who is faithful or expresses faith. If Paul meant the second option, objective genitive, we might translate *pistis christou* as "faith in Christ." That is, Christ is the object of a believer's faith; believers demonstrate faith in Christ. The difference between these two options can be as vast as the difference between heaven and earth, because the former (subjective genitive) signifies Christ's faith and the latter (objective genitive) refers to a believer's faith. However, most English Bibles translate *pistis christou* as "faith in Christ," considering it as an objective genitive. But this translation is problematic for the following reasons. First, readers are deprived of an opportunity to engage with this genitive case, particular if readers are not familiar with the Greek and the Bible text they are using does not inform them of the translation options. Surprisingly, the NRSV translates other genitive phrases such as *dikaiosynē tou theou* (Rom 1:16; 3:21) or *agape tou theou* (Rom 8:39) differently, as "the righteousness of God" and "the love of God," respectively. What does "the righteousness of God" mean? Readers have to wonder in what sense Paul used this genitive phrase. It can be God's righteousness (a subjective genitive) or "a righteousness from God" (an objective genitive). Likewise, "the love of God" may mean "God's love" or "our love for God." The final decision must be made by readers in consideration of the syntax (other words connected with the phrase or the sentence in which it occurs) and the literary contexts (the speech, chapter or book in which the phrase is found). Then, why does the NRSV treat *pistis christou* differently and translate it as "faith in Christ"? Why does it decide for readers? Actually, in view of Paul's theology and overall literary context of Romans and other letters written by Paul, most scholars believe that *pistis christou* must be a subjective genitive meaning: Christ's faith. For example, Rom 3:22 can be better understood if we translate *pistis christou* as Christ's faith: "God's righteousness came through Christ's faith for all who have faith." If Paul had meant our faith in Christ, he would have used *pistis en christou* ("faith in Christ"). Also, if he had meant believer's faith in Christ, he would not have added "for all who have faith" because this is redundant. However, you as the reader can also determine for yourself, and learning the Greek language can help make a better-informed decision.

Second, in another literary context, the Greek word *dikaiosynē* can and perhaps should be translated as *justice* and not as *righteousness*. For example in the Gospel of Matthew, people who hunger and thirst for justice (*dikaiosynē*) will receive justice (5:6). Those who are bullied and defamed, as were the prophets, will receive a great reward in the heavens (5:12); the kin*dom or *basileia* of the heavens has drawn near in Jesus. The kin*dom does not signify an otherworldly justice. Jesus came in human flesh to fulfill the law and the prophets, which he has summed up as loving God (the *greatest* commandment) and loving neighbor (the second *greatest* commandment) (5:17–20; 22:34–40; cf. 5:44).

Third, sometimes a word that is not in the Greek text is supplied in the English translation in order to complete the thought in a way that makes sense to the interpreter. For example, in the NRSV, 1 Cor 7:21 reads, "Were you a slave when called? Do not be concerned about it. Even if you can gain your freedom (*aleutheros*), *make use of your present condition now more than ever*." At issue is the last clause, which I (Mitzi) have italicized. Those ten italicized English words are a translation of just two Greek words: *mallon chrēsai*, which translates as "take more/greater advantage [of it]!" The question is, what is it that the slave should take advantage of or make use of, freedom or slavery? Translators decide how to complete the sentence, and some complete the sentence as the NRSV (also KJV or New Jerusalem Bible (NJB), for example) has done. But 1 Cor 7:21 reads differently in English Bible translations like the Christian Community Bible (CCB): "If you were a slave when called, do not worry, yet if you can gain your freedom, take the opportunity!" The Good News Translation (GNT) and the New American Bible (NAB) agree with the CCB. I (Mitzi) would think that both the larger literary context of 1 Cor *and* the context of the interpreter matters. As contemporary readers might imagine, proslavery advocates in the American South preferred the KJV version that encouraged the enslaved to be content with their enslavement once they became Christians. But anti-slavery advocates or abolitionists preferred an interpretation that encouraged the enslaved to take advantage of opportunities to gain their freedom.

Fourth, the New International Version (NIV, 1984 edition) translates *erga nomou* in Gal 2:16 as "observing the law." But *erga nomou* means "works of the law." We must interpret what Paul might have meant by the phrase "works of the law." But the NIV translates somewhat oddly because of the doctrinal concern with "justification by faith." Otherwise, "observing the law" is an interpretation, which is not seen in the text. This translation considers Judaism as a legalistic religion and the law as an impossible means of salvation.

Fifth, often our biases for or against a certain character in the Bible or our preunderstanding of who is evil and who is not and of who performs miracles and who does magic, impacts how we translate words. For example, in the Acts of the Apostles, the Pythian slave girl is described as a fortune-teller by translators, as if her oracles are false and lack power (16:16–18). This description automatically carries a negative connotation for contemporary readers. Thus, Paul is the good guy and she is automatically the evil one.

Sixth, the NRSV translates Gal 2:20 as follows: "And it is no longer I who live, but it is Christ who lives in me. And the life I now live in the flesh I live by *faith in the Son of God (en pistei zō tē tou hiou tou theou)*, who loved me and gave himself for me." The concern is the italicized part, which is made up of a genitive. Literally, we can translate it as "faith of the Son of God." Like other *pistis christou* phrases, Paul may mean Jesus's faith; that is, he says that he wants to live by Christ's faith.

Seventh, there is an issue of translation in 2 Cor 13:4 (NRSV): "For he was crucified *in weakness (eks astheneias)* but lives *by the power of God (ek dynameōs theou)*. For we are weak in him, but in dealing with you we will live with him by the power of God." In the plain sense, the preposition *eks* (or *ek*) connotes "from, out of, because of." But the NRSV translates *eks astheneias* as "in weakness." But the plain sense of *eks astheneias* is "from weakness" or "by weakness," as a similar prepositional phrase, *ek dynameōs theou*, in the same verse is translated as "by the power of God." If Paul had meant "in weakness," he would have used the preposition *en* ("in" in English) with "weakness": *en astheneias*.

Eighth, in Rom 16:1, Phoebe is called *diakonos*, which means "servant or minister." In Paul's time, the church was not yet institutionalized to include hierarchical church offices, and it did not much concern him since the end was imminent. As *diakonos*, Phoebe functioned like a local minister of the church in Cenchrea. She was not a deacon in the modern sense. But most English Bibles translate *diakonos* as a servant (NIV, NRSV, NKJV) or even as a deaconess (NJB).

Ninth, in John 1:5, we find the verb *katelaben* (from the root *katalambano*), which means "to obtain, make one's own, attain, come upon, overtake, seize." The NRSV and the NIV translate John 1:5 differently: "The light shines in the darkness, and the darkness did not *overcome* it" (NRSV); "The light shines in the darkness, but the darkness has not understood it"

(NIV). The NRSV makes better sense and translates *katalambano* properly and in context. But the NIV translates it as "understood," which is a bit of a stretch to stress the cognitive (thinking or perception) dimension of the gospel, namely the matter of understanding or accepting the gospel. But here *katalambano* conveys a broad spectrum of meaning that has to do with all kinds of darkness (human thought, behavior, society, or world that resists God's power).

Tenth, in Luke 15:1–7, Jesus tells a parable of the lost sheep. In it, the shepherd leaves the ninety-nine in *the wilderness* (*erēmos*) and searches for one lost sheep. The Greek noun *erēmos* in Luke 15:4 means "desert or wilderness." But the NIV translates it as "the open country," which is very surprising. By this translation, the NIV probably intends to mean that the shepherd did not abandon his sheep in a desert—a dangerous place, but that he left them in an open country. But this translation is problematic because a parable challenges readers to think differently. That is, readers have to wonder why the shepherd leaves the ninety-nine sheep in a desert.

Eleventh, some translators use euphemisms or words that give a more pleasant meaning or image than may have been intended or that does not reflect the context. For example, some translators prefer to translate the Greek word *doulos* as servant and not slave, but it obscures the fact of the pervasive and cruel reality of enslavement in the first century CE and beyond. Rome was a slave society. Sometimes other translators render Paul's use of *doulos* as *servant*. The NRSV has done this, for example, at Phil 1:1 where Paul refers to himself and Timothy as slaves (*douloi*, plural) of Christ Jesus. Some readers have begun to call Paul to task for appropriating the noun to describe himself without ever having had the experience of being enslaved. It is like he is pulling a Rachael Dolezal (to use an anachronistic term) on his readers.

Further Reading

Aland, Kurt, and Barbara Aland. *The Text of the New Testament: An Introduction to the Critical Editions and to the Theory and Practice of Modern Textual Criticism*. 2nd ed. Grand Rapids, MI: Eerdmans, 1995.

Callahan, Allen Dwight. "A Note on 1 Corinthians 7.21." *Journal of Interdenominational Theological Center* 17 (Fall 1989–Spring 1990) 110–14.

Ehrman, Bart, and Bruce Metzger. *The Text of the New Testament: Its Transmission, Corruption, and Restoration*. New York: Oxford University Press, 2005.

Gafney, Wil. "Reading the Hebrew Bible Responsibly." In *The Africana Bible*, edited by Hugh R. Page Jr., 45–51. Minneapolis: Fortress, 2010.

Harrill, Albert J. "Paul and Slavery: The Problem of 1 Corinthians 7.21." *Biblical Research* 39 (1994) 5–28.

Kim, Yung Suk. *Biblical Interpretation: Theory, Process, and Criteria*. Eugene, OR: Pickwick, 2013.

Metzger, Bruce. *A Textual Commentary on the Greek New Testament*. 2nd rev. ed. Peabody, MA: Hendrickson, 2005.

Neyrey, Jerome. "Lost in Translation: Did it Matter if Christians 'Thanked' God or 'Gave God Glory'?" *Catholic Biblical Quarterly* 71 (2009) 1–23.

Parker, Angela. "One Womanist's Understanding of Paul's Problematic Self-Identity in Galatians." *Journal of Feminist Studies in Religion* 34.2 (2018) forthcoming.

Section II

The Gospels and Acts

CHAPTER 9

"The Danger of a Single Story": The Synoptic Gospels

> Stories matter. Many stories matter; stories can be used to empower and humanize. They can be used to rob a people of their dignity, but they can also be used to repair. When we reject the single story, that there is never a single story about any place, we regain a kind of paradise.
>
> —CHIMAMANDA NGOZI ADICHIE

AWARD-WINNING NIGERIAN NOVELIST CHIMAMANDA Ngozi Adichie states the danger of creating a single story of a place or people and stereotypes is that they deprive a place and its people of human dignity. It matters who tells the stories and how stories are told. Adichie argues that the number of stories that are told is really dependent on power. "Power is to tell the story of another person [or place] and make it the definitive story."[1] Obviously, Jesus did not write his own story. Jesus said and did things, and eventually what he said and did was written down. In other words, an oral tradition preceded the written tradition. We have access to four canonical Gospels (Matthew, Mark, Luke, and John) and a number of noncanonical apocryphal Gospels about Jesus and his apostles (e.g., Gospel of Peter, Gospel of Mary, Gospel of Judas, Gospel of Thomas). What these multiple gospels tell us is that people perceived of Jesus (his life, ministry, words, death), his apostles and/or disciples, and the gospel differently; they sometimes agree, overlap, and diverge in substantial and not so significant ways. Readers are encouraged to honor their differences rather than submit to the impulse to harmonize the stories.

---

1. Adichie, "Danger of a Single Story." Chimamanda Ngozi Adichie is an internationally known multi-award winning Nigerian novelist.

Perhaps the existence of four canonical Gospels is a necessary gift given the fact that Jesus did not write his own story.

Despite the addition in the second century CE of titles attributing authorship of the Gospels to Mark, Matthew, Luke, and John, the identities of the authors are unknown. We do not have access to the original first century manuscripts of the NT. If an apostle or someone associated with a recognized and respected apostle was considered the author of a NT text, it was a significant factor in whether or not to include (or omit) that text in church canons (lists of authoritative texts; e.g., Marcion's canon, Muratorion canon). The unknown authors used sources to write their gospel narratives. An inquiry about sources that ancient writers may have used to construct their texts is called source criticism. It is concerned with written and oral sources or traditions. When ancient writers used sources to which they had access to compose their writings, they attempted to copy them verbatim and/or they revised them. Plagiarism was not an issue among the ancients. To inquire about how an author used, edited, or augmented his sources is referred to as editorial or redaction criticism.

> **Form criticism** identifies literary forms that authors of biblical texts used, such as prayers, hymns, exorcism stories, conflict stories, healing stories, beatitudes, passion narratives, genealogies, birth narratives, baptismal formulas, quotation formulas, letters, apocalyptic discourse, parables, wisdom sayings, and proclamation. Form criticism allows for readers to compare literary forms and interpret texts in light of their literary forms. Textual criticism considers the differences or variations in various manuscripts of the NT and how they might impact translation or interpretation.

The Gospels of Mark, Matthew, and Luke provide a similar synopsis of the life, ministry, and death of Jesus of Nazareth. Thus, they are called Synoptic Gospels, and they present a synoptic problem. They share some of the same content, sequence of events, or structure, but they also differ from each other in some significant ways. They share more in common with each other than they do with the fourth Gospel, the Gospel of John. This is not to say that there are no commonalities between the fourth Gospel and the synoptics, because there are many. For example, all four Gospels recounted that Jesus calls disciples, cleanses the temple, performs miracles, was crucified, left an empty tomb and ascended to the Father.

Two-Source Theory

In terms of source criticism and the Synoptic Gospels, most scholars accept the view that the authors of Matthew and Luke each used two common sources. One source that each used was the Gospel of Mark, a written narrative about the life and ministry of Jesus. The second source is referred to as Q, which derives from the German noun *Quelle* meaning *source*. Q is a hypothetical written document consisting mostly of the sayings of Jesus in Greek. Since Jesus spoke in Aramaic, Q was originally Aramaic, not Greek, although a few Aramaic words survive in the Gospels. This theory that identifies Q and Mark as sources for Luke and Matthew is called the *two-source hypothesis*, which is the commonly accepted solution to the synoptic problem. Thus, content and structure or the order in which the story unfolds in Mark is largely duplicated in Luke and Matthew. This use of Mark's narrative did not prohibit the writers of Luke and Matthew from slightly revising and/ or augmenting it. Under the two-source hypothesis, Mark is considered to have been written earlier than Luke and Matthew; this is Markan priority. In terms of date of writing, Mark's Gospel is dated between 68 and 70 CE. The later date is preferred by scholars that believe Mark wrote after the destruction of the Second Jewish Temple in 70 CE. Matthew and Luke are dated approximately between 80 and 100 CE, after Mark's text.

Table A below shows three examples of materials that Matthew and Luke borrowed from Mark and slightly revised. The episodes are: (1) the beginning of Jesus's ministry in Galilee (Mark 1:14–15//Matt 4:12–17// Luke 4:14–15); (2) the resuscitation of Simon's (Peter) mother-in-law (Mark 1:29–31//Matt 8:14–15//Luke 4:38–39); and (3) the healing of the man with Leprosy (Mark 1:40–44//Matt 8:1–4//Luke 5:12–14). Note that the material in brackets indicates what precedes and what follows each narrative, demonstrating how at times Matthew and Luke also maintain the order in which Mark told his story.

Table A

Mark	Matt	Luke
[Temptation of Jesus]	**[Temptation of Jesus]**	**[Temptation of Jesus]**
Mark 1:14–15: Now after John was arrested, Jesus came to Galilee, proclaiming the good news of God, and saying, "The time is fulfilled, and the kingdom of God has come near; repent, and believe in the good news."	Matt 4:12–17: Now when Jesus heard that John had been arrested, he withdrew to Galilee. He left Nazareth and made his home in Capernaum by the sea, in the territory of Zebulun and Naphtali, so that what had been spoken through the prophet Isaiah might be fulfilled: [quote Isa 9:1–2] From that time Jesus began to proclaim, Repent, for the kingdom of heaven has come near.	Luke 4:14–15: Then Jesus, filled with the power of the Spirit, returned to Galilee, and a report about him spread through all the surrounding country. He began to teach in their synagogues and was praised by everyone.
[Jesus calls first disciples.]		**[Rejection in Nazareth]**
	[Jesus calls first disciples]	
[Jesus heals man with unclean spirit in synagogue in Capernaum]	**[Jesus heals Centurion's slave]**	**[Jesus heals man with unclean spirit in synagogue in Capernaum]**
Mark 1:29–31: As soon as they left the synagogue, they entered the house of Simon and Andrew, with James and John. Now Simon's mother-in-law was in bed with a fever, and they told him about her at once. He came and took her by the hand and lifted her up. Then the fever left her, and she began to serve them.	Matt 8:14–15: When Jesus entered Peter's house, he saw his mother-in-law lying in bed with a fever; he touched her hand, and the fever left her, and she got up and began to serve him.	Luke 4:38–39: After leaving the synagogue he entered Simon's house. Now Simon's mother-in-law was suffering from a high fever, and they asked him about her. Then he stood over her and rebuked the fever, and it left her. Immediately she got up and began to serve them.
	[summary of healing persons possessed with demons and the sick in fulfillment of an Isaiah prophecy]	
[summary of healing sick and exorcising demons]		**[Crowds seek Jesus who went to a deserted place; they try to prevent him from leaving but he must preach in the synagogues and so he continued preaching.]**

"THE DANGER OF A SINGLE STORY": THE SYNOPTIC GOSPELS

Table A

Mark	Matt	Luke
[summary of Jesus preaching throughout Galilee in synagogues and casting out demons] Mark 1:40–44: A leper came to him begging him, and kneeling he said to him, "If you choose, you can make me clean." Moved with pity, Jesus stretched out his hand and touched him, and said to him, "I do choose. Be made clean!" Immediately the leprosy left him, and he was made clean. After sternly warning him he sent him away at once, saying to him, "See that you say nothing to anyone, but go, show yourself to the priest, and offer for your cleansing what Moses commanded, as a testimony to them." But he went out and began to proclaim it freely, and to spread the word, so that Jesus could no longer go into a town openly, but stayed out in the country; and people came to him from every quarter. [Jesus heals a paralytic]	[end of sermon on mount; building house on sand and rock and the amazement of crowd at his teaching with authority] Matt 8:1–4: When Jesus had come down from the mountain, great crowds followed him, and there was a leper who came to him and knelt before him, saying, "Lord, if you choose, you can make me clean." He stretched out his hand and touched him, saying, "I do choose. Be made clean!" Immediately his leprosy was cleansed. Then Jesus said to him, "See that you say nothing to anyone but go, show yourself to the priest, and offer the gift that Moses commanded, as a testimony to them." [Jesus heals a Centurion's slave]	[calling of first disciples] Luke 5:12–14: Once, when he was in one of the cities, there was a man covered with leprosy. When he saw Jesus, he bowed with his face to the ground and begged him, "Lord, if you choose, you can make me clean." Then Jesus stretched out his hand, touched him, and said, "I do choose, be made clean." Immediately the leprosy left him. And he ordered him to tell no one. "Go," he said, "and show yourself to the priest, and as Moses commanded, make an offering for your cleansing, for a testimony to them." But now more than ever the word about Jesus spread abroad; many crowds would gather to hear him and to be cured of their diseases. But he would withdraw to deserted places and pray. [Jesus heals a paralytic]

The Markan priority has hermeneutical implications or should impact how we interpret passages found in the Synoptic Gospels. We presume a narrative originated with Mark's Gospel if it is found in all the Synoptics. Markan priority means that interpreters will resist the impulse to harmonize the stories that appear in the synoptics. Instead, interpreters should observe the differences and consider where and why, for example, Luke or Matthew may have chosen to revise Mark's source. Any attempt to answer these questions requires that we read Matthew or Luke closely and consider changes to a particular Markan story in the literary context of Matthew or Luke. Matthew's literary context is the entire Gospel of Matthew; Luke's literary context is the entire Gospel of Luke. We also consider the stories or materials that immediately surround the story or passage in question in each Gospel. As an example, we will observe the differences in the story of the healing of Peter's mother-in-law. We will focus on Matthew's version and how the author edited his Markan source. In comparing Luke's and Matthew's versions with Mark's (as their source), readers should note differences among the above NRSV English translations (of course, demonstrated differently in the Greek text) both in terms of language and ordering or sequence of actions. Some differences may be minor and others more obviously noteworthy, but sometimes even seemingly minor changes or additions might not be theologically insignificant.

> For example, while Mark prefers to use the name Simon, Matthew changes it to Peter. Matthew omits that Jesus quickly left the synagogue and that James and John (and perhaps Andrew) were present. Matthew's Jesus saw Peter's mother-in-law lying on the bed, but Mark reports that Jesus was told about her. While Mark's Jesus took her hand and lifted her up causing the fever to leave, Matthew altered Mark so that Jesus simply touched her hand. In Mark she served "them" once she is healed; in Matthew she served "him," meaning Jesus. Luke, different from Mark, says she suffered from a high fever and that Jesus simply stood over her, rebuked the fever (as if a person, animate thing or a demon), and the fever left. Each understands Jesus's method for healing Simon/Peter's mother-in-law differently. Readers should investigate how each method fits in the overall portrait each paints of Jesus and healing, or even healing of women.

More About Q

Although Q is primarily a sayings source that is currently lost to us, scholars reconstruct Q for research purposes from Luke's narrative. Q material is identified as primarily sayings of Jesus that are present in both Matthew and Luke, but not present in Mark. Q is a source that Matthew and Luke share in common in addition to the Markan narrative source. For example, Q would

"THE DANGER OF A SINGLE STORY": THE SYNOPTIC GOSPELS

be represented as follows: Q (Luke) 15:3–7 // Matt 18:10–14; Luke 15:3–7 (the parable of the lost sheep). In addition to Q, another sayings source exists called the *Gospel of Thomas* (hereafter *GosTh*), which is a Christian apocryphal text consisting of the sayings of Jesus. While the prologue identifies the text as the secret words of the living Jesus written by the Apostle Didymos Judas Thomas (see John 11:16; 20:24–29), it is generally believed that *GosTh* was written in the mid-second century CE by an unknown author. The original language of *GosTh* was Greek but the extant or available text is in Sahidic Coptic.[2] A few scholars believe that the *GosTh* is Q, but most contend that Q is lost. The following are a couple of *GosTh* excerpts from Logia (sayings) 1, 3, 13, 31, 49, 100, 114 (*GosTh* consists of 114 Logia):

> *And He said*: Whoever finds the explanation of these words will not taste death. . . . *Jesus said*: If those who lead you say to you: "See, the Kingdom is in heaven," then the birds of the heaven will precede you. . . . But the Kingdom is within you and it is without you. . . . *Jesus said to his disciples*: Make a comparison to Me and tell Me who I am like. Simon Peter said to Him: Thou art like a righteous angel. Matthew said to Him: Thou art like a wise man of understanding. Thomas said to Him: Master, my mouth will not at all be capable of saying whom Thou art like. . . . *Jesus said*: No prophet is acceptable in his village, no physician heals those who know him. . . . *Jesus said*: Blessed are the solitary and elect, for you shall find the Kingdom; because you come from it, (and) you shall go there again. . . . They showed Jesus gold (coin) and said to Him: Caesar's men ask taxes from us. *He said to them*: Give the things of Caesar to Caesar, give the things of God to God and give Me what is Mine. . . . Simon Peter said to them: let Mary go out from among us, because women are not worthy of the Life. *Jesus said*: See, I shall lead her, so that I will make her male, that she too may become a living spirit, resembling you males. For every woman who makes herself male will enter the Kingdom of Heaven.[3] (Emphasis added)

Readers might note the similarities between *GosTh* sayings of Jesus and material from the Synoptic Gospels. Some *GosTh* sayings may be unfamiliar and even appear strange to readers acquainted with the canonical Gospels.

---

2. A Sahidic Coptic Codex dated about the fourth or fifth century CE of *The Gospel according to Thomas* was discovered in 1945 in the area of Nag-Hammadi in Upper Egypt.

3. Guillaumont et al., *Gospel According to Thomas*.

Matthew and Luke's Unique Material

Mark and Q do not account for all the material found in Matthew and Luke. The two-source theory continues that material found in each Matthew and Luke that is unaccounted for in Mark and Q and that Matthew and Luke do not share in common is material that is peculiar or special to each of them. In other words, in addition to Mark and Q, Matthew used his own material that scholars call *Special M*; and Luke had his own called *Special L*. For example, only Luke tells the stories of the priest Zechariah and the birth of John the Baptist (1:5–25); Jesus's visit at Mary and Martha's home (10:38–42); and the healing of the crippled bent-over woman in the synagogue on the Sabbath (13:10–17). Only Matthew's Gospel has the flight of Mary and Joseph to Egypt to escape Herod's death decree (2:13–15); the parable of the unforgiving slave (18:23–35); and the parable of the ten virgins (25:1–13).

Each Gospel should be respected as reflecting the author's literary and theological agenda or objective, his attempt to narrate the life, ministry, and death of Jesus from his perspective with the use of sources. Again, readers should resist the temptation to harmonize the Gospels. Differences may reflect the context or community to which each writer belonged, as well as their individual perspectives. Thus, differences among them also demonstrate that early believers in Jesus as God's Messiah or the Christ interpreted the events and people surrounding Jesus and his life, ministry, and death differently. These texts are testimonies both to the commonalities and diversity among early believers. We cannot know the full extent or content of the diversity among believers in the first century CE, since some texts like the *Gospel of the Ebionites* and the *Gospel of the Hebrews* are currently lost to us.

It matters where a story starts and has implications for how we interpret the story and the people in the story. Adichie states that if we start the story with the arrows of the Native Americans and not with the arrival of the British, we have an entirely different story. Start with the failure of the African state and not with the colonial creation of the African state, and we have an entirely different story. Each of the gospel writers start their story at different points. Mark begins his story by identifying his narrative as good news about Jesus, the Messiah (Christ) and son of God about whom the prophet Isaiah spoke. Matthew starts with Jesus's genealogy as God's Davidic Messiah showing how he was related to King David. Luke's story commences by informing his reader(s), the most excellent Theophilus, that his story has been thoroughly investigated and constitutes an orderly and truthful accounting and offers it as an addition to an already existing collection. John begins with a midrash or homily about Jesus as the pre-existent

Word (logos) that was with God from the very beginning of creation and who has come to disrupt darkness with light.

Further Reading

Adichie, Chimamanda Ngozi. "The Danger of a Single Story." TED Talk, 2009. https://youtu.be/D9Ihs241zeg.

Blount, Brian K. *Then the Whisper Put on Flesh: New Testament Ethics in an African American Context*. Nashville: Abingdon, 2001.

Borg, Marcus. *Jesus: The Life, Teachings, and Relevance of a Religious Revolutionary*. New York: HarperOne, 2015.

Bovon, François. *New Testament and Christian Apocrypha*. Edited by Glenn E. Snyder. Grand Rapids, MI: Baker, 2011.

Guillaumont, A., et al., trans. *The Gospel According to Thomas*. Leiden: Brill, 1959.

Harrington, Daniel J. *Interpreting the New Testament: A Practical Guide*. Collegeville, MN: Liturgical, 1979.

Hayes, John H., and Carl R. Holladay. *Biblical Exegesis: A Beginner's Handbook*. 3rd ed. Louisville: Westminster John Knox, 2007.

Kim, Yung Suk. *Biblical Interpretation: Theory, Process, and Criteria*. Eugene, OR: Cascade, 2013.

Klein, Robert H. *The Synoptic Problem: An Introduction*. Valley Forge, PA: InterVarsity, 1988.

Koester, Helmut. *History and Literature of Early Christianity: Introduction to the New Testament*. Berlin: Gruyter, 1987.

Meyer, Marvin W., ed. *The Nag Hammadi Scriptures: The Revised and Updated Translation of Sacred Gnostic Texts*. New York: HarperOne, 2009.

Powell, Mark Allan. *What Is Narrative Criticism?* Minneapolis: Fortress, 1990.

Robinson, James M. *Jesus According to the Earliest Witness*. Minneapolis: Fortress, 2007.

Robinson, James M., John S. Kloppenborg, and Paul Hoffmann, eds. *The Sayings Gospel Q in Greek and English with Parallels from the Gospels of Mark and Thomas*. English and Greek ed. Minneapolis: Fortress, 2002.

CHAPTER 10

Gospel of Mark

[A]n alternative reading [of Mark] suggests that Jesus's identity is evasive and that discipleship embraces this incomprehensibility. . . . A proper knowing of Jesus's identity is not a requisite for discipleship.

—Jin Young Choi[1]

I do not accept suffering as a divinely necessitated part of Jesus's ministry. However, I do acknowledge pain as an inevitable consequence of following Jesus. Consequently, a womanist hermeneutics of wholeness affirms that we will endure pain rather than forsake following Jesus, in order to bring about transformation in ourselves, our homes, our churches, our communities, and the world.

—Raquel St. Clair[2]

Jesus advanced an ethic of freedom, responsibility, and, above all, love for one's neighbor. This message of personal involvement shook social convention, creating a system that engages entirely the individual will: the coming kingdom, Jesus proclaimed, demands a willingness to serve that will not balk before suffering.

—François Bovon[3]

---

1. Choi, *Postcolonial Discipleship of Embodiment*, 14.
2. St. Clair, *Call and Consequences*, 83.
3. Bovon, *Last Days of Jesus*, 29–30.

Mark at a Glance

1. The author is unknown; we shall call him *Mark*.
2. Mark was likely Jewish and wrote for a mixed Jewish and Gentile audience.
3. Mark is dated sometime during the Jewish War (66–70 CE) and perhaps after the destruction of the Temple.
4. Mark's Gospel is the oldest written canonical Gospel.
5. Mark is the shortest of the four canonical Gospels.
6. Mark is the only NT text explicitly identified as a Gospel.
7. Mark's Jesus returns home often where his mother and siblings reside; home is significant.
8. The authority to exorcize demons/unclean spirits is central to Jesus's identity in Mark.
9. Jesus proclaims the good news of the nearness of God's *basileia* (rule or kin-dom).

Introduction

THE COPTIC ORTHODOX CHURCH believes that Saint Mark brought the Christ faith to Alexandria, Egypt, during the reign of the Roman Emperor Nero in the first century CE. Thus, the beliefs and/or doctrines of the Coptic Church are based on the Apostle Mark's teachings. Egyptian Coptic Christians claim Mark as their founder and their first patriarch. To Mark, of course, is attributed the authorship of the oldest canonical Gospel, the *Gospel of Mark*. The proof of this foundational claim, according to the Coptic Church, is the discovery of the NT writings in al-Bahnasa/Behnesa (Oxyrhynchus), in Middle Egypt, dated around 200 CE, which also included a small fragment of the *Gospel of John* written in the Coptic language (the final stage of the Ancient Egyptian language system) dated around the first half of the second century CE. Many believe that the founding of the church in Egypt is anticipated in Isaiah: "In that day there will be an altar to the LORD in the midst of the land of Egypt, and a pillar to the LORD at its border" (19:19).

Irenaeus, the second century CE Bishop of Lugdunum (now Lyons, France), claims in his *Against Heresies* that Mark as Peter's disciple and interpreter wrote what Peter preached (cf. Acts 13:5, 13; 15:37–40; Phlm 24; Col 4:10; 2 Tim 4:11; 1 Pet 5:13).[4] Nevertheless, most scholars consider the author of Mark's Gospel to be unknown; in this chapter we sometimes refer to the author of this oldest and shortest canonical Gospel as Mark. It is the only canonical Gospel that is explicitly identified as the Gospel (*euangelion*) of Jesus Christ, the son of God (1:1). Mark's Gospel contains no birth narratives; Jesus appears on the scene as a grown man ready for baptism. Mark's Gospel begins with a quotation introducing readers to John the Baptist as God's wilderness messenger who prepares a path for God's Messiah, as stated by the prophet Isaiah; however, the beginning of the quote is from Mal 3:1 (1:2; cf. Isa 40:3). Mark constructs a continuity between prophetic tradition of the Hebrew Scriptures and the ministries of Jesus and John. John baptized and preached the coming of one more powerful and worthy than himself and who would practice baptism of the Holy Spirit.

Mark's Jesus is a devout practicing Jewish man from Nazareth (a colonized rural Jewish town known for nothing in particular). He attends and participates in synagogue services, keeps the Sabbath as a holy day, reads and knows the Jewish Scriptures, and observes Jewish rituals and customs, even if not to every one's taste. Jesus's parents are Jewish peasants; his father is known to be a carpenter who may have found work in a nearby town. Jesus lives with his mother and siblings, whenever he returns home. He often refers to himself as the *son of man*, which some consider a divine title. However, when Mark's Jesus uses it, he is likely emphasizing his humanity; he is a human being or child of a human being.

Jesus ministers (performs exorcisms, healing miracles, teaches and preaches) in and around the region of Galilee, close to home, but also moves beyond Galilee and into Jerusalem. He chooses twelve apostles as his inner circle whom he mentors and commissions with the authority to do the same acts as he performs. He proclaims the good news of God's *basileia* (often translated *kingdom*, but perhaps closer to *reign* since the idea transcends a physical, earthly institution, at least from Jesus's perspective) in synagogues on the Sabbath, in homes (and at home), by the sea of Galilee, and seated in a boat anchored on the sea. Early in his ministry, some Pharisees and their scribes (the latter joined by the elders, chief priest, Herodians and their scribes) oppose Jesus's words and actions. He is a misunderstood Rabbi or Jewish teacher.

---

4. Irenaeus, *Against Heresies*, 3.1.1.

Some Jewish leaders dislogue and disagree with Jesus over issues of *halakhic* (legal rules and traditions that govern how Jewish people, or in this case a Jewish Rabbi and his disciples, ought to conduct themselves in terms of Sabbath observance, food preparation, pre-meal hand-washing rituals, and divorce and remarriage, for example). Jesus predicts his impending betrayal, death, and resurrection before setting his intentions to journey to Jerusalem where he will eventually be arrested, condemned, and crucified, but not before a number of preliminary events. On the first day of the week following his crucifixion, Mary Magdalene, Salome, and Mary the mother of James arrive early to anoint Jesus's body, but they find only an unsealed and empty tomb and a man robed in white who informs them that Jesus has been raised. God has raised Jesus. The oldest narrative ends at 16:8 with no appearance of the resurrected Christ to his disciples, although a reunion is anticipated in Galilee. Unfortunately, Mark's story ends with a depiction of the women as too scared and shocked to tell anybody about what they have seen (and not seen) and heard, despite being commissioned to tell it all.

Chapter Contents

1. The Good News of Jesus Christ
2. John the Baptist as Forerunner
3. The Selection of Twelve Apostles: Even Jesus Needs a Tribe
4. Silenced Demons/Unclean Spirits and the Unprecedented Authority of Jesus
5. Jesus Teaches in Parables
6. Home as Public Contested Space and Fluid Fictive Kinship Boundaries
7. Opposition and Death Conspiracies
8. Take Up Your Cross and Follow Me
9. Mark's Passion Narrative (Chapters 14–16)

The Good News of Jesus Christ

Christ (*Christos* in Greek) means anointed one or Messiah. In Mark, Jesus is both God's Messiah and son (1:1, 11; 8:29). As God's anointed one and son, Jesus preaches the goods news of God: "the time is fulfilled, and the *basileia* of God has come near; repent and believe in the good news" (1:15). The *basileia* of God is present on earth, and this makes it a political message. Unlike the Essenes that withdrew into the wilderness, Jesus brings the *basileia* of God to the people living in and around the towns and villages of Galilee. Jesus teaches the twelve that he called using parables so that they alone might know the mystery of God's *basileia*; he explains the meaning of them privately (4:11–12, 33). The *basileia* of God has drawn near in and through Jesus; he embodies good news through his ministry of powerful acts and words. Jesus embodies the *basileia* of God, but he does not restrict or contain it. The *basileia* of God has arrived with demonstrations of power (9:1). Eventually people figure out that Jesus is so powerful that they can experience healing by merely touching the hem or fringes of his cloak (6:56). Jesus shows that God's good news touches people in the places where they suffer and is realized in the body. Yet, it is not so easily experienced by everyone. Bringing a wealthy person into the *basileia* of God is like trying to thread a camel through a needle; it is not even humanly conceivable for Mark's or Jesus's audience—the hard working, low-wage earning peasants, the enslaved, and other peoples living in and around (or visiting) Galilee. But with God, Jesus declares, all things are possible (10:23–27); God sees from a different vantage point than human beings do, and God can do what seems impossible. The good news of the *basileia* is knowable and recognizable, and at the same time it is mysterious and incomprehensible. Perhaps, this complexity or ambivalence encourages a hermeneutical and epistemological humility.

John the Baptist as Forerunner

According to Mark, the prophet Isaiah anticipated John the Baptist's role as the forerunner that would prepare the way for Jesus as God's agent and Messiah (anointed one or Christ). John preached to those persons living in and around Jerusalem and Judea, exhorting everyone to repent of their sins and submit to a water baptism. Evidently, John preached repentance to kings *and* peasants. He apparently exhorted the Tetrarch (governor of one of four divisions under the Rome Empire) of Galilee and Perea, King Herod Antipas to repent of the sin of marrying his brother's wife (6:17–19). John indiscriminately preaching about sin got him killed, just as the consequence of Jesus's ministry will be his lynching. Through his preaching, John prepared the people for the impending appearance of Jesus from Nazareth of Galilee, a more powerful and worthy agent than himself. Isaiah's prophecy and John's role are confirmed at Jesus's baptism when the Spirit descends upon him and a voice from heaven identifies him as "my son, the beloved with whom I am well-pleased" (1:11). The Spirit compels Jesus into the seclusion of the wilderness for a forty-day fast during which time the adversary, Satan, tests him. This is Satan's traditional role, adversary and accuser of God's children (Job 1:6; Zech 3:1–2). Following the completion of the rites of passage and the arrest of John the Baptist, Jesus begins his ministry, not in Jerusalem, but in and around the region and sea of Galilee, not far from home (1:14). Galilee included Capernaum, Bethsaida, Cana, Tiberias, and Nazareth where Jesus lived.

Consider and discuss: How do you understand the Satan figure here in Mark? Do you think it is the same Satan from the book of Job? If so, is the Satan immortal like God or is he or she a created being? Could the Satan be understood metaphorically? The 1960–70s African American comedian Flip Wilson (1933–98) popularized the saying "the devil made me do it." Do we sometimes blame Satan for our own human frailties and shortcomings as well as systemic problems that oppress and make life difficult?

We are initially told that John was arrested, but not until chapter 6 do we discover what happened to John the Baptist while in custody. King Herod had John beheaded at the request of his wife Herodias. John, whom Herod feared because he was a holy and just man, had condemned Herod for marrying his brother's wife, Herodias, as mentioned above. At a banquet, Herod was so captivated with Herodias's dancing moves that he promised her anything she desired. After seeking her mother's advice (she must have been quite young or simply valued her mother's opinion), Herodias demands John's head on a platter. And Herod is obligated to grant her request (6:17–29). Herod created a situation for himself that he desperately wished he had not, somewhat like Jephthah who made a vow that resulted in the death of his daughter (Judg 11:29–40). Thus, as Jesus's reputation as an authoritative and powerful teacher, exorcist, and healer spread throughout the region, Herod is haunted by the unjust execution of John, assuming that Jesus is John the Baptist returned from the dead (6:14–16).

The Selection of Twelve Apostles: Even Jesus Needs a Tribe

While walking along the Sea of Galilee, Jesus chose his first four disciples before he performed his first public exorcism or miracle. He selected the first four men while they practiced their regulated and not very lucrative trade as fishermen: Simon (later named Peter, 3:16) and his brother Andrew and two other brothers James and John, the sons of Zebedee (1:16–20; cf. Acts 1:15–26). Three of the first four Jesus calls become a part of his intimate inner circle within a circle of twelve that he eventually chooses; Jesus needs a tribe too. For example, Peter, James, and John are asked to pray with Jesus at Gethsemane in Jesus's hour of agony as he prepares to face betrayal, arrest, and death; unfortunately, they fall asleep (14:32–42). Jesus also takes the three with him to experience his transfiguration on the mount of Olives where Moses and Elijah appear in conversation with Jesus (9:2–7). Perhaps their apparent closeness to Jesus gave James and John, the sons of Zebedee, the impression that proximity and intimacy translate into privilege (rather than greater responsibility), since they request that Jesus promise and reserve for them the privilege of sitting at his right and left side when he is glorified (10:35–45). No doubt when the rumor of their request reached the other apostles, the privilege they sought was not appreciated. Nevertheless, Jesus could not grant their request.

> **Consider and discuss:** Christians and other religious people often speak of God's favor (or blessing) in terms of material gains and/or experiences of survival when catastrophe or death strikes. Some sacred texts often lend themselves to such interpretations and others do not. Sometimes what we describe as favor or blessing is predicated upon privilege (e.g., access to higher education or education at all, inheritance of money, position, or other advantages of living in a developed nation, and so on). How can we express gratefulness and appreciation while recognizing our privilege and the responsibility that privilege demands to others who are less privileged or impacted by oppressions that we ourselves might not experience or experience differently?

The fifth disciple Jesus chooses is a tax collector, Levi (James), the son of Alphaeus with whom he also shares a meal; some scribes of the Pharisees condemn Jesus for doing so (2:13–17). That occasion gives rise to Jesus saying that the healthy do not need a physician but the sick do; Jesus's ministry is to/for sinners and not the righteous (2:17). Jesus has become quite famous in the region by the time he chooses other disciples that complete the twelve, whom he calls apostles. The noun *apostle* derives from the Greek verb (*apostellō*) meaning "I send"; the twelve are being groomed to embody and articulate the good news and to exercise authority over demons/unclean spirits. In addition to the five previously chosen, Jesus calls Philip, Bartholomew,

Matthew, Thomas, Thaddaeus, Simon the Cananaean, and Judas Iscariot; the latter is already identified as the one who will betray Jesus (3:19). And Simon Peter will deny Jesus twice after his arrest (14:30–31, 72). Tribes are not perfect and individual members sometimes let us down.

Silenced Demons/Unclean Spirits and the Unprecedented Authority of Jesus

The first powerful act that Jesus performs in Mark is an exorcism in the synagogue. After his baptism, wilderness testing, and selection of four disciples, Jesus immediately (Greek: *euthus*, a favorite Markan adverb) enters the synagogue and starts teaching, without invitation, it seems (1:21–28). Suddenly (*euthus*) a man with an unclean spirit enters the synagogue; the man cries out but the unclean spirits speak; that is what they do. They have usurped control of the man's body and voice: "Jesus of Nazareth, what do you want with us? Have you come to destroy us? I know who you are! You are God's Holy One" (1:24). They are many spirits, but they speak as one. This recognition scene shows that even if the people do not fully recognize Jesus or know what to make of the authority he demonstrates, the unclean spirits do. Synagogue meetings or worship emerge as contested sites of struggle where unclean spirits dare to contend with God's son. Perhaps like Satan/adversary in Job, they are "sons of God" too (1:6); it takes one to know one. In Mark, the authority and power that Jesus demonstrates over unclean spirits and/or demons is the ultimate symbol that the *basileia* of God is near in and through him. Jesus scolds the unclean spirits. Ordering them to be silent, he evicts them from the man's body. With a loud scream (*phonē megale*), the unclean spirits violently vacate the man's body causing convulsions, like a child throwing a temper tantrum. The exorcism is inextricably linked with Jesus's teaching. All who witness the exorcism conclude that what they have witnessed is a new authoritative teaching. Through a performative speech act (speech that accomplishes something), Jesus exorcised the unclean spirits. This first exorcism functions to uniquely contextualize Jesus's ministry, setting a pattern of silencing some unclean spirits or demons that recognize or identify him as God's son (3:11–12). It is difficult to know whether Mark's Jesus is struggling with the significance of his identity and/or if these recognition scenes are Mark's way of raising the consciousness of his readers about Jesus's identity and function as God's son and Messiah. Perhaps, it is both and more.

Other Deeds of Power and the Demand for Secrecy

Jesus demands secrecy or silence from others that he heals too, even when the healing takes place in public among the crowds. His fame spreads after the first exorcism (1:28). The fact that Mark's Jesus does not welcome the publicity draws our attention, as readers, to his attempts to silence the demons and/or unclean spirits and others, to keep his secret. The secret that is never really a secret! After Jesus heals a man afflicted with leprosy, he instructs him to present himself to the priest to offer the customary offering and to tell no one (1:40–45). This requirement is included in the Levitical laws (Lev 14). Unlike the demons and unclean spirits, humans ignore Jesus's demand for secrecy: understandably the man healed of leprosy freely publicizes the healing, as will the deaf man with the speech impediment whom Jesus heals (7:31–37; cf. 8:22–26). When Jesus resuscitates the synagogue leader Jairus's twelve-year-old daughter, he tells them not to make it known (5:21–43). The narrative is silent as to whether or not they comply. Similarly, when Peter, responding to Jesus's question, answers that Jesus is the Messiah/the Christ (anointed one), Jesus orders him and the others to tell no one (8:27–30; 9:2–9).

Cyrus, the Persian King, was also God's Messiah, and the only Gentile so named; he was regarded as a man of justice and he freed the Israelites from slavery (Isa 45:1, 13; Ezra 1:2–3). Of course, Messianic hopes tend to be political. They carry the expectation or anticipation for the destruction of the present hegemonic order and establishment of a new, just and favorable king and kingdom. The more Jesus performs powerful acts, the more popular and sought after he becomes. The crowds (consisting of the poor, the diseased, the demon possessed, tax collectors, and other "sinners," enslaved, and freedpersons) continue to swell and to find ways to touch or be touched by him. Jesus is like a just and compassionate mobile hospital with a perfect record and free health care.

Jesus embodies the good news of God for the most oppressed and afflicted when he expels demons or unclean spirits that have invaded human beings and taken up residence in their bodies; when he heals people from diseases that blind them, silence their tongues, dull their ears, cripple their legs, feet, and backs, tie their hands in knots, or turn their skin white with leprous sores. In Mark, Jesus's preaching, teaching, and powerful acts are intertwined; this amalgamation constitutes an authority not exercised by the scribes (1:22). The powerful acts Jesus performs demonstrate his authority, for example, to forgive sins. Jesus asks his detractors which is easier: the rhetoric of forgiveness or the demonstration of authority to forgive sins by making the carried-by-his-friends-bed-ridden-man whole again? (2:1–12).

Because of their faith, Jesus heals the paralyzed man. Yet Jesus does not always require faith before performing miracles; sometimes he is just moved with compassion for the dis-eased and hungry (1:41; 8:2).

This same authority that Jesus exercises, he gives to his disciples, as noted. However, on one occasion, the disciples are unable to expel a very violent and destructive unclean spirit from a man's son. Consequently, the man brings his son to Jesus (9:14–29). The disciples had not sufficiently prayed, it seems, in order to perform the miracle (9:29). Thus, authority and power are two different things or do not necessarily cohere. When Jesus responds that he can heal the father's son if he believes, the father replies, "I believe; help my unbelief" 9:24). Faith or belief is not the absence of unbelief.

Consider and discuss: Many religious people and Christians insist on putting God and Jesus in a box when it comes to healing. In other words, God only heals under certain conditions and only those who have a certain amount of unwavering faith or pay their titles or attend church regularly, and so on. Why do you think this is the case? What is the impact on us and how might such theologies/ideologies relieve us of the responsibility we have to promote health and wellness for all human beings?

Parallel Miracles

Some miracles occur twice in Mark: Jesus feeds the crowds that follow him (5,000 men and an untold number of women and children at 6:34–44; 4,000 people at 8:1–10). He soundly sleeps during a violent storm before silencing the sea in one episode and he walks on water and calms the stormy seas in another instance (4:35–41; 6:45–51). Jesus heals two blind men—one unnamed in Bethsaida (8:22–26) and one named Bartimaeus son of Timaeus in Jericho (10:46–52). The man in Bethsaida is brought to Jesus by his friends who beg Jesus to touch him. Jesus has to touch him twice to completely restore his sight. When Jesus lays his hands on Bartimaeus and puts saliva on his eyes, his vision is only partially restored. It takes a second laying on of hands to heal him. Bartimaeus is begging by the roadside when he hears that Jesus is approaching and he twice yells for him, despite attempts to silence him: "Jesus, Son of David have mercy on me. . . . Son of David have mercy on me!" (10:47–48). (Matthew's Jesus takes this phrase to a whole other level.) Jesus tells the crowd to summon the man, and when Jesus asks Bartimaeus what he wants, he replies, "My teacher, let me see again" (10:51). Bartimaeus's faith heals him. Jesus does not instruct him to keep the healing a secret. Perhaps, secrecy is no longer required at this point in the story, since Jesus enters Jerusalem immediately after this healing.

> **Extrabiblical Parallel Story: Caesar heals a blind man and a man with a withered hand.** When the Roman Emperor (Titus Flavius Caesar) Vespasian(us) Augustus (69–79 CE) was in Alexandria, Egypt, one summer, a commoner well known among the people for being blind approached Vespasian throwing himself at his mercy. Groaning, he begged Vespasian to restore his sight. According to the story, the Egyptian god Serapis compelled the blind man to approach Vespasian so that he might heal him by dabbing saliva on the man's eyes and cheeks. On another occasion, a man with a withered hand begs Caesar to restore his hand by trampling and stomping on it. Vespasian first responded with scorn and ridicule to these requests. When the man persists, Vespasian fears failure but also is inspired by the prospects of success. Thus, Caesar seeks the advice of the physicians as to whether or not each man has a hopeful prognosis; could human intervention help? The physicians advise that with the right technique applied to each they could each be restored. The gods wished it and perhaps the emperor had been chosen by the gods to heal them both and the glory would be Vespasian's. If he failed, the blame would be placed on the blind man and the man with the withered hand. Therefore, in the presence of eyewitnesses who had no advantage to lie, Vespasian healed each man as they had asked and they were fully restored. Tacitus, *Hist.* IV.81.

Jesus Teaches in Parables

Jesus primarily teaches using parables knowing that the crowds will not and do not fully comprehend their intended meaning. However, Jesus's disciples are privileged in that Jesus explains the meaning of the parables to them privately (4:33–34). Yet, sometimes Jesus appears frustrated when the disciples fail to understand. For example, Jesus tells the Pharisees and scribes that it is not what is ingested and digested that defiles a person, but it is the evil that comes from the heart and results in certain behaviors (e.g., sexual immorality, theft, murder, adultery, pride, and envy) that defiles. Subsequently, the disciples ask Jesus privately about the meaning of the parable (7:17–23). Jesus responds with at least mild irritation: "Then do you also fail to understand? Do you not see . . . ?" (7:18–19). This question is curious since it is Jesus's practice to explain his parables to the disciples privately. Of course, explanation does not automatically result in understanding. We do not know whether or not the twelve understand after Jesus provides them with further explanation. He will tell them three times about his death and resurrection, but it seems they cannot imagine it. They cannot imagine the intersection of Messiah, son of God, lynching, and resurrection.

Jesus uses a lot of images and/or metaphors to teach about the good news of the *basileia*. Paradoxically, although Jesus draws upon images that would be familiar to his audiences, he does not expect them to fully understand. Jesus's parabolic teaching includes sowers and seeds; lamps hid under bushels as a metaphor for how things hidden will come to light; mustard seeds said to be the smallest seeds produce the largest plant; the rich man who wanted to know how to inherit eternal life; and other brief and extended metaphors or parables. Jesus relates the parable of vineyard owner/slave master to the religious leaders who approach him while he is talking in the Jerusalem Temple, prior to his arrest (11:27–12:12). In that parable, a slave owner plants a vineyard (with the help of the slaves, of course) and leases it out in his absence. When the season of harvest arrives, the absentee landlord sends his slaves to collect his share of the produce. Each of the many slaves the owner sends to collect his share of the crop is beaten and/or murdered, but he keeps sending them. They are dispensable. When all his slaves have been maimed or killed, he sends his beloved son who is also murdered by the tenants; they hope that by killing the son they will gain access to his inheritance. When the landlord/slave master returns, the parable concludes that he will destroy the tenants and lease out the vineyard to others. Finally, Jesus invokes Ps 118:22–23 where the stone that the builders rejected became the head cornerstone. The religious leaders understand perfectly; they know the parable implicates them and they want to arrest Jesus on the spot. The religious leaders have conspired together and will solicit the assistance of the Roman authorities to destroy Jesus. But for the moment, for fear of arousing the crowds, they do nothing.

Home as Public Contested Space and Fluid Fictive Kinship Boundaries

The second healing miracle that Jesus performs, after the exorcism in the synagogue, occurs in the home of Simon's (Peter) mother-in-law (Simon evidently left his wife home to care for the household and any children and perhaps the mother-in-law too when he abandoned his fishing net to follow Jesus) (1:29–31). She is so sick that she is bedridden. Jesus simply takes her hand and lifts her out of the bed. Consequently, her fever subsides and she responds by serving them. The first two powerful acts that Jesus performs occur in the synagogue and in the home (synagogue assemblies could occur in homes as well). These two spaces emerge as sites of contestation and restoration.

Except for when he goes to Jerusalem, Jesus's ministry does not take him far from home. In fact, he is in and out of home. Sometimes home refers broadly to his hometown and other times, home is the residence where he lives with his mother, Mary, and his brothers Joses, James, Judas (Jude), and Simon and his three unnamed sisters (6:3). Like most women in Mark, the latter remain anonymous. Large crowds gather in Jesus's home, and they find creative ways to reach Jesus with their sick friends and family, even gaining access to his family home through the roof (2:1–12). On another occasion when Jesus arrives home and is confronted with a large crowd, for some reason people think he has lost his mind. His family arrives and attempts to constrain him (3:19b–22). When the crowd notices that Jesus's mother, sisters, and brothers are outside summoning him, Jesus takes the opportunity to expand the notion of family to include fictive kinship ties. His mother and brothers are those who perform God's will (3:35). Despite the large amount of time Jesus spends proclaiming the good news of God's reign at home, Jesus is compelled to declare that a prophet is without honor in his own home (6:4–6). His hometown people seem unable to reconcile the wisdom and powerful deeds Jesus performs and their familiarity with his family background or social class. Is he not the son of a carpenter, they ask. And is not Mary his mother? Still Jesus returns home often (3:35; 5:37; 9:2; 14:33). This desire for home and other psychological, spiritual, and material needs perhaps highlights Jesus's humanness. As noted above, Jesus refers to himself as the son of man (human being or child of a human being) (2:10, 28; 8:31, 38; 9:9; 10:33; 14:62). He requires rest and time away from the crowds and people in general; he needs or desires to pray in solitude and he cries; his gender and ethnic biases are revealed in conversation with foreigners (7:24–30).

Speaking of gender biases, with the exception of Jesus's mother Mary and other women named at the empty tomb scene (Mary Magdalene, Mary the mother of James, Salome), the women in Mark are nameless. These include Simon's mother-in-law, Jairus's daughter and the woman with the chronic hemorrhaging, Jesus's sisters, and the Syrophoenician woman and her daughter (1:30; 5:25–43; 6:3; 7:24–30; 15:47—16:1). Yet, most of these women demonstrate agency: the Syrophoenician woman finds Jesus, even though he does not want to be found, so he might heal her daughter. She refuses to let Jesus's negative response stand as the final word, and she persists until by her word her daughter is healed. She reclaimed her voice. The woman who had been hemorrhaging for twelve years (perhaps after having birthed a child the age of Jairus's daughter) braves the crowds to touch the hem of Jesus's garments (5:25–34). Perhaps her story motivated others who might not otherwise be able to access him in the large crowds to find healing in the same way (6:56).

Consider and discuss: How might you read between the lines, and against the grain of androcentric and patriarchal texts, and use your contextual and historical (re)imagination to (re)read any of Mark's stories about women in ways that can empower women and communities?

Opposition and Death Conspiracies

Jesus's opposition is primarily from some scribes, Pharisees, chief priests, and elders. As noted above, the first time Jesus experiences opposition is when he forgives the sins of the bed-ridden paralytic whose friends let him down through the roof so that Jesus might heal him (2:1–12). This first instance of opposition occurs in Jesus's home, but the synagogue (and later the Temple when he arrives in Jerusalem) is a site of conflict, especially on the Sabbath. Jesus has no problem allowing his hungry disciples to pick and eat grain on the Sabbath, but some Pharisees find it very problematic (2:23–28). Mark's Jesus recalls, albeit incorrectly, the time that David and his companions were so hungry that they ate the bread of presence off the altar in God's house when Abiathar was high priest (cf. 1 Sam 21:1–6). Jesus responds that the Sabbath was made for human beings and not human beings for the Sabbath; it is for the benefit of humans. When Jesus heals a man with a severely arthritic hand in the synagogue on the Sabbath, it is too much for some Pharisees to bear;

they conspire with a group called Herodians to destroy Jesus (3:1–6). Jesus makes their hit list early in his career. Later Jesus is accused of being insane and of being Beelzebub, the ruler of demons (3:21–23). Jesus responds to the accusations commonsensically: how can a house divided stand? In other words, how is it that he can expel demons *and* be a demon? Conversely, when Jesus's disciples inform him that they tried to stop someone from casting out demons in his name, he responds that they should not prohibit him from doing so; they are on the same side or will be (9:38–41).

Take Up Your Cross and Follow Me

As noted, Jesus's adversaries emerge early in his ministry and resolve to destroy him. He had taken up his cross when he began his ministry, as had John the Baptist. Jesus predicts his death three times (8:31–33; 9:30–32; 10:32–34) and during the last prediction he resolves to go to Jerusalem (10:33). He first announces his eventual death after Peter identifies him as the Messiah (8:27–30). The religious leaders (elders, chief priest, and scribes) will reject him, he will be killed, and he will rise after three days (8:31). Having just identified Jesus as God's Messiah, Peter could not accept Jesus's words and attempts to chastise Jesus. But instead Jesus rebukes Peter. In Peter's mind, this is not the way to reestablish the kingdom of Israel and to overthrow the Roman Empire. And crucifixion is a disgraceful death, reserved for criminals and the lower classes. Then Jesus announces to the disciples and the large crowd that if they would become his followers, they must deny themselves, take up their crosses and then follow him (8:34). What does it benefit one to obtain all that the world offers and yet lose one's life? The transfiguration scene six days later demonstrates the power of God over death and life (9:2–8). Peter, John, and James accompany Jesus up the mountain where the prophet Elijah and Moses appear speaking with Jesus. Peter's response is to offer to build a shrine for each of them as a memorial to the epiphany. The three disciples are instructed to keep the epiphany a secret until after Jesus is risen from the dead (9:9–13). The disciples do not understand what Jesus means when he states that he will rise from the dead (9:10, 32).

Jesus makes a royal-like entrance into Jerusalem on a colt, enters the Temple, looks around, and then leaves to go to Bethany (11:1–11). Between Jesus's entrance into Jerusalem and his arrest and crucifixion a lot transpires (chapters 11–12): Jesus curses a fig tree; he enters the Temple, cleansing it of thieves; he draws lessons from the fig tree that withered under his curse. The fig tree symbolizes the Temple; the Temple had become a corrupt system in which some of its leaders congregate like thieves and a poor widow sacrifices more of her finances and life than those who have more. Meanwhile, Jesus's opponents continue to concoct a case against him: the religious leaders question Jesus about the source of his authority as he enters the temple again; Pharisees and Herodians interrogate him about whether or not they should pay the emperor's taxes; some Sadducees question him about the resurrection; and a scribe asks Jesus to identify the greatest commandment. The greatest commandment is to love God with one's heart, soul, and mind, and the second is to love one's neighbor as one's self. It is not useful to know the first and fail to acknowledge and practice the second.

Chapter 13 is Mark's little apocalypse in which Jesus predicts the destruction of the Temple and the signs that precede the devastation: conflict, war, earthquakes, famines, persecution, darkening of the sun and moon, falling stars, false Messiahs and prophets, the second coming (*Parousia*) of the son of man, and the harvest. What good is the Temple if it does not serve God's purpose, but instead functions contrary to God's will and at the will of corrupt leaders and the Roman Empire? Like Jesus, the disciples will be arrested and tried before councils, governors, and kings, and they will be hated, betrayed, and beaten in synagogues as a consequence of spreading the gospel. The preaching of the Gospel is not dependent upon the existence of the Temple; it will be preached to all peoples (13:10).

The disciples are to remain alert because nobody but the Father knows the day and hour these things will occur. Of course, many scholars believe that Mark wrote in retrospect after (or during the period of) the destruction of the Temple. The "desolating sacrilege" at 13:14 is mentioned in Dan 11:31 and 12:11 where it is likely a historical reference to Antiochus Epiphanes, the Seleucid king, who erected a pagan altar to Zeus in the Temple. In Mark's context, it may refer to Eleazar, the rebel who in 67–68 CE desecrated the Temple by establishing his headquarters in its sacred precincts. It could also refer to the Emperor Caligula's intention to place an image of himself in the Temple.

Mark's Passion Narrative (Chapters 14–16)

Some regard chapter 11 as the start of the passion narrative when Jesus enters Jerusalem. However, in chapter 14, two days before the Passover and unleavened bread festivals, the chief priests and scribes resolve to kill Jesus, and the anointing of Jesus in Bethany gives the impression that his death is near. Because of Jesus's popularity among the people, they do not want to apprehend him during the celebrations so as not to cause an uproar among the people.

In the meantime, while in Simon's house (a man with leprosy, a skin disease), an unnamed woman anoints Jesus's head with expensive oils as he sits at the table. Others in the room object to the woman's use of costly oils to anoint Jesus, suggesting that better use could have been made of the oil if she sold it and received the equivalent of a day's wages (300 denarii) and contributed the money to care for the poor. How insensitive; Jesus himself was not wealthy. And he is facing a cruel and unjust death. Their objection may imply that the woman was well-off, demonstrating their bias against the wealthy. Jesus appreciated (perhaps he needed) her act of kindness, considering his impending death. Her act of kindness will be memorialized as a part of the good news. They will have (and have had) plenty of opportunities for showing tangible compassion toward the poor (14:7).

> **Consider and discuss:** What do you think of Jesus's response about the poor? How have these words been used as a way to avoid our responsibility to one another and to alleviate the systems that create poverty?

Judas agrees to betray Jesus for money. Regardless, Jesus celebrates with these twelve apostles the Passover feast commemorating the liberation of the Hebrew children from enslavement in Egypt (14:12–26; Exod 6:6). At the celebration, Jesus announces that one of them will betray him. Jesus serves the bread and wine, which symbolizes his body and blood poured out for many, respectively. The next time Jesus drinks wine will be in the *basileia* of God. After they sing a hymn, Jesus announces that they will all desert him. After supper and a walk to the Mount of Olives, Jesus predicts Peter's denial. Jesus takes Peter, James, and John to be with him at Gethsemane, expecting them to stay awake and pray, while he agonizes with his Abba (Aramaic for Father, which is similar to the Hebrew *'ab*; Jesus spoke primarily in Aramaic). Jesus acknowledges the power of the father to remove "the cup" (symbolic of his impending death) from him but yields to his Abba's will. And immediately (*euthus*), while still scolding the three about falling asleep as the hour of the son of man approaches, the Apostle Judas arrives with a sword-wielding, club-carrying mob, sent by the chief priests, elders, and scribes to arrest Jesus. Judas greets Jesus as a rabbi while kissing him, as a sign identifying him from among the others. One disciple resorts to violent resistance and slices off the ear of one of the chief priest's slaves. Jesus predicts that all his disciples will desert him.

Jesus is derided before the Sanhedrin and accused of blasphemy, and in the meantime Peter denies him three times as predicted. At the second meeting of the Sanhedrin, Jesus is bound over to Pilate, the governor representing the Emperor, who asks Jesus twice if he is the King of the Jews; the first time he responds "you say so" (15:2) and the second time he is silent. The text says it was customary for the crowds to ask Pilate to release a prisoner. No historical record of such a custom has been found. The religious leaders arouse the crowds, persuading them to ask for the release of Barabbas, a rebel who had committed murder during an insurrection. But regarding the one called "king of the Jews," they cried "crucify him!" (15:12, 14). Mark depicts Pilate as reluctant to crucify Jesus. Pilate questions Jesus's guilt: "What evil has he done?" (15:14). Nevertheless, he releases Barabbas, flogs Jesus, and orders him to be crucified. From after his arrest up to when he is sentenced to death, Jesus is humiliated; he is blind folded, spit on, slapped, beaten, and mocked. On the way to Golgotha, the place of the crucifixion, an African named Simon of Cyrene, a father of two sons named Alexander and Rufus, a foreigner and noncitizen of Rome passing through Jerusalem, is forced to carry Jesus's cross, as Jesus buckled under its weight.

In the passion narrative the title *King of the Jews* (or Israel) is evoked five times in reference to Jesus (15:2, 9, 12, 18, 32); the wooden cross to which they impale Jesus's body is engraved with the crime of which he was convicted: *King of the Jews*. Jesus is said to be guilty of blasphemy, but he is charged with treason; they claim he says he is a king. Rome crowns its own kings. Crucifixion constituted a disgraceful death reserved for slaves, freedpersons, war captives, revolutionaries, foreigners without Roman citizenship, and thieves; two bandits are crucified on either side of Jesus. Religious leaders, people who did not know him, and others mock and spit upon him as Jesus dies on the cross. Similarly, the lynchings of black people in the American South were public events and family affairs where people (parents and their children) celebrated the agonizing death of their victims.

Mark's Jesus speaks one last word from the cross: *Eloi, Eloi lema sabachthani*, which is translated, "My God, my God, why have you forsaken me?" It is a mixture of Aramaic and Hebrew, which may explain why the crowds misinterpret his words as a call for Elijah (15:34–35). All the disciples flee as predicted. When Jesus breathes his last breath with a heavy sigh, the Temple curtain is torn open, and a Roman centurion at that moment affirms that Jesus was God's son (15:37–39). Named (Mary Magdalene, Mary the mother of James, Joses, and Salome) and unnamed women who were disciples that followed Jesus throughout Galilee kept their distance from the cross (15:40–41). Joseph of Arimathea, a member of the council who anticipated God's *basileia*, asks Pilate for Jesus's body; Mary Magdalene and Mary the mother of Joses witness Jesus's body wrapped in linen cloth and buried in a private tomb. In Mark, Jesus is crucified on Friday and that evening, the day of preparation, Jesus is placed in the tomb (cf. John 19:14). In chapter 16, on the first day of the week, Sunday, after the Sabbath, the three named women arrive to anoint Jesus's body. When they arrive at the tomb, it is open and empty. A man in a white robe informs them that God has raised Jesus of Nazareth. He instructs the women to tell Peter and the disciples that Jesus will meet them in Galilee. But gripped with fear and shock, the women run from the scene and never tell anyone what they experienced; it becomes their secret.

Multiple Endings

Mark contains no ascension scene, but it has at least two other endings in the ancient manuscripts, a longer and a shorter denouement: (1) In the longer ending, Mary Magdalene is identified as a woman from whom Jesus exorcised seven demons; she tells others about having seen Jesus, but she is not believed. Jesus appears to two anonymous disciples and to the eleven separately before ascending back to heaven (16:9–20); and (2) a shorter additional ending consists of the women reporting to Peter and his friends about what happened, and Jesus commissionong his disciples.

Summary

1. John the Baptist prepared the way for Jesus's ministry with his own.
2. Jesus is the Son of God who embodies the *basileia* of God.
3. Jesus is a very human Messiah (anointed agent of God).
4. Jesus returns home often and home is a site of struggle and contestation.
5. Jesus is a Jewish man who observes Jewish customs and rituals and is (mis)understood by some religious leaders.
6. Jesus anoints and commissions his disciples with authority to cast out demons, but authority does not guarantee power.
7. The demons/unclean spirits recognize Jesus, but Jesus silences them.
8. People that Jesus heals are told not to publicize their experience.
9. Jesus is crucified by the Romans for treason.
10. Mary Magdalene, Mary the mother of Joses, and Salome are disciples of Jesus with personal knowledge of his empty tomb.

Further Reading

Blount, Brian K. *Go Preach! Mark's Kingdom Message and the Black Church Today*. Maryknoll, NY: Orbis, 1998.

Card, Michael. *Mark: The Gospel of Passion*. Downers Grove, IL: InterVarsity, 2012.

Cartlidge, David R., and David L. Dugan. *Documents and Images for the Study of the Gospels*. 3rd ed. Minneapolis: Fortress, 2015.

Choi, Jin Young. *Postcolonial Discipleship of Embodiment: An Asian and Asian American Feminist Reading of the Gospel of Mark*. New York: Palgrave Macmillan, 2015.

Cone, James. *The Cross and the Lynching Tree*. Maryknoll, NY: Orbis, 2013.

Crossan, Dominic. *The Historical Jesus: The Life of a Mediterranean Jewish Peasant*. San Francisco: Harper Collins, 1991.

Dewey, Joanna. "Mark." In *Searching the Scriptures*. Vol. 2, *A Feminist Commentary*, edited by Elizabeth Schüssler Fiorenza, 470–509. New York: Crossroad, 1994.

Evans, Craig A. *Fabricating Jesus. How Modern Scholars Distort the Gospels*. Downers Grove, IL: InterVarsity, 2006.

France, R. T. *The Gospel of Mark*. Grand Rapids, MI: Eerdmans, 2014.

Isasi-Diaz, Ada María. "Kin-dom of God." In *In Our Own Voices: Latino/a Renditions of Theology*, edited by Ada María Isasi-Diaz, 171–89. Maryknoll, NY : Orbis, 2010.

Kim, Yung Suk. *Messiah in Weakness. A Portrait of Jesus from the Perspective of the Dispossessed*. Eugene, OR: Cascade, 2016.

Lettsome, Raquel S. "The Gospel of Mark." In *The New Testament: Fortress Commentary on the Bible*, edited by Margaret Aymer, Cynthia Briggs Kittredge, and David A. Sánchez, 173–215. Minneapolis, Fortress, 2014.

Levine, Amy-Jill, ed. *A Feminist Companion to the Gospel of Mark*. Sheffield, England: Sheffield, 2001.

Liew, Benny Tat-Siong. "Haunting Silence: Trauma, Failed Orality and Mark's Messianic Secret." In *Psychoanalytic Meditations between Marxist and Postcolonial Readings of the Bible*, edited by Benny Tat-Siong Liew and Erin Runions, 99–128. Semeia Studies. Atlanta: Society of Biblical Literature, 2016.

———. *Politics of Parousia. Reading Mark Inter(Con)Textually*. New York: Brill, 1999.

Myers, Ched. *Binding the Strong Man: A Political Reading of Mark's Story*. Maryknoll, NY: Orbis, 2008.

Newheart, Michael. *"My Name is Legion": The Story and Soul of the Gerasene Demoniac*. Collegeville, MN: Liturgical, 2004.

Pae, Keun-Joo Christine. "Minjung Theology and Global Peacemaking." In *Reading Minjung Theology in the Twenty-first Century*, edited by Yung Suk Kim and Jin-Ho Kim, 164–83. Eugene, OR: Pickwick, 2013.

Pallares, Jose Cardenas. *Poor Man Called Jesus: Reflections on the Gospel of Mark*. Maryknoll, NY: Orbis, 1986.

Powery, Emerson. "Mark." *True to Our Native Land: An African American New Testament Commentary*, edited by Brian K. Blount et al., 121–57. Minneapolis: Fortress, 2007.

Rhoads, David, Joanna Dewey, and Donald Michie. *Mark as Story: An Introduction to the Narrative of a Gospel*. 3rd ed. Minneapolis: Fortress, 2012.

Sánchez, David Arthur. "Ambivalence, Mimicry, and the *Ochlos* in the Gospel of Mark." In *Reading Minjung Theology in the Twenty-First Century*, edited by Yung Suk Kim and Jin-Ho Kim, 134–47. Eugene, OR: Pickwick, 2013.

Slater, Thomas. "Son of Man." In vol. 2 of *Oxford Encyclopedia of the Bible and Theology*, edited by Samuel Balentine, 316–21. New York: Oxford University Press, 2015.

St. Clair, Raquel. *Call and Consequences: A Womanist Reading of Mark*. Minneapolis: Fortress, 2008.

CHAPTER 11

Gospel of Matthew

Many and varied are the interpretations dealing with the teachings and the life of Jesus of Nazareth. But few of these interpretations deal with what the teachings and the life of Jesus have to say to those who stand, at a moment in human history, with their backs against the wall.

—Howard Thurman[1]

Never forget that justice is what love looks like in public.

—Cornel West

Jesus was not a Roman citizen.... If a Roman soldier pushed Jesus into a ditch, he could not appeal to Caesar; he would be just another Jew in the ditch.

—Howard Thurman[2]

Matthew at a Glance

1. Author is an unknown Jewish, colonized male who wrote in the first century CE; we shall call him Matthew.
2. Written between 80 and 85 CE, possibly from Antioch in Syria (or Egypt?).

---

1. Thurman, *Jesus and the Disinherited*, 11.
2. Thurman, *Jesus and the Disinherited*, 33.

3. Matthew likely used the following sources: Mark's Gospel, Q in common with Luke, and special material peculiar to Matthew (M).
4. Originally written in Greek; no extant original first century manuscript.
5. Only Matthew describes the virginal conception of a baby to be named Emmanuel and Jesus.
6. Contains more chapters than any other canonical Gospel.
7. Only Gospel that mentions the Greek word *ekklēsia* (meaning *assembly* but often translated anachronistcally as *church*).
8. Only Gospel beginning with a genealogical book identifying Jesus at both ends as the Messiah or *Christos* (anointed one).
9. Themes include: justice/righteousness, fulfillment of Torah and prophetic words, and good/wicked slaves.
10. Prefers the phrase "kingdom of the heavens" to "kingdom of God."

Introduction

THE AUTHOR WHOM WE call Matthew was likely a colonized Greek-speaking Jewish male who lived and wrote in the first century CE when Rome ruled the then known world. As we read Matthew's Gospel we bring to bear our own contexts, questions, and concerns. We will discuss theological, ideological, and narrative content of the Gospel. Also of significance to us are representations of hybridity, empire, race, gender, class, and othering. Special attention will be given to some texts found only in Matthew, as well as traditions on which Matthew relied (source criticism). We also consider how Matthew redacted or revised his sources (redaction criticism).

Most traditional readings of Matthew foreground Jesus's role as Jewish rabbi/teacher with an inner circle of twelve male disciples/students and a larger crowd of followers. We address the content of Jesus's teaching and how his teaching, life, and ministry are interconnected. The Matthean Jesus was more than a teacher/rabbi, he was God's Messiah and prophet. During crises such as periods of colonization and oppression, people often look to their teachers for insight/answers about tradition, justice, survival, and hope. We find this fulfilled in Matthew's representation of Jesus as a political revolutionary prophet, God's son, and God's Messiah. Prophetic, revolutionary teaching is risky business. The teacher/rabbi does not just pour knowledge into a human vessel, but he is opening up what was closed to *derash* (study, practice, dialogue; *Greek, anoigō*, see Matt 13:35), namely imaginative, innovative, performative aspects of Torah interpretation; revolutionary, liberating teaching breaks open the student and perhaps challenges the teacher too.

As we read Matthew's Gospel, beginning with his book of lineage (*biblos geneseōs*), we seek to understand how Jesus sought to shape his disciples. Also, we discuss how some oppressive systems, relationships, and behaviors might be reinscribed, supported, or foundational. We do not, of course, undertake a comprehensive examination of Matthew, but we focus on particular texts, themes, constructions, and interpretative perspectives of importance for colonized, minoritized, and/or oppressed people, not dissimilar from Jesus and his first-century followers.

Chapter Contents

1. Opening Matthew's Book of Lineage: Mulatto Messiah and Son
2. The Birth of the Mulatto Messiah
3. The Matthean Performative Fulfillment Formulae
4. Matthew's Jesus: Son of Refugees and Colonized Revolutionary Prophet
5. Kingdom of the Heavens and Kingdom Rhetoric
6. Matthew's Distinctive Use of Mark's Gospel
7. Matthew's Distinctive Use of Q
8. Matthew's Special Material
9. Matthew's Passion Story: False Accusations, Deception, and the Crucifixion

Opening Matthew's Book of Lineage: Mulatto Messiah and Son

Matthew's genealogy (*geneseōs*) informs us that Jesus will be a Messiah King; his birth is a fulfillment of the prophetic tradition, not in the sense of being the first Messiah, no more than the first Jewish child named Jesus. He is a type. By beginning his Gospel with a patrilineal (father dominated) genealogy, Matthew provides both a continuity with the past, or with tradition, while also disrupting it (cf. Gen 5:1—6:8; Exod 1:1-6). Non-Jewish females and second-born males dot the genealogy. God is a God of disruption. God's disruptions encompass and transcend race/ethnicity, class, gender, and empire. In Jesus we see racial/ethnic, class, and gender boundaries, but such boundaries are sometimes fluid and constructed. Although similar to other genealogies found in the Hebrew Bible, Matthew's record departs from the norm in several respects. Males and their first-born male progeny usually dominate the patrilineal tradition. Women, such as Sarai, are sometimes included in genealogies, and they can be matrilineal, but seldom are foreign women mentioned (see Gen 11:27–32). Genealogies make assertions about kinship identity and social status in relation to others. They map individual, intra- and intergroup social, political, cultural, ideological, and economical commitments.

In the genealogy with which Matthew opens his book, Jesus is identified in relation to the Messianic tradition, God, and humanity (1:1). Jesus is identified as Christ (*Christos*) or anointed one from the Hebrew word *masiach*. Because the Matthean Jesus is biologically both the son of God and a son of human beings, literally born of the Spirit and the flesh, we could characterize Jesus as a mulatto. He is mixed, a combination of two kinds/races (*genos*). Jesus's mixed-race lineage is also demonstrated by the inclusion of non-Jewish women in the genealogy, namely, Tamar, a Canaanite woman who "played the role of a prostitute" (Gen 38) and Rahab who was a Canaanite prostitute, mentioned only here as Boaz's mother (Jos 2:1–21; 6:22–25) (it seems no other extant source dared remember her as Boaz's mother); Ruth, a Moabite woman (also a Canaanite), compelled to seduce Naomi's heir to ensure Naomi's lineage (Ruth 2–4); and Bathsheba who is mentioned not by name but as "wife of Uriah" taken by David, bearing his son Solomon. Each named woman sought some sort of justice for herself or for another. Womanist or feminist readings of the genealogy see the inclusion of the women as positive, instructive, and/or problematic. Their presence disrupts the would-be all male lineup but also might function to reinscribe constructions of women and foreigners as outsiders within, as well as the putative dichotomous nature of women as either sexually illicit or sexually pure. Additionally, Jesus is conceived in a woman and by God's Holy Spirit (1:20). Like most peoples with a history of colonization, Jesus is of mixed "race." Unlike African slaves enslaved in America for whom birth records were not generally kept, Matthew has provided a precise genealogy or record of birth.

Jesus is identified as Messiah in the first and final lines of the genealogy. The last line of the genealogy disrupts the pattern created with the words:

"[male] father of [male]." Instead as noted, we read "Joseph the husband of Mary, from whom Jesus was born, the one called Christ" (1:16). He is identified as Messiah prior to any demonstrated connection to David and yet his link to the Davidic dynasty is significant. One might say that the purpose of the genealogy is to show what kind of Messiah Jesus will be: He is human royalty and divinity. Jesus's divinity is not bestowed after death like most Caesars but in life like the Egyptian Pharaohs. Jesus as a son of Israel is connected by marriage to Israel's first patriarch, Abraham. Jesus has roots in royalty as a son of David and other Kings of Judah, the worst and the best; the infamous and the celebrated (e.g. Solomon, Rehoboam, Abijah, Uzziah, Hezekiah, Manasseh, Josiah). Jesus's ancestry includes foreigners, particularly women who were taken as wives of patriarchs and/or who had their babies. Jesus's relatives have been migrants, immigrants, refugees, colonized, exiles, and the enslaved. Few of his ancestors are above reproach. Born today, few might avoid the criminal (in)justice system.

Matthew's birth record ends by identifying Joseph as Mary's husband and *not* as Jesus's biological father. Jesus is related to Joseph's bloodline by marriage. Mary shares this in common with the other women in the genealogy; they too are included by marriage and the children produced by their wombs. Jewish women, by birth or marriage, were considered full members of the community. Thus, Jesus as God's Messiah is legitimately linked to King David.

The name Joseph might remind Matthew's readers of the patriarch Joseph, Jacob's son, through whom Israel's ancestors began a long and complex history with Egypt (Hebrew: *Mizraim*). In fact, Mary's Joseph has four dreams; the patriarch Joseph had many dreams prior to being sold into Egyptian slavery and while in Egypt (2:19; Gen 37-50). The patriarch Joseph also married an Egyptian woman named Asenath through whom he had two children, Manasseh and Ephraim (Gen 41:50-52). Egypt is implicated throughout the birth narrative. Matthew is the only Gospel to mention Egypt as part of Jesus's birth story.

Consider and discuss: Is it possible that Matthew's Gospel was written in Egypt rather than in Antioch of Syria as many scholars argue? Could the original author have been a Jewish (or God-fearing) man (or woman) from Egypt? How might affirmative answers to these questions impact how we read Matthew?

Matthew divides Jesus's birth lineage into three neatly construed dispensations of fourteen generations each: from Abraham to David, from

David to the Babylonian Exile, and from Babylonian Exile to the Messiah (1:17). However, the list of generations Matthew provides does not precisely add up. Readers might find it curious that Matthew's genealogy does not favor first born sons. He may favor those with more historical favorability and/or that fit his ideological and theological agenda. Matthew is selective. For example, the listing from Abraham to King David (1:2–6a) names thirteen father-son pairs; however, if we count Zerah as Perez's twin, we have fourteen named sons, but not fourteen generations. Also Jacob, Judah, and Aram were not firstborn sons. Judah's first born son was named Er who was conceived with the unnamed daughter of a Canaanite man named Shua; Tamar was Er's first wife (Gen 38:1–6). Some have suggested the numerical value of the Hebrew consonants in David's name equals fourteen. David's name only appears in two of the "fourteen generations." Yet, all roads lead to and from King David. The second division lists the Kings of Judah from David to Jeconiah but, as with the previous unit, omits individuals in order to claim fourteen generations. For example, Kings Ahaziah, Joash, Amaziah, and Queen Athaliah's usurping of the throne are excluded (2 Chr 22–25). Skipping the former three kings in the genealogy, Matthew claims Joram as the father of Uzziah (a.k.a. Azariah, 2 Chr 3:11–12), rather than as his great-great-grandfather. Matthew's objective is not historical accuracy. For historical precision and perfection in human pedigree are not priorities or prerequisites for divine anointing.

The final division in the genealogy after the Babylonian deportation from Jeconiah to Jesus is fourteen generations if we include Jesus. Perhaps "fourteen generations" is a metaphorical designation meaning all that is necessary to fulfill or demonstrate the constructed lineage and its significance. Matthew's theology reflects upon history and is often indebted to history but it is not bound by or tethered to the historical. Using historical theology, Matthew attempts to show that Jesus is the Messiah, but a certain kind of Messiah. Perhaps it is the inconsistencies, the continuities and discontinuities, insider and outsider connections, the hybridities, the perfection and imperfection that allow this Messiah to be God's Messiah and not just a Messiah for the Jewish people. So that the "us" in "God with us" refers to whoever will accept this Messiah.

Matthew shows how God honors and yet transcends biology and human lineage. Jesus, as born of a woman and the Holy Spirit is ontologically marked by hybridity and yet his hybridity is not tragic in sense of the "tragic mulatto" among African Americans in American history. Through his birth Jesus disrupts the boundaries of possibility and impossibility, which had already been reconfigured with the inclusion of the non-Jewish women in the genealogy and the shift away from the first born as representative of the lineage and the focus on Judah. Hybridity is not denied and racial purity is not asserted. A hybrid being is not a dichotomous being but a fluid one; there is no pure division.

Consider and discuss: Are there certain forms of hybrid identities that are more acceptable in our society than others? If so, what are they and how can we overcome these biases?

The Birth of a Mulatto Messiah

The very first image evincing the hegemonic presence of the Roman Empire is Matthew's mention of King Herod, which contrasts with King David mentioned in Jesus's ancestral lineage (1:6; 2:1). Jesus's birth takes place in the historical context of the puppet king Herod (the Great) who ruled over Roman Judea from 37 BCE to 4 CE. The puppet kings were placed over conquered Roman provinces and colonies, ruling at Rome's pleasure. Ultimate power remained with the Caesar or Roman Emperor. Not only was Herod frightened at the thought of a Jewish king being born in Bethlehem but all Jerusalemites were as well (2:3).

As previously noted, the final line of the genealogy disrupts the pattern created with the words: "[male] father of [male]." Instead we read "Joseph the husband of Mary, from whom Jesus was born, the one called Christ" (1:16). This incongruity is explained at 1:18–15 beginning with the words: "the birth of Jesus Christos happened in this way." Matthew inserts tension into his narrative with the disruption. However, does he resolve the tension here or is it heightened, creating further unresolved tensions? Mary, a virgin, conceives a baby while engaged to be married to Joseph. As a just (*dikaios*) man, Joseph attempts to save Mary from public humiliation by secretly dissolving their relationship. Joseph's plans are disrupted by an angelophany (angel appearing to a human being). Yahweh's messenger (*angelos*) informs Joseph that Mary has not been sleeping around; she is simply having the Holy Spirit's baby! In the dream, Joseph is either reminded or for the first time discovering that he is a "son of David"; he is royalty. Like other Jewish fathers, Joseph will be able to name Mary's son and the name will carry a salvific meaning connected with the life purpose of Mary's son to save his people. The precarious situation in which the Holy Spirit places Joseph and the revelatory divine angelophany to Joseph (and not to Mary) is summed up using the language of prophetic fulfillment. Although the prophet is unnamed, readers familiar with the Hebrew Scriptures might recognize the scripture and perhaps its origin from Isaiah. Of course the sacred writing has been slightly modified to reflect the current context: "Look, the virgin (*parthenos*) will conceive and bear a son and they will call his name Emmanuel" and Jesus (1:23, 25; 7:14). Mary has no say in the situation, but is totally dependent upon Joseph to act justly, to save her and her child from public disgrace. Joseph prefigures his son who will rescue his people "from their sins." Joseph is never again mentioned beyond the birth narratives.

The name "Emmanuel" meaning "God [is] with us" may be a title or reflect the type of prophetic Messiah Jesus would become. The Isaiah scripture from the Masoretic Text does not read "virgin" (*bethulah*) but "young girl" (*'almah*) (Isa 7:14). During the time of the Syro-Ephramite crisis (in the eighth century BCE the Northern Kingdom of Israel/Ephraim joined forces with Syria against the Southern Kingdom of Judah for its refusal to align with them against Assyria). Yahweh gave King Ahaz of Israel a sign, which was a young woman giving birth to a baby boy whom she would name Emmanuel (Isa 7:14). That child was a sign as well that God was with God's people during the time of Assyrian aggression (Isa 7:17; 8:7); the prophet declared, "God is with us" (Isa 8:10). That young woman appears to be a prophetess and quite possibly the wife of Isaiah of Jerusalem (Isa 8:1–8). The Septuagint (Greek translation of the HB/OT), however, has (re)interpreted "young girl" (*'almah*) as "virgin" (Greek: *parthenos*), which is also applied to Mary in Matthew. In fact *'almah* can be translated young woman or virgin; of course, a virgin is normally a young woman. Historically, in times of oppression, distress, and uncertainty God was always assuring God's chosen leaders and the people that God was with them. For example, when God instructed Joshua, God's anointed one, to lead the Israelites across the Jordan, God told Joshua that he would exalt him so that the people would realize that "I will be with you as with Moses" (Jos 3:7). And so in continuity with the character and presence of God in the HB, the God of the NT in the era of the Roman Imperial rule assures Israel that God is with them, among them, or embodied in the soon-to-be-born Jesus, child of Mary whose husband is Joseph.

Only in Matthew is Mary's baby visited by magicians/magi or wise men (Greek, *magoi*) from the East. Magic/magician is a term often reserved for the other, as opposed to one's own miracle workers. It is likely the magi's skill for reading the stars (their astrological science) that informs them that the king of the Jews has been born; they arrive in Jerusalem from the East after his birth. Herod's advisors were obviously not aware of Jesus's birth. After the magi question the town folk, word reaches Herod that a baby has been born whom wise men from the East claim to be the King of the Jews. In fact, their inquiry, "Where is the child who has been born King of the Jews?" constitutes the first question in the NT. The magi have come to worship or honor (*proskuneō*) the future King; Herod later feigns his own desire to worship (*proskuneō*) the king of the Jews. Scholars assume that the magi are pagan or non-Jewish men. But nothing in the text requires this deduction. They could be wise God-fearers or they could be Jewish magi from Egypt. Simon in the apocryphal Acts of Peter and likely in the canonical Acts as well is a Jewish magus/magician (*APt* 2.51; Acts 8). That Herod summons the Jewish leaders for details about the Messiah's birth place does not preclude the magi from being Jewish. It is Herod who sends the wise men/magi to Bethlehem, and not any of the ordinary Jewish inhabitants of Jerusalem whom the magi questioned. Luke also places Jesus's birth in Bethlehem (Luke 2:4, 15; cf. John 7:42). Neither the Jews living in Jerusalem nor magi from the East know where the child has been born. News of the birth of a child who is to assume the position as king over Judea is subversive to the Roman Empire and to Herod as the King appointed by the Empire to reign over Judea. Herod's quick actions betray the credibility of magi. The magi continue to be led by the star, which hovers over Bethlehem.

Consider and discuss: What theological or social presuppositions and/or assumptions about magic and miracles do we bring to our interpretations of the biblical text? How can we free ourselves of such presuppositions and open ourselves up to other interpretative possibilities? How might doing so also help us to be less judgmental of others today?

It is significant that the birth of the baby Jesus, king of the Jews, is announced by magi or wise men from the East. Matthew tends to limit directions from which people come to share a meal in the kingdom to east and west (8:11), whereas Luke extends it to include not only east and west but north and south (13:29). Perhaps, Matthew views the world dualistically in terms of the (East), with particular emphasis on Egypt, and all the rest of the Roman Empire as the West.

Jesus is wisdom personified in Matthew. In comparing John the Baptist's meager dietary habits with Jesus's eating and drinking, Jesus is identified as wisdom (*sophia*) whose works (*erga*) are vindicated (11:19). The grammatically feminine Greek noun *sophia* is linked with Jesus as a Jewish male. Jesus's eating and drinking is associated with "sinners and tax collectors," which is not what would normally be expected of the Messiah for whom John paved the way. Despite Solomon's renowned wisdom (*sophia*), Jesus is greater (12:42), as wisdom personified. When Jesus returns to his hometown of Nazareth and teaches in the synagogue, the locals, knowing his family, are amazed at Jesus's wisdom (*sophia*) and powerful deeds (*dunameis*) (13:54–55). It seems that works with *sophia* or *sophia* with works is inevitable and inseparable in Jesus. The first century Jewish historian Josephus wrote that Jesus was a wise man and one who did wonderful works (*AntJ* 18.3.63).

The baby Jesus apparently had been born in a small house (*oikia*). As planned, upon entering the house, the magi worship (*proskuneō*) the child, as is normally done when one enters into the presence of God or royalty. The very expensive gifts of gold, myrrh, and frankincense presented to the child may reveal the lucrative and effective nature of the magi's astrological endeavors and/or the land from which they traveled. Like Joseph, the magi receive a divine dream warning them to avoid Herod as they return home.

Matthew does not describe the actual birth of Jesus; Luke provides more details. Even more particulars are given by the second century apocryphal text *The Protoevangelium of James* (The First Gospel of James, the brother of Jesus). In the latter text, Mary's mother is named Anna, and Mary is subjected to a virginity test after giving birth to the baby Jesus. There Mary's pregnancy is even more scandalous. Her mother Anna placed her in the care of the temple at the age of twelve. The Temple priest entrusts Anna to Joseph's care, and in his care, at age sixteen, Anna is impregnated by the Holy Spirit.

The Matthean Performative Fulfillment Formulae

Matthew uses the language of fulfillment more than any other Gospel. He most often uses it to introduce Jewish Scripture citations, primarily from the Prophets; Mark employs the language more sparingly and in reference to the fulfillment of time, Scripture, or events (1:15; 13:4; 14:49; cf. Luke 4:21). In John's gospel fulfillment language refers to scripture and introduces scripture on a few occasions, but primarily from the Psalms (13:18; 17:12; 19:24, 36). Not all scripture quotations in Matthew are introduced using fulfillment language nor is the language limited to scripture quotations (2:5; 3:3; 13:35; 15:7; 21:13).

The typical fulfillment formula resembles the following: "this took place to fulfill what had been spoken by the Lord through the prophet." But the language can vary slightly (1:22; 2:23; 21:4; 26:56). Most often cited is Isaiah (4:14; 8:17; 12:17; 13:14) or Jeremiah (2:17; 27:9). In Matthew the prophets or prophetic literature are sacred texts that demonstrate the fulfillment of certain events in Jesus's life and ministry. This does not preclude that these events had their own prior historical contexts. The first time that Matthew inserts a fulfillment formula concerns the virgin conception and birth of Jesus (1:22). There, he employs the characteristic formula followed by a quotation. Here "fulfill" signifies both a realized event and a recontextualization; as noted above, the original scripture has its own historical context. Another example is when Jesus protests John the Baptist's refusal to baptize him, arguing that it must be done in order to "fulfill all justice" (3:15). Here, we interpret the Greek noun *dikaiosunē* as justice rather than as *righteousness* (of course, many interpreters prefer the latter sense). While John considers it an injustice or dishonor for Jesus, as God's Messiah, to submit to a baptism of repentance, Jesus's words and submission are a reversal of what is honorable by human standards. Jesus does not use his anointed status to avoid a ritual that is required of other human beings.

We might say that particular prophetic and Messianic traditions inscribed in Israel's sacred Scriptures are renewed and performed in Jesus's birth, life, and ministry as God's Messiah among God's people living in the first century CE under Roman rule. The fulfillment citations construct historical, theological, literary, and semantic links between the Jewish Scriptures and Jesus's birth, baptism, powerful acts, teachings, death, and resurrection. The Scriptures provide the meaning and trajectory for Jesus's birth, life, and ministry. The fulfillment citations also demonstrate that Jesus is a type of certain Hebrew Bible characters like Elijah, Moses, and of course the Emmanuel baby born to the young female prophetess as a sign of God's presence with God's people.

Matthew's Jesus: Son of Refugees and Colonized Revolutionary Prophet

The portrait we shall construct of Jesus is drawn from Matthew's narrative as an organic whole; it is not an excavation in search of the historical Jesus. This is a literary and theological construction. What is it that we understand Matthew's text to say about Jesus? How might we, as contemporary readers of Matthew, perceive of Matthew's Jesus, through our own context and considering the historical and literary context of Matthew's Gospel?

Son of Refugees: *Out of Egypt Have I Called My Son*

Joseph has a second angelophany compelling him to take his new family and flee to Egypt because of Herod's attempt to destroy the child king (2:13). Overnight, the pair and their child become refugees fleeing Judea to find a safe haven in Egypt. This is a reversal of Moses and the Hebrews' flight from Egypt and Egyptian slavery into the wilderness; a pivotal event in Jewish history that Israel is constantly admonished to remember. To escape Herod's death decree, Yahweh's angel instructs Joseph to take his family and flee to Egypt. In the first century when Jesus's family fled to Egypt to save him from Herod's death grip, Egypt had been under Roman control for about thirty years. We do not know to what part of Egypt the young family fled, but according to Matthew they were able to escape Herod's slaughter of innocent children in Bethlehem. Their success demonstrates the limits of Herod's power and reach as Rome's puppet king. Had Herod's efforts been supported by the Roman Empire and had the emperor viewed the baby Jesus as a national threat, surely the family would not have been able to cross the border into Egypt and remain there without being sent back to Judea or detained. The text does not tell us whether the family had the assistance of some "underground railroad" similar to the one that assisted runaway Africans enslaved in America to escape to freedom in the North, but it is not an impossibility.

> **Consider and discuss:** How often do we focus on the one child who escaped the infanticide in Bethlehem and forget about the many slaughtered children? There is a brief pause in the text that allows for grief or mourning. To be fair, it is an inconsolable grief. How might we have been desensitized to the deaths of innocent children as a means to an end? Can you think of contemporary situations comparable to this slaughter of innocents?

The first century Jewish historian Josephus informs that Egypt had a population of over seven million, excluding the intellectual and cultural capital of Alexandria; that number is based on poll-tax returns (*War*, 2.385). Egypt's population exceeded that of other regions in the then-known inhabited world, the *oikumenē* (Diodorus Siculus, 1.31.6–8). Egypt's vast population would have been an ideal place for the refugees to blend in. In addition, Egypt and Alexandria were called home to a sizeable Jewish population. According to the Jewish writer Philo of Alexandria (ca. 20 BCE–40CE), no less than one million Jews called Egypt home (*Against Flaccus* 43). Thus, it might not have been difficult for the young Jewish family to hide and/or to find sympathizers and allies in Egypt. Israel has a history of seeking refuge in and assistance from Egypt with whom they have had a long relationship characterized by both hospitality and hostility, feast and famine, oppression and liberation. They have intermingled through marriage and slavery (Gen 41:45; 46:1–4; 50:22–26).

If Jesus was born around 3 or 4 BCE and Herod died in 4 CE, Jesus might have been around seven years of age when his family returned to Judea. It seems that Joseph is told in a third angelophany that it is safe to return to Israel. Herod the great had died and his son Archelaus replaced him as King of Judea but instead of tetrarch (ruler of a fourth of a division) was appointed ethnarch (national leader) over Samaria, Idumea, and Judea. Joseph surmised that the threat was not buried with Herod; it was not about the person but about the position of King over Judea. Guided once more by his dreams, Joseph takes a detour and settles in Nazareth. When Mary and Joseph return from Egypt after Herod's death, their exodus is a fulfillment of scripture: "out of Egypt have I called my son" (2:15; Hos 11:1). In this scripture Hosea's "son" is symbolic of Israel. Historically, God had promised Jacob that he would bring him out of Egypt and later made the same promise to Moses (Gen 46:4; Exod 3:12). Thus, this is not the first time in Israel's history that God has called God's "son" out of Egypt.

Colonized Political Revolutionary Prophet

To say that Jesus was a revolutionary is not to suggest that he was the first or last Jewish revolutionary contemporary or prior to his life. Nor is it to suggest that the only revolutionaries were Jewish men. Not all of God's chosen and anointed servants were Jewish. Cyrus, King of Persia, and Nebuchadnezzar, king of Babylon, were called God's anointed servants or Messiahs. But just as Matthew, and other gospels, places Jesus within the Jewish prophetic tradition, we might also understand him to place Jesus within the tradition of zealots or revolutionaries. Here, of course, we use the word *zealots* in all lower case, since the Zealots as a formal political party did not emerge until the latter half of the first century CE and after Jesus's lifetime.

Jesus is a colonized revolutionary prophet as a member of a race/ethnic group conquered by and subject to the Roman Empire (see 3 Maccabees). As mentioned above, Jesus's life, ministry, and death fulfill or perform/(re) enact certain events that occurred or are mentioned in Israel's prophetic tradition. When Jesus demonstrates too much authority and/or power among the masses because of his powerful deeds (*dunameis*) and his proclamation that the kingdom of heaven is near in him, he is viewed with suspicion and as a possible threat to certain established Jewish authorities and Roman order. Because many colonized people assimilate and submit in order to live a more peaceful life with their colonizers, they too might become suspicious and feel threatened when a zealot or revolutionary prophetic figure arises. We also see the impact of Jesus's status as a colonized Jewish man when he is asked about paying taxes to Caesar (the Roman government). Hybridity is an escapable reality for colonized and colonizers, both of whom are mutually impacted as they interact and intermingle. Sometimes the colonizer forces some aspect of a foreign culture on the colonized as with the imposition of Greek language and culture (hellenization) under the Romans.

As a hybrid revolutionary prophet, Matthew's Jesus sometimes attempted to alleviate the systemic reasons for people's sufferings. For example, Jesus attempts to replace an oppressive kingdom with God's kingdom of heaven and its focus on justice and love of neighbor and enemy. But the relationship between colonized and colonizer is complex and sometimes fluid. At other times, it appears that Matthew's Jesus offers no critique of unjust systems and instead reinscribes systemic oppression. For example, in many of the Matthean parables, slavery and stereotypical slave-master relationships are employed, indiscriminately and uncritically, as paradigms for God and behavior suitable for persons wishing to participate in the kingdom of heaven. This is discussed more fully below.

As a revolutionary prophet, like those who preceded him, Matthew's Jesus requires that his disciples do or act with justice and love. Their justice should exceed that of some of the scribes and Pharisees (5:20; 9:13): no ostentatious piety (6:1ff.) and to treat others as one would like to be treated (7:12). Jesus demonstrated his *God-with-us-ness* in his dealings with the crowds and some Jewish leaders and sects whom he encountered and who pursued him. Matt 12:15–21 (and the embedded Isa 42:1–4 quotation) and its immediate context, demonstrates a difference between injustice and justice, namely, some Pharisees' concern for strict halakic observance and their concomitant unjust treatment of the people versus Jesus's own understanding of Torah observance and the justice he embodied and engendered among the people. Following Matthean summaries (8:14–17; 12:15–21) we find quotes from Deutero-Isaiah's servant songs (Isa 53:4; 42:1–4), focusing on the justice of God and the unjust treatment of the servant. In both 8:14–27 and 12:15–21, Jesus's healing and/or exorcism activities are said to fulfill a portion of the servant songs (Isa 53:4; 42:1–4). Thus, Jesus's disciples are to teach others the justice and love that they practice (5:19). Matthew focuses on Jesus as the anointed of God, the Messiah or Christ, and not primarily as a teacher only; he is a Messiah who is both a teacher and a prophet. The justice Jesus embodies and teaches through embodiment is contrary to the ways of the colonizer/oppressor within and without. The first century Roman historian Tacitus (ca. 57–117 CE) wrote the following: "The Romans are deadly pillagers of the world; they have exhausted the land by their indiscriminate plunder, and now they ransack the sea. A rich enemy excites their greed; a poor one, their lust for power. East and West alike have failed to satisfy them. They are the only people on earth to whose covetousness both riches and poverty are equally tempting. To robbery, butchery, and rape, they give the lying name of 'government'; they create a desolation and call it peace."[3]

As a revolutionary Messiah, Jesus is concerned with and engenders the justice and love of God, teaching others to embody and engage in embodied teaching of the same. Matthew establishes for his readers the character of Joseph as a just (*dikaios*) man who is engaged to the pregnant young girl, Mary; and Joseph is not the father. Implicitly, the justice of God prevails in the wise men's decision not to report back to Herod upon finding the baby Jesus (2:12). Conversely, injustice is committed when Herod orders the murder of all children two years old and under in and around Bethlehem (2:16). Herod as Rome's puppet King is the antithesis of Jesus as God's political revolutionary Messiah. Acts of justice and injustice are weaved, implicitly and explicitly, throughout the story, the narration of the story, and in Jesus's words and deeds. If Matthew begins with the just Joseph, it ends with Jesus's brother James "the just" emerging as leader of the Jerusalem council (27:56; cf. Acts 1:13; 15:13; Jude 1).

Matthew's Jesus does not apologize to his hometown folks for preaching prophetic words that astound and offend (13:54b–57a). Herod Antipas (21 BCE–39 CE, son of Herod the Great), tetrarch of Galilee, was also disturbed by the powerful acts Jesus performs, thinking he might be a resurrected John the Baptist (14:1–2). Matthew revises Mark's version: He adds that fear of the crowd (*ochlos*) that regards Jesus as a prophet prevents Herod from assassinating Jesus (14:5; Mark 6:17–20). Like other zealots and revolutionaries, Jesus had large crowds as well as disciples following him. And some Jewish authorities attempt to keep the Roman peace, including curtailing possible revolts (*stasis*), which seems to be more of a concern in Matthew. The powerful and unapologetic acts Jesus performs among and for the crowds of mostly common folks, and without charge, make him the paradigmatic revolutionary prophet and teacher. Jesus's actions exceed and embody his words. This is possibly why some attribute to him a superior authority. An injustice is committed when we offer people what they need but we place it beyond their economic and physical reach. For example, a business might open a grocery store in a poor neighborhood but the prices of the fresh produce are so inflated that the residents cannot afford to purchase it. Or the geographical location of the store requires that all residents have cars and/or can afford to purchase gas for their cars.

---

3. Tacitus, "Calgacus' Address to the Caledonians," 80–81.

Did Jesus fail as a revolutionary, as some assert? The answer to this depends on how we understand Jesus's role and goal as a revolutionary. Was his goal to assume the mantle of a revolutionary prophet like Elijah, fulfill his purpose and then commission his disciples to continue? If this is the case, then we could say that Jesus did not fail. If Jesus's disciples (female and male) fail, then the hope is for others to rise up and willingly risk the consequences of doing revolutionary deeds and speaking prophetic truths to power. If the kingdom was within and had come near in Jesus, how is it a failure if he embodied it to the best of his ability as a son of Abraham and of Mary? Was Jesus's success in Matthew dependent upon an expectation that Jesus initiate and/or accomplish the replacement of one kingdom with another kingdom? Kingdoms in and of themselves are oppressive. But it appears that through his embodied teaching and promotion of an embodied Gospel, Jesus hoped to dismantle oppression brick by brick, challenging kings and religio-political authorities as well as common people's thinking and actions. We might perceive Matthew and Matthew's Jesus in terms of hybridity and sometimes assimilation (some assimilation is both unconscious and unavoidable) in the adoption of kingdom rhetoric, for example. It appears, however, that Matthew espoused and envisioned (and Matthew's Jesus engendered) justice.

Consider and discuss: What is the relationship between movements and movement leaders? Can revolution occur without the crowds willing to stir up the status quo at the risk of freedom and life? Why or why not? Reflect on historical, current, and recent movements like the abolitionist movement, women's suffrage movement, the US farm worker's movement, the labor movement, the Black Lives Matter and Me Too movements. What should be our response to or involvement in such movements?

Kingdom of the Heavens and Kingdom Rhetoric

The phrase "kingdom of the heavens" is peculiar to Matthew. God's kingdom transcends any and all conceptualizations and levels of the heavens. It is both earthly and heavenly, and it bridges the two. With the imprisonment and execution of John the Baptist, the kingdom of the heavens suffered violence (11:12). When the least in the kingdom suffer from imprisonment, homelessness, hunger, sickness, and injustices, Jesus as royal revolutionary Messiah suffers too (25:35–46). He too is the political prisoner, the hungry refugee, the rejected immigrant, and the stranger. Since the kingdom bridges and transcends heaven and earth, Jesus's word will stand even when heaven and earth pass away (24:35). The diabolos offers Jesus all the kingdoms of the world (4:8); but God's one kingdom encapsulates, overcomes, and transcends them all. At Jesus's baptism, the Father's voice of acknowledgement and approval is heard from the heavens (*ouranoi*) (3:17).

Peculiar to Matthew is a trilogy of brief parables to help Jesus's disciples envision and understand the kingdom of the heavens (13:44–50). Each parable begins with "the kingdom of the heavens is like." Central to all three parables is an emphasis on doing the just/right(eous) thing in specific contexts. These acts consist of finding or catching and buying, selling or catching something of tremendous value to the subject. The trilogy of parables may characterize the kingdom participant who relinquishes everything for the kingdom. But the kingdom is not some abstract notion. The enduring idea of "kingdom" carries with it certain concrete notions and relationships that betray Israel's long history as colonized and colonizers. It references the story of a people, or at least the elites among them who tell the story, wanting a king like other nations, so that they might rule instead of being ruled. But within any kingdom, the rulers and the ruled exist together in hierarchal relationships of oppression and subordination. This trilogy appeals to those likely to be subjects, the ruled, and not the kings: it features fishermen and their work and dreams to discover hidden treasure and to score the big catch. The evil and bad are dispensable. Jesus, as a scribe of the kingdom, trained his scribes by reinterpreting old and familiar images (14:51–52). But a possible downside of interpreting old and familiar images is that some of the old oppressive meanings attached to the old and familiar survive and invade one's theology and anthropology.

John the Baptist and Jesus's kingdom rhetoric demonstrate their desire to overthrow and/or transform systems of oppression and replace them with a more just and justice-making realm on earth, embodied in human beings and institutions, including religious institutions. Even as we critique the rhetoric from our postmodern perspective, we recognize in Matthew an intent to subvert an existing colonizing imperial system of oppression.

Consider and discuss: "Kingdom" is an ancient word/concept. What other ideologies and social realities are historically associated with kingdoms that may conflict with how we understand the character of God, Jesus, and the Holy Spirit? What contemporary words would parallel the word and conception of "kingdom"? What are the pros and cons of employing such contemporary metaphors as symbols of the presence and activity of God and God's Spirit in the world?

Matthew's Distinctive Use of Mark's Gospel

Some of the ways that Matthew has used Mark as a source have been mentioned in previous sections. We have noticed that when Matthew borrows from Mark, he edits those traditions to reflect his own theological purposes and emphases. As in Mark, four of Jesus's disciples are chosen prior to the commencement of his teaching; a rabbi (teacher) must have disciples (4:18–22; Mark 1:16–20). Here we mention some additional texts that reflect the different ways that Matthew revises Mark's material. We will briefly discuss the wilderness rite of passage (4:1–11); Jesus's encounter with the Canaanite woman (15:21–28; cf. Mark 7:24–30); and the feeding of the 5,000 plus crowd in the desert (14:13–21; cf. Mark 6:32–44; Luke 9:10–17).

The Wilderness Rite of Passage (4:1–11//Mark 1:12–13; Luke 4:1–13)

While Mark devotes only two verses to Jesus's wilderness testing, Matthew expands the narrative to eleven verses. Both agree that the Spirit initiated the encounter, but in Matthew the Spirit orchestrates or leads Jesus into the wilderness to encounter the adversary (4:1). They also agree that the purpose was so that the devil or Satan (4:1, 10) would tempt or test (*peirazomai*) him; he would be in the desert forty days (4:2//Mark 1:13); Matthew adds "forty nights." Both Gospels appear to pattern the event after Israel's forty years in the wilderness upon escaping from Egyptian bondage (Deut 8:2). Matthew more precisely replicates Moses's forty days and nights on Sinai and Elijah's forty days and nights journey to Horeb to meet God (Exod 24:18; 1 Kgs 19:8). According to Matthew, the tempter did not appear until after Jesus had fasted for the forty days and nights and was famished. Jesus is physically weak and vulnerable when he submits to a three-question oral examination. The first two require that he prove he is the son of God: Feed yourself by turning the stones to bread. To which Jesus responds by quoting Deut 8:3 that bread is not a mortal's sole sustenance, but every word of God sustains him. If he is not going to feed himself, he might as well attempt suicide by throwing himself off the highest point of the Temple and expect God to save his son. This time it is the devil that quotes the scripture (Ps 91:11–12) about how God would catch him and not permit so much as his foot to be harmed. Jesus disrupts the Scripture that the devil evokes with his own Scripture quotation, one that prohibits testing God (Deut 6:16). Finally, the Devil/Satan offers Jesus wealth and the ultimate political power in return for Jesus's worship. But Jesus dismisses Satan and verbally commits to honor (*proskuneō*) and worship only God, demonstrating his commitment despite his famished body. By electing to be confined to the boundaries of his humanity and not transgress them (trying to be God), Jesus engenders and embodies the justice of God in the wilderness and in his ministry (being like and honoring God). Matthew agrees with Mark that following the temptation, the angels ministered (*diakoneō*) to Jesus (4:11; Mark 1:13).

Matthew's Jesus demonstrated that he would claim solidarity with his fellow humans living in food and water deserts. Jesus does not yield to the temptation to sell out in exchange for a small part of "kingdoms of the world and their splendor." Jesus knows hunger, pain of poverty, and the false hope that comes from promises thwarted by unjust systems. Jesus refused to capitalize on his privilege. Even when privilege (e.g., "white privilege") is handed to a person, she can reject it in favor of solidarity with the least of these. Now Jesus can commence his ministry among those Galilean peasants and the rest of the ninety-nine percent living under the oppression of the Roman Empire who know hunger, despair, and poverty and the temptations and multiple forms of violence that accompany them. Jesus can empathize and sympathize; he has and will continue to live and minster in solidarity with the most marginalized.

Jesus's Encounter with the Canaanite Woman (15:21–28//Mark 7:24–30)

Matthew follows Mark in placing the story of the Canaanite woman's encounter with Jesus after he teaches the crowds and his disciples, presumably in public space, about defilement: what comes out of the body/heart is more defiling than what one consumes (15:10–20). However, in Mark that discussion occurs in the private space of a house (Mark 7:17). Unlike Mark, Matthew's story is followed by Jesus, pursued by large crowds and their sick, descending a mountain. But differently, Mark's story of the Syrophoenician woman, as he calls her, is followed by the healing of a deaf man with a speech impediment (15:29–31; cf. Mark 7:31–37). Matthew's preference for "Canaanite" as a description of the woman's ethnicity ensures that his readers know without further description that she is a Gentile; whereas Mark adds that she is Greek or a Gentile so that his readers might not mistake her for a Jewish woman living and perhaps born in Syria or Phoenicia. Also, Matthew knows the district as a combination of Tyre and Sidon; Mark, as simply Tyre. Later we find that Jesus did not perform many powerful deeds in Tyre and Sidon as had been done in Capernaum and Chorazin (11:20–24); therefore, the latter will be judged more harshly.

In both Gospels the woman is anonymous. Both ethnic descriptors "Canaanite" and "Syrophoenician" are reminiscent of hostilities between them and the Jewish people. Matthew foregrounds certain behaviors absent from Mark's story: She is a shouting woman, characterized so by both the narrator and the disciples; like other characters in Matthew she shouts, "Have mercy on me, Son of David" (cf. 20:29–34); a demon torments her daughter (only Mark initially calls it an "unclean spirit," 7:25); and Jesus acknowledges her great faith. By calling Jesus "son of David," the woman is acknowledging and/or submitting to Jesus as a descendant of David, which could simply mean she recognizes him as a Jewish man and possibly of royal lineage. Matthew may mean it as a double entendre, having two meanings; his readers should again see Jesus as expressing his purpose and loyalty as God's Messiah. Mary's husband, Joseph, is also described as the "son of David" by the angel of the Lord no less (1:20). There, of course, it refers to his ancestry in the line of King David and by extension Mary's son as well.

"Son of David" occurs more frequently in Matthew's Gospel than in any other. The two blind men who approach Jesus for healing also shout the same phrase as the Canaanite woman: "Have mercy on us, Son of David" (9:27; cf. 20:29–34; 21:9; Mark 10:46–52). In both instances, faith comes into play. Amazed at Jesus's healing of a blind and mute demon-possessed man, it is publicly asked whether Jesus might be the "son of David" (12:23). Even the children in the Temple shout "Hosanna to the son of David" (21:15; cf. 22:41–42).

Only in Matthew are the disciples present urging Jesus to dismiss the Canaanite mother because of her persistent shouting (cf. Acts 16:16–18 where Paul is annoyed by the Pythian slave girl). In Matthew, prior to the dialogue about tables, crumbs, and dogs, the woman and Jesus engage in a *tête-à-tête*: Jesus declares that he is only sent to the lost sheep of the house of Israel. The woman's response is to prostrate herself before him, asking for help. The most significant dialogue from Mark begins with Jesus saying, "It is not fair to take the children's food and throw it to the dogs" (v. 26b; Mark 7:27–28). To which the woman responds: "Yes, Lord, yet even the dogs eat the crumbs that fall from their masters' table," v. 27. (See chapter 10, "The Gospel of Mark," for a further discussion of this dialogue and dogs/

pets among ancient Romans and Semitic peoples.) Matthew's Jesus is more exclusionary; both prioritize Israel. Finally, both versions seem to attribute the power that healed the woman's daughter to something within her: in Matthew it is her "great faith" and in Mark, her word (*logos*).

A Way Out of No Way in the Desert
(14:13–21; cf. Mark 6:32–44; Luke 9:10–17)

Following Mark's chronology, Matthew places the feeding of the 5,000 after the story of Herod's execution and before the narrative of Jesus walking on the sea. Also like Mark, Matthew includes both feeding stories, the 5,000 and later the 4,000. Matthew's Gospel appears to promote seeds of institutionalism with its mention of the Greek noun *ekklēsia* (*assembly* but often translated anachronistically as *church*) with Jesus as its foundation, rather than Peter (16:18). The *ekklēsia* is a broader cultural idea of a political, religious, and supposedly democratic gathering concerned with the peace or wholeness of a community. Matthew's feeding story seems to further this notion of *ekklēsia*. The Matthean episode begins when Jesus, mourning John the Baptist's death, removes himself to a deserted place but is unable to escape the crowds who followed him. When Jesus sees the multitudes following him, presumably out of their many needs, he has compassion on them. In Mark's version he demonstrates compassion as well, but his compassion compels him to *teach* the crowds, seeing them as sheep without a shepherd. But Matthew's Jesus, whom so many like to call the ultimate teacher, does not follow Mark here. Instead, the Matthean Jesus's compassion leads to him to heal the sick. He addresses their very physical needs. We might understand Jesus and his disciples here as a collective, in institutional terms, as laying the foundation of the *ekklēsia*. The crowd makes this collective aware of their needs; they feel comfortable doing so because Jesus has made it his business to be among them (as God with us). Jesus has experienced their stories and intervened in them in helpful, healthful, and restorative ways. The disciples, as in Mark, call Jesus's attention to the obvious: it is getting late, they'd been there a long time healing folks, and everybody's hungry. The disciples urge Jesus to dismiss the crowd so that they might obtain food, leaving the disciples to have their own little private dining experience. The majority of these people who have followed Jesus, if not all, are by no means wealthy. Jesus calls upon this emerging, fledgling institution of thirteen, including Jesus himself, to use what they have to feed this hungry crowd. The twelve want to know where Jesus expects them to get enough to feed this community. Jesus asks them how much they have.

He does not ask them about what they don't have, even though that is where their hunger pains force them to focus. Seven loaves and a few small fish, as opposed to Mark's five loaves and two fish (Mark 6:38). Without hesitation Jesus makes a way in the desert; the dust of the earth becomes their table and they recline together. Jesus thanks God for what they have to work with. Next, Jesus breaks the bread and orders the disciples to feed the crowds. Jesus is doing what the Roman government sometimes did; it provided free bread for the poor. This distribution of food may have been limited to the poor in the cities. Compassion and charity are necessary interventions, but structures that create poverty must be dismantled.

Those Jesus enlists to minister to the needy crowd did not go hungry. That there was something left is as much a testimony to Jesus as to the crowds. As in Mark, all had their fill and twelve baskets full remained. The crowds did not insist upon devouring every single crumb; they too only wanted enough to meet their needs. Too often the crowds are deemed untrustworthy. Without knowing or getting to know their stories, the crowds are often criticized and impugned for their deficiencies. Personal transformation in this instance involves being concerned with and meeting the needs of others without casting blame.

Consider and discuss: Some people argue that it is the government's responsibility to feed the poor and hungry. Do you agree or disagree and why or why not? What systems help create poverty? What can we do to help put an end to poverty?

Matthew's Jesus later declares that what we do for the "least" we do for Jesus (25:38–40): For I was a hungry child living on the streets with my family and you gave me food; I was a Flint, Michigan, resident and you gave me clean water to drink; I was a Syrian or a Haitian refugee and you welcomed me; I was naked, stripped of dignity and justice, and you clothed me; I was overcome with sickness and medical bills, and you took care of me; I was in prison and you visited me, not knowing whether I was innocent or guilty, repentant or unremorseful. But more than this you fought for policies (e.g., a living wage, hospitality, rehabilitation, accessible quality education for all) for the least and you dismantled unjust systems (e.g., for-profit prisons, privatization of water).

Another significant difference between Mark's version of this story and Matthew is the mention of women and children in the crowd. Matthew seems to be concerned to include the most vulnerable in our society, poor women and children.

Matthew's Distinctive Use of Q

Again, we propose to provide examples of how Matthew has used material from Q and made it his own through revisions and additions. Matthew shares the Q material in common with Luke; it is a common hypothetical and non-extant sayings source from which the two draw. Sometimes Matthew's use of Q is basically the same as Luke's. For example, Jesus's prayer of thanks to the Father for revealing things to him that are not revealed to others is exactly the same in both Matthew and Luke (11:25–27// Luke 10:21–22). Another example occurs in Jesus's lament over Jerusalem (23:37–39//Luke 13:34–35) where we see only a few minor differences; perhaps the most significance is Matthew's insertion of the word "desolate" to describe the final condition of the Temple/house. Noteworthy Q material is what many call "the sermon on the Mount," which we will refer to as a mountaintop manifesto (5–7).

Mountaintop Manifesto (5–7)

Chapters 5–7 are the first of five extensive discourse segments in Matthew (also chapters 10, 13, 18, and 23–27). This Matthean manifesto comes from Q. In his manifesto delivered on the mount (known as "the sermon on the mount"; as opposed to Luke's on the plain), Matthew presents this first lengthy discourse as a unified teaching block; Luke's is scattered throughout his Gospel. We shall focus on particular themes in this manifesto. A manifesto is a public declaration of an individual or group's positions and/or views, goals, and objectives. Jesus begins with describing nine types or ways that people are blessed. The first assertion describes the poor in spirit as blessed; to them belong the kingdom of heaven. It is not the aristocratic landowners who control the kingdom, in contrast to the Roman Empire. The insertion of the prepositional phrase *in spirit* after the word *poor* need not be perceived as a spiritualizing of poverty. People trapped in poverty often experience broken spirits and loss of hope. Conversely, a crushed spirit can result in economic poverty. The fourth beatitude assures that those who hunger and thirst for justice (*dikaiosunē*) will be satisfied (5:6; also 5:10). While the Romans conquered and then strove to keep the peace to maintain power, Jesus states that the peacemakers are the children of God. Strategically, the beatitudes are followed by two significant metaphors used to instruct the crowds: "the salt of the earth" and the "light of the world" (5:13–14). This instruction links the promise of justice for the poor in spirit with the global obligation to engender justice. No other synoptic Gospel connects justice for the poor in spirit and personal and/or corporate responsibility to the rest of the world as Matthew does (Mark 4:21; 9:50; Luke 8:16; 11:33; 14:34–35).

Jesus has come to fulfill or perform, reenact Torah, which is summed up in love of God and neighbor. He presents a series of teachings based on the following pattern: "You have heard . . . but I say to you" (5:21–48). Jesus's teaching is somewhat stricter than what they have heard. For example, to lust after a woman is to commit adultery. Also, it is not enough to refrain from swearing falsely; one should not swear at all. It is no longer acceptable to just love one's neighbors, but Jesus admonishes the crowd to love their enemies as well and pray for their persecutors. Ostentatious giving, praying, and fasting are to be avoided. God knows what they need before they ask, but it doesn't hurt to pray for daily food, mutual forgiveness of debts, and the establishment of the Father's kingdom on earth.

Jesus informs the crowds and his disciples that God cares that they are nourished and clothed. This is reiterated in chapter 25 in the context of Jesus's teaching about the final execution of justice. If God dresses and feeds the birds, certainly God desires to do the same for human beings regarding their mundane temporal needs (6:25–34; cf. 7:9–10). God cares about social justice. Therefore, the disciples can with confidence prioritize their participation in God's kingdom, since the people's needs are a priority of the kingdom. Justice is an intrinsic and organic divine objective; the mandate to prioritize God's reign does not invite or construct an untenable dichotomy between temporal needs and the nearness and proclamation of God's kingdom in Jesus.

While some things have been nuanced, other things are presented as black and white, less complex. These include false prophets, and good and bad trees that bear good and bad fruit respectively. Significantly, Matthew's Jesus prefaces the summation of the Torah's requirement to love God and neighbor with the words "in everything"; Luke does not (7:12; Luke 6:31). The expectation that Jesus's followers would treat others as they would expect to be treated is a synopsis of God's instruction and commandments in the prophets as well as in the Torah. Jesus's life and ministry embody God's love and love of our fellow human beings. In Jesus this love is fulfilled; it is performed. The least in the kingdom are those who break the commandments (5:17–20); they neglect to love God and neighbor. Those described as "least" in Jesus's eschatological (final events) discourse are different from the least who break Torah. The breakers of Torah are not said to be excluded but have a diminished place in the kingdom. Perhaps this is because this is a warning and an opportunity for transformation and not the final judgment.

Consider and discuss: Is there any social reversal evident in the manifesto or throughout Matthew's text? Does Jesus demonstrate reversal of present social distinctions, roles, and statuses? If not, when is that not the case and why do you think he does not? How do we as contemporary believers live in the tension of the promises in the manifesto and the often oppressive reality that we or others experience?

Jesus's words about entering into the narrow gate is framed within the polarities of life and destruction (7:13–14//Luke 13:22–24). The wide and easy gate leads to destruction; while the narrow and hard way leads to life. Readers might understand the latter route as the way of justice/ righteousness or the way that God and Jesus as God's Messiah advocate. The way of destruction, the easy and wide road, might signify the way of the Roman Empire. Rome built many roads, allowing for easy travel and commerce throughout the empire. Few people find the less accessible and more rugged route.

Matthew's Special Material

Certain sayings, teachings, narrative episodes, and parables are peculiar to Matthew's Gospel, some of which we have already noted. Materials special to Matthew are neither a revision of other extant sources nor do they appear in any other Gospel tradition (e.g. Mark, Luke, John). Here we shall briefly discuss the following three extended Matthean narratives: (1) the conversation with the temple tax collector about paying taxes (17:24–27); the parable of the unmerciful slave (*doulos*) (18:23–25); and the parable of the ten virgins (25:1–13).

Does Your Teacher Pay His Tax (*didrachma*)? (17:24–27).

This tax is a testament to the imposition of a temple tax on Jewish people, in addition to the general taxes paid to the Emperor. The temple tax collector addresses Peter, asking whether his Rabbi pays his temple taxes. (Peter appears to be prominent or exalted in texts that diminish women like Mary Magdalene, particularly in the empty tomb scenes.) When Jesus arrives in Capernaum, Jesus asks Peter whether the earthly kings exact taxes from their own children or from others. Peter provides the obvious answer. It is from others. The burden of taxes is the social reality of the colonized, oppressed, and slaves. Thus, Jesus sends Peter fishing with the instructions that he is to find a coin in the mouth of his first catch with which he is to pay their temple tax. The reason Jesus gives for paying the tax is so that they might not offend (*skandalizō*) the Romans. Later in Matthew's narrative Jesus is approached by some disciples of the Pharisees and Herodians who question Jesus directly about paying the emperor's taxes. Jesus does not carry coins, it seems, but asks his interrogators to produce one. They produce a denarius and Jesus flips it to the obverse, which is the side where the image of the emperor's head is imprinted, demonstrating authority and ownership. Thus, Jesus asserts that people give to Caesar what belongs to him and to God what is due God. That episode is from Matthew's Markan source (22:15–22//Mark 12:13–17//Luke 20:20–26). Different from Mark, Matthew describes them as motivated by maliciousness or wickedness (*ponēria*); in the Synoptics all agree that Jesus openly calls them hypocrites.

> **Consider and Discuss:** At times Jesus and/or Matthew's Gospel appears as unapologetically subversive toward the Roman Empire. But at other times Matthew's Jesus does not want to offend the Roman authorities. How do you explain this ambivalence? Is this ambivalence a result of the author's or Jesus's hybridity? Is Jesus promoting an imperialist agenda? Are there circumstances in which the colonized and/or foreigners or even citizens should refuse to pay taxes; why or why not?

The Parable of the Unmerciful Slave (*doulos*) (18:23–25).

The master/slave relationship in the slave parables in the Gospels represents the social reality of living in a slave society. They further reinscribe stereotypical master and slave behavior and relationships. This Matthean parable is one of many introduced with these words: "for this reason the kingdom of heaven is likened to." The king in the parable owns slaves and each owe him money. He wants to settle or balance his books. Since the first slave was unable to repay his 10,000 talents, the king proceeds to sell him, his wife, and their children to satisfy the debt. A slave owner/master selling slaves was under no obligation to keep a family together. This was one of the greatest fears of Africans enslaved in America, to have their spouses and children sold away from them. Unexpectedly and perhaps unrealistically, the parable represents the king as having pity on the begging slave, and he cancels his debt. However, later that same released slave violently attempts to collect a lesser debt of 100 denarii (a day's wage) from a fellow slave. This is a poignant reminder of how the oppressed can become oppressor or imitate the ways of their oppressors. When the slave pleads for more time to pay his debt, the forgiven slave has him imprisoned. There seems to be a presumption that the imprisoned slave had the money, but he refused to pay. Whereas the king/master had no such presumption of the slave who owed 10,000 talents. Of course, 10,000 talents is a significantly larger amount than 100 denarii. How could a slave amass such an enormous debt, except that his master extort him by charging him exorbitant amounts for food, clothing, shelter, and so on? Conversely, perhaps the debt the slave owed the forgiven slave was a legitimate debt that the forgiven slave desperately needed to recoup. Other slaves who witness one slave imprison another for nonpayment of a debt get word to the forgiven slaves' master, the king. The king, like other slave masters, had the power to renege on his promise to release the slave of his enormous debt. And the enslaver submits the slave's body to torture until the entire debt is paid, which could be years. The king represents a heavenly Father who will submit to torture those who fail to forgive their brothers and sisters and will renege on his offer of mercy.

Consider and discuss: What is the upside or the downside of comparing the heavenly Father or God with the king-slave master in this parable? Where does the parable break down in its ability to be liberating? For whom would or should this parable be most troublesome (and least so) and why?

The Parable of the Ten Virgins (25:1–13)

This Matthean parable is the second in a set of three; it is part of a trilogy. Scholars clearly recognize the preceding parable and the one that follows this one as slave parables. We suggest that this one arguably is a slave parable as well. Thus, ten females that are both slaves and virgins wait for the bridegroom to arrive. The parable does not mention a bride. Could this possibly be a portrayal of a nobleman or king taking for himself a number of virginal slave women as brides? (cf. Judg 21:1–12). Five of the virgins are defined as foolish because they fail to carry more than enough oil in anticipation of the groom's late arrive. The other five are wise because they are more than prepared and are thus able to enter into the wedding festivities (or consummation of the marriage?) with the groom. The five wise refuse to share their oil with the foolish virgins who consequently leave to buy more oil. Upon their return, the groom denies them entrance with the words, "I do not know you." The verb "know" sometimes refers to knowing someone sexually.

In the immediate context, the parables about the faithful and wise slave (24:45–51) and the slave master who entrusts his slaves with talents (money) (25:14–30) precede and follow, respectively, the story of the ten virgins. The first and last parables in the trilogy culminate with the wicked or worthless slave being thrown into a place characterized by "weeping and gnashing of teeth" or torture (24:51; 25:30). This parable of the ten virgins, as well as the other two in the trilogy, function to demonstrate the importance of remaining watchful or awake since the Son of Man will return unexpectedly. Only the Father in heaven knows when the parousia (coming) will occur, and he has not revealed any precise knowledge even to the son (24:36). All three parables, as well as other slave parables in the Gospels, reinscribe master-slave stereotypes (22:1–10/Luke 14:15–24; 24:45–51/Luke 12:42–46; 25:14–30; Luke 19:11–27). Masters are cruel and exacting. Slaves are to be obedient and their bodies accessible to the master at his whim. They must stay awake. Yet, such parables assist in teaching disciples what it means to participate in the kingdom of heaven.

Matthew's Passion Story: False Accusations, Deception, and the Crucifixion

Matthew generally follows Mark's passion narrative in terms of chronology and content. We will discuss some places where Matthew diverges from Mark and some possible reasons for those differences. Like Mark, Matthew's passion narrative begins after his embedded apocalypse. For Matthew it is Jesus's fifth and final discourse and it addresses the destruction of the Temple, the coming of the Son of Man, and three parables illustrating the importance and consequences of being vigilant concerning the unexpected return (*parousia*) (24–25). The Passion story begins at chapter 26 with Matthew's formulaic words that mark the end of all his major discourses: "When Jesus had finished saying all these things." Two days before the Passover celebration Jesus predicts his crucifixion. A woman with an alabaster box of precious oil anoints Jesus's body, after which he is betrayed by one of his own disciples, Judas. Matthew inserts a detail in the Judas story not found in Mark: Judas betrays Jesus for a specific amount of money, thirty pieces of silver (26:15).

This additional information becomes the basis of an entire Matthean episode, fulfilling Jeremiah's prophetic utterance (27:3–10). But prior to that, Matthew demonstrates further Judas's deceitfulness and naiveté. At the Passover dinner where Jesus reveals to the twelve disciples that one of them will betray him, Matthew adds and highlights a brief dialogue between Jesus and Judas: "Surely not I, Rabbi?" feigned Judas. And [Jesus] replied, "You have said so" (26:25). So Judas's passion story, we might say, is interweaved in Matthew with Jesus's passion narrative. Perhaps Judas thought his betrayal would go unnoticed because Jesus would save himself! Significantly, the latter possibility is broached when Matthew's Jesus addresses his ally who with his sword sliced off the high priest's slave's ear. Jesus asks his defender whether he has considered that Jesus's Father would commission twelve legions of angels if he appealed to him for help (26:52–53). God's legions could trump Caesar's. But the scriptures must be fulfilled.

Readers naturally want to know what Judas did with his blood money. Repentant for his part in the sentencing of his innocent Rabbi to death, Judas attempts to return the money to the chief priests and elders; they reject it as a violation of Torah. Judas tosses the money on the Temple floor, rushes out, and commits suicide by hanging himself. The money is scooped up off the floor and used to purchase a cemetery ("potter's field") for burying indigent foreigners and named the "field of blood."

Consider and discuss: A connection exists between poverty and violence. What impact do you think poverty (Jesus's, Judas's, or others) had on the events leading up to and culminating in Jesus's death and crucifixion? What historical and contemporary events in America and beyond might we compare with Jesus's passion narrative?

At the Passover dinner after Jesus drinks from the cup symbolizing his blood, Jesus interprets it as being for the forgiveness of sins; this cup he will drink afresh with them in his "Father's kingdom" (26:28–29). Judas is not the only disciple who will need Jesus's forgiveness. In Mark, Jesus insists that Peter will deny him before the cock crows twice; Matthew simply says before the cock crows (26:34; Mark 14:30). Peter is of course at Gethsemane with Jesus, together with the two sons of Zebedee (James and John, in Mark) (26:37). Judas arrives with a large crowd to betray Jesus with a kiss signaling him as the one the authorities should arrest. The Matthean Jesus responds by, so to speak, "turning the other cheek": "Friend (*hetairos*), do what you are here to do" (26:50; cf. 5:39; Luke 6:29).

Jesus does not "unfriend" Judas! Perhaps the forgiveness symbolized by the cup is for both Judas and Peter, as well as many others.

In Matthew two different slave girls (*paidiskē*) approach Peter (as opposed to the same slave girl accusing him twice in Mark), one asking whether he accompanied Jesus the Galilean and the other confident that Peter did accompany "Jesus of Nazareth" (26:69–71; Mark 14:66–69). And as Jesus warned, Peter denied knowing and being a friend or follower of Jesus three times before the cock crowed once; Peter wept intensively.

Consider and discuss: How does society view Peter's and Judas's betrayal differently? How do you understand suicide in the context of Christian faith? In our contemporary historical past and in the not-so-distant past, most of us know of someone who in extremely difficult times and/or when suffering from a mental illness has resorted to suicide. Africans enslaved in America committed suicide as the only means to escape the cruel realities of enslavement; some even committed infanticide so that their female children would not be subjected to sexual abuse and rape. Does or should our Christian faith allow for forgiveness for such individuals? How do you think Matthew's Jesus viewed Judas's suicide?

When Jesus is taken before the Council and the High Priest Caiaphas, Matthew is specifically aware of two false witnesses that testify that Jesus said he would destroy the Temple (26:61; Mark 14:53–63). The High Priest in Matthew not only wants to know if Jesus is the Messiah, but also whether he is the "son of God," to which Jesus replies, "You say so" (26:64). Jesus's trial before the Roman Governor Pontius Pilate is interrupted in Matthew by a cameo appearance from Pilate's wife. She is not named, but she intervenes based on a troubling dream about Jesus and his innocence (27:19). Pilate appears to be impacted by his wife's words and he wishes to prevent a riot among the Jewish people (the crowds that the chief priests and elders are attempting to stir up). Only Matthew inserts the dramatic scene of Pilate washing his hands of Jesus's blood while declaring his own innocence. Conversely, the crowds arrogantly claim responsibility for Jesus's death sentence and crucifixion; they accept the blame for themselves and their posterity.

The journey to the cross for Jesus, who is charged with sedition against the Roman Empire, continues with floggings; soldiers strip him of his own clothes, stuffing his body into a costume worthy of "the king of the Jews." In Matthew the robe is scarlet or red (27:28); in Mark it is purple. In both Mark and Matthew, Jesus is struck with a reed. But in Matthew the soldiers also place a reed in his right hand and mockingly show obeisance, kneel before him. When the soldiers have completed their sport, they again strip Jesus, forcing his body back into the ordinary attire of a Galilean peasant. The fact that Simon of Cyrene, compelled to carry Jesus's cross, has two sons is not important for Matthew.

While hanging on the cross, Jesus is taunted by the crowds, together with his two companions from their crosses, in words reminiscent of Judas's frustrated and tragic gamble: "If you are the Son of God, come down" and "he trusts in God; let God deliver him now, if he wants to, for he said, 'I am God's son'" (27:40–43). Matthew records an earthquake, tombs opening, and resurrected bodies of previously sleeping saints appear walking around in the Holy City, Jerusalem. The same women in Mark are present in Matthew. The Joseph of Arimathaea who claims the body of Jesus to place in his own tomb is a rich man and one of Jesus's disciples in Matthew. Since the birth narratives, readers have not heard the name Joseph. On the second day, afraid that Jesus's disciples would steal his body in order to support the deception that Jesus had been resurrected, some Pharisees and chief priests ask Pilate for permission to secure the tomb. In this Matthean episode, Pilate acquiesces, seemingly to prevent an uproar among the people. Ultimately, it is the chief priests and elders who bribe the soldiers to keep quiet about the empty tomb, deceiving the people.

The Empty Tomb, Resurrection Appearances, and Witnesses

On the first day of the week, the two Marys go to Jesus's tomb where they experience an earthquake. The quake is explained as resulting from the angel of the Lord's descent from heaven and unsealing the tomb. The guards posted at the tomb fall unconscious at the sight of the brilliant angelophany. The two Marys remain conscious and able to receive the angel's words, although obviously needing the angel's assurance so as not to be overcome with fear. Despite their fright, mixed with joy, they quickly depart to testify to the disciples that Jesus has been raised. But the risen Jesus intercepts them, allowing the women to receive a commission directly from Jesus, while clutching his body and worshiping him.

Only Matthew includes a summary or final commissioning scene of the eleven disciples. The two Marys are eyewitnesses to the empty tomb and are the only disciples to receive the good news directly from the angel entrusted with opening the tomb. Yet their commission from the angel and later from Jesus is limited, at least in the narrative, to telling the disciples.

The women as the first eyewitnesses are excluded from the final scene. Yet, the fact that they were eyewitnesses cannot be taken away from them; it is likely that they told whoever would listen. When the eleven meet the risen Jesus in Galilee, as a result of the women's testimony, Jesus instructs them to go, make disciples, and baptize. Possibly the mention of the trinity represents an early baptismal formula. Jesus's final promise is to be with them always, as God with us.

Summary

1. Jesus is God's Messiah from the beginning to the end of the narrative; he is a Davidic Messiah who is related to King David through the marriage of his mother to Joseph.

2. Jesus is a mulatto and hybrid Messiah, born of a woman and of God's Spirit and with both Jewish and Canaanite ancestors.

3. The significance of Egypt is specific to Matthew. Egypt could be the provenance of the wise men as well as the place from which the author wrote his narrative.

4. Jesus as God's Messiah is a revolutionary prophet and a teacher who embodies and engages in embodied teaching.

5. Jesus fulfills, performs, or re-presents in his life, ministry, and death certain prophetic utterances, which are recontextualized in Matthew.

6. In Matthew the justice of God and love of neighbor and enemy are central to Jesus's existence and purpose.

7. Matthew contains a number of slave parables to describe participation in the kingdom of heaven; those parables reinscribe typical master-slave behaviors.

8. In Jesus's rite of passage in the wilderness, we see demonstrated Jesus's loyalty to God and his fellow human beings and a rejection of worldly power, authority, and position.

9. In his manifesto on the mount, Jesus argues for the priority of the kingdom of heaven because of its commitment to social justice for the individual and in the world.

10. Matthew's passion narrative weaves together two stories: the story of Jesus's suffering and crucifixion and the story of Judas's betrayal, anguish, and suicide.

Further Reading

Aslan, Reza. *Zealot: The Life and Times of Jesus of Nazareth*. New York: Random House, 2013.

Bantam, Brian. *Redeeming Mulatto: A Theology of Race and Christian Hybridity*. Waco, TX: Baylor University Press, 2010.

Beaton, Richard. "Messiah and Justice: A Key to Matthew's Use of Isaiah 42:1–4?" *Journal for the Study of the New Testament* 75 (1999) 5–23.

Brock, Ann Graham. *Mary Magdalene, the First Apostle: The Struggle for Authority*. Harvard Theological Studies 51. Cambridge: Harvard Divinity School, 2003.

Brown, Michael Joseph. "The Gospel of Matthew." In *True to Our Native Land: An African American Commentary of the New Testament*, edited by Brian Blount et al., 85–120. Minneapolis: Fortress, 2007.

Byron, Gay L. "Black Collectors and Keepers of Tradition: Resources for a Womanist Biblical Ethic of (Re)Interpretation." In *Womanist Interpretations of the Bible: Expanding the Discourse*. Edited by Gay L. Byron and Vanessa Lovelace, 187–208. Atlanta: Society of Biblical Literature, 2016.

Collins, John J. *The Scepter and the Star: The Messiahs of the Dead Sea Scrolls and Other Ancient Literature*. New York: Doubleday, 1995.

Crowder, Stephanie Buckhanon. *When Momma Speaks. The Bible and Motherhood from a Womanist Perspective*. Louisville, KY: Westminster John Knox, 2016.

Dube, Musa W. *Postcolonial Feminist Interpretation of the Bible*. St. Louis: Chalice, 2000.

France, R. T. *The Gospel of Mark*. Grand Rapids, MI: Eerdmans, 2014.

Glancy, Jennifer A. *Slavery in Early Christianity*. Minneapolis: Fortress, 2006.

Hendricks, Obery M., Jr. *The Politics of Jesus: Rediscovering the True Revolutionary Nature of Jesus's Teachings and How They Have Been Corrupted*. New York: Three Leaves, 2006.

Jarvis, Cynthia A., and E. Elizabeth Johnson, eds. *Feasting on the Gospels: A Feasting on the Word Commentary*. Vol. 1, *Matthew, Chapters 1–13*. Louisville: Westminster John Knox, 2013.

Kim, Yung Suk. *A Transformative Reading of the Bible: Explorations in Holistic Human Transformation*. Eugene, OR: Cascade, 2013.

Levine, Amy-Jill. "Gospel of Matthew." In *Women's Bible Commentary: Twentieth-Anniversary Edition*, edited by Carol A. Newsom, Sharon

H. Ringer, and Jacqueline E. Lapsley, 465–77. Louisville: Westminster John Knox, 2012.

Luz, Ulrich. *Matthew 1–7: A Commentary.* Hermeneia. Minneapolis: Fortress, 2007.

Osman, Ahmed. *Out of Egypt: The Roots of Christianity Revealed.* London: Arrow, 1999.

Reid, Barbara. *The Gospel According to Matthew.* Vol. 1. New Collegeville Bible Commentary. Collegeville, MN: Liturgical, 2005.

Smith, Mitzi J. "Slavery, Torture, Systemic Oppression, and Kingdom Rhetoric: A Womanist Reading of Matt 25:1–13." *Insights from African American Biblical Interpretation,* edited by Mark Alan Powell, 77–97. Eugene, OR: Cascade, 2017.

Smith, Mitzi J., and Lalitha Jayachitra, eds. *Teaching All Nations: Interrogating the Matthean Great Commission.* Minneapolis: Fortress, 2014.

Sri, Edward, and Curtis Mitch. *The Gospel of Matthew.* Catholic Commentary on Sacred Scripture. Grand Rapids, MI: Baker Academic, 2010.

CHAPTER 12

Gospel of Luke

De Lawd Sperit da libe een me an gee me powa. Cause e done pick me fa tell de good nyews ta de po people. E done sen me fa tell dem wa ain't free, say, "Oona gwine be free." E sen me fa tell de bline people, say, "Oona gwine see gin." E sen me fa free dem wa da suffa. An e sen me fa tell de people say, "De time done come wen de Lawd gwine sabe e people."

—DE GOOD NYEWS BOUT JEDUS CHRIST WA LUKE WRITE [IN GULLAH SEA ISLAND CREOLE][1]

Of their call, we have no record. We do not always know where they were born, nor do we know what happened to them after he was gone. Painful as it is to admit, we do know that an untold number of women followed Jesus—even at the risk of anonymity and of being misunderstood.

—RENITA WEEMS[2]

Mother Catherine's conception of the divinity of Christ is that Joseph was his foster father as all men are foster fathers, in that all children are of God and all fathers are merely the means.

—ZORA NEALE HURSTON[3]

---

1. American Bible Society, *Gospel According to Luke*, 21–22. My translation: "The Lord's Spirit is alive in me and gives me power. Because he has picked me to tell the good news to the poor people. He has sent me to tell them that we are not free, [but to] say, 'you are going to be free.' He sends me to tell the blind people that 'you are going to see again.' He sends me to free those who suffer. And he sends me to tell the people that 'the time has come when the Lord is going to save his people'" (Luke 4:18–19).
2. Weems, *Just a Sister Away*.
3. Hurston, *Sanctified Church*, 27.

Luke at a Glance

1. Written in the last decades of the first century CE by an unknown author that we shall call Luke.
2. In addition to his own material, Luke used Mark's narrative and the Q source.
3. Luke includes his own version of Jesus's genealogy and birth story.
4. Luke is the only canonical Gospel that narrates Jesus's early childhood.
5. Luke might have been a Gentile who worshipped the God of Israel, also known as a Godfearer.
6. Luke's Greek vocabulary is diverse and extensive.
7. Most scholars believe that Luke's Gospel is the first in a two-volume work; the *Acts of the Apostles* is the sequel.
8. Some themes in Luke include God's visitation, anticipation, or expectation of the Messiah, (im)proper attitude toward "sinners," and the power of the Holy Spirit.

Introduction

A COLONIZED PEOPLE LIVING and surviving under what seems like impossible circumstances characterized by oppression and violence look to their God to accomplish what they cannot do for themselves or to empower them to do the impossible. For Luke's God, nothing is impossible or anything is possible. Luke begins by telling the story of a husband and wife, Zechariah and Elizabeth, who have done all in their power to conceive and birth children, and yet they are unable to produce a child together. God steps in and does what is otherwise impossible. The impossible that God performs for them serves as a prelude to the rest of Luke's story. God is just warming up. Even more impossible, than an elderly husband and wife unable to produce a child is a woman conceiving without the help of a man (before Viagra and in vitro fertilization). Inconceivably, God's Spirit will cause Mary to conceive.

It matters who writes the story; each story may tell a different truth and serve a different function. Luke's Gospel begins with a prologue dedicated to "the most excellent Theophilus" (1:1–4). Theophilus (from *theos* meaning God and *philos* meaning friend or lover) may refer to some unknown noble person familiar to the author or it may be a collective noun for all persons who consider themselves a friend or lover of the God of Israel. Or perhaps it is both. According to Luke, many narratives had already been written based on eyewitness or first-hand traditions about Jesus's life and ministry. Luke adds to that body of literature. After a thorough investigation of those sources, Luke felt compelled to write an accurate recounting so that the most excellent Theophilus might know "the truth" about all that occurred.

The birth narratives in Luke and Matthew are their own contributions (1:5–2:39//Matt 1:18–2:23). Luke tells about the birth of both John the Baptist and Jesus. Both Matthew and Luke provide genealogies showing Jesus's ancestry with each starting and ending with different persons or with God. Only Luke provides a glimpse of Jesus's early childhood. But in many respects Luke (and Matthew), as a Synoptic Gospel, follows the structure and re-presents the content of Mark's Gospel. Jesus is baptized by John who enters the wilderness to be tested by the devil; preaches his first sermon in the synagogue; performs an exorcism of and silences unclean spirits in the synagogue; selects his first few disciples; and commences his ministry in and around Galilee, after John the Baptist's arrest (and death). Jesus's early opponents are Pharisees and their scribes. Jesus preaches the good news of the *basileia* of God and repentance, and he performs miracles up to and even after he heads toward Jerusalem (9:51) to be crucified.

Luke demonstrates that he has a consciousness of the political and religious context in which the visitation and hospitality of God occurs. Luke continues to demonstrate the visitation and hospitality of God and other themes found in the first few chapters: Jesus's association with "sinners and tax collectors," anticipation or expectation of the Messiah, and the power of God's Spirit on Jesus. God does the unconventional and the impossible or inconceivable. To the community, perhaps, already in the womb, Jesus is guilty by association with "sinners," his mother Mary being unmarried when she conceives; people can count!

Chapter Contents

1. Political-Religious and Religious-Political Context
2. Birth Narratives: With God Nothing is Impossible
3. Jesus's Early Childhood and the Beginning of His Ministry
4. Guilty by Association: Hospitality Among Sinners

5. Parables and Other Lessons About Rich People and Slaves
6. More of Luke's Special Material
7. Long Journey to Jerusalem and Luke's Passion Narrative

Political-Religious and Religious-Political Context

After Luke's prologue (1:1–4) and the beginning of the birth narratives through verse 3:1, Luke provides the historical context for his story by naming the political and religious leaders holding office at the time of John and Jesus's births and that will also be present when Jesus is arrested, sentenced, and crucified: Herod Antipas is Tetrarch over Galilee (his brother Philip is Tetrarch of Ituraea and Trachonitis; Lysanius is Tetrarch of Abilene) and Pontius Pilate is governor of Judea (he will later try and sentence Jesus to death, 23:1–25). In terms of the religious leaders connected with the Temple, Annas (6–15 CE) and Caiaphas (18–36 CE) are high priests. All of these individuals serve at the appointment and/or will of Rome. Caesar Augustus, known as son of god and savior of the world, is the Roman Emperor (27 BCE–14 CE) that orders a census of all those living under the Rome Empire for purpose of collecting taxes (2:1), a census not confirmed by external sources to be a historical fact. In the fifteenth year of Tiberius Caesar's rule or hegemony as Emperor (14–37 CE) Jesus will be crucified.

> **Consider and discuss:** Luke has done his research to know the historical and religious contexts of Jesus's life, ministry, and death and the historical and social context in which the gospel was preached. How important is it for people of faith to know what is going on in the world as they attempt to live, teach, and preach the gospel or good news of God? How does knowing or not knowing one's local community and the global contexts impact our preaching and ministry and the way we live as human beings and people of faith in the world?

Birth Narratives: With God Nothing is Impossible

Luke's birth narratives demonstrate that God can do what is impossible for human beings to accomplish. Luke retells the birth of John the Baptist, who will serve as the forerunner to God's Messiah, and the birth of the Messiah.

The parents of both John and Jesus conceive under impossible circumstances. The Jewish priest Zechariah and his wife Elizabeth are elderly and have not been able to conceive and produce children. Elizabeth's predicament mirrors that of Hannah the mother of Samuel in the Hebrew Bible (2 Sam 2:1-10). Both are identified as righteous and blameless according to Jewish law, and they pray to be able to conceive and birth children. Thus, Elizabeth's inability to bear children thus far is not because of any sin she has committed. Zechariah and Elizabeth continue to pray for children. The degree to which they might expect their prayers to be answered given their ages and their history is another thing. They at least go through the motions of offering up their prayers before God; sometimes this is the most that one can do. On the day that he is chosen by lot to serve in the sanctuary to offer the incense that accompanies the prayers of the people, the angel Gabriel (1:19) appears (an angelophany) to a startled and fearful Zechariah as he stands before the altar of incense. While the incense serves as a visual image of the people's prayers ascending to God, Gabriel is the evidence that God has heard Zechariah and Elizabeth's prayers. In spite of the impossibility of conception, Elizabeth will conceive and birth a son whom Zechariah is instructed to name: John. Gabriel further informs Zechariah that John will be no ordinary child: many will celebrate at his birth; he will be great in Yahweh's eyes; and he will turn Israel's attention toward God (1:14-17). In Elizabeth's womb, John will be filled with the Spirit; God will anoint him (1:15). Similarly, Jesus, the baby in Mary's womb, will attest to the Spirit in Elizabeth's fetus when she visits Mary (1:41); both women carry the evidence of God's visitation in their bodies. As an adult John will baptize Jesus, but God will anoint him as well. When Jesus eventually enters the synagogue for the first time as a man he announces that God's Spirit is upon him (4:16-18).

In terms of post-natal care, Gabriel advises Zechariah that his child John should avoid fermented wine and other strong drink. Understandably, Zechariah questions Gabriel wanting to know how he will know that this is true, given their ages. Gabriel refuses to provide Zechariah with the proof he needs. At this point the angel reveals that his name is Gabriel, the position he occupies in God's presence, and that God commissioned him to deliver this good news. Perhaps, as created beings, angels become annoyed with human beings too. Mary will ask for proof as well, but she is not scolded. Zechariah is condemned for asking a perfectly reasonable question; his request is considered an act of disbelief. Consequently, Gabriel renders him mute until the child is born and named (1:20). When Zechariah exits the temple, unable to talk and explain why he was in the sanctuary so long, the people conclude he has seen a vision. Perhaps they reached this conclusion by reading Zechariah's hand gestures, facial expressions, and lips. Luke says nothing about Elizabeth's response when Zechariah returns home unable to speak. He simply fast-forwards to the fifth month of Elizabeth's pregnancy. On the one hand, Elizabeth appears ashamed of her pregnancy and her growing belly; she stays in seclusion for five months. Perhaps, people continued to gossip in light of Zechariah's age, supposing that she had been with a younger man. Yet her words demonstrate that she herself knows the truth that her pregnancy is because Yahweh has noticed her situation and removed her disgrace (1:25). Perhaps it is more bearable to let people think she is dishonored than to actually be dishonored.

When Elizabeth is six months pregnant, the angel Gabriel visits Mary in Nazareth of Galilee. She is a virgin engaged to Joseph. Gabriel states that Mary is a woman who has received the grace of God because Yahweh is *with her* and she has nothing to fear (1:28–29). Mary receives news of her pregnancy directly, not by way of Joseph; of course, Joseph has nothing to do with the process. Like Elizabeth, Mary will likely be the subject of gossip; people can count. She too will conceive a son, and she will name him Jesus (1:31). Like John, Jesus will be great, but he is the son of the Most High and will assume the throne of his ancestor David. Ironically, Joseph is related to David in the genealogy, not Mary; but Joseph is not the biological father. It is not biology that makes Jesus royalty. Of course, no one has legitimately sat on the throne of David and ruled over Israel as a nation since King Zedekiah; the Babylonian Empire conquered Judah in 586 BCE and appointed a government over Judah (2 Kgs 24–25). For a brief period in the first century BCE the Hasmonian kings ruled in Jerusalem (1–2 Macc). And as was promised to David, Jesus's reign will be eternal (2 Sam 7:16; 1 Chr 17:14). This Lucan promise is made while the Jewish people are a colonized people living under the oppressive rule of the Roman Empire.

Mary's response to the news is not so different from Zechariah's, but she is not met with the same condemnation. Instead, Gabriel is more sympathetic and patient. Perhaps this is because she is a young inexperienced virgin. Gabriel explains to Mary that the Holy Spirit will visit her, resulting in conception. Consequently, Mary will give birth to the son of God. Mary is informed that Elizabeth is already pregnant. Perhaps the latter news, given Zechariah's age and Elizabeth's predicament, is a source of encouragement for Mary. If they can be expecting a child, perhaps what is happening to her is not so inconceivable. These two birth announcements are summed up at 1:37: "Nothing is impossible with God." Perhaps these words are the lens through which we are to view Luke's entire narrative. God does what God chooses, visits with whom God chooses, and so will Jesus as God's son.

With the knowledge of Elizabeth's miraculous pregnancy, Mary quickly visits her. As soon as the baby in Elizabeth's womb hears Mary's voice, the baby John jumps with joy in his mother's womb. Filled with the Holy Spirit, Elizabeth blesses Mary and her child. Elizabeth is informed of Mary's pregnancy through the child who has been anointed in her womb as the one to proclaim the appearance of the baby Jesus. Mary breaks out in a song of praise to Yahweh for looking upon her with mercy and grace. Mary's song is traditionally named the *Magnificat*, a Latin translation of the third word in her song: "My soul magnifies the Lord" (1:46–56). In some manuscript traditions, the song is attributed to Elizabeth and not Mary. A prominent theme in the song is the reversal of circumstances or social status: God has scattered the proud and humbled or dethroned the powerful. The Mighty One lifted up the lowly and filled the hungry with good things, but the rich are dispersed empty-handed.

Consider and discuss: Many readers regard the reversal signified in Mary's song as restructuring and redistribution of power, position, and wealth, as a form of social justice. Perhaps knowing that God sees and gives one the ability to reimagine one's life in more powerful ways that are not characterized by oppression and subordination is a blessing that can lead to self and community empowerment. Mary imagines and sings about a reordering of society in which she is no longer at the bottom. Unless one can imagine a different reality, one is not likely to accept it as a possibility. For whom in the first century CE context, other than Mary and Elizabeth, might Mary's song of reversal be regarded as good news? For whom in our contemporary context might it be understood as good news or bad news? How might such a reversal not address the issue of poverty, inequity, subordination/hierarchy, oppression, and injustice, but perpetuate it?

After John's birth, Zechariah, filled with the Holy Spirit, prophesies about Jesus as the coming savior from David's house, the prophet of the Most High who brings knowledge of salvation to his people, and shines a light on/for those in darkness (1:67–80). (In Luke's sequel, the Acts of the Apostles, the Pythian slave girl identifies the Apostle Paul and Silas as slaves of the Most High God; this truth seriously annoys Paul, 16:16–18). Zechariah's speech is traditionally called the *Benedictus* (*Latin* for blessed), which is the first word of his prophesy. Zechariah's prophesy parallels, Mary's song.

Jesus is born in a manger or feeding trough in Joseph's ancestral homeland of his distant relative King David of Bethlehem (2:1–20). According to Luke, when Augustus Caesar was Emperor and Quirinius was governor of Syria, Caesar issued a decree requiring everyone to register with the census for the purpose of taxation. Thus, Joseph left Nazareth in Galilee, apparently when Mary was close to her due date, and traveled to Bethlehem, likely by donkey. They are still engaged when the baby is born. Meanwhile, an angel appears to shepherds tending their flocks in the fields and announces the good news of the birth of God's Messiah and Savior in the city of David. The angelophany causes fear but the announcement of good news evokes a glorious, heavenly choral response. As instructed, the shepherds visit the baby and his parents and share the good news they received from the angel.

Luke inserted a third prophecy in the birth narratives, which is attributed to Simeon, a righteous and devote man who anticipates the coming of the Messiah; the Holy Spirit promised that he would not die before seeing the Messiah (2:25–38). When Jesus's parents bring Jesus as their firstborn son to the Temple to perform the rites of purification (Lev 12), Simeon takes the baby into his arms and announces the fulfillment of the Spirit's promise. Jesus is the agent of God's salvation and "a light of revelation to the Gentiles for the glory" of Israel (2:29–32). This speech is traditionally called the *Nunc Dimittis*, which is Latin for the first few words Simeon speaks, *now you are dismissing* (your servant in peace) (2:29). Simeon further blesses Jesus as the one "destined for the falling and rising of many in Israel, and to be a sign that will be opposed so that the inner thoughts of many will be revealed—and a sword will pierce your own soul too" (2:34–35). Perhaps this prophecy refers partially to the opposition that Jesus will experience as he embodies, preaches, and teaches a gospel inclusive of "sinners and tax collectors." Simeon parallels the prophetess (*prophētis*) Anna. This is the only use of the Greek feminine for *prophet* in the Gospels (2:36; at Rev 2:20 Jezebel is a *prophētis*). Anna is an eight-four-year-old widow who never leaves the Temple (cf. *Protoevangelium of James*). Although Anna is a prophetess, no direct speech is attributed to her.

According to Jewish law and tradition, both John and Jesus are circumcised on the eighth day after their birth and they are both named as the angel Gabriel instructed (1:59; 2:21). John the Baptist develops and is strengthened in Spirit and enters the wilderness in preparation for his public ministry to Israel (1:80). Jesus likewise matures, but increases in wisdom and in favor among humans and God (1:40, 52). Jesus increases in and is filled with wisdom (from the Greek feminine noun, *Sophia*). "Wisdom (*Sophia*) is vindicated by all her children" (7:35).

Jesus's Early Childhood and the Beginning of His Ministry

Every year for twelve years, Jesus's parents take him to Jerusalem to celebrate the Passover, the feast in remembrance of the liberation of the Hebrews from Egyptian slavery (2:41–52). Having traveled to Jerusalem in the company of a group of friends and relatives, Jesus's parents do not realize he is not with the group until they have traveled a full-day's journey from Jerusalem. Jesus is in the Temple for three days before his parents locate him back in Jerusalem. They find Jesus in intense dialogue with the teachers in the Temple; the latter are impressed with Jesus's answers and questions. Jesus's parents are confounded when he responds to their words of concern by asking if they didn't know that he must be about his father's business.

Ministry of John the Baptist

As in Mark, John preaches a baptism of repentance (*metanoia*) and forgiveness of sins. The salvation of God occurs in the lives of real people within the historical, political, and cultural contexts of their lived experience. People are to expect or anticipate (Greek word *prosdexomai* or *prosdokeō* (2:21, 25, 38; 3:15; cf. 4:20) God's visitation through the Messiah, Angels, and God's Spirit. John shames the crowds who come to him for baptism, calling them vipers. When they ask what it is they should do, John replies that they should stop taking advantage of people under their authority. The tax collectors should stop cheating people and the soldiers should stop extorting money from them (3:10–14). The people are filled with anticipation or expectation (*prosdokeō*) of the Messiah, and wonder if John the Baptist is the one (3:15–16). Like Jesus, John the Baptist can read their hearts or thoughts, but he is not the Messiah. The Messiah will baptize them with the Holy Spirit and with fire.

Following a brief note about the arrest of John the Baptist, Jesus is baptized (3:18–20). John is arrested because of his rebuke of Herod for marrying his brother's wife Herodias and for his cruelty. When John baptizes Jesus, the Spirit lights on him in bodily form and God's voice approves of him as God's "beloved son" (3:22).

Consider and Discuss: Oppressed peoples tend to expect, anticipate, or hope for a Messiah figure to help deliver them from their oppression. How is this problematic and how does this expectation perhaps demonstrate a misunderstanding of what makes a successful revolutionary movement?

First Things First: Genealogy and Testing

Luke says that Jesus was thirty years old when he began his ministry (3:23). He is the son of Joseph, presumably, and the son of God. Jesus's genealogy is similar to those we find in the HB/OT. Jesus is related to prophets, kings, priests, and the first male human being Adam through his father Joseph, despite the fact that Joseph is not his biological father. He is related to Amos, Nahum, Obed, David, Jacob, Isaac, Abraham, Methuselah, Noah, Enoch, Adam, others, and God; no women are named in Luke's genealogy of Jesus, not even Mary. Some people named are unknown or not identifiable.

Luke's Jesus is full of the Holy Spirit when the Spirit leads him into the wilderness to be tempted by the devil for forty days (4:1–12//Matt 4:1–11//Mark 1:12–13). At the end of the testing, no angels visit Jesus as in Mark and Matthew. Jesus is filled with the power of the Spirit after his forty-day testing and when he starts his ministry in Galilee in the region of his hometown of Nazareth.

Jesus's Sermon in the Synagogue

Jesus's sermon in the synagogue is the first lengthy narrative of his ministry (4:16–30). We do not know the full content of the sermon or Midrash that Jesus presents in the synagogue. He seems to draw from both Isa 61:1–2 and 58:6 of the Greek translation of the Scriptures (the Septuagint). He is anointed with Yahweh's Spirit for the purpose of preaching good news to the poor (*ptochos*), release to the captives or the conquered, restoration of sight to the blind, relief to the weakened, broken, or oppressed, and to proclaim the acceptable year of Yahweh. He omits the phrase to bind up the broken hearted and to announce a day of vengeance. Finally, Jesus announces to his hometown synagogue audience that the Scriptures he read are fulfilled before their eyes (4:21); he is the anointed one. The audience has a difficult time reconciling Jesus's claim with the man who stands before them whom they know as Joseph's son. Apparently, sensing their discomfort, Jesus addresses their doubts—that doctors (or prophets) are unable to heal themselves and their need to see him do what he has done in Capernaum in his home town. Amazing words and eloquent preaching is insufficient for the hometown folks to believe he is the one about whom the Scriptures testify. Finally, Jesus reminds them of God's prophets whom God sent to non-Israelites to experience the healing power of God: Elijah to the widow of Zarephath in Sidon (1 Kgs 17:1–16), and Elisha to Naaman the leper (2 Kgs 5:1–14). The more Jesus talks, the more enraged the crowd becomes (4:28). The response to Jesus's sermon is an inhospitable one, to say the least. The people run Jesus out of town and attempt to throw him off a cliff (4:29). Jesus, however, manages to slip through their fingers. One might view this as Jesus's first miracle.

Jesus preaches the good news of the *basileia* of God. Like Mark, Jesus calls his first few disciples after performing his first exorcism. However, Simon sees himself as unworthy of following Jesus because he is a sinful man (5:8). Luke's Jesus also silences the unclean spirits and demons who know his identity, but he does not tell those he heals, like the man with the withered hand, to keep silent (6:6–11). It is through the power of Yahweh that Jesus heals (5:17). As in Mark, Pharisees and scribes emerge early as Jesus's opponents. When the Pharisees have a problem with Jesus's disciples plucking and eating grain on the Sabbath, Jesus announces that the son of man (the human being) is master (*kurios*) of the Sabbath (6:5). Like John the Baptist, Jesus can read people's thoughts (6:8).

Jesus chooses the rest of his twelve disciples and reveals that Judas will betray him. After completing his inner circle, Jesus begins teaching large crowds of disciples while standing on level ground (6:17—7:1). People from all around Galilee, from Judea, Jerusalem, Tyre, and Sidon come to hear Jesus teach and to experience healing. Jesus's power is contagious; the people experience healing just from touching him (6:19). Jesus's teaching includes beatitudes or blessings; he pronounces a blessing upon the poor (not the poor in spirit) that they will be fed; people who are hungry now will be satisfied now; those who weep in the present will laugh. He also pronounces judgment through woe oracles upon the rich, those who laugh now, and the recipients of much flattery, presumably because of their high social status. Jesus teaches the crowds to love their enemies and not to judge others. The bottom line is to treat others in the same way one would like to be treated (6:27–31). Further, it is no big deal to love those who love you, even sinners do this. Disciples do not surpass their teacher, but if they are fully qualified they will be like their teacher. Here, and elsewhere so far, Jesus teaches using short parables. Can the blind lead the blind? Good trees cannot yield bad fruit and vice versa (6:39–45//Matt 7:16–20; cf. 5:34–36).

Consider and discuss: The parable of the good tree and bad tree sets up a good/bad polarity. In what instances does this polarity not ring true? What might be the impact of using such a polarity to judge as a measure of our own lives and other people's lives and even groups of peoples?

> **Consider and discuss:** What are the implications of Jesus's teaching about loving one's enemies? Do you think Jesus's discourse on loving one's enemies applies to the Rome Empire, to oppressive systems that rob peoples of freedoms and material necessities? Why or why not? Does contemporary society expect the oppressed, colonized, racial/ethnic minoritized peoples, and women to bear the burden of forgiveness and love more so than others? Why or why not?

For the first time in Luke, we find out the names of women who followed Jesus (8:1–3). Luke's Jesus travels with the twelve and some women whom Jesus delivered from demon possession and illnesses. Mary Magdalene is described as having had seven demons; Joanna is a wife of Herod's Steward (perhaps she is of an elite class), and the last one named is Susanna; many more women disciples remain unnamed. These women were perhaps patrons of Jesus and his Twelve, supplying their daily needs. Yet, the women were not simply patrons, they were also disciples with access to Jesus. Mary Magdalene, Joanna, and an additional Mary, the mother of James, are the first to proclaim the news of the empty tomb, even if they are not believed (24:10–11). It is difficult to tell when the women began following Jesus. It is possible that the women are among the first crowds that flock to Jesus to be freed of unclean spirits and demons and to be healed, even before Jesus invites Simon Peter, James, and John (sons of Zebedee) to follow him (4:40–41). As early followers of Jesus, this would make the women more or less eligible to replace Judas Iscariot in the *Acts of the Apostles*, but Peter strikes first to prevent this possibility by specifying that Judas's replacement must be a male (1:21–26).

Guilty by Association: Hospitality Among Sinners

Recall that some of John the Baptist's disciples were tax collectors and soldiers. So, it is no surprise that Jesus invites Levi the tax collector to follow him (5:30–32//Mark 2:13–22//Matt 9:9). In Jesus's public discourse about John the Baptist, Jesus argues that God's messengers are condemned regardless of whether they fast, as John did, or eat and drink, as Jesus does. The former is accused of being demon-possessed, and Jesus is called a friend of "tax collectors and sinners" (6:33–34). Associating with tax collectors and sinners was a sure way to garner the disrespect and ridicule of some Pharisees and scribes. Perhaps the accusation early in Luke's narrative functions to stereotype Jesus as an enemy and/or misfit among his own people. The collocation "tax collectors and sinners" functions as a politics of disgust. A politics of disgust encourages antipathy or hatred toward a people or persons based on false, unfair, and constructed stereotypes. A politics of disgust preserves the power and dominance of the stereotype, silencing the voices of those objectified by the stereotype and destroying any possibility of political solidarity between the majority and the oppressed or the one it seeks to oppress. Perhaps Luke's Jesus attempts to deconstruct and to expose this political tactic when he exhorts the crowds to love those they perceive as enemies.

Consider and discuss: In what ways are Christians encouraged to see non-Christians as sinners and thus as their enemies? What people in our society are stigmatized in such a way that associating with them can result in one's own reputation being called into question?

Luke extends and puts a different spin on Mark's story of the woman who anoints Jesus with expensive oils (7:36–50//Mark 14:3–9//Matt 26:6–13; John 12:1–8). Mark positions the story at the beginning of his passion narrative before Jesus's arrest, trial, and crucifixion, but Luke places it early in Jesus's ministry. In Mark, the scene occurs in the home of Simon, a man with a leprous condition; but in Luke an anonymous woman identified as a sinner approaches Jesus at the house of a Pharisee, named Simon, a disciple of Jesus. In Mark's narrative, the woman is not a sinner, but she is judged as inconsiderate of the poor and extravagant to a fault. Luke's Simon is anonymous until he speaks (7:39–40). The woman never speaks, but is spoken about, by both Simon and Jesus. The nameless woman labeled a sinner washes the Lucan Jesus's feet with her tears and dries them with her loose hair. Ancient eastern Mediterranean social codes may apply here. A woman with loose hanging hair could represent a woman not bound to one man, unmarried and therefore a danger to men and society; a woman's loose hair could be associated with conjury and ecstatic states of frenzy. However, nothing in the narrative unequivocally signifies that she is a prostitute or a loose woman. She is called a "woman of the city, who *was* a sinner." This unnamed city woman *was previously* identified as a sinner, and perhaps others convinced her to see herself in the same light. Some people do not want other people to forget their past, and a person's past is not always what people perceive or construct it to be. Nothing states that the woman arrived with loose hair; she could have loosened her hair to dry Jesus's feet once her tears fell on them. Kissing Jesus's clean feet, the unnamed woman anoints them with the oils. Allowing his audience to read the Pharisee's thoughts, Luke writes that the man criticized Jesus, questioning his role as a prophet because he does not seem to know that the woman touching him is a sinner. Discerning Simon's thoughts, Jesus responds with a parable of the creditor who forgave two debtors who owed him different amounts of money, one more than the other. Jesus asks which debtor will love the creditor more. Of course, Simon answered, the one who owed and is forgiven the most. Jesus likens the woman to the debtor who owed the most. She did for Jesus what Simon failed to do when Jesus entered his home. Her hospitality is impeccable; his missed the mark. The reason she shows Jesus such great love through her hospitality (in someone else's home!) is that her sins were (past tense) many and have been forgiven. "The one to whom little is forgiven [or perceives he has little to be forgiven] loves little" (7:47b). Although the woman demonstrated love because she had been forgiven, in Simon's house, in the presence of the man who stigmatized her because of her past (whatever that was), ironically Jesus announces that her sins are forgiven. This becomes the second time that Jesus is identified as a forgiver of sins. Jesus acknowledges the woman's faith and releases her in peace.

Consider and discuss: Individuals and peoples may have a sense of their own dignity and self-worth and yet be stigmatized in society or by dominant groups who have the power to exclude them from certain circles and from access to power, knowledge, networks, and resources. How, where, and to whom do you see this happening in our religious institutions, in our communities, and globally? How and when have we been complicit? What can we do to empower ourselves and to empower others who are stigmatized?

On his way to Jerusalem (9:51), Luke's Jesus is asked about the relationship between fatal tragedies and sin (13:1–5). Evidently, the Roman governor Pilate earned a reputation for being cruel. He apparently killed some Galileans as they offered meat sacrifices. Some people from among the crowds ask whether those killed suffered such a fate because they were worse sinners than other Galileans. Or what about the eighteen Jerusalemites who died when the tower of Siloam fell on them? Jesus's answer seems to be an unequivocal *no*, until he adds that if they fail to repent, they too will perish like those in Galilee and Jerusalem. John the Baptist's message connected repentance and sin, but perhaps Jesus does not (cf. 3:3). Are committing sin and being identified in society as a sinner the same in Luke? Perhaps not.

Eventually the "tax collectors and sinners" gravitate toward Jesus's teaching; they show up in large numbers to hear Jesus, to the dislike of some Pharisees and scribes (15:1–2). They must be experiencing Jesus's message as good news. At 15:2, the two groups are conflated as "sinners" that Jesus welcomes (*prosdexomai*) and eats with. People considered "sinners" by others who do not see themselves as "sinners" are the ones that Jesus treats with hospitality and who do the same for Jesus. The Lucan parable of the woman who owns ten coins, but loses one, makes this point (15:9–10). She lit a lamp, searched for the one coin, and when she found it, she celebrated with her friends and neighbors. Luke's Jesus announces that God's angels rejoice when one sinner repents. People who see themselves as sinners or whom others stigmatize as sinners find relief from that burden through repentance (cf. 18:13). The thing to do if one believes a person to be a sinner is to relieve them of that burden rather than to increase it. Thus, to see sin in others (based on rumor and/or easily identifiable behaviors unacceptable to one's self) but to neglect to see the sin in one's own life is perhaps the sin that cannot find repentance in Luke. Luke's Jesus shared an entire parable about sinners and tax collectors for the benefit of those who consider themselves more worthy or righteous than others by comparing themselves to others (18:9–14); tax collectors see themselves as sinners. Fasting and tithing religiously do not make one better than another person who does not do such things. Fasting and tithing are often treated as a race to the top or to heaven. Here, Jesus uses status reversal language, as in Mary's song; those who exalt themselves will be humbled, and vice versa.

Tax Collectors were often what we would call independent contractors that the Empire contracted to collect taxes. Perhaps they were accompanied at times by soldiers who sometimes extorted people along with some tax collectors. Those contracted to collect the public revenues procured among the most lucrative government contracts. Private individuals and corporations could bid for the contracts. Public revenues included harbor taxes, customer tariffs, indemnity, and poll taxes. The indemnity tax was a large sum conquered nations were required to pay Rome as compensation for the expense Rome incurred in fighting a war. Poll taxes were paid annually to Rome to reimburse it for maintenance of a governor or military force in the province. Poll taxes were determined by census returns; heads of households were required to return to their places of origin to affirm their census data. Luke shows that perhaps the practice of cheating and extorting tax payers was so prevalent that anyone performing the task was seen as a sinner.

Another story peculiar to Luke's Gospel, is the narrative of the encounter between a chief tax collector named Zacchaeus and Jesus (19:1–10). A short man, Zacchaeus climbs a tree to get a glimpse of Jesus among the crowds. Jesus notices Zacchaeus and summons him out of the tree because he must stay at his house. The onlookers grumble because they view Zacchaeus as a sinner and have a problem with Jesus eating with sinners. Zacchaeus confesses that he has cheated people and proposes to make amends by giving half of his earnings to the poor to repay 400 percent interest to anyone he has defrauded. Salvation has arrived at Zacchaeus's house; his occupation does not negate his status as a son of Abraham. Jesus came to save the lost. In the end, Jesus is not delivered into the hands of tax collectors, but into the hands of "sinners" who hire the tax collectors (24:7).

Jesus Commissions the Twelve and Seventy to Receive Hospitality

When Jesus sends out his apostles with power and authority, he instructs them to take nothing for their journey—no staff, no luggage, no food, no money, but to depend on the hospitality of others (Luke 9:1–6). Part of this instruction is reversed later when Jesus faces death and prepares them for his departure (22:24–38). They are to take on the status of a person with no home or homelessness and to rely upon the hospitality of others. They are sent to cities and villages to preach and heal. Herod hears about their work and is anxious to know Jesus's identity. The sending of the seventy (or seventy-two) is peculiar to Luke (10:1–20; cf. Matt 9:37–38; 10:7–16). Jesus appoints seventy in addition to the twelve and sends them by pairs to every town and place where he intended to go; he realizes his own limitations. The Messiah cannot do it all. Strangely, they are to greet no one on the road. When they enter a house, they should greet those residing in the home with "peace on this house." They are to eat what is given them. They are to preach that the *basileia* of God has come near; it is near in Jesus, but also near in others who embody the power and authority of God as revealed in Jesus. If they are not welcomed in the houses, then they should proclaim the Gospel in the streets (where they shall also live whenever no household receives them). Regardless of whether they are rejected or received with hospitality, the *basileia* of God has come near. God's *basileia* is not banished by human rejection. The seventy return with a praise report: Demons submitted to them! But Jesus cautions that their greatest joy should come from knowing that their names are written in heaven.

Consider and discuss: There is often a tension between providing for the needs of women and men called to ministry and men and women becoming wealthy off the backs of those to whom they minister and garnering a standard of living that exceeds many in their congregations. How do we strike a balance so that we do not necessarily demand that persons called to ministry become impoverished and the idea that ministers should be wealthy as a symbol of God's favor? What is our responsibility as people of faith in eliminating poverty for all and not just the minister whom we often set on a pedestal?

Parables and Other Lessons About Rich People and Slaves

The Lukan Jesus teaches using parables too, and some of them are only found in Luke. For example, the parables of the wayward or prodigal son (15:11–32), the Good Samaritan (10:29–37), the rich fool (12:13–21), the wedding banquet (14:7–14), the rich man and Lazarus (16:19–31), and the rich slave owner's unjust manager/overseer (16:1–13) are a few only found in Luke. Many of Jesus's parables use slavery or the enslaved and rich people to teach moral and ethical lessons about acceptable and unacceptable behavior in certain situations (e.g. 17:7–10). Matthew and Luke's Gospels contain many slave parables that are attributed to Jesus. Did the historical Jesus teach using these parables or did the authors of the Gospels put them in Jesus's mouth? Well-behaved slaves should be imitated by others, and vice versa (19:11–27). Stereotypical master and slave relationships and behavior are reinforced: the cruelty of slave masters toward disobedient and disloyal slaves and overseers; the expectation of productivity from slaves regardless of the circumstances and whether the master is absent or present; the objectification of the slave body; the slave body as always accessible to the slave master; the lazy slave as evil; the good slave as submissive. Rich people are also stereotyped. They are greedy, lack compassion, and end up in Hades.

More of Luke's Special Material

A Roman centurion in Capernaum requests that Jesus heal his unnamed slave who is near death (7:1–10; cf. Naaman the Leper, 2 Kgs 5:1–14). This must have been a very useful, obedient, and loyal slave, for those were the only slaves valued and worth saving. The centurion, as slaveowner, sent the Jewish elders to request Jesus come and heal the slave. The Jewish elders testify to the centurion's worthiness as the reason that Jesus should heal the slave. The centurion loves the Jewish nation; he has built them a synagogue (he is a patron). Ironically, the centurion views himself as unworthy to be in Jesus's presence and asks him just to conjure a healing word for his slave from a distance; his unworthiness is based on the position of authority he holds over soldiers and slaves. When the messengers return to the house, they find the slave's health restored.

The story of the resurrection of the widow of Nain's son also demonstrates the visitation and hospitality of God through Jesus (7:11–17). Some regard this story as parallel with the story of Elijah's encounter with the widow of Sidon (1 Kgs 17:1–16). As usual, when Jesus enters the city a large crowd gathers. When Jesus nears the city gate, the widow's dead son is being carried out for burial. Jesus tells the woman not to cry. This is not because she should not mourn and weep for her dead son; it is because Jesus is about to resurrect the boy. Out of compassion for the mother, Jesus resurrects the young man by touching the coffin, causing the pallbearers to freeze. The young man gets up and eats; it is as if he were asleep for a few days and was famished. The response is "a great prophet has risen among us" and "God has concerned himself with or visited (*epeskepsatō*) his people" (7:16).

Jesus's ministry in the region of Galilee ends with the challenge for his disciples to take up their cross (9:18–50). However, Luke's Jesus inserts the word "daily"; they should take up their crosses daily. They are to live and practice their faith and vocations daily in such a revolutionary way that each day their actions and voices threaten a status quo that naturalizes exclusion of people based on their occupation, gender, social class, ethnicity/race, religious affiliation, sexuality, or dis-ability. Jesus revisits the cost or consequences of being a disciple or apostle (14:25–35). One cannot be a disciple without a willingness to bear the cross or the consequences of following Jesus. In Luke, this also means a willingness to redistribute one's wealth to alleviate poverty.

GOSPEL OF LUKE 157

Long Journey to Jerusalem and Luke's Passion Narrative

Half way through the narrative, Luke's Jesus "set his face to go to Jerusalem" (9:51; 13:22; 17:11). As Jesus makes his way to Jerusalem, he commissions seventy disciples, visits with Mary and Martha, teaches his disciples to pray, casts out demons, teaches and heals in the synagogues, straightens out the body of the nameless woman who had been bent over for eighteen years (13:10-17), and many other things. Jesus is informed that Herod the Fox wants to kill him, but Jesus predicts his own death. Herod has no power over his life. In the meantime he will continue on his way: "it is impossible for a prophet to be killed outside of Jerusalem. Jerusalem, Jerusalem the city that kills the prophets and stones those who are sent to it," Jesus laments over Jerusalem (13:31-35). By way of the Mount of Olives, Jesus makes a triumphal entry through Bethany; he is hailed as a king and God is praised for all the powerful acts demonstrated before the people (19:20-40). Again, Jesus laments over Jerusalem (19:41). After entering Jerusalem, Jesus teaches in the Temple while the religious leaders (chief priests and scribes) conspire to kill him (19:47-48; 21:37-38)

Luke's passion narrative differs quite a bit from Mark's. As noted above, the woman with the expensive oils anoints Jesus early in Luke's story. Luke's Jesus instructs the Twelve to memorialize the supper before he signifies that Judas will betray him (22:14-20). The last meal that Jesus shares with the Twelve includes a farewell discourse about what constitutes greatness, and the revelation that Peter will deny Jesus three times before the cock crows (22:24-34). Before Jesus is betrayed by Judas and arrested, he agonizes in the Mount of Olives; sweat pours from his body like drops of blood. Jesus would like for the cup of his suffering to be removed; nevertheless, he will do the Father's will (22:39-46). Some scholars have argued that perhaps Luke based his passion narrative on a separate source similar to or the same as the author of the Gospel of John used. Luke likely used his own special material and Mark's passion narrative.

Following their last meal, Jesus is arrested (22:47—23:5). While Jesus is detained and appears before the Sanhedrin, Peter denies him three times, as Jesus predicted, even when the slave girl (*paidiskē*) recognizes him. Finally, Jesus is tried by the Roman governor Pontius Pilate and sentenced to death by crucifixion, a disgraceful and generally slow death reserved for thieves, slaves, and others of the lower social classes. Luke's special material can be found again when Jesus, because he is a Galilean, is sent by Pilate to Herod Antipas, tetrarch of Galilee. Jesus is condemned by Pilate and Barabbas is released. On the way to the cross, Simon of Cyrene is seized and compelled to carry Jesus's cross (23:6–43). Mourning women of Jerusalem follow Jesus to the place of the skull, and he turns to bless all women unable to give birth to children. Only Luke allows his readers to eavesdrop on the conversation between Jesus and the thieves with whom he shares his last hour on the lynching tree. Only Luke narrates Peter's visit to the empty tomb, Jesus's encounter with two disciples on the road to Emmaus, the resurrected Jesus's appearance to the Eleven, and Jesus's ascension (24:12–53). Some of the same religious and political leaders that Luke mentions in his birth narratives emerge in the passion narrative; the religious is political and the political are religious. This collusion frames Luke's narrative.

Summary

1. God visits God's people through angels, the Spirit, and Jesus.
2. God performs the impossible.
3. Jesus associates and embraces "sinners and tax collectors" to the dismay of many.
4. Jesus is full of wisdom and is wisdom.
5. Jesus empowers and commissions his disciples, women and men, with the same authority and power he himself exercises.
6. Jesus is full of God's Spirit and is anointed by God.
7. Both John the Baptist and Jesus can read the thoughts of other human beings.
8. Women were among the earliest followers of Jesus, perhaps they were the first.

Further Reading

Adewale, Olubiyi Adeniyi. "An Afro-Sociological Application of the Parable of the Rich Man and Lazarus." *Black Theology* 4 (2006) 27–43.

Borg, Marcus. *Jesus: The Life, Teachings, and Relevance of a Religious Revolutionary.* New York: HarperOne, 2015.

Bovon, François. *Luke 1: A Commentary on the Gospel of Luke 1:1—9:50.* Hermeneia. Minneapolis: Fortress, 2002.

———. *The Last Days of Jesus.* Louisville: Westminster John Knox, 2006.

Byrne, Brendan. *The Hospitality of God: A Reading of Luke's Gospel.* Collegeville, MN: Liturgical, 2000.

Carey, Greg. *Sinners: Jesus and His Earliest Followers.* Waco, TX: Baylor University Press, 2009.

Crowder, Stephanie Buckhanon. "Gospel of Luke." In *True to Our Native Land: An African American New Testament Commentary*, edited by Brian L. Blount et al., 158–85. Minneapolis: Fortress, 2007.

Dickerson, Febbie. *The Widow and the Judge: A Womanist Investigation of Jesus' Parable*. Womanist Readings in Scripture Series. Edited by Mitzi Smith and Gay Byron. Fortress/Lexington, forthcoming.

Gonzáles, Justo L. *The Story Luke Tells: Luke's Unique Witness to the Gospel*. Grand Rapids, MI: Eerdmans, 2015.

Green, Bridgett A. "'Nobody's Free until Everybody's Free': Exploring Gender and Class Injustice in a Story about Children (Luke 18: 15–17)." In *Womanist Interpretations of the Bible: Expanding the Discourse*, edited by Gay L. Byron and Vanessa Lovelace, 291–310. Semeia Studies 85. Atlanta: Society of Biblical Literature, 2016.

Green, Joel B. *Conversion in Luke-Acts: Divine Action, Human Cognition and the People of God*. Grand Rapids, MI: Baker Academic, 2015.

———. *The Gospel of Luke*. The New International Commentary on the New Testament. Grand Rapids, MI: Eerdmans, 1997.

Gupta, Nijay K. "Teach Us, Mary: The Authority of Women Teachers in the Church in Light of the Magnificat (Luke 1:46–55)." *Pricilla Papers* 29 (2015) 11–14.

Hendricks, Obery M., Jr. *The Universe Bends Toward Justice: Radical Reflections on the Bible, the Church, and the Body Politic*. Maryknoll, NY: Orbis, 2011.

King, Karen L. *The Gospel of Mary of Magdala: Jesus and the First Woman Apostle*. Santa Rosa, CA: Polebridge, 2003.

Kinukawa, Hisako. "The Miracle Story of the Bent-Over Woman (Luke 13:10–17): An Interaction-Centered Interpretation." In *Transformative Encounters: Jesus and Women Reviewed*, edited by R. Kitzberger, 292–314. Leiden: E. J. Brill, 2000.

Levine, Amy-Jill. *The Misunderstood Jew: The Church and the Scandal of the Jewish Jesus*. New York: HarperOne, 2006.

———. *Short Stories by Jesus: The Enigmatic Parables of a Controversial Rabbi*. New York: HarperOne, 2015.

McKenna, Megan. *Luke: The Book of Blessings and Woes*. Hyde Park, NY: New City, 2009.

Menéndez-Antuña, Luis. "Male-Bonding, Female Vanishing: Representing Gendered Authority in Luke 23:26—24:53." *Early Christianity* 4 (2013) 490–506.

Nadella, Raj. *Dialogue Not Dogma: Many Voices in the Gospel of Luke*. New York: T. & T. Clark, 2011.

Phanon, Yuri. "Is She a Sinful Woman or a Forgiving Woman? An Exegesis of Luke 7:36–50." *Asian Journal of Pentecostal Studies* 19 (2016) 59–84.

Powell, Mark Allan. "Jesus and the Pathetic Wicked: Re-visiting Sanders's View of Jesus's Friendship with Sinners." *Journal for the Study of the Historical Jesus* 23 (2015) 188–208.

———. *Jesus as a Figure in History: How Modern Historians View the Man from Galilee*. Louisville: Westminster John Knox, 1998.

Reid, Barbara. "The Gospel of Luke: Friend or Foe of Women Proclaimers of the Word?" *Catholic Biblical Quarterly* 78 (2016) 1–23.

Rieger, Joerg. "Reclaiming People Power." In *Unsettling the Word: Biblical Experiments in Decolonization*. edited by Steven Heinrichs, 208–9. Manitoba, Canada: CommonWord, 2018.

Rhoads, David, David Esterline, and Jae Won Lee, eds. *Luke-Acts and Empire: Essays in Honor of Robert L. Brawley*. Princeton Theological Monograph Series 151.Eugene, OR: Pickwick, 2011.

Schüssler Fiorenza, Elisabeth. *Jesus: Miriam's Child, Sophia's Prophet. Critical Issues in Feminist Christology*. New York: T. & T. Clark, 2015.

Sell, Nancy A. "The Magnificat as a Model for Ministry: Proclaiming Justice, Shifting Paradigms, Transforming lives." *Liturgical Ministry* 10 (2001) 31–40.

Sobrino, Jon. *Christ the Liberator: A View from the Victims*. Maryknoll, NY: Orbis, 2001.

Spencer, F. Scott. *Salty Wives, Spirited Mothers, and Savvy Widows: Capable Women of Purpose and Persistence in Luke's Gospel*. Grand Rapids, MI: Eerdmans, 2012.

Thurman, Howard. *Jesus and the Disinherited*. Boston: Beacon, 1976.

Upkong, Justin. "Luke." In *Global Bible Commentary*, edited by Daniel Patte, 385–94. Nashville: Abingdon, 2004.

———. "Parable of the Shrewd Manager (Luke 16:1–13). An Essay in Inculturation Biblical Hermeneutic." *Semeia* 73 (1996) 189–210.

Vakayil, Prema. *Women Shall Prophesy (Joel 2:28): Anna, the Prophetess (Lk. 2:36–38), A Study in Luke's Biblical Perspective*. Bangalore: Asian Trading Corporation, 2007.

Weems, Renita. *Just a Sister Away*. West Bloomfield, MI: Warner, 2005.

———. *Showing Mary: How Women Can Share Prayers, Wisdom and the Blessings of God*. New York: Warner, 2005.

CHAPTER 13

Gospel of John

Darkness cannot drive out darkness; only light can do that. Hate cannot drive out hate; only love can do that.

—Martin Luther King, Jr.[1]

There are no "Christians" there [in John's Gospel]; they are all Jews.... The gospel is one side of a bitter family quarrel.... The arguments are heated, even exaggerated, and the literary form for a heated and exaggerated form is a polemic.

—Peter J. Gomes[2]

John at a Glance

1. The Gospel of John is also called the Fourth Gospel.
2. Tradition claimed that John, the disciple of Jesus, wrote John, but the author is unknown.
3. John is different from the Synoptic Gospels in terms of source and writing style.
4. John does not include Jesus's birth narrative, water baptism, and parable teaching.
5. The absence of the above does not mean that John is less historical than the Synoptics. It contains early Jesus traditions and historical information about the Johannine community.

---

1. King, *Where Do We Go*, 67.
2. Gomes, *Good Book*, 115.

6. John can be understood from the Johannine community's experience of separation from the synagogue.
7. Traditionally, John has been read as "the spiritual Gospel" because of its intimate spiritual language coupled with the role of the Spirit ("Advocate," *Paraklētos*).
8. Historically, John has been read through the eyes of high Christology. But this reading can be challenged if we read Jesus as the Jewish Messiah who does the work of God.
9. Thus, traditional incarnation theology based on John 1:14 also can be challenged. Namely, "the Logos became flesh" can be read as Jesus's embodiment of God's word.
10. Jesus may be better compared to Moses than to God.

Introduction

TRADITIONALLY, THE FOURTH GOSPEL has been cherished as the "spiritual gospel" featuring individual salvation, high Christology, and exclusivism. Namely, to believe in Jesus is everything needed for individual salvation once and for all. High Christology came out of the so-called Logos theology in that God became a human being. John 1:14 has been understood literally; that is, God became flesh, which is Jesus. In this view, Jesus was God himself, and vice versa. He was preexistent with God, leaving the heavenly glory and coming to earth to redeem humanity through his sacrifice. Thus, Jesus should have died to accomplish the salvation of humanity. Likewise, Johannine exclusivism is emphasized based on John 14:6: "I am the way, and the truth, and the life. No one comes to the Father except through me." But the Fourth Gospel goes beyond the above traditional interpretation. Salvation is more than an individual dimension and seeks multiple dimensions: personal, communal, and cosmic salvation. Likewise, faith is more than what one believes about Jesus and involves trusting relationships with God and commitment to the way of God and of Jesus. The main image and role of Jesus is the Jewish Messiah who does the work of God and testifies to the truth (18:37). He brings the light and life to the world through his work of God. In this regard, the Johannine Jesus can be better compared to Moses than to God, and both are sent by God to carry out God's special task. While Moses is sent by God to deliver Israelites from the hands of Pharaoh, Jesus is sent by God to deliver people from darkness and to provide them with light.

Likewise, John 14:6 ("I am the way, and the truth, and the life. No one comes to the Father except through me") can be read differently as descriptions of his work as the Messiah. That is, Jesus reveals the way of God, testifies to the truth of God, and provides the abundant life of God.

We will also read John as the literature of community development in times of crisis. The Johannine community behind this Gospel goes through various stages of development after separation from the synagogue in late first century CE. Thus, we will attend to this community's experience and explore how it responds to difficult moments of life in the community.

Chapter Contents

1. The Historical Context of the Gospel
2. Logos and Jesus
3. "I Am" (*Egō Eimi*) Sayings of Jesus
4. John 14:6 and Exclusivism
5. Faith, Discipleship, and Transformation

The Historical Context of the Gospel

The Fourth Gospel is the product of the Johannine community dealing with expulsion from the synagogue. There are several clues in John that reflect this painful experience of separation: 9:22; 12:42; 16:2. In these places, we find that some people were put out of the synagogue because of their faith. Scholars believe that these references to the expulsion reflect the Johannine experience of expulsion. All this implies that the Fourth Gospel reveals "a two-level drama," one during Jesus's time and the other during John's time.[3] It is generally believed that the Johannine community goes through stages of community development. The first stage has to do with internal evangelism within the synagogue where the Johannine members stay and share the good news about Jesus with their fellow Jews. John 1:39–43 reflects this activity of evangelism in the synagogue. In this passage, we find sayings about evangelism such as "come and see" and "we have found the Messiah." The second stage involves a time of conflict in the synagogue due to the Johannine members' continuous evangelism. Ultimately, they are expelled from the synagogue. The third stage involves a post-separation experience. Once separated, Johannine members have to find themselves strong in Christ. On

---

3. Martyn, *History and Theology*, 35–66.

the one hand, they need a sacred, safe space where they feel at home. On the other hand, they have to defend their position from the synagogue. In this complex, polemical context, the Johannine dualisms, for example, between light and darkness (12:35, 46), or relatively high Christology can be understood (6:33–35; 8:58; 9:27–34).

John's Difference with the Synoptic Gospels

Apparently, the Fourth Gospel does not have parables, exorcisms, beatitudes, water baptism of Jesus, temptation story in the wilderness, and Jesus's birth narrative. This implies that the Fourth Gospel does not depend on the synoptic sources such as Mark or Q. Rather, it includes different sources such as signs source, farewell sources, or the Prologue. It also has some unique materials such as the story of Nicodemus (3:1–21), a Samaritan woman (4:1–42), and a man born blind (9:1–41). There are many differences between the Synoptic Gospels and the Fourth Gospel. In the Synoptic Gospels, Jesus has a one-year public ministry, but in the Fourth Gospel, he performs three years of public ministry, and observes three Passovers (2:13; 6:4; 11:55). In the Synoptics, Jesus makes one journey from Galilee to Jerusalem, but in the Fourth Gospel, he makes multiple visits to Jerusalem (2:13; 5:1; 7:10). John makes better sense because multiple visits to Jerusalem is more realistic than a single visit. The Synoptic Gospels seem to dramatize Jesus's one journey from Galilee to Jerusalem.

Regarding eschatology, while the Synoptic Gospels emphasize future eschatology, the Fourth Gospel focuses on present eschatology ("eternal life," 3:36; 5:24; 6:47–54). In the Synoptics, the Last Supper is the Passover meal, but in John, it occurs before the Passover (13:1; 18:28). Likewise, in the Synoptics, Jesus was crucified on the day of Passover, but in the Fourth Gospel, he was crucified before the Passover. This implies that the Fourth Gospel considers Jesus's death a paschal lamb, slaughtered before the Passover (19:14, 31, 42).

Although there are many differences between the Synoptic Gospels and the Fourth Gospel, they share core traditions about Jesus and his teachings about the kingdom of God. The common view is that John does not have teachings about the kingdom of God, but the Fourth Gospel also teaches about the kingdom of God. For example, Jesus tells Nicodemus that "no one can see the kingdom of God without being born from above" (3:3). Jesus's point is that people have to be born from God and follow the way of God. While there are no parables in the Fourth Gospel, the "I am" sayings of Jesus plays a similar role to parabolic teaching. Through these sayings, he encourages his audience to rethink the significance of the word of God and their place in the world. For example, he talks to the Jews in John 6:51: "I am the living bread that came down from heaven. Whoever eats of this bread will live forever; and the bread that I will give for the life of the world is my flesh."

Logos and Jesus

In Hellenistic philosophy, *logos* is a rational mind or reason, which is the basis of the universe. It means more than "the word," as is usually translated. The corresponding concepts in the Hebrew Bible include *dabar* (the word [of God]), *hokmah* (wisdom), or *ruach* (Spirit). Philo, the Jewish philosopher in Alexandria in first century CE, considers the Logos as the divine mind being immanent in the world. So when God creates the world by speaking the word, it is none other than the work of the Logos.

John begins with the phrase *en archē*, just as in Gen 1:1 but in Hebrew: *bereshit*. Both of these mean "in a certain beginning." There is no definite article between "in" and "beginning." So here, "the beginning" does not seem to refer to the beginning of all beginnings. *En archē* or *bereshit* means the real old time or the sense of "once upon a time." That is why the NRSV translates Gen 1:1 as follows: "In the beginning when God created the heavens and the earth." John's point is that God is the beginning of all, including human beings.

In the Johannine prologue, John introduces the Logos to the world. It originates not in this world but in God. The Logos connotes God's word, work, and Spirit. In John 1:1–14, the Logos is not directly associated with Jesus though it may be presumed so by readers. In John 1:1, John simply says that once upon a time there was the Logos—the divine word or Spirit. John explains the work of the Logos. That is, the Logos has come down to the world, but it was rejected because people were evil, seeking their own power and glory. John the Baptist also came to teach about the Logos but he failed. John's judgment about this situation is summarized in 3:19–21: "And this is the judgment, that the light has come into the world, and people loved darkness rather than light because their deeds were evil. For all who do evil hate the light and do not come to the light, so that their deeds may not be exposed. But those who do what is true come to the light, so that it may be clearly seen that their deeds have been done in God."

Finally, in John 1:14, the Logos is connected to the work of Jesus. The invisible, preexistent Logos became flesh and was embodied through Jesus. Therefore, the traditional incarnation theology based on high Christology needs a reevaluation. Here the point is not that God became Jesus but that the Logos became visible and felt through Jesus's life. In fact, throughout the Johannine narrative Jesus always says that he is sent by God to do the work of God. Otherwise, he never claims that he is God or equal to him. Rather, he says that God is greater than he (10:34). Even if he says that the Father and he are one, it does not mean that he is equal with God, but it means that they work together in unity (10:30). When Jews charged him with a charge of blasphemy, he does not accept their charge because his argument is that he worked for God as the Son of God, which is his main title. Even if Thomas calls Jesus "my God," that does not mean that he is the same as God because someone may be called god in the Hebrew Bible (John 6:34–35; cf. Ps 82:6). Overall, John's portrayal of Jesus is the Jewish Messiah who embodies the Logos.

"The Logos became flesh" is a metaphorical statement, which has the form of "A is B." In this formula, A and B are two disparate things that are linked together to reveal new meaning. But the meaning is not so obvious as it seems because the disparate relations are many and therefore need the reader's deliberation. "A" is called the target domain, and "B," the source domain. In metaphorical expressions, A is explained through B. But in a plain sense, A is not B. For example, when Jesus says, "I am the bread that came down from heaven" (6:51), he does not mean that he is the bread literally. Here he means that he enriches a person's life. Just as food is necessary for people, his work for God will be their food.

Similarly, "the Logos became flesh" can be read metaphorically. The Word (*logos*) and flesh are two disparate things. The Logos (the target domain) can be explained through flesh (the source domain). The abstract idea of the Logos is explained through the image of flesh, which evokes real human life and a vulnerable world. That is, the invisible wisdom or word of God became known, seen, felt, and touched in this shaky world through somebody's life—Jesus who testified to the truth of God (18:37) and delivered "the Logos of God" (17:6, 14, 17) to his disciples. Otherwise, the Logos is not the same as Jesus but is incarnated in him. Jesus always makes it clear that his job is to do the work of God (10:25, 37–38).

Consider and discuss: Usually, Jesus in the Fourth Gospel is read through high Christology and exclusive incarnational theology. Namely, the claim is that Jesus is God and that he is the only truth and salvation. This exclusive gospel was preached to the third world and minoritized communities, denying other religions and cultures. But if we interpret Christology and incarnational theology differently, there might be a space for conversations with other religions or cultures. That is, Jesus is the Son of God, who is not the same as God or the Logos. He embodies God's word (Logos). We may understand John 1:14 differently: "the Logos was manifested through Jesus's life." The Christian gospel is not meant to defeat other cultures or religions. What do you think about this alternative interpretation?

"I Am" (*egō eimi*) Sayings of Jesus

Unlike the Synoptic Gospels, John has unique forms of sayings of Jesus, the so-called "I am" sayings. We find two kinds of "I am" sayings of Jesus in the Fourth Gospel: "I am" without the predicate (the grammar that follows the subject and verb (i.e., "I am"), which includes the object of the verb and prepositional phrases attached to it (i.e., "the bread of life") and "I am" with the predicate. In the former, Jesus says "I am" to the disciples who are terrified at his walking on the water and he simply affirms his identity: "It's me."[4] In the latter, there are seven "I am" sayings of Jesus with the predicate:

- "I am the bread of life/living bread (6:35–51)
- "I am the light of the world" (8:12; cf. 9:5)
- "I am the gate of the sheepfold" (10:7–9)
- "I am the good shepherd" (10:11–14)
- "I am the resurrection and the life" (11:25)
- "I am the way, the truth, and the life" (14:6)
- "I am the vine/true vine" (15:1–5)

---

4. Examples of this type of the "I am" sayings are in John 4:26; 6:20; 8:24; 8:28; 8:58; 12:26; 13:13; and 13:19.

All the above "I am" sayings consist of metaphorical expressions, having the structure of "A is B." For example, Jesus is not the bread literally, but he (the target domain) needs to be understood through the bread (the source domain). Readers must grapple with this "arbitrary link" between Jesus and the bread. Likewise, other "I am" sayings need to be interpreted in the same manner. The question is in what sense does Jesus become the light of the world, the gate, the shepherd, the resurrection, the way, the truth, the life, and vine? One very plausible way of reading these sayings is to interpret them as the description of his work, not as the sign of his divinity. Namely, Jesus is the bread in the sense that his work for God gives hope and abundant life to the needy. As the Son of God, he embodies God's word and delivers it to his disciples (cf. 17:6–17). Likewise, "the light of the world" is the source domain to which Jesus's work needs to be linked. He is not the light himself but brings the light of God to people dwelling in darkness. Namely, he is not the light himself in the plain sense, but his advocacy for the marginalized sheds new light on someone's life. The man born blind recovered his sight through Jesus's work. Similarly, Jesus is not the gate himself because he is the heavenly gate. The gate may symbolize ways of justice shown by Jesus. The shepherd as the source domain also helps us understand Jesus's work in terms of shepherding. Whereas thieves or bad shepherds sacrifice the sheep, the good shepherd takes care of them. When Jesus says that "I am the resurrection," this is a metaphorical statement. Through Jesus's work, people are hopeful of their situation and will not give up on the present conditions of life. Other source domains such as the way, the truth, the life, and the vine also have to do with Jesus's work in one way or another. Jesus shows the way of God, testifies to the truth, and liberates the life stuck in darkness.

Often, Jesus's "I am" sayings are associated with the revealed divine name in Exod 3:14 in support of high Christology (Jesus is Divine or God). But that reading seems futile because the context and message of Exod 3:14 is not really a revelation of God's name. Exod 3:14 (*'ehyeh 'asher 'ehyeh*) is hard to translate. Typically, it is translated as "I am who I am" or "I shall be that I shall be." The Septuagint has an interesting translation: "I am the one who exists" (*egō eimi ho on*), which reflects Hellenistic ontology. But the Hebrew text does not deal with such an ontology. There are other ways of translating and understanding this verse. One alternative translation may be through "the same for same" (*idem per idem*) strategy. Stating the same thing twice is a refusal to answer the question asked by a person. Moses asks God for his name, but God does not give him what he requests. Instead he says: "I am that I am." No other answers would adequately explain who God is. Another alternative translation is made in an eschatological sense: "I shall be that I shall be." This translation emphasizes God's presence with Moses no matter what happens to him. As we see above, the context and content of Exod 3:14 does not have to do with divine name revelation. Rather, it should be understood in the larger context of oppression (Exod 3:7–8). Moses is sent by God to deliver the Israelites from slavery in Egypt. God says to him: "I have made you like God to Pharaoh" (Exod 7:1; cf. 4:16). When Moses is uncertain about his calling (Exod 3:11), God affirms his presence as "I am" with him. Thus, Jesus is better compared to Moses than to God. Both of them do the work of God.

John 14:6 and Exclusivism

John 14:6 ("I am the way, and the truth, and the life. No one comes to the Father except through me") has been read from the perspective of exclusivism. The literal, traditional reading goes like this: "Jesus is the way to heaven; he is the truth because he is God; he is the life because he died for sinners. So nobody can be saved except through Jesus." But this reading is inadequate. This statement is part of the "I am" sayings of Jesus, and it must be understood metaphorically. First, we need to understand this verse in view of the Johannine community context where members struggle to understand their place due to separation from the synagogue. The Johannine Jesus comforts the community members and reassures them of their place in him. Thus, Jesus begins in 14:1: "Do not let your hearts be troubled. Believe in God, believe also in me." Because of the need to comfort them, Jesus says that he is the way in the sense that his teaching and life is the way to God. Also, he says to them that their way is a good one. Namely, John 14:6 is given to those who are troubled because of expulsion from the synagogue. It is not given to triumphalist believers but it helps troubled believers deal with their situation well.

Second, John 14:6 can be read as descriptions of Jesus's work. That is, Jesus is the way because he lived an exemplary life for God, discerning what is good to follow. Jesus is the way because he walked the way of God until he died. In that sense, Jesus's way leads to God, but at the same time, it is a difficult road that requires a cost and patience. Likewise, Jesus is the truth because he testified to the truth of God through his life. But this truth was not accepted in the world, and his testimonial work of God led to his death. Jesus is the life because he revealed the way and the truth of God. In this respect, "No one comes to the Father except through me" can be paraphrased as follows: "All those who want to live abundantly in God must seek the way I lived, the truth to which I testified, and the abundant life I fought for." Read in this way, John 14:6 does not sound imperialistic or exclusivist. Rather, the

Johannine Jesus engages in the world to make sure that people discern what is right, testify to the truth, and live abundantly in God.

> **Consider and discuss:** America is not the place of a single race, culture, or religion. Muslims, Buddhists, Christians, and other religionists live together. Yet, non-Christian people or non-Western cultures are often discriminated against and pressured to adopt the view of the dominant culture or religion. When you meet non-Christian friends or other people and happen to talk about religion and society today, what views of other religions do you express to them or what would you say about John 14:6? Do you believe that John 14:6 is an exclusive statement about salvation or that it may provide space for interfaith dialogue? If you can find common ground with other religions, what would that be?

Faith, Discipleship, and Transformation

Faith

Faith, discipleship, and transformation are key concepts in the Fourth Gospel. Faith (*pistis* in Greek and *emunah* in Hebrew) is used variously in John. One sense is a mental agreement with someone's word or work. For example, Jesus says in 1:50: "Do you believe because I told you that I saw you under the fig tree? You will see greater things than these." Similarly, he says in 3:12: "If I have told you about earthly things and you do not believe, how can you believe if I tell you about heavenly things?" The other use of faith in the Fourth Gospel is to accept Jesus as the Messiah (3:18; 5:38; 6:29; 9:35–36), which involves knowledge about him, and commitment to his teaching. But still in other places, faith is focused on trusting or following God or Jesus. For example, Jesus says in 12:36: "While you have the light, believe in the light, so that you may become children of light." "To believe in the light" means "you have to trust the light and follow it." This notion of trusting faith prevails in John (3:16–18; 11:25, 48; 14:1). Jesus often asks people to believe in him because he does the work of God. The Johannine Jesus does not separate faith from work: "If I am not doing the works of my Father, then do not believe me. But if I do them, even though you do not believe me, believe the works, so that you may know and understand that the Father is in me and I am in the Father" (10:37–38). This kind of trusting faith also applies to God, as Jesus says in 14:1: "Do not let your hearts be troubled. Believe in God, believe also in me." God is the primary place of trust. He is the one who sent the Messiah and loved the world. Jesus is also the place of trust because he showed who God is through his life.

Discipleship

Discipleship requires ongoing faith and commitment to Jesus's teaching: "As he was saying these things, many believed in him. Then Jesus said to the Jews who had believed in him, 'If you continue in my word, you are truly my disciples; and you will know the truth, and the truth will make you free'" (8:31–32). Some Jews believed that his teaching was right, but they did not commit to his teaching. Mere belief in him or knowledge of his teaching is not enough to become his disciples. He tells them that they must know and keep his teaching. Jesus's teaching must be reconstructed from all he said and did in the Gospel. Only then can they become his disciples and live as children of God. In this regard, discipleship is conditional in that if they follow the teaching of Jesus, they are truly his disciples. They do not become his disciples once and for all.

The episode of Nicodemus also illustrates what true discipleship means (3:1–12). Nicodemus is an ambiguous or imperfect character, who knows Jewish tradition very well but does not understand what Jesus teaches. Jesus says to him: "Very truly, I tell you, no one can see the kingdom of God without being born from above" (3:3). True disciples should be born from above. But Nicodemus does not understand this spiritual language of Jesus and asks: "How can anyone be born after having grown old? Can one enter a second time into the mother's womb and be born?" (3:4). This misunderstanding is partly caused by the ambiguous adverb *anōthen*, which means "above or again." But Jesus means "above," as he corrects Nicodemus: "Very truly, I tell you, no one can enter the kingdom of God without being born of water and Spirit" (3:5). Here, "being born of Spirit" means "born from above" because the Spirit comes from above. "Being born of water" is a bit difficult to understand since it may represent either water baptism or physical birth. In either case, however, "the Spirit" is key to the kingdom of God. Since the Spirit comes from above, Jesus emphasizes one's spiritual birth from above. That is, to live in the kingdom of God, they have to trust God and follow the Spirit from above. Jesus further explains the nature of the spiritual birth in 3:8; it is like the wind that "blows where it chooses, and you hear the sound of it, but you do not know where it comes from or where it goes. It is with everyone who is born of the Spirit." Jesus's point is that the Spirit does not discriminate against race, gender, ethnicity, or any determinants. Likewise, the spiritual person is led by the Spirit and treats all the same. As the wind is invisible yet seen by its work, a person of the Spirit must be the same. Such a person must be humble, as Jesus says: "Very truly, I tell you, unless a grain of wheat falls into the earth and dies, it remains just a single grain; but if it dies, it bears much fruit" (12:24). Jesus's washing of his disciples' feet is also an example of service and discipleship (13:1–7).

Transformation

Transformation in the Fourth Gospel involves multiple aspects of change in life: personal, communal, and cosmic dimensions. A personal dimension has to do with accepting Jesus as the Messiah and following his teaching. The Samaritan woman is a good example of personal transformation. She is an anonymous woman who faces hardships, given that she has no husband now. Jesus knows that she had five husbands before and even the one she has now is not hers (4:17–18). When she met Jesus in the wilderness, she was thirsty in many ways: economically, socially, religiously, and spiritually. But she was very engaging with him and entered a series of conversations that led to her own change of life and her community as well. She found a new Messiah who has an interest in her life. Her view of the religion and the messiah also changes in ways that she now understands the importance of wellbeing of all people. She hears: "God is spirit, and those who worship him must worship in spirit and truth" (4:24). Then she rushes to her village to share the good news about him with her village people.

The other example of personal transformation is the man born blind in John 9:1–41. He lived a miserable life because he was blind. He was also stigmatized by society and labelled a sinner. Jesus's disciples do not sympathize with him; they think that he was born blind because of his parents' sin or his own (9:2–3). But Jesus rejects such a parochial theology and uses this opportunity of meeting him as a moment of glorifying God. Jesus opens his eyes, and he is cleansed at Siloam because he has faith that he would be healed. This blind man now sees a new world full of light and life. Yet his new life faces opposition from his village people and other leaders of society. That is an ironic reality that he must face. Initially, he does not know who healed him, but he testifies about his experience of being healed. Eventually, he meets Jesus face to face again and understands him better. All this implies that his transformation experience is not easily accepted in the community and larger society. He must still deal with hostile conditions of life even after he becomes a new person of God.

Also, we may consider the Johannine community in terms of communal and cosmic transformation. As an isolated community, its members could have stayed in their comfort zone in Christ. But they did not hide in a cave, as the Fourth Gospel presents a new way of transformation for both the community and the world at large. The Johannine community engages in the world, very different from the Qumran community, which is a very sectarian community living in a desert. In John, Jesus's disciples are sent into the world to love it through the love of God. The Johannine world is not a place of judgment by God. It is the world that God loved so much and sent his Son to save it (3:16).

We also see the importance of the world as God's mission place in Jesus's farewell speech. Jesus asks his disciples to stay in a hostile world: "I am not asking you to take them out of the world, but I ask you to protect them from the evil one. They do not belong to the world, just as I do not belong to the world. Sanctify them in the truth; your word is truth. As you have sent me into the world, so I have sent them into the world" (17:15–18). The world is God's mission field to which Jesus's disciples are sent to transform. In this regard, the vision of transformation in John is cosmic and involves the change of the world.

The way of transforming the world is not by knowledge about Jesus but through the discipleship that follows his teaching rooted in the love of God and love of the world. This kind of discipleship does not demonize others or other religions because God loved the world and the people in it. God's love is bigger than any human thought. Thus Jesus's disciples are invited to engage in dialogue with others and walk with them through the love of God. If the Logos mission is performed through this careful engagement in the world, the Fourth Gospel will be a gospel of inclusion rather than of exclusion.

If the Johannine community follows the above logic of God's love in the world, this community is supposed to be a community of transformation. This very community started out with separation from the synagogue. Members experienced pain and trauma due to the recent conflict with and expulsion from the synagogue. But they overcome difficult times and feel sure about their place in Christ. At the same time, they do not stay in their comfort zone. Rather, they feel the mission of God's love through Christ. They are sent into the world in which they are hated and persecuted. But they do this mission gladly because it is their joy that people turn to God.

Summary

1. The Fourth Gospel is very different from the Synoptic Gospels, but that does not mean that it is less historical than them. It also contains important information or traditions about Jesus and the Johannine community.
2. The author is unknown, but the beloved disciple, whose identity is also unknown, may have something to do with the foundation of the Johannine community.
3. The Fourth Gospel reflects the Johannine community's experience: its separation from the synagogue, its survival, and growth.
4. This community undergoes the process of transformation because of their painful experience of separation from the synagogue.
5. The Johannine Jesus came to testify to the truth of God (18:37). Truth telling is an important part of God's work done by Jesus, as he says: "You will know the truth, and the truth will make you free" (8:32).
6. Traditional Logos theology or high Christology needs to be reinterpreted because the Johannine Jesus is close to the Jewish Messiah who does the work of God.
7. Jesus never claims that he is God. He is closer to Moses than to God because both are sent by God to do a special task.
8. The "I am" sayings of Jesus can be understood as the descriptions of his work of God.

Further Reading

Blount, Brian K. *Then the Whisper Put on Flesh: New Testament Ethics in an African American Context*. Nashville: Abingdon, 2001.

Callahan, Allen Dwight. "John." In *True to Our Native Land: An African American New Testament Commentary*, edited by Brian Blount et al., 186–212. Minneapolis, MN: Fortress, 2007.

Cannon, Katie, Emilie Townes, and Angela Sims, eds. *Womanist Theological Ethics: A Reader*. Louisville, KY: Westminster John Knox, 2011.

Culpepper, Alan. *The Gospel and Letters of John*. Nashville, TN: Abingdon, 1998.

Hylen, Susan. *Imperfect Believers: Ambiguous Characters in the Gospel of John*. Louisville, KY: Westminster John Knox, 2009.

Kim, Yung Suk. *Truth, Testimony, and Transformation: A New Study of the "I Am" Sayings of Jesus in the Fourth Gospel.* Eugene, OR: Cascade, 2014.

Kysar, Robert. *John the Maverick Gospel.* Louisville, KY: Westminster John Knox, 2007.

Levine, Amy-Jill. *Feminist Companion to John.* Vol. 1. New York: Sheffield, 2003.

Martyn, J. Louis. *History and Theology in the Fourth Gospel.* Louisville, KY: Westminster John Knox, 1968.

Newheart, Michael. *Word and Soul: A Psychological, Literary, and Cultural Reading of the Fourth Gospel.* Collegeville, MN: Liturgical, 2001.

O'Day, Gail. "The Gospel of John." In *Women's Bible Commentary: Revised Edition*, edited by Carol Newsom et al., 517–30. Louisville, KY: Westminster John Knox, 2012.

Park, Kyung-mi. "John." In *Global Bible Commentary*, edited by Daniel Patte, 401–11. Nashville, TN: Abingdon, 2004.

Schneiders, Sandra. *Written That You May Believe: Encountering Jesus in the Fourth Gospel.* New York: Crossroad, 2003.

Smith, Mitzi J. "Water is a Human Right, but It Ain't Free: A Womanist Reading of John 4:1-42." In *Womanist Sass and Talk Back: Social (In)Justice, Intersectionality and Biblical Interpretation*, 7–27. Eugene, OR: Cascade, 2018.

CHAPTER 14

The Acts of the Apostles

From one ancestor [God] made all peoples to occupy the whole earth.

—Acts 17:26a

Whether he's white as a sheet or black as a skillet, out of one blood God made all nations.

—Fannie Lou Hamer (1917–77), African American Civil Rights Activist[1]

Acts at a Glance

1. Acts is widely considered the sequel to Luke's Gospel.
2. Acts was written between 80 and 90 CE; some scholars argue for an earlier or later date.
3. The Acts of the Apostles is the only text of its kind in the NT.
4. Acts is addressed to Theophilus.
5. The author may be an unknown Gentile God-fearer.
6. Acts primarily focuses on activities of the Apostles Peter and Paul.
7. The primary actor is God.
8. The kerygma (preaching) of the early believers was that "God raised Jesus."

---

1. Mills, *This Little Light of Mine*, 306.

9. Acts covers the period from Jesus's death (about 27–33 CE) to about 64 CE.
10. Acts 1:8 is considered the programmatic text that reveals the geographic advancement of the missions.

Introduction

ONE OF THE MOST quoted biblical texts among African Americans during the civil rights movement was Acts 17:26; it was a favorite text of civil rights activist Fannie Lou Hamer. Hamer invoked it when she asserted that the church, like Christ, was sent to all people regardless of race.[2] Returning by bus from a civil rights training session in Charleston, South Carolina, Fannie Lou Hamer and others on a bus were arrested in Winona, Mississippi, and jailed. During this brief and unjust incarceration, Hamer was brutally beaten and denied medical treatment. June Johnson remembers Fannie breaking out in song; she would particularly sing "When Paul and Silas Were Bound in Jail." It baffled Fannie to hear that the jailer and his wife were reportedly Christians, considering the ruthless beatings they received. Hamer spoke with the jailer's wife and requested that she read two scriptures, Prov 26:26 and Acts 17:26. The jailer's wife wrote the scriptures down, but she never returned to speak with Hamer.[3]

Hamer conjured Acts as a source of resistance, motivation, and inspiration. But scholars have identified Acts as an ancient historical monograph or biography, similar to Greco-Roman romance novels, and an epic like Homer's *Iliad*. The Acts of the Apostles is the only text of its kind in the NT, although a number of noncanonical Christian apocryphal Acts survive (e.g., *Acts of Thomas*, *The Acts of Paul and Thecla*, *The Acts of Peter*, *The Acts of Peter and the Twelve*). Like the canonical Acts, the apocryphal Acts focus on the ministry of one or two main protagonists or characters, their miracles, travels, preaching, converts, and the opposition. The canonical Acts recounts the ministry of the Apostle Peter (and John) primarily in Jerusalem in the first half of the narrative. And Acts focuses on activities of the Apostle Paul and his colleagues in the second half. Some readers assert that Acts is about the acts of the Holy Spirit; however, the primary actor is God, the Father. Overall, Luke attempts to show that despite opposition, the apostles preached the gospel undeterred and thousands of people joined the Jesus movement.

2. Riggs, *Can I Get a Witness?*, 179.
3. Mills, *This Little Light of Mine*, 56–58, 60, 65.

Internal and external opposition and conflicts arise throughout the narrative and some are settled in shocking and unpredictable ways. Nevertheless, the spread of the gospel is unhindered. God is on the side of the gospel.

Chapter Contents

1. Authorship, Date, and Sources
2. Theophilus, the Addressee
3. The Promise and Outpouring of the Spirit
4. God as Primary Actor
5. Violence, Unjust Incarceration, and Internal Conflict
6. Gifted, Agentive, and Silenced Women
7. Some Conversion Narratives: Simon, Ethiopian Eunuch, Cornelius, and Lydia
8. The Holy Spirit
9. Saul's Call, Commissioning, and Diaspora Mission

Author, Date, and Sources

The place of composition and the author are unknown. Suggestions about authorship include Luke the evangelist and Luke the physician and co-worker of the Apostle Paul (Col 4:14; 2 Tim 4:11; Phlm 24; Irenaeus, *Against Heresies* 3.14.1). Luke is likely a Gentile God-fearer; some argue that he was Jewish. Some scholars argue that the author, whom we shall call Luke, consulted or used several sources to compose his narrative: A Palestinian document about the Jerusalem *ekklēsia* and Peter's (and John's) activities; an Antiochene tradition about the *ekklēsia* in Syrian Antioch and the commissioning of the apostles Paul, Barnabas, and others there; and finally a *We* travel diary that is detectable when the narrator is represented with first person plural pronoun *we* (16:1–17; 20:5–15; 21:1–18; 27:1—28:16). Luke may have constructed the speeches and summaries. Act contains three major summaries (2:42–47; 4:32–35; 5:12–16) and quite a few minor and numerical summaries (e.g., 1:14; 2:41; 4:4; 5:14; 6:1, 7; 9:31–32; 11:21, 24; 12:24; 14:1; 16:5; 19:20; 28:30–31) that provide succinct descriptions of the activities and growth of the early *ekklēsia*. In his first volume, the Gospel of Luke, Luke knew and used Mark's Gospel, which is dated shortly before or after the destruction of the Jewish Temple in 70 CE. Scholars believe Acts was written shortly after (or perhaps at the same time) Luke's Gospel between 80 and 90 CE.

Theophilus, the Addressee

According to Acts 1:1, Luke composed a first book about the teaching and ministry of Jesus for a man named Theophilus. Luke's Gospel was addressed to the "most excellent Theophilus" in order to provide him with a truthful and orderly account of the events about which others had already instructed him; Luke supplements an existing collection on the subject (Luke 1:1). The identity of Theophilus (*Theo* meaning God in Greek; *philos* meaning friend or lover) is unknown. Perhaps Theophilus was a Roman official (and God-fearer) like Cornelius or the noblest King Festus (governor of Judea) who is knowledgeable of the events surrounding Jesus (10:2; 26:25–28). The name Theophilus might be a collective noun referring to people (Jewish or Gentile) that consider themselves a friend or lover (worshipper or patron) of the God of Israel (e.g., the Ethiopian Eunuch, a royal official, 8:27b; Cornelius the Roman centurion, 10:2). Thus, Acts was addressed to a broad audience, which makes sense given the commission to take the good news to the ends of the earth (1:8).

The Promise and Outpouring of the Spirit

Acts begins by recounting Jesus's post-empty tomb/resurrection appearance and his ascension. The story differs in some respects from Luke 24. In Luke's Gospel, Jesus spends a day with some unnamed disciples and the eleven apostles, but in Acts Jesus instructed only the eleven apostles for forty days before his ascension (1:3–11). The forty days of instruction allows Luke to account for activities of the apostles between Passover and Pentecost. The eleven apostles are instructed to return to Jerusalem (from the Mount of Olives; Bethany mentioned in Luke was on the slope of the mountain) and wait for God's promised outpouring of the Spirit at Pentecost (*Shavuot*) (1:2–5). The eleven apostles still anticipate that Jesus would establish God's kingdom on earth and want to know when, but Jesus responds that only God has the authority and knowledge and has not revealed it (1:6–7). Interestingly, the Kingdom of God is seldom the subject of preaching in Acts. When the Kingdom of God is preached, the Twelve do not proclaim it; the Apostle Paul or one of the other Hellenists preach the Kingdom (8:12; 14:22; 19:8; 28:31).

The purpose of the outpouring of God's Spirit at Pentecost is to anoint the apostles and other women and men disciples to act as God's witnesses in Jerusalem, Judea, Samaria, and toward the ends of the earth (1:8). Acts 1:8 is considered the text that set the geographical itinerary for the mission; it reveals the territorial advancement or expansion of the missional activities of God's witnesses. It is not a strictly linear progression but it demonstrates movement from the Jerusalem center outwards. Although the story culminates in Rome with Paul under house arrest (28:16), Rome is only one of the ends of the earth. The plural word *ends* signifies multiple geographical destinations. In chapter 8, the Ethiopian eunuch's return to his homeland after his conversion can be understood as one of the *ends* of the earth; Ethiopia was considered by ancient writers and historians to be located at the far extremes of the earth. Perhaps Luke leaves the possibilities open precisely to signify that the story itself is open-ended, to be continued.

We might also identify more than one programmatic text that signals how the narrative will unfold in addition to the geographical mapping of place. The legal scholar, Pharisee, and member of the Council, Gamaliel admonishes his peers not to hinder Peter and the other apostles, arguing as follows: "So in the present case, I tell you, keep away from these men and let them alone; because if this plan or this undertaking is of human origin, it will fail; but if it is of God, you will not be able to overthrow them—in that case you may even be found fighting against God!" (5:38–39, NRSV). The apostles face opposition and/or competitors in the public spaces where they preach and teach the resurrection of Jesus and grace of God. In those spaces their theology and Christology is opposed. Yet, they prevail.

In the second floor or upper room, the eleven apostles, Mary the mother of Jesus, Jesus's brothers James and Judas, and other unnamed women (and men), totaling about 120 people, commit themselves to prayer and waiting. While waiting, Peter assumes the leadership role and initiates a process for replacing Judas. Judas's replacement is required to be a male (*anēr*) who followed Jesus from his baptism to his ascension (the statement implies that more than the eleven were at the ascension, 1:15–22). Based on this delimiting criteria the eleven apostles choose two male candidates, pray, and cast lots to demonstrate the divine selection of a man (*anēr*) named Matthias to replace Judas (1:23–26).

When Pentecost arrives, the Spirit visibly enters the room and sits on each one—the twelve apostles, Mary, James, Judas, and the other women and men present. The Spirit's entrance impacts all the human senses: their sight, touch, hearing, and speech. The Spirit feels and sounds like a strong wind, looks like tongues of fire, and causes all present to speak in the languages of those present at the Pentecost celebration. The crowd of diverse ethnicities is drawn to the sound of a multilingual symphonious recital of the mighty acts of God. Some are amazed but others accuse them of being drunk (2:1–13).

> **Consider and discuss:** The verbal demonstration of the Holy Spirit is in diverse languages. The Holy Spirit did not insist upon one language. Many countries outside of the USA require students to learn both their native language and English. In October 2017, a New Jersey high school teacher was videotaped telling her Latina/o students to stop speaking Spanish but to speak "American" because people died in combat so that they could be in America. How can we demonstrate a commitment to and love of diverse peoples and their languages in our society, schools, and churches through our attitudes and practices regarding foreign languages and language acquisition?

This demonstration in the upper room marks the beginning of the testimony about the risen Jesus in Jerusalem, the headquarters of the movement. Significantly, when the persecution breaks out in Jerusalem because of Stephen's speech, only the Hellenists flee Jerusalem. The Twelve remain despite the assertion that the persecution was against the *ekklēsia* in Jerusalem (8:1–3). The Twelve rarely leave Jerusalem except to exercise authority over other evangelists and their converts. For example, Peter and John go to Samaria when they hear that some Samaritans are converted in response to Philip's preaching and miracles (8:4–25). The Council that convenes to decide on what basis Gentiles will be received into the movement is located in Jerusalem (chapter 15). The Jerusalem prophet Agabus travels from Judea to Caesarea to warn Paul through prophetic performance not to go to Jerusalem, despite the presence of Philip's prophesying daughters in the home (21:8–11). The Twelve apostles belong to the *ekklēsia* in Jerusalem. The Apostle Saul/Paul, Barnabas, Simon called Niger, Lucius of Cyrene, and Manaen are associated with the *ekklēsia* at Antioch, Syria (different from Pisidian Antioch in Asia) (chapter 13).

> **Consider and discuss:** Where do you see inclusion and exclusion in the beginning of the movement? What should we replicate and what should we critique and do differently in our contemporary setting? What contemporary movements have begun with diversity and end up as monolithic? What movements began as

monolithic and became more diverse? What accounts for such changes and what can we learn from them?

God as Primary Actor

Peter's Pentecost speech is the first by an apostle and is regarded as paradigmatic or the model missionary speech. At Pentecost, the Apostle Peter emerges as the spokesperson for the Twelve. As we have seen, God the Father both promised and poured out the Holy Spirit upon the earth (1:4; 2:17, 33). A common *kerygma* or proclamation in the speeches to Jewish (Israelites) and mixed audiences of Jews and Gentiles is that *God raised Jesus*. That kerygma is the primary content whether the preacher is Peter or Paul (2:24, 32; 3:15, 26; 5:30; 13:30, 37); the *kerygma* is not found explicitly in the speeches of Stephen, Philip, or Apollos. Recall that in the synoptic Gospels the primary *kerygma* is *The Kingdom of God is near*. However, in Acts it is the equally bold assertion that *God raised Jesus*.

In the speeches in Acts, God also foreknows, promised, pours out God's Spirit, approved of Jesus, made Jesus both Lord and Christ, glorified and exalted Jesus, made a covenant, swore to David, spoke through Jesus, shows no partiality, and anointed and ordained Jesus. God, the creator of heaven and earth and everything in them, does not dwell in human-made shrines. God is the god identified in the altar inscription that reads, "To the unknown god," in Athens (17:23–25).

Violence, Unjust Incarceration, and Internal Conflict

People in authority afflict violence upon subordinates in Acts. These authorities include the Emperor Claudius, some Jewish leaders, *the Jews* (Greek: *hoi Ioudaioi*), crowds of Jews and Gentiles, Saul/Paul, the Council, Roman officials, and certain unnamed apostles. Following the public stoning of Stephen in chapter 7, Paul pursued, persecuted, and jailed members of the *ekklēsia* (*assembly* or anachronistically translated *church*) or the Way (8:3; 9:2). The violence committed against the *ekklēsia* is both verbal and physical. Verbal violence leads to physical violence as when some Jews are persuaded to bear false witness against Stephen (6:8–12). Peter (and John) and Paul and Silas are incarcerated unjustly (4:3–17; 16:19–23). Saul/Paul is never legally tried and punished for persecuting and murdering women and men of the Jesus movement, which is ironic given Stephen's stoning. Prisca and Aquila were expelled from Rome along with other Jews under the Emperor Claudius around 54 CE (8:2; cf. 11:28). King Herod Agrippa I, Rome's puppet King of Judea, physically abuses members of the *ekklēsia,* murders James the brother of Jesus with the sword, and unjustly imprisons Peter (12:1–5).

The construction of *the Jews* as the primary opponents of the Apostle Paul's missionary activities in the synagogues and their violent behavior toward him ostensibly demonstrates an anti-Jewish attitude, even though the phrase *the Jews* functions as a literary device to create a consistent and hostile opponent against the spread of the gospel in the Diaspora and among Gentiles. Paul primarily preaches in Jewish synagogues to both Jews and Gentiles and people from both groups join the movement even as *the Jews* stir up the crowds against Paul and his coworkers.

At times Paul's opponents are not *the* Jews. For example, when Paul and Silas cross the border into Macedonia (Europe) where they encounter the Pythia slave girl (*paidiskē*), Paul expels a spirit from her simply because he is annoyed by her speech and presence. Perhaps Paul is the violent one here? This act constitutes an economic loss to her slave owners (and a loss to her, especially if perhaps she received any of her peculium (slave earnings controlled by the master) with which she might eventually purchase her own freedom and/or use for personal needs. Because of the loss of earnings from Paul's exorcism, the Pythian girl's slave owners accuse Paul and Silas of being Jews (foreigners) who are promoting customs that are illegal for Romans to keep, and they succeed in having them imprisoned. This episode parallels the imprisonment of Peter and John in the first half of the narrative. Of course, Acts ends with Paul under house arrest in Rome.

Consider and discuss: In Acts, religious characters on both sides of the Jesus movement commit violent acts in the name of God. Before Paul joined the Jesus movement he persecuted members of the Way in the name of loyalty to the God of Israel. In our contemporary society, Christians and members of other religions commit verbal and physical violence against other human beings. What do we do with sacred texts that seem to condone violence? How do we construct a nonviolent theology and ethics from such texts?

Internal Conflict

Those who oppose Peter and John in the first half of Acts, however, are some of the Jewish leaders. The abuse from the Jewish leaders against Peter and John in Jerusalem for preaching about the resurrected Jesus as God's messiah is in one sense an example of internal conflict, since the Jesus movement was still a sect within Judaism. But the first example of conflict among members of the Jesus movement is the Ananias and Sapphira episode, which scholars identify as a punishment miracle (5:1–11). Acts contains a number of literary parallels—normally between Peter and Paul but also between minor characters. The preceding story about Barnabas (later Saul/Paul's partner) parallels the Ananias and Sapphira episode as a positive example of compliance to community rules (4:36–37). Barnabas sells all his goods and lays all the profits from the sale at the apostles' feet in fulfillment of the community's expectations (perhaps informal), which is that the members share all things in common so that none of them is impoverished. Scholars question whether or not this goal was an ideal and romanticized view of communal sharing or an achieved reality. If it was an ideal, it was perhaps one worth working toward. Ananias and Sapphira are depicted as lying to the Holy Spirit when they, according to Peter, fail to deposit the full proceeds of the sale of their property with the apostles. This indictment begs the question of whether or not the community rule was voluntary; if voluntary, why the fatal consequences? Peter confronts each separately and both husband and wife drop dead. The husband dies first and the wife, not knowing her husband has died, appears before Peter and lies about the sale price. The narrator announces that the Holy Spirit revealed the lie to Peter. She immediately drops dead and is carry out and buried beside her husband. Would the community deal with all dissenters in the same manner? As a result (or regardless?) the following summary states explicitly that men *and* women joined the *ekklēsia* (5:14); many are undeterred by the couple's fate.

Considering the Ananias and Sapphira episode, readers might not expect the controversy that arose about the neglect of the Hellenist widows in chapter 6. A problem arises when some of the Hellenist widows are being neglected in the service of daily meals. No direct solution is offered, it appears, to the presenting problem. Instead, the apostles decided on a hierarchical solution: The apostles will not serve any tables; they will dedicate themselves solely to the preached word and designate others to perform the ministry (*diakoneō*) of tables. Consequently, seven Hellenist men (*anēr*) full of the Spirit and of Wisdom (Stephen, Philip, Prochorus, Nicanor, Timon, Parmenas and Nicolaus) are selected to do table ministry. However, Stephen and Philip obviously do more than serve meals; both preach the Gospel. In chapter 7, after being falsely accused (6:9-15), Stephen delivers the longest speech in Acts culminating in what could be described as a mob lynching; he is stoned to death. Stephen accused his fellow Jews of murdering the prophets, including Jesus. Stephen further asserts that the Most High does not dwell in houses made with human hands and accuses the Israelites of being "uncircumcised" and of opposing the Holy Spirit.

In chapter 15, as a result of the spread of the Gospel to the Gentiles and their conversion and reception of God's Spirit, a dispute occurs over what the community should require of Gentiles who joined the movement. Some Pharisees and men from Judea want to force the Gentile believers to submit to circumcision (practically speaking such a requirement could be painful, perhaps fatal, and could negatively impact the missional activities among the Gentiles). The leaders of the Jerusalem *ekklēsia* (James the brother of Jesus and other members of the Council including Simon Peter) summon Paul and Barnabas to appear before the Jerusalem Council to report about their experience as missionaries about the Gentiles. They report that the Gentiles received the Spirit just like the Jewish believers. After some discussion, James reaches a decision. The only requirements for the Gentile believers who are turning to God will be to refrain from eating foods offered to idols and from animal flesh not properly killed and drained of its blood (15:19-20). Judas and Silas accompany Paul and Barnabas to Antioch with a letter detailing the Council's decision concerning the Gentile believers in Antioch and Syria (15:23-29).

Gifted, Agentive, and Silenced Women

Although readers are generally enouraged by the number of women included in Acts (and its prequel the Gospel of Luke), feminist scholars note that women in Luke-Acts are silenced; very little, if any, direct speech is attributed to them and when it is, it is negative or ridiculed, as with Sapphira or Rhoda the slave girl (5:7-10; 12:12-17). Recently, some womanist and feminist scholars have attributed more agency to Rhoda and Dorcas, reading them through the complexity of the lived experiences of women of color and women in general. Philip's four prophesying daughters do not prophesy even when the opportunity arises. When the Apostle Paul visits their home and is determined to risk returning to Jerusalem, the prophet Agabus, who travels all the way from Judea to Philip's home in Caesarea to prophesy, warns Paul about the dangers that await him; the daughters are eerily silent (21:8-14). A hermeneutics of suspicion, historical reimagination, and reading between and behind the lines can help restore agency to the women that the narrative has silenced or eclipsed. Perhaps in reality Philip's four daughters did use their prophetic gift and prophesied in support of Paul's decision to go to Jerusalem; but Agabus arrived from Judea to speak a contrary prophetic word.

Prisca remains a positive example of women's agency in Acts; her name is mentioned most often before her husband Aquila's. She appears to take the lead when teaching the eloquent Alexandrian Jewish man Apollos more accurately about the way of God (18:24–28). Perhaps Prisca is at least as eloquent and knowledgeable as Apollos in preaching the scriptures. Although the western manuscript tradition characterizes the unnamed women at Pentecost as wives with their children supporting their men, in the Alexandrian manuscript tradition they are disciples and members of the inner circle; they felt, saw, heard, and received the promise of Holy Spirit just like the apostles in the upper room. This means the women at Pentecost also proclaimed the mighty acts of God in the languages of the diverse visitors gathered to celebrate the feast. When women participated in the early Jesus movement, they did so as gifted and agentive disciples and apostles, even if they are silenced in the text.

Some Conversion Narratives: Simon, Ethiopian Eunuch, Cornelius, and Lydia

When the Hellenist evangelist Philip flees Jerusalem after the outbreak of persecution, the first person he encounters in Samaria is a gifted and powerful man named Simon, who is practicing efficacious magic (8:4–23). Stories about Simon appear in other texts as well such as the apocryphal *Acts of Peter*. Prior to Philip's arrival as a refugee in Samaria, Simon had already developed a positive and admired reputation among the people. In fact, the people, from the least to the greatest, referred to Simon as "the power of God called Great" (8:10; cf. 28:6). Nothing in the narrative implies that Simon's activities were lucrative or predatory. Nevertheless, Philip's powerful acts and preaching surpassed those of Simon. Thus, Simon submits to Phillip's deeds and preaching and is baptized along with many others in Samaria. However, when Peter and John in Jerusalem hear about the mass conversion in Samaria, they arrive to lay hands upon the converts so that they might receive the Holy Spirit. Simon is even more impressed and requests to purchase the power to also lay hands on people in similar manner. Peter rebukes Simon for his wickedness and exhorts him to repent.

Consider and discuss: Imagine yourself in Simon's place as a new believer or as someone who mentors new believers. How might you understand Simon's actions differently from the way Peter understood them? Have you had a similar experience and how did you feel?

Some scholars have argued that the Ethiopian eunuch is the first Gentile convert in Acts, but consider the Roman centurion Cornelius as the first *significant* Gentile convert (8:26–40; chapter 10). The unnamed Ethiopian Eunuch can be understood as a parallel of the Cornelius household conversion story (and Lydia in chapter 16). Both are Gentiles and both are officials and representatives of empire—the eunuch is the chief treasurer of the Candace (queen) of Ethiopia, and Cornelius is a centurion in the Roman military. Both are God-fearers. The eunuch has returned from worshipping in Jerusalem, and owns and is familiar with the Jewish Scriptures; Cornelius is identified as a devout man who fears God. Both Philip and Peter meet the Ethiopian eunuch and Cornelius, respectively, through the divine intervention of an angel.

Both Cornelius and the Ethiopian eunuch's stories can be understood as parallels of the conversion of Lydia and her household. The Apostle Paul visits Lydia as the result of a vision in which a man from Macedonia (Europe) summons him to come and assist them (16:10–15). On the Sabbath, Paul and Silas visit Lydia's synagogue (assembly) of women down by the river worshipping God. Lydia is a worshipper of God, an independent business owner who perhaps both manufacturers and sells purple dyes. Purple signifies royalty and Lydia's customers may be from the upper classes, and thus she may be financially well-off herself. She is also the head of her household and of the women's synagogue that meets by the river. Lydia and her household (like Cornelius and his household) are baptized in response to Paul's preaching. Like the Ethiopian eunuch, there is no mention of them receiving the Holy Spirit. These Gentile conversion narratives represent the missional activities of Philip (one of the Seven and a Hellenist), Peter (Jerusalem), and Paul (Antioch).

The Holy Spirit

In Acts, the Holy Spirit behaves in various ways. At Pentecost, as noted, the Spirit appeared as tongues of fire having entered the room like a powerful wind and rested on each person with the result that they spoke in other languages. This is not a pattern in Acts. People sometimes receive the Holy

Spirit after baptism and the preached word; at other times, people receive the Spirit before baptism. Gentiles and Jews receive the Spirit. Sometimes people speak in other languages and sometimes they do not. Sometimes people receive the Spirit from the laying on of hands and other times this is not the case. In chapter 13, the Holy Spirit personally instructs the prophets and teachers in the *ekklēsia* at Syrian Antioch to lay hands on Paul and Barnabas to consecrate them for their ministry. There is no manifestation of speaking in languages and those who lay hands on them are not among the Twelve. It is God who anointed Jesus with God's Spirit (10:38).

Saul's Call, Commissioning, and Diaspora Mission

Saul is a Jewish name and Paul is a Roman name. God does not change Saul's name when he receives his call on the Damascus Road where he encounters the risen Jesus (chapter 9). Saul/Paul is a devoted Jew throughout the narrative and believed he was demonstrating loyalty to God when he persecuted the members of the *ekklēsia*. Through a blinding light a voice calls Saul's name twice and asks why he is persecuting him. Saul responds, "Who are you, Lord?" The voice responds, "I am Jesus, who you are persecuting" (9:5). Jesus instructs Saul to find the disciple Ananias in Damascus; he will lay hands on him, causing him to see again. The light blinded Paul. The two men with Paul lead him into the city, a three-day journey without food or drink, where Ananias lays hands on him and he receives his sight. At the *ekklēsia* in Syrian Antioch the Apostles Paul and Barnabas are anointed for their work among the Gentiles.

Paul begins his ministry in the synagogue in Damascus where he is recognized and feared by *the Jews* and must escape at night assisted by some disciples (9:19–25). Paul continues and a pattern is developed whereby Paul preaches in the synagogues to Jews and Gentiles and is opposed. Although some scholars insist that Paul completed three missionary journeys in Acts; this is misleading. The gospel is not spread in linear fashion. Paul visits some places more than once and other places he avoids altogether or temporarily. Sometimes the Spirit hinders Paul from entering a region (16:6–7), a man or the Lord in a vision summons him to come or to stay a while (16:9–10; 18:8–11), or Paul is chased out of town because of his preaching and/or people plot to harm him or conspire to kill him (17:5–10; 20:3), among other reasons. Throughout Paul's Diaspora ministry, *the Jews* oppose his proclamation to the Gentiles. On three occasions Paul vows that he is turning to the Gentiles because of opposition from *the Jews*, but each time he returns to preach to Jewish and Gentile audiences in the local synagogues

(13:46; 18:6; 28:8). This depiction of *the Jews* is anti-Jews, even though the term does not refer to the entire Jewish people. Many Jews and Gentiles joined the movement and the apostles themselves are Jewish. The Jesus movement is identified as a sect or party (like the Pharisees, Sadducees, and Essenes) within Judaism to the very end of the narrative (28:24).

Similar to Jesus in the Gospel of Luke, Paul is eventually compelled to go to Jerusalem and is not dissuaded by the prophet Agabus from Judea (Luke 9:51; Acts 19:21). From Jerusalem, Paul will eventually arrive in Rome. Between Jerusalem and Rome Paul will recount his call narrative twice in his defenses before the Roman governor Festus (who succeeded Felix) (22:3–21) and before King Agrippa I (26:9–23). Paul's journey to Rome is punctuated with storms, shipwreck, deliverance, and miracles. But he and the ship's crew arrive safely, and Paul is placed under house arrest where he continues to preach (chapters 27–28).

Although the story ends with Paul under house arrest in Rome, Acts does not give the impression that the spread of the Gospel ceased there, that Rome was the ultimate destination, or that Paul would be the only apostle or evangelist to share the gospel to the ends of the earth. We imagine the Ethiopian eunuch returned to Ethiopia, at one of the farthest ends of the earth, with the conviction that Jesus was God's Messiah mentioned by the prophet Isasiah.

Summary

1. God fulfilled God's promise to send the Holy Spirit.
2. Twelve Apostles served as God's witnesses primarily in Jerusalem and Judea.
3. The Gospel is preached in Jerusalem, Judea, Samaria, and toward the ends of the earth.
4. The Hellenist evangelists and the Apostle Paul and his coworkers proclaim the Gospel in the Diaspora.
5. The Jerusalem *ekklēsia* functions as the headquarters of the Jesus movement.
6. The *ekklēsia* in Syria Antioch serves as the headquarters for the Apostles and Evangelists in the Diaspora.
7. The primary content of the preaching or kerygma is that God raised Jesus.
8. God is the primary actor.

9. God's Spirit is active in diverse ways in Acts.
10. Women are gifted, agentive members of the Jesus movement.
11. Although the mission is consistently opposed, it is undeterred.
12. The story ends in Rome but the preaching of the Gospel does not.

Further Reading

Aymer, Margaret. "Outrageous, Audacious, Courageous, Willful: Reading the Enslaved Girl of Acts 12." In *Womanist Interpretations of the Bible: Expanding the Discourse*, edited by Gay L. Byron and Vanessa Lovelace, 265–90. Semeia Studies. Atlanta: Society of Biblical Literature, 2016.

Bonz, Marianne Palmer. *The Past as Legacy: Luke-Acts and Ancient Epic*. Minneapolis: Fortress, 2000.

Bovon, François. *New Testament and Christian Apocrypha*. Edited by Glenn E. Snyder. Grand Rapids, MI: Baker, 2011.

Calpine, Teresa J. *Women, Work and Leadership in Acts*. Tübingen: Mohr Siebeck, 2014.

Dickerson, Febbie. "Acts 9:36–43: The Many Faces of Tabitha, a Womanist Reading." In *I Found God in Me: A Womanist Biblical Hermeneutics Reader*, edited by Mitzi J. Smith, 297–312. Eugene, OR: Cascade, 2015.

Fitzmyer, Joseph A. *The Acts of the Apostles*. Anchor Bible 31. New York: Doubleday 1998.

Gaventa, Beverly. *Acts*. Abingdon New Testament Commentaries. Nashville: Abingdon, 2003.

González, Justo L. *Acts: The Gospel of the Spirit*. Maryknoll, NY: Orbis, 2001.

Jennings, William James. *Acts*. A Theological Commentary on the Bible. Louisville: Westminster John Knox, 2017.

Levine, Amy-Jill, ed. *A Feminist Companion to the Acts of the Apostles*. Cleveland: Pilgrim, 2004.

Martin, Clarice J. "Acts of the Apostles." In *Searching the Scriptures*. Vol. 2, *A Feminist Commentary*, edited by Elisabeth Schüssler Fiorenza, 763–99. New York: Crossroad, 1994.

———. "A Chamberlain's Journey and the Challenge of Interpretation of Liberation." *Semeia* 47 (1989) 105–35.

Matthews, Shelley, and Benny Tat-Siong Liew. *The Acts of The Apostles: An Introduction and Study Guide: Taming the Tongues of Fire*. New York: T. & T. Clark, 2017.

Pervo, Richard I. *Acts of the Apostles*. Hermeneia. Minneapolis: Fortress, 2009.

Reimer, Ivoni Richter. *Women in the Acts of the Apostles: A Feminist Liberation Perspective*. Minneapolis: Fortress, 1995.

Skinner, Matthew L. *Intrusive God, Disruptive Gospel: Encountering the Divine in the Book of Acts*. Grand Rapids, MI: Brazos, 2015.

Smith, Mitzi J. *The Construction of the Other in the Acts of the Apostles: Charismatics, the Jews, and Women*. Princeton Theological Monograph Series 154. Eugene, OR: Pickwick, 2011.

———. "Epistemologies, Pedagogies, and the Subordinated Other: Luke's Parallel Construction of the Ethiopian Eunuch and the Alexandrian Apollos." In *Womanist Sass and Talk Back: Social (In)Justice, Intersectionality and Biblical Interpretation*, 46–69. Eugene, OR: Cascade, 2018.

Williams, Demetrius K. "The Acts of the Apostles." *In True to Our Native Land. An African American Commentary of the New Testament*, edited by Brian Blount et al., 213–48. Minneapolis: Fortress, 2007.

Section III

Pauline Epistles

CHAPTER 15

Significance of Paul as a Jewish Man in Diaspora

AFTER JESUS, PAUL IS the most important yet controversial figure in the NT. It is often believed that he wrote thirteen letters in the NT. Typically, they are divided into three groups: Paul's undisputed letters (Romans, 1–2 Corinthians, Galatians, Philippians, 1 Thessalonians, and Philemon); Deutero-Pauline Letters (Ephesians, Colossians, and 2 Thessalonians); and the Pastoral Epistles (1 Tim, 2 Tim, and Titus). But modern scholarship doubts Paul's authorship of the last two groups, which have different writing styles and conflicting theological views. For example, whereas Paul affirms women's place in the *ekklēsia*, the Pastoral Letters teach that women are subordinate to men. Whereas Paul discourages marriage, the Pastoral Letters encourage it. The truth is that he was very influential to early believers during and after his life. That is why these later epistles were written in his name.

Paul was admired as a great missionary and theologian during and after his life. But he was also a controversial figure because of his gospel of faith, which has often been misunderstood as a law-free gospel. While some Jews thought that he was a betrayer to their tradition, some Gentiles thought that he paved a new way of salvation through faith, not by the law. But he does not agree with either position. Paul accepted Jesus as the long-awaited Jewish Messiah and interpreted Jewish scriptures from the perspective of Jesus's life and death.

Paul's Early Life in Diaspora

Paul's undisputed letters give us some information about his former life and family background (Phil 3:4–6; Gal 1:13–14). He was a Pharisee and zealous about the law. Because of his zeal for God and the law, he persecuted the *ekklēsia* of God. Paul also says that he comes from the esteemed lineage of a

Jewish family. As a Pharisee, he was supposed to know well the traditions of the fathers and keep them thoroughly. This means that he kept Jewish laws and rituals, including circumcision and dietary regulations. He maintained a purity boundary between Jews and Gentiles. He was supposed to live a life of privilege as a learned Jew in the Diaspora. In the Acts of the Apostles, it is repeatedly stated that Paul is a Roman citizen, which grants him rights and privileges others do not have (chs. 21-23); his letters are silent on this issue. Silence neither affirms nor disputes.

In the Diaspora world, Judaism was highly regarded by the Roman authorities and populace. In general, Jews were given the privilege of self-rule in their communities. They maintained their tradition and cooperated with the Roman authorities. In this very hospitable environment, members of the early *ekklēsia* are part of or engage with (in the case of Gentiles) the Jewish communities. Jewish leaders felt a threat or challenge because this newly emerging *ekklēsia* could replace them. In fact, these new believers talked about the God of Jews and Jewish scriptures and claimed that Jesus, the crucified one, was the Jewish Messiah. So Paul, as a Pharisee, was also intolerant of their view of God and the Messiah. He went out to disrupt the *ekklēsia* gatherings, violently persecuting the *ekklēsia* or *Way* of God (Gal 1:13). Paul may be compared to the young Jewish law student, Yigal Amir, who assassinated the prime minister Yitzhak Rabin in 1995 who tried to make a peace deal with Palestinians. Amir felt that Rabin violated the Jewish law concerning the promised land.

Paul as an Apostle for the Gentiles

But something happened to Paul. He says God revealed the Son to him (Gal 1:16). However, we do not know exactly what happened to him from his own letters. Acts tells us about the dramatic experience of meeting the risen Lord on the Damascus Road (9:3-8; 22:6-11; 26:13-19). But scholars believe that *Acts* portrays Paul as a perfect missionary or an ideal apostle. Whatever happened to him, his word is simple that God revealed the Son to him (Gal 1:16). Since then, he changed the course of his life with full dedication to the new mission for the Gentiles. Through his revelatory experience, he changed a few of his views about God, God's Messiah, and the world. First, Paul confesses that he was unenlightened because of a zeal for God (Rom 10:2). He thought that his God was for Jews only and that God made a special covenant with them only. But he realizes that God is the God of both Jews and Gentiles, as Rom 3:29-31 says:

> Or is God the God of Jews only? Is he not the God of Gentiles also? Yes, of Gentiles also, since God is one; and he will justify the circumcised on the ground of faith and the uncircumcised through that same faith. Do we then overthrow the law by this faith? By no means! On the contrary, we uphold the law.

As a Jewish Diaspora man, he always believed that God was for Jews only. But now as an enlightened Jewish man he sees God differently. God is the God of all. Paul's call is for this good news about God, as he states in Rom 1:1: "Paul, a slave of Jesus Christ, called to be an apostle, set apart for the good news of God." His fundamental conviction is that God loved the whole world and that God's covenant is extended to the Gentiles. Second, Paul thought that Jesus could not be the Messiah for Jews because he was crucified and failed to bring God's *basileia* to Israel. But now he believes that the crucified Jesus is the Messiah, the Son of God, who demonstrated God's righteousness or justice to the world through faith (Rom 1:1–17; 3:21–26). Paul is very much impressed by Jesus's faith that embodies God's rule on earth. Third, he senses that his new call from God is for the Gentiles. From beginning to end, he worked as an apostle for the Gentiles, considering Peter to be an apostle to the Jews (Gal 2:8; Rom 11:13). His last will is to go to Spain—considered to be one of the ends of the earth—to preach the good news of God. We do not know whether he made his final mission trip to Spain or not. Most probably, he could not make it, because according to church tradition, he was martyred in Rome about 65 CE during Nero's reign as Emperor (Eusebius, *Eccl. Hist.* 2.25.5). The most important change in Paul's life is his unwavering passion for the Gentiles. He became the apostle for the Gentiles. With a new understanding of God, the Messiah, and the Law, Paul lived a simple life and spent all his energy and time on the good news of God through Jesus Christ. His diasporic life experience as a Pharisee turns to embracing the whole world as a Diaspora. In other words, for him, now the world must seek and turn to God. His Hellenistic philosophy and culture may have also impacted his mission in the sense that the world is one.

The Centerpiece of Paul's Gospel

Paul as an apostle for the Gentiles propagates his gospel (2:16; 16:25) featuring three mutual elements: "the righteousness of God" (*dikaiosynē tou theou*), "faith of Christ" (*pistis christou*), and "the body of Christ" (*soma christou*). First, I take the interpretative position that "the righteousness of God" means God's righteousness and not a righteousness from God. God is the one who is righteous, steadfast, and faithful (cf. Rom 1:16–17; 3:21–26).

For Paul, God is the beginning and end of the good news. Even Jesus is subordinate to God (cf. 1 Cor 15:28). In Rom 1:1 and 15:16, God is the good news (the good news of God as God's good news). The good news is that God's righteousness is revealed from faith to faith (Rom 1:16). Second, the phrase "faith of Christ" (Rom 3:21–22; Gal 2:16) means Christ's faith and not the believer's faith in him. Christ is the one who exemplified the love of God and revealed God's identity or character. He was faithful to God and advocated for the poor and marginalized. The result is his death, which ironically reveals the power and wisdom of God (1 Cor 1:25). In other words, Jesus was crucified because he challenged the wisdom of humans and the world. The cross of Jesus is both a tragic and loving event. It is tragic because Jesus was killed by Roman authorities; it is loving because he did not give up on proclaiming the good news of God. All Jesus did had to do with "the gospel of Christ" (Gal 1:7; Phil 1:27).

Third, the phrase "the body of Christ" in 1 Cor 12:27 means a Christic body in the sense that the Corinthians must embody Christ. Traditionally, "the body of Christ" in 1 Cor 12:27 has been understood as a metaphorical organism: a body (like the *ekklēsia*) belonging to Christ. But in 1 Cor 12:12–27, Paul understands "the body of Christ" mainly as Christ's own body and Christ-like body. The former refers to his crucified body, and the latter to believer's embodiment of Christ. The point is that Christians (followers of Jesus) must follow the way of Christ, which means to be led by the Spirit, as Rom 8:13–14 says, "For if you live according to the flesh, you will die; but if by the Spirit you put to death the deeds of the body, you will live. For all who are led by the Spirit of God are children of God."

For Paul, Christian means to die with Christ and live to God. His logic about Jesus's death is not that "because Jesus died, I do not die" but that "because he died, I also died." Second Corinthians 5:14–15 presents this idea: "For the love of Christ urges us on, because we are convinced that one has died for all; therefore all have died. And he died for all, so that those who live might live no longer for themselves, but for him who died and was raised for them."

The above threefold gospel of Paul is seen in 1 Cor 1:9: "God is faithful; by him you were called into the fellowship of his Son, Jesus Christ our Lord." Christians are called into the fellowship (*koinōnia*) of Jesus whom God sent. Similarly, it is also seen in Rom 3:22: "God's righteousness through Jesus Christ's faith for all who have faith." This means that Christ's faith alone is not enough for God's righteousness. People must have faith through which they participate in God or in Christ so that God's righteousness would be effective to them.

Faith and the Law

Regarding faith and the law, Paul never says that faith overthrows the law; rather, he affirms the law in Rom 3:31: "Do we then overthrow the law by this faith? By no means! On the contrary, we uphold the law." The law is not wrong by itself as if it were an imperfect means of salvation. Rather, what is wrong with it is zeal for it. In other words, the law should not be a condition or hindrance to becoming children of God. Indeed, the very first thing that people need is not the law but God's grace and promise. For example, God called Abraham who was an alien, old, and weak (Gen 12:1–4). Then Abraham's faith follows God's grace. The law was given later through Moses to guide and bless the Israelites. What comes first is God's grace, which is followed by faith. While the law is holy and good, it cannot precede faith. Faith has been working through God's people, from Abraham to Jesus and to all Christians. So even the law must be kept through faith. Faith is working for both Jews and Gentiles, as he says: "God is one; and he will justify the circumcised on the ground of faith and the uncircumcised through that same faith" (Rom 3:30).

Therefore, for Paul, the problem is not the law *per se* but the Jews' unenlightened mind that does not see the importance of God's love for all. In addition, they must accept Jesus as the Jewish Messiah who fulfilled the law's purpose. Gal 5:14 reads: "For the whole law is summed up in a single commandment, 'You shall love your neighbor as yourself'" (cf. Rom 10:4; 13:9). Otherwise, Jesus did not repeal or replace the law but fulfilled it (cf. Matt 5:17).

Considering the above clarification, "justification by faith" needs to be reevaluated. It does not mean that the law is an impossible means of salvation. The law is still holy and perfect in the sense that it is God's gift. Faith means to trust God and live by it. That is what Hab 2:4, as quoted in Rom 1:17, says: "The one who is righteous lives by faith." If faith and the law are understood this way, Paul's gospel does not repudiate the place of Israel, as he vehemently argues in Rom 9–11. Earlier, he clearly said that the faithlessness of Jews cannot "nullify the faithfulness of God" (Rom 3:3). Even though many Jews still do not accept Jesus as the expected Messiah, he still believes that God will save them (Rom 11:26).

Further Reading

Bassler, Jouette. *Navigating Paul: An Introduction to Key Theological Concepts.* Louisville, KY: Westminster John Knox, 2006.

Charles, Ronald. *Paul and the Politics of Diaspora*. Minneapolis, MN: Fortress, 2014.

Kim, Yung Suk. *A Theological Introduction to Paul's Letters: Exploring a Threefold Theology of Paul*. Eugene, OR: Cascade, 2011.

Lopez, Davina. *The Apostle to the Conquered: Reimagining Paul's Mission*. Minneapolis, MN: Fortress, 2008.

Sanders, E. P. *Paul: The Apostle's Life, Letters, and Thought*. Minneapolis, MN: Fortress, 2015.

Stendahl, Krister. *Paul among Jews and Gentiles and Other Essays*. Minneapolis, MN: Fortress, 1976.

CHAPTER 16

The Body of Christ

THE "BODY" (*SOMA*) IS a complex term in Paul's letters. It refers to the human body, the community, and the site of life. Even if Paul refers to the community as a body, the meaning is not obvious because we need to determine how he uses it. Two options of interpretation are possible. One is the traditional reading in that "the body of Christ" is read as a metaphorical organism. Thus "the body of Christ" is an *ekklēsia*/community that belongs to Christ. The other is an alternative reading in that "the body of Christ" may be read as a metaphor for a way of living. Thus, "the body of Christ" is Christic body. We will see more about this later.

The Body in the Greco-Roman World

Stoicism is a dominant philosophy in the Roman Empire and views the body as a hierarchical organism. Therefore, society is also seen as hierarchical just as the body is. Elites rule the body and all others are ruled by them. The head is the control tower that governs other parts in the body. In this system, people are to serve this unified one body whose head is Roman Emperor. In this body, unity or concord (*homonoia*) is emphasized to prevent people from demanding justice and equality. In this regard, unity is the language of control. Here is what the fable of Menenius tells: "Life is not unfair because you eat all the time without working. We are not going to work for you any longer." Then the belly said it like this: "That is fine with me if you do not work any longer; but you have to know that if you do not work, I will starve to death and then you will also die." Here, the rhetorical emphasis is that the lower classes must stay in their place without complaining.

In the Roman Empire, some slaves were tortured and crucified by Rome, as Jesus was. We can hardly talk about Jesus's cross without thinking about the suffering and torturing of human bodies in this time. They were considered no-bodies even though they were worthy of living a good life.

Roman satirists such as Horace and Juvenal wrote about the slaves' deaths and their horrifying scenes of the crucifixion.[1] Chariton also recorded the crucifixion of a group of slaves.[2] We also must know that Roman philosophers and elites avoided the topic of crucifixion or suffering altogether because it was too hard even to think about it.

Paul's Body Politics

Paul's body politics differs from that of the Stoics. In 1 Cor 12:12–26, he articulates the Christ-like community where all parts, including the head, are treated equally. All parts, wherever they are attached, are one because they suffer and rejoice together. For him, the body is one because everybody is taken care of equally in the community. The body is one not because all parts are placed in one organism but because they are all taken care of equally and respectfully. The weaker part is honored more because it needs recovery. Paul states this in 1 Cor 1:26–29: "Consider your own call, brothers and sisters: not many of you were wise by human standards, not many were powerful, not many were of noble birth. But God chose what is foolish in the world to shame the wise; God chose what is weak in the world to shame the strong; God chose what is low and despised in the world, things that are not, to reduce to nothing things that are, so that no one might boast in the presence of God" (1 Cor 1:26–29).

"The Body of Christ" in Paul's Undisputed Letters

First, "the body of Christ" means Christ's physical body. For example, "the body of Christ" at the Lord's Supper (1 Cor 10:16; 11:20–30) is his real body that was given for the love of God. A similar use is also found in Rom 7:4: "In the same way, my friends, you have died to the law through *the body of Christ*, so that you may belong to another, to him who has been raised from the dead in order that we may bear fruit for God." Here "the body of Christ" is Jesus's real body, especially his crucifixion. For Paul, the crucifixion of Jesus is important to Christian faith because it shows the wisdom and strength of God, as he says in 1 Cor 1:23–25: "but we proclaim Christ crucified, a stumbling block to Jews and foolishness to Gentiles, but to those who are the called, both Jews and Greeks, Christ the power of God and the wisdom of God. For God's foolishness is wiser than human wisdom, and God's weakness is stronger than human strength."

---

1. Horace, *Satires* 1.8.8–13; Juvenal, *Satires* 14.77–78.
2. Chariton, *Chaereas and Callirhoe* 4.2.

There is another use of "the body of Christ" that refers to the community. Here, we have two options for interpretation. On the one hand, the body is understood as a metaphorical organism, as we saw before: "a body as the church belonging to Christ." Here the body is perceived as a social body. But there is an alternative reading, based on a different conception of the body: that is, the body as a site of living. "The body of Christ" means "Christ-like body" (or Christic body). This use of the genitive case is called an "attributive genitive," as in Rom 6:6: "the body of sin" as "the sinful body." In this attributive genitive reading, the body is understood not as a social body but as Christic body. This alternative reading of "the body of Christ" is found in 1 Cor 12:27 and Rom 12:5 to which we now turn.

In 1 Cor 12:12-27, Paul talks about the human body as an analogy and relates it to Christ: "For just as the body is one and has many members, and all the members of the body, though many, are one body, so it is with Christ" (1 Cor 12:12). This saying sounds like Stoicism's rhetoric of unity (*homonoia*). But that is not the case because Paul perceives the body differently as a site of mutual care and solidarity, as is with Christ. In Christ, all different members work together and take care of each other. They are led by the one Spirit; therefore, they are one body: Jews or Greeks, slaves or free (1 Cor 12:13). He goes on to say in 12:14-26 that many members work together to help each other and do not control others. In this community, the weaker parts are indispensable, the less honorable parts are clothed with greater honor, and the less respectable parts are treated with greater respect (12:22-23). God is the center of the community since "God arranged the members of the body, each one of them, as he chose" (12:18). All parts, including the head and feet, are under God. No part can claim that "I am superior to you." In Christ, there is no dissension within the body because all are united to Christ. So Paul says, "If one member suffers, all suffer together with it; if one member is honored, all rejoice together with it" (12:26). Finally, in 12:27, he says, "Now you are the body of Christ and individually members of it." If we take "the body of Christ" as an attributive genitive (Christic body), this statement is an exhortation to the Corinthian community. An alternative translation of 12:27 will be as follows: "You are a Christic body and have to embody Christ individually and communally." This sense of the body is also found in 1 Cor 6:20: "Glorify God in your body."

In Rom 12:4-5, Paul has a similar idea about "the body of Christ" as in 1 Cor 12:12-27: "For as in one body we have many members, and not all the members have the same function, so we, who are many, are *one body in Christ*, and individually we are members one of another." These words in Rom 12:4-5 sound like Stoicism. But it is not so because the community must be maintained "in Christ," which is a modal dative: Christly manner.

That is, the community as one body must imitate Christ in his spirit. In Rom 12:15–17, Paul advises the Roman *ekklēsiai* to live according to this manner of Christ: "Rejoice with those who rejoice, weep with those who weep. Live in harmony with one another; do not be haughty, but associate with the lowly; do not claim to be wiser than you are. Do not repay anyone evil for evil, but take thought for what is noble in the sight of all."

"The Body of Christ" in the Deutero-Pauline Letters

"The body of Christ" also appears in the Deutero-Pauline Letters whose Pauline authorship is disputed. In these letters, "the body of Christ" is clearly used as a metaphorical organism and it refers to the *ekklēsia*. In Paul's undisputed letters, he never places "the body of Christ" with the *ekklēsia* side by side. Rather, he makes a distinction between "the body of Christ" and the *ekklēsia*. While the church is being built up (1 Cor 14:4, 5, 12), "the body of Christ" refers to Christ's real body or Christ-like body. But in the Deutero-Pauline Letters, "the body of Christ" is understood as a metaphorical organism. That is, "the body of Christ" is the *ekklēsia* whose head is Christ (Eph 4:12). For example, Col 1:24 says, "For the sake of his body, that is, the church." Also, in Col 1:18, Jesus is "the head of the body, the church." Similarly, Eph 1:22–23 confirms this use of the body: "And he has put all things under his feet and has made him the head over all things for the *ekklēsia*, which is his body, the fullness of him who fills all in all." It is very interesting to see that these letters do not draw on Christ's real body or crucifixion.

Further Reading

Bryant, K. Edwin. *Paul and the Rise of the Slave: Death and Resurrection of the Oppressed in the Epistle to the Romans*. Boston, MA: Brill, 2016.

Copeland, M. Shawn. *Enfleshing Freedom: Body, Race and Being*. Minneapolis: Fortress, 2009.

Kim, Yung Suk. *Christ's Body in Corinth: The Politics of a Metaphor*. Minneapolis, MN: Fortress, 2008.

Martin, Dale B. *The Corinthian Body*. New Haven, CT: Yale University Press, 1995.

Welborn, Laurence. *Paul's Summons to Messianic Life*. New York: Columbia University Press, 2015.

CHAPTER 17

Romans

One has not only a legal but a moral responsibility to obey just laws. Conversely, one has a moral responsibility to disobey unjust laws.

—Martin Luther King Jr., *Letter from a Birmingham Jail*

God loves human beings. God loves the world. Not an ideal human, but human beings as they are; not an ideal world, but the real world. What we find repulsive in their opposition to God, what we shrink back from with pain and hostility ... this is for God the ground of unfathomable love.

—Dietrich Bonhoeffer[1]

Romans at a Glance

1. Romans is the longest letter Paul wrote.
2. It was sent to Christians in Rome.
3. Paul never visited Rome and did not found any assemblies there.
4. Church tradition says that Peter was the first bishop of the Roman church. We do not know how Roman Christianity began or who led it.

---

1. Bonhoeffer, *Ethics*, 84.

5. Romans is also a situational letter dealing with some local *ekklēsia* issues such as Jews-Gentiles relations or misunderstanding about faith and the law.
6. Paul defends his gospel of faith that does not reject the law or Israel.
7. Paul wants to receive support from the Roman Christians when he goes to Spain for the last mission trip.
8. The grand theme of the letter is "the gospel" (*euangelion*) for which Paul says he was called and set apart.
9. Paul's gospel has a threefold aspect: God's gospel, Christ's gospel, and his gospel that talks about God and his Son.
10. Rom 1:16–17 identifies the themes of the letter: "For I am not ashamed of *the gospel*; it is *the power of God* for salvation to everyone who has *faith*, to the Jew first and also to the Greek. For in it *the righteousness of God* is revealed through faith for faith; as it is written, 'The one who is righteous will live by faith..'" Therefore, it is very important to understand "the good news of God," "the righteousness of God," and "faith of Christ."

Introduction

ROMANS IS THE MOST well-known, cherished letter among other letters of Paul. Paul never visited Rome and did not found churches there. But he was supposed to know the Roman *ekklēsia* situation through believers expelled from Rome due to the edict of Claudius (ca. 50 CE). The most burning issues in Rome are two-fold: Gentile arrogance that negates the place of Israel in God's salvation drama and their misunderstanding about God's gospel. For example, Gentile believers tended to become antinomian (lawless) and rejected the law. But Paul affirms both the law and the place of Israel. In this chapter, we will see the occasion and purpose of Romans and explore some crucial theological concepts such as "the good news of God" (*euangelion tou theou*), "the righteousness of God" (*dikaiosynē tou theou*), and "faith of Christ" (*pistis christou*). We will also examine Paul's view of sin, law, and freedom. Most importantly, we explore Paul's passion for the Gentile mission and his universal vision of salvation for all.

Chapter Contents

1. The Occasion and Purpose of the Letter
2. "The Good News of God" (*euangelion tou theou*)
3. "The Righteousness of God" (*dikaiosynē tou theou*)
4. "Faith of Christ" (*pistis christou*)
5. Sin, Law, and Freedom
6. Salvation Drama
7. Paul and Politics

The Occasion and Purpose of the Letter

Paul writes Romans to defend his gospel and garner support for his final mission to Spain in the future. He thinks that he covered the eastern part of the hemisphere with his gospel preaching (Rom 15:19) and aims to go to Spain by way of Rome. He sees himself as "a minister of Christ Jesus to the Gentiles in the priestly service of the gospel of God" and believes the Gentiles are an acceptable offering to God (Rom 15:16). Since Spain is the end of the west, he wishes to finish his mission there. To do that last job, he knows that he needs support from the Roman Christians. More importantly, he also needs their understanding about his gospel. In fact, some Romans misunderstood his gospel as law-free in the sense that faith alone matters. But his gospel is not law-free. Rather, his gospel is a law-affirming, law-discerning, law-fulfilling gospel, based on Christ's work and God's righteousness.

Paul also deals with other issues in the Roman assemblies. Even though he did not found assemblies there, he heard about them through some Jewish Christian missionaries such as Prisca and Aquila, who were possibly expelled from Rome due to the edict of Claudius. These issues include Gentile arrogance and the negation of Israel. Gentile Christians think that their faith alone matters and that they do not need the law. But Paul disagrees with them and vehemently defends his gospel of faith in Rom 1–8. He also defends the place of Israel in Rom 9–11, based on God's promise for Israelites. After Rom 9–11, he moves to other issues in the community such as how to live as members of the community (Rom 12), how to deal with governing authorities (Rom 13), and how to make one united community in Christ (Rom 14–15).

"The Good News of God" (*euangelion tou theou*)

In Rom 1:1, Paul says that he is "a slave of Jesus Christ, called to be an apostle, set apart for the good news of God." Namely, his mission is for the good news of God. "The good news of God" means God's good news or the good news about God. God is the good news because he is faithful and righteous. God makes a covenant with Abraham and his descendants. Moreover, he extends his covenant to Gentiles through Jesus Christ. God is the good news because he cares for the poor and weak. God is the source and initiator of the good news. See below how God is characterized by Paul:

- God has the power for salvation (1:16; 11:23)
- God is righteous (1:17; 3:21–22, 25; 10:3)
- God shows no partiality (2:1)
- God is faithful (3:3; 11:1–8)
- God is justice (3:5)
- God is grace (5:15)
- God is steadfast (8:39; 15:5)
- God is merciful (9:15–33; 11:30–31; 12:1; 15:9)
- God raised the dead (10:9)
- God is sovereign (11:33)
- God's rule is about righteousness (14:17)
- God is the truth (15:8)

God's good news is proclaimed and lived out by Jesus, "who was descended from David according to the flesh and was declared to be Son of God with power according to the spirit of holiness by resurrection from the dead" (1:3–4). Paul says that Christians "have received grace and apostleship to bring about the obedience of faith among all the Gentiles for the sake of his name" (1:5). God's good news is exemplified by Jesus, and what Christ did for God constitutes "the good news of Christ" (1:9; 15:9). Paul's gospel is to proclaim God's good news through Jesus. Thus, we may think of three aspects of gospel: God's gospel, Christ's gospel, and Paul's gospel. These are linked with one another. The starting point of the gospel is God. Jesus as the Son of God revealed God's righteousness through his faith. Paul's gospel is to proclaim this gospel of God and of Jesus Christ through his word and action. He is convinced that the gospel is "the power of God for salvation to everyone who has faith, to the Jew first and also to the Greek" (1:16). In the gospel, "God's righteousness is revealed through faith for faith; as it is written, 'The one who is righteous will live by faith'" (1:17). He is not ashamed of this gospel because it is God's power for salvation. For this gospel, he does everything he can and wants to go to Spain—the end of earth (15:19–20).

The Greek Genitive Case

Unlike English, Greek has a case that tells us a noun's function. The genitive case is one of the five cases in Greek: nominative case, genitive case, accusative case, dative case, and vocative case. The nominative case speaks of the subject. The genitive case involves possessive relations. While the accusative case speaks of the direct object, the dative case points to the indirect objective. The vocative case has to do with addressing someone. Our concern is about the genitive case, which regulates possessive relations: "A of B." In English, the possessive relation is expressed with the preposition "of"; for example, "the love of God." But in Greek, there is no preposition "of," and therefore, the genitive case (the corresponding suffix to a noun) is used. Namely, "of God" is made in one word "God" with a suffix attached. So in Greek, the love of God is expressed as follows: *agapē theou*. The word *theou* corresponds to "of God." But the real issue is how to translate or interpret the Greek genitive phrases. For example, "the love of God" can be either a subjective genitive case or an objective genitive case, depending on its context. If "the love of God" means God's love, this genitive is called a subjective genitive because God is the subject of love ("God loves us"). An example of this is found in Rom 8:39, as Paul says that nothing shall "separate us from the love of God." On other occasions, "the love of God" can mean our love for God. If this is the case, this genitive case is an objective genitive because God is the object of love ("We love God" or "God is loved by us"). In the end, the difference between the subjective genitive and objective genitive is the heaven-and-earth difference because while in the former God loves us, in the latter we love God.

In Romans, there are important genitive cases that we need to tackle and explore: "the righteousness of God" (Rom 1:17; 3:21–26); "faith of Christ (Rom 3:22; cf. Gal 2:16). But the meaning of these genitive phrases must be decided, based on their context. "The righteousness of God" can mean "God's righteousness" (a subjective genitive) or "a righteousness from God" (an objective genitive). God's righteousness means that God is righteous. "A righteousness from God" means that a righteousness comes from God so that a person may possess it. Here, the question is: With whose righteousness are we concerned: God's or an individual's? Again, the difference between these two is like the heaven and earth difference. We need to know in what sense Paul used this genitive phrase and will come back to this issue later.

Likewise, "faith of Christ" needs to be examined whether it is "Christ's faith" (a subjective genitive) or "faith in Christ" (an objective genitive). What does Paul mean by this genitive phrase? For example, how can we translate and interpret Rom 3:22, which has two genitive cases: "the righteousness of God" and "faith of Christ Jesus"? Does he say that God's righteousness came through Christ's faith? In this case, both genitive cases are treated as the subjective genitive. Or does he say that God's righteousness came through faith in Christ? Or does he mean that an individual's righteousness came through faith in Christ? Most English translations render "faith of Christ" as "faith in Christ." But this translation can be challenged because Paul does not seem to mean the believer's faith. We will come back to this issue later.

"The Righteousness of God"
(*dikaiosynē tou theou*)

"The righteousness of God" (*dikaiosynē tou theou*) is a central theme in Romans. It appears in Rom 1:17, which is considered a thematic verse, and in 3:21–22, which repeats the idea expressed in 1:16–17. Before exploring what this means in Romans, let us examine the Hebrew word *tsedeq*, which means steadfast love or righteousness; sometimes it can be translated as justice. This word is used to describe who God is or what he did, and indeed, it is one of the most frequently appearing nouns in the Hebrew Bible. In other words, God is the one who is steadfast and righteous. There are several ways of describing God's righteousness in the Hebrew Bible. First, God's covenantal faithfulness stands out as he makes a covenant with Abraham and his descendants. Abraham was not worthy to be called by God. It is God's initiative of love and call that makes him start a new life. Second, God's justice and righteousness stand out as he deeply cares about justice in society. God speaks through Amos: "But let justice roll down like waters, and righteousness like an ever-flowing stream" (Amos 5:24). God does not want rich sacrifices at the altar but wants his people to live justly in honor of each other. This is because God is holy, they must live accordingly (Lev 20:26). God also speaks through Micah and demands justice, kindness, and a humble mind: "O mortal, what is good; and what does the LORD require of you but to do justice, and to love kindness, and to walk humbly with your God?" (Mic 6:8). Third, God's righteousness also can be understood as his promise of salvation and justice in the future when his people were under unspeakable, horrendous suffering. This is the issue of theodicy in that God's justice is questioned: Where is God when his people suffer? In this kind of a senseless world, God promises the news of salvation to them. Dan 12:1–2 may be read in that light when Israelites need hope in God when they were under foreign domination and many innocent people were killed. God will reward the righteous ones and punish the evil ones. This expectation about God's dealing with the future developed further, and people aspired for the future deliverer of Israel. This is the messianic expectation that Jews have had for a long time until first–second centuries CE.

Paul uses the Greek *dikaiosynē*, an equivalent for Hebrew *tsedeq*, with God in the form of the genitive case: *dikaiosynē tou theou* ("the righteousness of God"). What does he mean by this phrase? Does he mean God's righteousness (a subjective genitive)? Or does he mean "a righteousness from God"? The answer seems clear: it is God's righteousness, just as the Hebrew Bible describes God as the one who is righteous. Throughout his letters, Paul's theology is God-centered. In other words, his faith is in God who is righteous. This idea of God's righteousness is the main theme of Romans. For example, Rom 1:17 reads: "In it the righteousness of God is revealed through faith for faith; as it is written, 'The one who is righteous will live by faith.'" God is the one who is righteous and his goodness can be seen and felt through faith. In other words, through faith for faith, one can live, and that life is a righteous one. That is what Hab 2:4 means: The righteous one shall live by faith. It is not the other way around, as Luther understands this verse and translates it from a doctrinal perspective of "justification by faith": "The one who is righteous by faith shall live." But the original context and syntax of Hab 2:4 does not support Luther's translation here. Habakkuk's concern is about God's silence against rampant evil and the righteous person's suffering, and so he complains to God. Then God answers him that no matter what happens to God's people, they must live by faith.

In Rom 3:21–22, "the righteousness of God" also appears and must be God's righteousness, too: "But now, apart from law, the righteousness of God has been disclosed, and is attested by the law and the prophets, the righteousness of God through faith of Jesus Christ for all who believe." "The righteousness of God" is used twice. In verse 21: God's righteousness has been disclosed. This saying of Paul may be close to what Jesus said in Mark 1:15: "The time is fulfilled, and God's rule or reign has come near." Paul, just like Jesus, thinks that now is the time of salvation because God appeared in the world. God's rule or God's righteousness has come into the world. Therefore, the idea is that God, not the Roman Emperor, must be the center and source of life. In verse 22, Paul repeats God's righteousness but makes it clear that it came through Christ's faithfulness.

Faith

The Hebrew word *emunah* and the Greek word *pistis* connote similar concepts of fidelity, steadfastness, or trust. In the Hebrew Bible, "living by faith" is important, as Hab 2:4 says, "The righteous shall live by their faith (*be emunato*)." In other words, faith and life are inseparable from each other. Paul also quotes from Hab 2:4 and says similarly in Rom 1:17: "The righteous one shall live by faith." Paul agrees with Habakkuk that faith is not a concept of belief alone, but it is faithful living or trusting God. In the Gospels, Jesus has faith in God and proclaims the good news of him. Paul also has faith in God and in Christ. For Paul, faith is "work-in-action" because of Jesus. After Paul, this concept of faith shifted to a concept of teaching or knowledge (Col 1:4; 2:7; Eph 1:15; 2:8–9; 3:12–17; 4:5–13; 1 Tim 1:5, 13–14; 4:6; 2 Tim 3:15).

"Faith of Christ" (*pistis christou*)

We have explored "the righteousness of God" as God's righteousness, which has been disclosed through Christ's faith ("faith of Christ" as Christ's faith). Namely, *pistis christou* in Rom 3:22 must be a subjective genitive. It is Christ's faith that demonstrated God's righteousness in the world. Therefore, the traditional translation and interpretation of *pistis christou* as "faith in Christ" is hard to accept. Jesus Christ revealed who God is through his life and death. All Jesus did was to testify to God's righteousness. If Paul wanted to emphasize the believer's faith in Christ, he would have used a prepositional phrase *pistis en christo*, which plainly means "faith in Christ." Furthermore, if he had meant an objective genitive sense of *pistis christou*, he would not need the last part "for all who have faith" because this is redundancy.

A better reading in Rom 3:22 would be from a threefold gospel formula: God's righteousness, Christ's faith, and the believer's faith. That is, God's righteousness came through Jesus's faith and it would be effective for all who have faith of Jesus. Christians must identify their faith with Christ. Jesus's faith alone is not enough because God's righteousness cannot be a reality if they do not participate in Christ. In Rom 3:26, again, Paul says: "it was to prove at the present time that he (God) himself is righteous and that he justifies the one who has the *faith of Jesus*."

Hilasterion (Rom 3:25)

"Whom God put forward as a sacrifice of atonement by his blood, effective through faith. He did this to show his righteousness, because in his divine forbearance he had passed over the sins previously committed" (Rom 3:25, NRSV).

In traditional Christian theology, Jesus's death is understood from the theories of traditional atonement such as penal substitution theory and ransom theory. Rom 3:25 is often read as a proof text to strengthen such theories. In this verse, there is an unusual Greek word *hilasterion*, which appears only one other time in Heb 9:5. This word connotes various things, as will be seen below. In Greek culture, *hilasterion* means expiation or propitiation. That is, a sacrifice is given to a deity to placate him or her. If this view is taken, Jesus's death is considered a soothing sacrifice to appeal to God for the forgiveness of sins. But there is no strong indication that Paul means such an idea in his letters. Then we will need to look into the Hebrew concept of atonement, *ha-kapporet*, which means "the mercy seat" (Exod 25:17). When this Hebrew word is translated into Greek, *hilasterion* is used. *Ha-kapporet* is a golden lid to the ark of the covenant, which symbolizes God's presence on the Day of Atonement (*Yom Kippur*). On this day, Jews gather together and give sacrifices to God, which has to do with atonement (mending of the broken relationship with God). If Paul drew on this idea of "the mercy seat" and applied it to Jesus's death, what did he possibly mean? One very plausible interpretation is that God considers Jesus's death as "the mercy seat," likely on the day of atonement, and deals with all the sins committed in the past because of his sacrifice through faith. Jesus's death becomes a moment of God's presence (the mercy seat) because Jesus showed faith ("effective through faith" in 3:25). Because of this act of Jesus's sacrifice, God declares that now is a new time that people may live righteously because of Jesus. Namely, God's love is known, felt, and touched through Jesus's faith. Therefore, Jesus makes God be righteous, and God justifies those who have Jesus's faith. This conclusion is well stated in Rom 3:26: "It was to prove at the present time that he (God) himself is righteous and that he justifies the one who has the *faith of Jesus*."

Consider and discuss: In the history of interpretation, *pistis christou* in Paul's letters has been translated as the *objective* genitive meaning: "faith in Christ," which implies exclusive Christology and salvation. This kind of Christian gospel was preached to the third world and minoritized communities, deemphasizing Christian ethics or moral obligations to others. That is, what was emphasized through "faith in Christ" is only the faith of believers, which is none other than the salvific knowledge that Jesus made a perfect sacrifice for them. Otherwise, there is no real emphasis on Christian faith that imitates Christ. But if we interpret *pistis christou* in the *subjective* genitive sense: "Christ's faith," which is what Paul seems to mean, the emphasis of faith is not on believers but on Jesus, whose faith is the foundation of Christian life. A mere belief in God or in Jesus is not sufficient. We must consider how Jesus lived. Which sense of the genitive do you think Paul intended, the objective genitive or the subjective genitive and what is the significance for your life?

Sin, Law, and Freedom

In Rom 3–8, sin, law, and freedom are complexly related to each other. Sin appears very frequently in Romans (forty-six times), and its form is always singular except for a few verses (3:25; 4:7; 5:14; 11:27). See below the list of sin, which covers the most important places where it appears:

- Sin came into the world through one man (5:12).
- People are under the power of sin (3:9).
- Through the law, sin is known (3:20).
- Sin was before the law (5:13).

- Sin as power exercises dominion in death (5:21; 6:12, 14).
- Sin rules the body (6:6).
- Sin dwells within a person (7:17, 20).
- Sin seizes an opportunity in the commandment to produce covetousness (7:8–9, 11). So the law is not sin (7:7).
- Sin makes people die (7:13).
- Sin enslaves persons (6:17; 7:14).

As we see above, sin is variously described as the power that infects and enslaves people. Sin as a collective power exercises dominion in the body. The problem is sin, not the law per se or the body itself. Paul's view of the law is nuanced. Nevertheless, he says the law is holy and good. It is a gift of God. The human body is also a gift of God. The distinction between sin and the law, and between sin and the body must be made in Paul's thinking. If sin is a problem, what can humans do? There is a way out of the power of sin. It is by dying to sin, as in Rom 6:2, 7, 10–11. Dying to sin means not to follow sin's way and "to put to death the deeds of the body" (8:13). In this regard, Jesus's death alone cannot make children of God free from sin because sin is power. The only thing one can do is to die to sin. Otherwise, one cannot get rid of it. Jesus did not remove sin by his death. The only way of undoing sin's power is to die to it. Jesus followed the law of the Spirit and did not submit to the law of sin (8:1–4). For those who live according to the spirit of Jesus, there will be no condemnation because "the law of the Spirit of life in Christ Jesus has set you free from the law of sin and of death" (8:1–2). The way of freedom is through the law of the Spirit, which was followed by Jesus. If one lives in Christ, one can get free from the law of sin. Thus, Christians should "set their minds on the things of the Spirit," which is life and peace (8:5–6). They have to live up to "the law of God" (8:7) or "the law of the Spirit" (7:23, 25; 8:2).

Salvation Drama

Traditionally, Rom 1–8 have been read as chapters of faith, and Rom 12–16 have been read as chapters of exhortation. The former deals with "justification by faith," and the latter with Christian ethics. In this traditional reading, Rom 9–11 is hard to fit because these chapters do not stay with the traditional doctrine of "justification by faith." In these chapters, Paul seems to waver in his position about the gospel of faith because he opens a way for unbelieving Jews and affirms the place of Israel. But in fact, these chapters are pivotal to Paul's theology and gospel because his belief is that God's salvation drama must be inclusive to both Jews and Gentiles. He emphasizes that his gospel does not negate Israel even if his Jews are faithless, not accepting Jesus as the Messiah. He believes that God will save all Israel according to his time plan (11:26). Before that time, he also believes that God will fill his house with Gentiles. It is his hope and prayer that God will save all, as he says: "For God has imprisoned all in disobedience so that he may be merciful to all" (11:32). Paul believes that God can do this all because he is sovereign and merciful. He praises such a wonderful God: "O the depth of the riches and wisdom and knowledge of God! How unsearchable are his judgments and how inscrutable his ways! For who has known the mind of the Lord? Or who has been his counselor?" (11:33–34). Until when God accomplishes what he wants to make it happen, no one can condemn others to destruction.

Paul and Politics

Often, Paul is viewed as socially conservative or as the one who is largely unconcerned about politics and this world. He is often championed as a great theologian who forged the truth of the gospel based on "justification by faith." He is also considered a theologian who aims to save souls from damnation. In this view, this world and politics are not a major concern for him. But this view can hardly make sense if we read Paul seriously. First, he is egalitarian, as he says in Gal 3:28. In his view of community, different social classes, ethnicities, and genders are gathered together and treated equally in Christ. He is not a revolutionary or abolitionist. Since his ethics are informed by the imminent return of the Lord, he does not attempt to change social systems. Nevertheless, he arguably does not promote slavery or gender hierarchy unlike the later epistles after him (household codes in the Deutero-Pauline and Pastoral letters regulate harsh relationships among different classes).

Second, Paul is not a promoter of a dualistic gospel between this world and next world. He expects that God will restore God's creation in the end. In the meantime, the children of God must participate in God's work through Christ.

Third, Paul did not found the doctrine of justification by faith. The problem for Jews is not the law but their unwillingness to accept Jesus as the Messiah and their zeal for the law. For Paul, faith means to trust God and Jesus. The law can be informed and discerned by faith. The law can be fulfilled through the faithful life.

Fourth, regarding Paul's view of the state, Rom 13:1–7 is often used to support the authoritarian government. But this is not true. In Rom 13:1–7, Paul talks about God and the governing authorities. From a surface reading, he seems to support the idea that the *ekklēsia* must submit to all powers, including even dictators, as he says in 13:1–2: "Let every soul be subject to the governing authorities. For there is no authority except God, and the authorities that exist are appointed by God. Therefore, whoever resists the authority resists the ordinance of God, and those who resist will bring judgment on themselves." Some suggest that this text is an interpolation (meaning an insertion by later editors) because it is very different from his other texts. For example, in 1 Cor 7:23, he advises the members of the community not to become slaves of human masters. But most scholars believe that this text comes from Paul. Even if he wrote it, he does not deal with the doctrine of church and state but addresses local issues in the Roman house assemblies. With this context in mind, we may come up with three possibilities of interpretation. First, Paul admonishes some enthusiasts in the Roman house assemblies who believe their salvation is already accomplished and they are free to do anything, and thus do not submit to governing authorities. Namely, Paul worries about their radical view of eschatology and the negligence of their civic duty. Second, the entire passage may be understood against the taxation issue. Some people do not want to pay their taxes. Thus, Paul is concerned because if they do not pay taxes, not only will they as individuals incur the wrath of the government but the *ekklēsia* will be threatened. Third, Paul worries about a Jewish independence movement in Palestine. If Jewish Christians in Rome do not pay taxes to Rome or participate in the governing authorities, they may be sympathetic to the Jewish independence movement in Palestine. Thus, Paul worries about possible political situations in which the foundation of the churches in Rome may be threatened. We do not know exactly what he thought of when he gave these instructions to the churches in Rome. But the bottom line is that we should not read Rom 13:1–7 as a blank statement about the doctrine of church and state, even if it lends itself in some way to such a problematic interpretation.

Phoebe in Rom 16:1

Phoebe is an influential leader in the Jesus movement along with Paul. She is a *diakonos* of the *ekklēsia* at Cenchreae (16:1). *Diakonos* is often translated as deacon, but this translation is problematic if it means the title of deacon in the assembly of believers. During Paul's time, church offices were not developed due to the expectation that the Lord would return soon. *Diakonos* means "minister" like a pastor in the modern-day church. He or she is a minister of God, who is responsible for an individual *ekklēsia*. Phoebe is a female minister at Cenchreae in Corinth. After Paul, women's role and position in the *ekklēsia* were severely limited, as we see in 1 Tim 2:11–14.

Junia in Rom 16:7

During Paul's time, did female apostles exist? The answer is *yes*. The evidence is in 16:7: "Greet Andronicus and Junia, my relatives who were in prison with me; they are prominent among the apostles, and they were in Christ before I was." Paul calls a Jewish couple prominent apostles. Junia is the wife of Andronicus, but she is also an apostle. As time goes by, the *ekklēsia* becomes conservative and women are relegated to domestic works. Suddenly, in the later manuscripts containing this verse 16:7, her name changed to Junias, which is a male name. The reason is that women could not become apostles.

Summary

1. Romans is not a book of systematic theology but a letter that deals with issues facing Paul and the Roman house assemblies.

2. The occasion and purpose of the letter are twofold: preparing for his final mission to Spain and dealing with some issues such as Gentile arrogance and misunderstanding about his gospel.

3. Paul's gospel begins with the gospel of God, which has power for salvation. In the gospel, God's righteousness is revealed through faith for faith. This gospel is also about his Son, who revealed "the righteousness of God" (God's righteousness). So *pistis christou* (faith of Christ) must be Christ's faith, which also must be shared by his followers.

4. What is wrong with Jews is not the law per se or Judaism but their unwillingness to accept Jesus as the Messiah and their zeal for the law.

5. In Paul's gospel, faith is the universal law through which both Jews and Gentiles can live righteously before God.

Further Reading

Brooten, Bernadette J. "Junia—Outstanding among the Apostles (Romans 16:7)." In *Women Priests: A Catholic Commentary on the Vatican Declaration*, edited by J. Leonard and Arlene Swidler, 141–44. New York: Paulist, 1977.

———. *Women Leaders in the Ancient Synagogue*. Providence, RI: Brown Judaic Studies, 1982.

Bryant, K. Edwin. *Paul and the Rise of the Slave: Death and Resurrection of the Oppressed in the Epistle to the Romans*. Boston, MA: Brill, 2016.

Davies, W. D. *Paul and Rabbinic Judaism: Some Rabbinic Elements in Pauline Theology*. Philadelphia: Fortress, 1965.

Elliott, Neil. *The Arrogance of Nations: Reading Romans in the Shadow of Empire*. Minneapolis, MN: Fortress, 2008.

Elliott, Neil, and Mark Reasoner, eds. *Documents and Images for the Study of Paul*. Minneapolis, MN: Fortress, 2011.

Epp, Eldon Jay. *Junia: The First Woman Apostle*. Minneapolis, MN: Fortress, 2005.

Gaventa, Beverly. *Our Mother Saint Paul*. Louisville, KY: Westminster John Knox, 2007.

Hoyt, Thomas L., Jr. "Romans." In *True to Our Native Land: An African American Commentary of the New Testament*, edited by Brian Blount et al., 249–75. Minneapolis: Fortress, 2007.

Jewett, Robert. *Romans*. Hermeneia Commentary. Minneapolis, MN: Fortress, 2007.

Johnson, Luke Timothy. *Reading Romans: A Literary and Theological Commentary*. Reading the New Testament. Macon, GA: Smyth & Helwys, 2013.

Kim, Yung Suk. *A Theological Introduction to Paul's Letters: Exploring a Threefold Theology of Paul*. Eugene, OR: Cascade, 2011.

Lopez, Davina. *The Apostle to the Conquered: Reimagining Paul's Mission*. Minneapolis, MN: Fortress, 2008.

Patte, Daniel. "Romans." In *Global Bible Commentary*, edited by Daniel Patte, 429–43. Nashville, TN: Abingdon, 2005.

Sanders, E. P. *Paul and Palestinian Judaism: A Comparison of Patterns of Religion*. Philadelphia, PA: Fortress, 1977.

Smith-Christopher, Daniel L. "Resistance with Love." In *Unsettling the Word: Biblical Experiments in Decolonization*, edited by Steve Heinrichs, 234–35. Manitoba, Canada: CommonWord, 2018.

Stendahl, Krister. *Paul among Jews and Gentiles and Other Essays.* Minneapolis, MN: Fortress, 1976.

Stubbs, Monya. *Indebted Love: Paul's Subjection Language in Romans.* Eugene, OR: Pickwick, 2013.

Tamez, Elsa. *The Amnesty of Grace: Justification by Faith from a Latin American Perspective.* Translated by Sharon H. Ringe. Nashville, TN: Abingdon, 1993.

Yeo, K. K., ed. *Navigating Romans through Cultures: Challenging Readings by Charting a New Course.* New York: T. & T. Clark, 2004.

CHAPTER 18

1 Corinthians

The ethical base of Christianity is love. This should be performed from the side of poor and oppressed *ochlos* recovering their rights.

—Ahn Byung-Mu[1]

But God chose what is foolish in the world to shame the wise; God chose what is weak in the world to shame the strong; God chose what is low and despised in the world, things that are not, to reduce to nothing things that are.

—1 Cor 1:27–28

---

1 Corinthians at a Glance

1. First Corinthians was sent to the *ekklēsia* in Corinth, the Roman province of Achaia, part of the Corinthian correspondence.

2. The Corinthian *ekklēsia* is a storehouse of problems, ranging from division to sexual immorality to resurrection.

3. Paul received oral and written reports about the Corinthian *ekklēsia* and letters from the Corinthians.

4. The centerpiece of Paul's advice to the Corinthian *ekklēsia* is to imitate Christ by remembering his faith and sacrifice for the community, as he says in 1 Cor 2:1: "When I came to you, brothers and sisters, I did not come proclaiming the mystery of God to you in lofty words or wisdom. For I decided to know nothing among you except Jesus Christ, and him crucified."

---

1. Kim and Kim, *Reading Minjung Theology*, 96.

5. "Body" infuses 1 Corinthians; therefore, it is important to understand various uses of the body in the letter: the human body, Christ's body, and the community as a body.

6. "The body of Christ" (*soma christou*) in 1 Cor 12:27 and that of Rom 12:4–5 may be interpreted together. Both are about Christ and the community. The issue is how to interpret this metaphor.

7. In the Corinthian *ekklēsia*, both women and men are free to participate in Christian worship, receiving gifts of the Spirit.

8. Regarding the resurrection body, Paul says that flesh and blood will not inherit the kingdom of God. Instead, he reimagines a different body of the resurrection: a spiritual body, which is an oxymoron.

9. 1 Cor 14:33b–36 is considered an interpolation (a text inserted by later editors). This passage is similar to 1 Tim 2:11–15, which is considered a non-Pauline text.

Introduction

THE CORINTHIAN *EKKLĒSIA* REVEALS a wide array of issues: division (1:11); sexual immorality (chapters 5–6); marriage-related issues (7:1–40); food offered to idols (8:1–13; 10:1–33); Paul's apostleship (9:1–27); head veiling at worship (11:1–16); the Lord's Supper (11:17–34); spiritual gifts and the community (chapters 12–14); resurrection (chapter 15). All these above issues need to be resolved in the *ekklēsia* as soon as possible. Thus, Paul responds to these issues one after another.

Chapter Contents

1. The Occasion and Purpose of the Letter
2. Division and Paul's Response (1 Cor 1–4)
3. Other Issues and Paul's Response
4. Head Veiling (11:1–16) and Women in the *Ekklēsia* (14:33b–36)
5. "The Body of Christ" (*Soma Christou*) in 1 Cor 6 and 1 Cor 12
6. Resurrection (1 Cor 15)

The Occasion and Purpose of the Letter

The most fundamental problem in the Corinthian *ekklēsia* has to do with division of the community. People came from Chloe and reported the issue about four factions: a party of Paul, of Apollos, of Cephas, and of Christ (1:11–12). Paul is very concerned about this issue and takes the time to explain why unity or union with Christ is important and how it can be achieved. His basic response to them is to imitate Christ and participate in his faith and death. He reminds the Corinthians that the foundation of the *ekklēsia* is not an apostle or any human being but Christ who gave his life for them. But it is God who laid the foundation of the *ekklēsia*. In Paul's ecclesiology, the *ekklēsia* belongs to God, not to Christ. Paul's favorite language about the *ekklēsia* is "the church of God" (1 Cor 1:2; 10:32; 11:22; 15:9). He also reminds the Corinthians that salvation is not done yet and that they still must bear the cross of Jesus in their lives.

Division and Paul's Response (1 Cor 1–4)

Regarding the issue of division in the *ekklēsia*, Paul exhorts the Corinthians to bear the cross of Christ. On the one hand, he acknowledges that they are called "saints" who are sanctified in Christ (1:2). On the other hand, he also reminds them that their new membership in the *ekklēsia* must be rooted in Jesus. In 1 Cor 1:9, Paul says, "God is faithful; by him you were called into the fellowship of his Son, Jesus Christ our Lord." His point is twofold: The Corinthians are called by God (he is faithful) and called into the fellowship (*koinōnia*) of his Son, Jesus Christ. Namely, they must know who called them and where they are rooted. *Koinōnia* of Christ is none other than participation in his life and death. Their problem is a lack of union with Christ. That is, they did not follow Jesus's spirit and the way he lived. Therefore, Paul says in 1 Cor 1:10: "Now I appeal to you, brothers and sisters, by the name of our Lord Jesus Christ, that you all speak the same thing and that there be no divisions among you, but that you be united in the same mind and the same purpose." This verse is the thesis of the letter. He appeals to them that they must be "united in the same mind and the same purpose" of Christ. "Speaking the same thing" does not necessarily mean that they have the same thought in all aspects of life. Rather, the point is that the Corinthians must be on the same page in their understanding of God, Jesus, *ekklēsia*, and the world. That is, they must be informed "by the name of our Lord Jesus Christ." Their thought and action should be based on Christ's faith and spirit.

In 1 Cor 1:13—4:21, Paul further explores what it means to have the same mind with Christ or to have fellowship with him. He says, "We proclaim Christ crucified, a stumbling block to Jews and foolishness to Gentiles" (1:23; cf. 2:2). "The message about the cross" is "the power of God" (1:18). The world seeks power and wisdom to save themselves and sacrifices others who are poor and weak. But Jesus challenges the system of domination in the empire, and thus, he is crucified. On the one hand, his cross is the evidence that he did not stop proclaiming God's righteousness. On the other hand, evil people and authorities are held accountable for his death. Paradoxically, this seeming failure of the cross of Jesus shows God's wisdom and power, as he says, "For God's foolishness is wiser than human wisdom, and God's weakness is stronger than human strength" (1:25). God seems foolish or weak to the eyes of the world because he advocates for the least. In a dominant society, the wise and the strong advocate for themselves at the sacrifice of the lower classes. But in an alternative community in Christ, "God chose what is foolish in the world to shame the wise . . . what is weak in the world to shame the strong . . . what is low and despised in the world" (1:27–28). What Paul says here is that the Corinthians are called and chosen by God and that Christ exemplified God's love in the world through his faith. Paul's view of the community and the world at large is radical because the weak and the marginalized are preferred by God.

Other Issues and Paul's Response

Some Corinthians are so confident about their status in public life (8:1–13; 10:1–33) and eat food offered to idols. They argue that food is clean and given by God. Thus, they say that they are free in Christ and therefore can eat anything. Idols are not God and all food is clean. Paul acknowledges their good knowledge but he does not agree with their irresponsible act toward the weak, who are conscious about food offered to idols and troubled by those who exercise freedom irresponsibly. So his advice to the Corinthians is that they exercise freedom responsibly for edifying the community, as he says: "Knowledge puffs up, but love builds up" (1 Cor 8:1).

Enthusiasts argue that their salvation is done and that they are wise in Christ and free to do anything (4:1–10). So they say, "All things are lawful" (6:12; 10:23). They think that their bodies do not matter because their souls were already saved. Some of them were involved in sexual immorality (5:1–13; 6:9–20). But Paul says, "Not all things are beneficial" (6:12; 10:23). This means that the Corinthians must know how to use their body responsibly. The conclusion is in 6:20: "For you were bought with a price; therefore glorify God in your body."

At the Lord's Supper (11:17–34), we see a clear conflict between those who came early and those who came late. The former group was supposed to be the rich, and the latter group to be the poor. On this important community gathering, union/unity must be seen and achieved. But ironically, there is a division with uncaring behavior in the community. The rich members bring something to share and eat them up before the poor members come. He reminds them of the purpose of the Lord's Supper, which is not to celebrate Jesus's victorious resurrection but to remember his death. They must reflect on the meaning of his death and take care of each other.

Head Veiling (11:1–16) and Women in the Ekklēsia (14:33b–36)

Head Covering

1 Cor 11:1–16

Be imitators of me, as I am of Christ. I commend you because you remember me in everything and maintain the traditions just as I handed them on to you. But I want you to understand that Christ is the head of every man, and the husband is the head of his wife, and God is the head of Christ. Any man who prays or prophesies with something on his head disgraces his head, but any woman who prays or prophesies with her head unveiled disgraces her head—it is one and the same thing as having her head shaved. For if a woman will not veil herself, then she should cut off her hair; but if it is disgraceful for a woman to have her hair cut off or to be shaved, she should wear a veil. For a man ought not to have his head veiled, since he is the image and reflection of God; but woman is the reflection of man. Indeed, man was not made from woman, but woman from man. Neither was man created for the sake of woman, but woman for the sake of man. For this reason a woman ought to have a symbol of authority on her head, because of the angels. Nevertheless, in the Lord woman is not independent of man or man independent of woman. For just as woman came from man, so man comes through woman; but all things come from God. Judge for yourselves: is it proper for a woman to pray to God with her head unveiled? Does not nature itself teach you that if a man wears long hair, it is degrading to him, but if a

> woman has long hair, it is her glory? For her hair is given to her for a covering. But if anyone is disposed to be contentious—we have no such custom, nor do the churches of God.

Head covering is hard to understand because the context in which Paul writes is unclear. On the one hand, he affirms the hierarchical view of gender, as he says in 11:3: "But I want you to understand that Christ is the head of every man, and the husband is the head of his wife, and God is the head of Christ." After this, he goes on to say that men should not wear a head covering while women should wear it because of gender hierarchy in God's creation (11:4–10). But on the other hand, he relativizes gender hierarchy in the *ekklēsia* as he says in 11:11–12: "Nevertheless, in the Lord woman is not independent of man or man independent of woman. For just as woman came from man, so man comes through woman; but all things come from God."

There are a few options to interpret this complex passage. First, some women's refusal to wear head veilings at worship service is considered a challenge to the gender difference in the church. If this is the case in the Corinthian *ekklēsia*, Paul's advice is to maintain a gendered community at least in worship service. He wants the *ekklēsia* to conduct business orderly and decently in honor of gender differences.

Second, women's refusal to wear the head covering is considered a challenge to gender hierarchy. Probably, some women practiced radical gender equality in ways that they refused to wear head veiling at worship. They depended on Paul's teaching in Gal 3:28 in which there is radical equality in the *ekklēsia* between different social classes, between ethnicities, and between genders. If this is the situation in the Corinthian *ekklēsia*, Paul's advice is to control such a radical equality in the *ekklēsia*.

Third, another interpretive option is to consider a local *ekklēsia* situation where some women disturbed an orderly worship service. Namely, some pagan women joined the new Christian community and brought their hairstyle to the *ekklēsia*. It is possible that their acts of worship with different hairstyle disrupted otherwise the normal worship service. If this is the situation, Paul's advice is to deal with the *ekklēsia* incidents through a peaceful, orderly service. In other words, he does not talk about gender difference or gender hierarchy.

Fourth, this passage is considered an interpolation (an inserted text; that is non-Pauline), given the fact that Paul's view of women is positive in his authentic letters. Indeed, in the Corinthian *ekklēsia*, both men and women receive the same Spirit (1 Cor 12:11) and freely participate in the *ekklēsia*.

Consider and discuss: Paul is a controversial apostle whose view of society, women, or slaves is very complex. Issues reflected in 1 Cor 11:1–16 is unclear; therefore, it is not easy to decide about Paul's view of women or community. Some see him as socially conservative because of this text and do not allow women's leadership in the *ekklēsia*. First Cor 14:33–36 is used to support their view. But the other text of Gal 3:28 has a very different egalitarian voice. What do you think is going on in the Corinthian *ekklēsia* that Paul addresses here? What is Paul's view of women or gender relation in the *ekklēsia*? What is your view of gender in the *ekklēsia* and society?

Women in the *Ekklēsia* (1 Cor 14:33b–36)

1 Cor 14:33–36

> For God is a God not of disorder but of peace. (As in all the churches of the saints, women should be silent in the churches. For they are not permitted to speak, but should be subordinate, as the law also says. If there is anything they desire to know, let them ask their husbands at home. For it is shameful for a woman to speak in *ekklēsia*. Or did the word of God originate with you? Or are you the only ones it has reached?)

First Cor 14:33b–36 is considered an interpolation. Nowhere else does he say a text or something like this: "Women should be silent in the churches or that they are not permitted to speak, but should be subordinate, as the law also says." Rather, the evidence for supporting women's place in the *ekklēsia* overflows. In the Corinthian *ekklēsia*, both women and men pray and prophesy (11:4–5). He worked with women leaders (for example, Phoebe was a minister; Junia was an apostle). It is no doubt that Gal 3:28 is an oft-cited text to support his egalitarianism. Interestingly, 1 Cor 14:33b–36 has a parallel with 1 Tim 2:11–15, which is considered a non-Pauline text. Because of this parallel, scholars believe that this text came from a later post-Pauline *ekklēsia* that wants to check women's place or participation in the church. That is, they did not like Paul's view of equality in the *ekklēsia* and inserted this text right after 14:33a: "for God is a God not of disorder but of peace." Maybe because Paul mentions the issue of "disorder" in 14:33a, the insertion text occurs after that verse. But in fact, this "disorder" does not have to do with women's teaching or speaking in the *ekklēsia*. Before 14:33a, the issue is regarding spiritual gifts. Namely, some people boasted about their gifts and did not care about the whole community. Because of this concern, Paul asks the Corinthians to edify the community.

Consider and discuss: Is it possible to see this text 14:33b–36 as an interpolation? Compare it to 1 Tim 2:11–14.

1 Cor 14:33–36	1 Tim 2:11–15
For God is a God not of disorder but of peace. (As in all the churches of the saints, women should be silent in the churches. For they are not permitted to speak, but should be subordinate, as the law also says. If there is anything they desire to know, let them ask their husbands at home. For it is shameful for a woman to speak in church. Or did the word of God originate with you? Or are you the only ones it has reached?)	Let a woman learn in silence with full submission. I permit no woman to teach or to have authority over a man; she is to keep silent. For Adam was formed first, then Eve; and Adam was not deceived, but the woman was deceived and became a transgressor. Yet she will be saved through childbearing, provided they continue in faith and love and holiness, with modesty.

"The Body of Christ" (*Soma Christou*) in 1 Cor 6 and 1 Cor 12

In chapter 16, we have briefly explored "the body of Christ" in Paul's letters. Stoicism views the body as a metaphorical organism in which unity and hierarchy are emphasized. In this view, the focus is not parts but the whole of the body. That is, for the sake of the whole, the individual parts must serve and sacrifice themselves. But Paul's body metaphor, as in 1 Cor 12:12–27, is very different from Stoicism. For him, the different parts of the body, though different in terms of honor or power, are duly respected and taken care of equally. He also recognizes that some parts of the body are less honorable or less respectable. But they are to be clothed with great honor and greater respect because they are in the same body. In the body, all parts rejoice and suffer together.

1 Cor 6:12–20

"All things are lawful for me," but not all things are beneficial. "All things are lawful for me," but I will not be dominated by anything. "Food is meant for the stomach and the stomach for food," and God will destroy both one and the other. The body is meant not for fornication but for the Lord, and the Lord for the body. And God raised the Lord and will also raise us by his power. Do you not know that your bodies are members of Christ? Should I therefore take the members of Christ and make them members of a prostitute? Never! Do you not know that whoever is united to a prostitute becomes one body with her? For it is said, "The two shall be one flesh." But anyone united to the Lord becomes one spirit with him. Shun fornication! Every sin that a person commits is outside the body; but the fornicator sins against the body itself. Or do you not know that your body is a temple of the Holy Spirit within you, which you have from God, and that you are not your own? For you were bought with a price; therefore glorify God in your body.

In 1 Cor 6:12–20, Paul argues that the body is for the Lord and it should not be used for fornication or other irresponsible purposes. Some Corinthians argue that they can do anything with their bodies because they were already saved. But Paul says that the body is for God and the Lord. To glorify God, they must use the body responsibly and know that their body is a temple of the Holy Spirit. Christ is a good example that he used his body responsibly for God's righteousness. So the Corinthians must become one spirit with Jesus (6:17). "One spirit with him" means that they must share his vision and follow his faith and life. Paul asks rhetorical questions regarding the Corinthians' ethical duty: "Do you not know that your bodies are members of Christ? Should I therefore take the members of Christ and make them members of a prostitute? Never!" (1 Cor 6:15). In this verse, "members of Christ" are to be understood figuratively in view of the human body. In other words, "members of Christ" are body parts (*mele*) that constitute Christ, who is the whole body. The principal image here is union of parts to the body, which is Christ. The idea of union is clarified in 6:16: "Do you not know that whoever is united to a prostitute becomes one body with her? For it is said, 'The two shall be one flesh.'" All in all, what Paul tries to say is that the Corinthians must know how and where to use their body: it is for God and the Lord. Similarly, the union of the body is found 1 Cor 12:12–27. In this passage, Paul exhorts the Corinthian community to embody Christ individually and communally.

1 Cor 12:12–27

> For just as the body is one and has many members, and all the members of the body, though many, are one body, so it is with Christ. For in the one Spirit we were all baptized into one body—Jews or Greeks, slaves or free—and we were all made to drink of one Spirit. Indeed, the body does not consist of one member but of many. If the foot would say, "Because I am not a hand, I do not belong to the body," that would not make it any less a part of the body. And if the ear would say, "Because I am not an eye, I do not belong to the body," that would not make it any less a part of the body. If the whole body were an eye, where would the hearing be? If the whole body were hearing, where would the sense of smell be? But as it is, God arranged the members in the body, each one of them, as he chose. If all were a single member, where would the body be? As it is, there are many members, yet one body. The eye cannot say to the hand, "I have no need of you," nor again the head to the feet, "I have no need of you." On the contrary, the members of the body that seem to be weaker are indispensable, and those members of the body that we think less honorable we clothe with greater honor, and our less respectable members are treated with greater respect; whereas our more respectable members do not need this. But God has so arranged the body, giving the greater honor to the inferior member, that there may be no dissension within the body, but the members may have the same care for one another. If one member suffers, all suffer together with it; if one member is honored, all rejoice together with it. Now you are the body of Christ and individually members of it.

In 1 Cor 12:12, the body is associated with Christ: "so it is with Christ." The Corinthian community as a body should be united to Christ. The Corinthians, whoever they are or wherever they come from, are parts/members of Christ, who is the body. Therefore, they must remain with Christ, following his spirit and faith. In this Christ-informed community, all members rejoice and suffer together. With the idea of union in a body, 1 Cor 12:27 can be translated and understood differently: "You are a Christic body and have to embody Christ individually and communally." Here, the concept of the body is a way of living. Thus, "the body of Christ" can be translated as "Christic body." A similar example is found in Rom 6:6: "the body of sin" as "the sinful body." This alternative reading is very different from the traditional interpretation focused on a metaphorical organism in that "the body of Christ" is interpreted as "a community belonging to Christ."

1 Cor 12:28–31

> And God has appointed in the church first apostles, second prophets, third teachers; then deeds of power, then gifts of healing, forms of assistance, forms of leadership, various kinds of tongues. Are all apostles? Are all prophets? Are all teachers? Do all work miracles? Do all possess gifts of healing? Do all speak in tongues? Do all interpret? But strive for the greater gifts. And I will show you a still more excellent way.

In 1 Cor 12:28–31, Paul talks about different functions in the Corinthian body. Traditionally, these verses have been understood through the lens of a metaphorical organism. That is, a hierarchy is arranged by different functions in the community: "apostles are first, prophets are second, and teachers are third" (12:28). But the cardinal numbers of "first, second, or third" do not necessarily refer to a hierarchy. It is also possible he simply lists different works one after another. Earlier, in 12:12–26, he perceives the Corinthian community as a system of mutual support and care in which all are considered equal. That is, different functions do not lead to a hierarchy. What is essential to the community is not who is more gifted than others but with what attitude the Corinthians work. In 1 Cor 12:31, Paul introduces a new theme of love, which is a more excellent way than any gifts. In 1 Cor 13, he continues to talk about love. The true unity/union is not by gifts or functions but through love rooted in Christ.

Consider and discuss: In the contemporary church, "the body of Christ" is taught and preached based on a metaphorical organism. The usual emphasis is, therefore, the unity of the *ekklēsia*. In the name of Jesus, diversity is downplayed or denied. Doctrine precedes diversity. The *ekklēsia* is considered the only place of salvation and unity. There are two kinds of people, according to this view of the organism: those who are in the *ekklēsia* belonging to Christ and those who are outside of the *ekklēsia*. Jesus becomes the boundary of the community without much engaging in the world. Other religious people are outside of the *ekklēsia*. They do not belong to Jesus. Consequentially, there is no mandate to serve others. But what if we interpret "the body of Christ" differently, as a Christic body? Individuals and the community alike may live like Christ (Christ-like body). What do you think about this alternative interpretation about the body?

Resurrection (1 Cor 15)

Some Corinthians doubt the resurrection of the dead because in Greek philosophy the body is rotten and the soul is immortal. So the resurrection message is nonsense for them to accept. But Paul affirms the resurrection of the dead. Resurrection is done by the power of God (2 Cor 13:4); therefore, it is not impossible for God to raise the dead. Regarding the question by the Corinthians: "How are the dead raised? With what kind of body do they come?" (1 Cor 15:35), Paul's response is nuanced. On the one hand, he acknowledges that the flesh and blood cannot inherit the kingdom of God (1 Cor 15:50). This means that his concept of the resurrection is not bodily (flesh) and that the perishable cannot inherit the imperishable. On the other hand, he affirms a different kind of resurrection, which is not bodily but spiritual. Thus, he coins a new term, "a spiritual body"—an oxymoron (1 Cor 15:44). In Greek dualism, it is impossible for the body and spirit to go hand in hand. But Paul combines two impossible elements together. In doing so, he affirms God's power of resurrection. There will be a new spiritual body. Paul's resurrection language is spiritual and pastoral in the sense that God has power to raise the dead. He comforts the Corinthians to stay in faith under any circumstances.

Consider and discuss: In the Apostle's Creed, we find this expression: "the bodily resurrection." What does this bodily resurrection mean to Christians? What can Paul say about this issue of the bodily resurrection?

Interim Ethics

Paul believes that the Lord would return soon. Until the end, Christians must devote themselves to God because the time is short, not being so preoccupied with worldly matters. While living in the present and experiencing the Spirit, they must look to the ultimate end. This attitude of interim ethics is the basis of Paul's theology and ethics. For example, in 1 Cor 7:1–40, there are disputes about marriage, divorce, celibacy, slavery, and circumcision, and these issues are dealt with this view of interim ethics. That is, they should think and act as if they live in the last days now. Similarly, they are advised to live a life of simplicity, adopting celibacy if they can. Also, his advice is not to think too much of the current social condition such as slavery because eventually they will be all liberated from all human masters. Likewise, circumcision is also a matter of passing. Since Paul anticipates the Lord to return very soon, he does not attempt to change social conditions.

Nevertheless, his interim ethics is not apolitical in the sense that salvation is only spiritual or otherworldly. While the end did not come yet, he still believes that the present should be lived well. His conclusive advice to those who are uncertain or worry about their social status is found 1 Cor 7:24: "In whatever condition you were called, brothers and sisters, there remain with God." Here "to remain with God" is a key to understanding his view of social relations and therefore, they should not become slaves of human masters (1 Cor 7:23).

Consider and discuss: Household codes reflect a very conservative view of gender and community. They appear in the Deutero-Pauline and Pastoral Letters, whose Pauline authorship is disputed (Col 3:18—4:1; Eph 5:21—6:9; Titus 2:1-10; cf. 1 Peter 2:18—3:7). There are significant differences between Paul's authentic letters and these later epistles where the household codes appear. Nonetheless, many Christians read all the traditional Pauline letters together and argue that Paul is a conservative person. Why do some of us still read this way?

Summary

1. First Corinthians was written to respond to various issues in the community, ranging from division to sexual immorality to resurrection.
2. The main theme of the letter is found in 1:9-10: "God is faithful; by him you were called into the fellowship (*koinōnia*) of his Son, Jesus Christ our Lord. Now I appeal to you, brothers and sisters, by the name of our Lord Jesus Christ, that all of you speak the same thing and that there be no divisions among you, but that you be united in the same mind and the same purpose."

3. Paul's body analogy in 12:12–27 is very different from *homonoia* (unity) speeches in Stoicism. He emphasizes suffering and rejoicing together in the human body and community as well. But Stoics see the body and community through a metaphorical organism to maintain a community of unity and hierarchy.

4. 1 Cor 12:27 can be translated and interpreted differently through the alternative lens of the body: the body as a site of life and as a metaphor for a way of living: "You (the Corinthians) are a Christic body and you have to embody Christ individually and communally." Namely, "the body of Christ" can be an attributive genitive: Christic or Christ-like body.

5. The Corinthian *ekklēsia* enjoys the gifts of the Spirit; both men and women are free to participate in the *ekklēsia*. But because of this freedom through the Spirit, some members do not edify the community, thinking that all things are lawful.

6. Issues of head veiling in 11:1–16 are hard to interpret. The various options are to be considered.

7. The Cornithain passage at 14:33b–36 is considered an interpolation because it is very similar to 1 Tim 2:11–14. Paul never uses this kind of misogynistic language elsewhere in his undisputed letters.

8. Paul emphasizes the resurrection of the dead, not the resurrection of the body.

Further Reading

Badiou, Alain. *Saint Paul: The Foundation of Universalism*. Translated by Ray Brassier. Stanford: Stanford University Press, 2003.

Bassler, Jouette. "1 Corinthians." In *Women's Bible Commentary: Revised Edition*, edited by Carol Newsom et al., 557–65. Louisville, KY: Westminster John Knox, 2012.

Georgi, Dieter. *Remembering the Poor: The History of Paul's Collection for Jerusalem*. Nashville, TN: Abingdon, 1992.

Horsley, Richard. *1 Corinthians*. Abingdon, TN: Abingdon, 1998.

Ibita, Ma. Marilou. "A Conversation with the Story of the Lord's Supper in 1 Corinthians 11:17–34." In *1 and 2 Corinthians: Texts @ Contexts*, edited by Yung Suk Kim, 97–114. Minneapolis: Fortress, 2013.

Janssen, Claudia. "Bodily Resurrection (1 Cor 15)? The Discourse of Resurrection in Karl Barth, Rudolf Bultmann, Dorothee Soelle and

Contemporary Theology." *Journal for the Study of the New Testament* 79 (2000) 61–78.

Kim, Yung Suk. *Christ's Body in Corinth: The Politics of a Metaphor*. Minneapolis, MN: Fortress, 2008.

———. "'Imitators' (*Mimetai*) in 1 Cor. 4:16 and 11:1: A New Reading of Threefold Embodiment." *Horizons in Biblical Theology* 33 (2011) 147–70.

King, Karen L. *What is Gnosticism?* Cambridge: Harvard University Press, 2005.

Martin, Dale B. *The Corinthian Body*. New Haven: Yale University Press, 1995.

Meggitt, Justin. *Paul, Poverty, and Survival*. Edinburgh: T. & T. Clark, 1998.

Odell-Scott, David. *Paul's Critique of Theocracy: A Theocracy in 1 Corinthians and Galatians*. New York: T. & T. Clark, 2009.

Pagels, Elaine. "Paul and Women: A Response to Recent Discussion." *Journal of the American Academy of Religion* 40 (1972) 538–49.

Pathrapankal, Joseph. "1 Corinthians." In *Global Bible Commentary*, edited by Daniel Patte, 444–50. Abingdon, TN: Abingdon, 2004.

Punt, Jeremy. "Identity and Human Dignity amid Power and Liminality in 1 Corinthians 7:17–24." In *1 and 2 Corinthians: Texts @ Contexts*, edited by Yung Suk Kim, 9–30. Minneapolis: Fortress, 2013.

Sanders, Boykin. "1 Corinthians." In *True to Our Native Land: An African American New Testament Commentary*, edited by Brian Blount et al., 276–306. Minneapolis, MN: Fortress, 2007.

Smith, Mitzi J. "'Love Never Fails': Rereading 1 Cor 13 with a Womanist Hermeneutic of Love's Struggle." In *Theologies of Failure*, edited by Roberto Sirvent and Duncan Reyburn. Eugene, OR: Cascade, forthcoming.

Welborn, Laurence. *Paul, the Fool of Christ: A Study of 1 Corinthians 1–4 in the Comic-Philosophic Tradition*. New York: T. & T. Clark, 2009.

Wire, Antoinette Clark. *The Corinthian Women Prophets: A Reconstruction through Paul's Rhetoric*. Minneapolis, MN: Fortress, 1990.

Yeo, K. K. "Pauline Theological Counseling of Love in the Language of the Zhuangzi." In *1 and 2 Corinthians: Texts @ Contexts*, edited by Yung Suk Kim, 117–28. Minneapolis: Fortress, 2013.

CHAPTER 19

2 Corinthians

Proximity has taught me some basic and humbling truths, including this vital lesson: Each of us is more than the worst thing we've ever done.

—Bryan Stevenson[1]

The community of the saints is not an "ideal" community consisting of perfect and sinless men and women, where there is no need of further repentance. No, it is a community which proves that it is worthy of the gospel of forgiveness by constantly and sincerely proclaiming God's forgiveness.

—Dietrich Bonhoeffer[2]

---

2 Corinthians at a Glance

1. Second Corinthians is not a single letter but a composite letter.
2. It is made up of at least four or five letters, which are as follows: a letter of the collection (2 Cor 8); a letter of defense of Paul's ministry (2 Cor 2:14—7:4); a letter of tears (2 Cor 10–13); a letter of reconciliation (2 Cor 1:1—2:13; 7:5–16; 13:11–13); another letter of the collection (2 Cor 9).
3. The Corinthian *ekklēsia* did not improve much after Paul's letter (1 Cor).

---

1. Stevenson, *Just Mercy*, 17–18.
2. Bonhoeffer, *Cost of Discipleship*, 287.

4. The new issues include the arrival of charismatic leaders (called super-apostles) and harsh negation of Paul's apostleship.
5. The centerpiece of Paul's advice to the *ekklēsia* is not different from 1 Corinthians. That is to imitate Christ and follow his gospel based on God's grace. We also see his very much emotionally charged words in the letter of tears.
6. In the letters of the collection, we continue to see Paul's passion for helping the poor saints in Jerusalem. We need to interpret why he is very much concerned about this collection project even though there was some misunderstanding or resistance from the church.
7. Because 2 Corinthians is a composite letter, we must read possible individual letters separately in context.

Introduction

AFTER SOME TIME PASSED since he wrote 1 Corinthians, Paul decides to visit again Corinth to check how the *ekklēsia* is doing and defend his gospel and apostleship. But his visit was not successful; he was insulted and humiliated publicly (2 Cor 2:5–8; 7:12). Then he returned to Ephesus in disgrace (2 Cor 12:21) and wrote the letter of tears to express his bitter feelings about his visit, hoping to correct wrongdoing in the *ekklēsia* (2 Cor 2:4; 10:1—13:10). In this letter, he emphasizes the power of weakness and service to others, saying that salvation is not done yet and that Christians must suffer for the gospel of God and of Christ until the end (2 Cor 11:20–31). After this, there was reconciliation between Paul and the Corinthians because there was repentance. In fact, he wrote a few more letters after this tearful letter. We need to see his correspondence relationships with the *ekklēsia*, including his visits:

- Paul's first visit to Corinth (2 Cor 1:19)
- Paul's first letter (1 Cor 5:9), which was lost
- The Corinthians' first letter to Paul (1 Cor 7:1)
- Paul's second letter (1 Cor)
- Paul's third letter (2 Cor 8)

- Paul's fourth letter (2 Cor 2:14—7:4): defense of his apostleship to false teachers
- The arrival of the super-apostles (2 Cor 11:5)
- Paul's second visit to Corinth (2 Cor 2:1-4)
- Paul's fifth letter (2 Cor 10-13): the "painful" letter
- The Corinthians repenting of the pain they caused Paul (2 Cor 2:5-11; 7:5-12)
- Paul's sixth letter (2 Cor 1:1—2:13; 7:5-16; 13:11-13): the letter of reconciliation
- Paul's seventh letter: more instructions about the collection (2 Cor 9)

Chapter Contents

1. Letter of the Collection for the Poor Saints (2 Cor 8)
2. Letter of Defense of Paul's Ministry (2 Cor 2:14—7:4)
3. Letter of Tears (2 Cor 10-13)
4. Letter of Reconciliation (2 Cor 1:1—2:13; 7:5-16; 13:11-13)

Partition Theories

According to partition theories, 2 Corinthians is not a single letter but a composite document comprising of several separate letters, originally written at different times for different purposes. There are clues that 2 Corinthians is not a single letter. First, 2 Cor 1:1—2:13 is conciliatory in nature, but the tone changes suddenly in later chapters, 2 Cor 10-13. The best explanation about this difference may be because he wrote two different letters originally. That is, he wrote a "painful" letter first, and sometime later, the Corinthians repented of their sins. This led to his writing of another letter of thanksgiving. Second, 2 Cor 8 looks like a separate letter sent to Corinth to deal with the collection project. Second Cor 2:14—7:4 also looks like a separate letter about the defense of his ministry. Third, there is another collection letter, 2 Cor 9, which repeats the same theme of the collection with a different tone.

Letter of the Collection for the Poor Saints (2 Cor 8)

Second Cor 8 is a letter of the collection for the poor saints in Jerusalem. Paul writes this letter to request voluntary offerings for those poor people. In doing so, he appeals to the spirit of voluntarism, as exemplified in the Macedonian churches. In the history of interpretation, 2 Cor 8 has been read differently: for example, through the lens of charity, ecclesiology, soteriology, eschatology, and friendship. The lens of charity is the most popular one taken by most readers. Without addressing other social justice issues, they emphasize the need of help for the poor. The ecclesiological lens highlights the unity between Gentile Christians and Jewish Christians. Here the issue is more than charity, and what is hoped for is the bond between Jews and Gentiles through this collection project. The soteriological lens emphasizes God's grace and salvation that are shown through the collection. That is, the Corinthians must show the love of God through their giving, as they received gifts from others. The eschatological lens emphasizes the importance of gentile mission because on the last day Gentiles as gifts may be brought to Jerusalem.

The lens of friendship emphasizes the Hellenistic concept of friendship. Aristotle thinks of two kinds of equality in friendship: between equals and between unequals. While the former is numerical, the latter is proportional. That is, while equals must have the same amount of wealth, unequals have their share proportionally, as in the patron-client system, where benefactors have more share than beneficiaries. Some think of Paul's meaning of equality with this concept in mind. That is, he asks for a reciprocal exchange between unequal friends: the relationship between benefactors and beneficiaries. In this case, the Jerusalem church is a benefactor who recognizes Paul's Gentile *ekklēsia*, and in return, Paul gives monies to the poor in Jerusalem. This view of friendship may be seen in 2 Cor 8:4, 6, 12, but it is very questionable that he primarily addressed this kind of reciprocation between unequal friends. In his view, both Jews and Gentiles are equals before God (for example, Gal 3:28). Others see Paul's concept of equality as an equality between equals. But Paul's audiences in Corinth and Jerusalem are not equals.

All the above readings do not take seriously equality (*isotes*), as is shown in 2 Cor 8:13–15: "I do not mean that there should be relief for others and pressure on you, but it is a question of *an equality* between your present abundance and their need, so that their abundance may be for your need, in order that there may be *an equality*. As it is written, 'The one who had much did not have too much, and the one who had little did not have too little.'" Paul's concern is to foster equality between different social classes because they are all people of God. This concept of equality requires

Gentile Christians to share what they have with others because God is the source of life and equalizer among different peoples. The churches in Macedonia understood this and participated in God's grace by sharing voluntarily "according to their means, and even beyond their means" (2 Cor 8:2–3). When other Christians suffer wherever they are, they also need God's grace through which they may experience equality in terms of economic means. Paul clearly addresses the issue of poverty and emphasizes equality between the Gentiles and the poor saints in Jerusalem. In doing so, he says, "I do not mean that there should be relief for others and pressure on you, but it is a question of an equality between your present abundance and their need, so that their abundance may be for your need, in order that there may be an equality" (2 Cor 8:13–14). Otherwise, he does not say that there must be a numerical or mechanical balance between them. Rather, all this good work should be done voluntarily to participate in God's grace, which is open to all, especially for the deficient. What matters is equality between different classes and among different peoples because God cares for all. God's creation needs to be sustained with a fair distribution of resources. This sharing must be done voluntarily, based on people's need: "The one who had much did not have too much, and the one who had little did not have too little" (2 Cor 8:15; cf. Exod 16:18).

Consider and discuss: Why is Paul very much concerned about the collection for the poor people in Jerusalem? What is his theological point about this collection project? Does he simply care about charity, so to speak? Or, does he consider this act as a symbolic gesture that Gentiles would pay what they owe Jews because salvation comes from them? Or, does he care about equality between different communities or between social classes? Or, does he consider this collection as a part of eschatological gifts made on to the altar of Jerusalem? It is important to understand Paul's motif of helping the poor saints in Jerusalem because sometimes a person helps others to prove that he/she is better or stronger than them. Or, in some situation, he/she shares something with others to preach an uninformed, naïve gospel.

Letter of Defense of Paul's Ministry (2 Cor 2:14—7:4)

Some Corinthians ridiculed Paul's ministry because he did not receive financial gifts from the wealthy. His gospel was not popular because he did not preach the gospel of prosperity. Some even belittled him because his physical look was not so impressive with his poor speech. Many Corinthians rejected his ministry and apostleship. Thus, in 2 Cor 2:14—3:18, he defends his ministry and apostleship based on "the Spirit of the living God" (2 Cor 3:3). As he writes in Galatians, his basic argument is that his call is not from Jerusalem or by human authorities, but from God. Similarly, in this letter of defense (2 Cor 2:14—7:4), he argues that his ministry is rooted in "the Spirit of the living God." Here he emphasizes the Spirit and God. Otherwise, he does not say that his gospel is based on the Torah or Jewish tradition or on Jerusalem apostles. He distinguishes between God and all other elements such as the Torah or any human authorities. Certainly, he does not say that the latter is wrong but it must be informed by God who is the source of life.

Then, he argues that the Spirit of God works through the ministry of Jesus, which becomes "a new covenant, not of letter but of spirit" (3:6). Paul's referral to the new covenant derives from Jer 31:31-34 in which the Lord speaks through Jeremiah: "I will make a new covenant with the house of Israel and the house of Judah. It will not be like the covenant that I made with their ancestors when I took them by the hand to bring them out of the land of Egypt—a covenant that they broke, though I was their husband" (Jer 31:31-32). Here, Jeremiah makes clear that the new covenant is for Jews. The prophecy continues in Jer 31:33-34: "But this is the covenant that I will make with the house of Israel after those days, says the LORD: I will put my law within them, and I will write it on their hearts; and I will be their God, and they shall be my people. No longer shall they teach one another, or say to each other, 'Know the LORD,' for they shall all know me, from the least of them to the greatest, says the LORD; for I will forgive their iniquity, and remember their sin no more." But surprisingly, Paul applies the new covenant in Jeremiah to Jesus who does the work of the Spirit. If the laws were written on the tablets of stone, a "letter of Christ" is "written not with ink but with the Spirit of the living God, not on tablets of stone but on tablets of human hearts" (2 Cor 3:3). "Letter of Christ" means Christ's letter that Jesus wrote through his faithful obedience to God. It also may mean a letter about Christ—words and deeds about him. Now this letter of Christ is written on tablets of human hearts. Jesus's letter or good news about him must be lived out through his followers.

Since Christ exemplified God's love through his life and death, Paul argues that now the Corinthians must continue to carry this letter of Christ originally written by Jesus, prepared by Paul. In other words, the Corinthians are a letter of Christ that they have to carry to become good news to others. Because of a new covenant through Jesus's work, Paul has confidence in Christ and follows him. Thus, he contrasts between Moses's ministry with Christ's. His point is not that Moses is wrong but that Christ as the Son of God (and as the Messiah) exemplified God's love and fulfilled the law. Furthermore, to those who stick to Mosaic laws and deny that Jesus is the Messiah, Paul claims that Jesus demonstrated who God is through his faithful work. Accordingly, he declares, "Now the Lord is the Spirit, and where the Spirit of the Lord is, there is freedom" (2 Cor 8:17).

In 2 Cor 4:1–18, Paul professes his faith in the merciful God and proclaims the gospel of Christ under any circumstance. His proclamation of Jesus is not by words only but through the death of Jesus, so that the life of Jesus may be visible to Christians (2 Cor 4:10). Even if hardships or suffering remain in the community, he advises the Corinthians not to lose heart because the ultimate transformation is under way: "Even though our outer nature is wasting away, our inner nature is being renewed day by day" (2 Cor 4:16). He also says, "We look not at what can be seen but at what cannot be seen; for what can be seen is temporary, but what cannot be seen is eternal" (2 Cor 4:18).

In 2 Cor 5:1–21, Paul explains what it means to follow Jesus Christ. First of all, he declares, "For the love of Christ urges us on, because we are convinced that one has died for all; therefore all have died. And he died for all, so that those who live might live no longer for themselves, but for him who died and was raised for them" (2 Cor 5:14–15). Christ's death has to do with his love of God and people ("For the love of Christ urges us on"). Paul's theology is that since Christ died for all, therefore, all have died. He does not say we do not die because Jesus died. His death is an example of moral sacrifice. That is, to follow Christ means to die with him, and to die with him means to live a life of the Spirit. Those who follow the Spirit can live no longer for themselves. Only when the Corinthians have died in Christ, they are a new creation: "everything old has passed away; see, everything has become new!" (2 Cor 5:17). Here "in Christ" must be a modal dative, which emphasizes a way of living like Christ.

In 2 Cor 6:1—7:4, Paul exhorts the Corinthians to move away from partnership with the ungodly (cf. 2 Cor 27:1), maintaining the Spirit of God. He also says in 2 Cor 6:13-14: "In return—I speak as to children—open wide your hearts also. Do not be mismatched with unbelievers. For what partnership is there between righteousness and lawlessness? Or what fellowship is there between light and darkness?" Paul wants them to live ethically, worthy of God's grace and call. The reason is they are the temple of the living God (2 Cor 6:16–17).

Consider and discuss: Paul contrasts Christ's ministry and Moses's. Does this contrast sound anti-Semitic? Is there a way of speaking the truth without anti-Semitism? If there is, what would that be?

Consider and discuss: 2 Cor 5:17 is one of the most often-cited verses: "So if anyone is in Christ, there is a new creation: everything old has passed away; see, everything has become new!" What does "a new creation" mean to Paul? What does it have to do with Christ? How can it happen to Christians? What is the content or nature of a new creation? Does it include various aspects of transformation in human life and society? Can we include embodied theology proposed by womanist or feminist theologians?

Letter of Tears (2 Cor 10–13)

After a painful visit to Corinth, Paul writes a long letter of tears. His emotion erupts from one stage to another, expressing his concerns and frustrations about the Corinthians, rebuking them harshly, defending his character and work of Christ. He knows that his speech is weak and his physical look is not so impressive. He also knows that he did not receive financial support from the wealthy and that he lacked charisma in his ministry, as compared with the super-apostles (2 Cor 11:5–6). He acknowledges that he is foolish or weak, and lists many hardships and difficulties he had during his travels and ministry (2 Cor 11:23–27). But he changes the meaning of weakness and considers it the source of power (2 Cor 11:30). Through his weakness, God's power is revealed, as he says: "Three times I appealed to the Lord about this, that it would leave me, but he said to me, 'My grace is sufficient for you, for power is made perfect in weakness" (2 Cor 12:8–9). He goes on to say that all hardships are for the sake of Christ (2 Cor 12:10) and confesses: "for whenever I am weak, then I am strong" (2 Cor 12:10). Through nothingness-like experience, he gains more strength; therefore, he is not at all inferior to them (2 Cor 12:11). So he does not agree with his opponents that he is weak or foolish. Rather, he argues that his knowledge is sound and good; his conscience is devoted to lifting up the Corinthians; his spiritual experience is deep; his lineage is very Jewish; and his spirit is rooted in Christ (10:1). Furthermore, he says his gospel is free and does not give burden to people. Through this letter of tears, on the one hand, he wants to win the love of the Corinthians, but on the other hand, he threatens those who are joining together an evil person and are engaging in all immoral things (2 Cor 12:21). This letter is a heavy one for Paul since his emotional roller-coasters move fast, sometimes calling his opponents Satan.

Consider and discuss: Let us think about the role of a painful letter. Obviously, Paul's letter of "tears" is very emotional and judgmental. What are the pros and cons of this kind of letter? Is an emotionally charged speech or letter working most of the time and effective to the audience today?

Letter of Reconciliation
(2 Cor 1:1—2:13; 7:5–16; 13:11–13)

Finally, Paul writes a letter of reconciliation because the Corinthians repented and the wrongdoer was punished. In this letter, he calls the Corinthian *ekklēsia* "the church of God," which means that the *ekklēsia* belongs to God, not to Jesus or Paul or to any Christian leaders. For this God's house, he says he "behaved in the world with frankness and godly sincerity, not by earthly wisdom but by the grace of God—and all the more toward you" (2 Cor 1:12). He reminds the Corinthians that God is merciful and consoles his people. He asks the Corinthians to forgive an identified wrongdoer since he was punished. He also asks them to reaffirm their love for him, so that they will not fall in Satan's designs (2 Cor 2:11). Likewise, he expresses his regret that he grieved them with a letter of tears. But he also believes that eventually, grief led to repentance (7:9). He makes a distinction between godly grief and worldly grief. While the former "produces a repentance that leads to salvation," the latter "produces death" (7:10). Lastly, he makes farewell in 13:11 and exhorts the Corinthians to have the same mind of Christ and live in peace.

Summary

1. Second Corinthians is a composite letter.

2. It is made up of at least two or maximum four letters: a letter of the collection (2 Cor 8); a letter of defense of Paul's ministry (2 Cor 2:14—7:4); a letter of tears (2 Cor 10-13); a letter of reconciliation (2 Cor 1:1—2:13; 7:5-16; 13:11-13); another letter of the collection (2 Cor 9).

3. These letters were written over a period to deal with different issues, as seen above.

4. With these various letters combined, it will be helpful to account for the history of Paul's relationship with the Corinthian community.

5. New situations developed in later times in the Corinthian *ekklēsia*: the arrival of the super-apostles, who are from Jewish ancestry, showing splendid colors of charisma and rhetorical abilities.

6. As 2 Cor 8-9 shows, Paul has a consistent and persistent desire to help the poor in Jerusalem. So it is important to explain why he was so eager to help them.

Further Reading

Cannon, Katie, Emilie Townes, and Angela Sims, eds. *Womanist Theological Ethics: A Reader*. Louisville, KY: Westminster John Knox, 2011.

Georgi, Dieter. *Remembering the Poor: The History of Paul's Collection for Jerusalem*. Nashville, TN: Abingdon, 1992.

Kim, Yung Suk. *A Theological Introduction to Paul's Letters: Exploring a Threefold Theology of Paul*. Eugene, OR: Cascade, 2011.

Love, Sechrest. "Identity and the Embodiment of Privilege in Corinth." In *1 and 2 Corinthians: Texts @ Contexts*, edited by Yung Suk Kim, 9-30. Minneapolis: Fortress, 2013.

Martin, Dale B. *Sex and the Single Savior: Gender and Sexuality in Biblical Interpretation*. Louisville, KY: Westminster John Knox, 2006.

Roetzel, Calvin. *2 Corinthians*. Abingdon, TN: Abingdon, 2007.

Welborn, Laurence. "Paul and Pain: Paul's Emotional Therapy in 2 Corinthians 1.1-2.13; 7.5-16 in the Context of Ancient Psychagogic Literature." *New Testament Studies* 57 (2011) 547-70.

———. "That There May Be Equality: The Contexts and Consequences of a Pauline Ideal." *New Testament Studies* 59 (2013) 73-90.

CHAPTER 20

Galatians

> There is no easy walk to freedom anywhere, and many of us will have to pass through the valley of the shadow of death again and again before we reach the mountaintop of our desires.
>
> —Nelson Mandela

Galatians at a Glance

1. Galatians was sent to the churches of Galatia, the Roman province of Asia Minor.
2. The location of these churches is a matter of debate. While some suggest that Paul wrote to a Celtic people in the northern part of the province, others think that he wrote to the southern part of the province during his first missionary journey (Acts 13–14).
3. Galatians is the only letter that Paul does not give thanks to his addressees. The reason is that the Galatians accepted a different gospel that he did not proclaim.
4. Paul defends his gospel of faith, based on God's grace or promise. The law is holy but it cannot be a condition of justification.
5. He also defends his apostleship, based on God's call, not by the human commission or authorities.
6. Justification and freedom are among the most important themes of Galatians.

Introduction

GALATIANS IS AN "ANGRY" letter in which Paul expresses his dissatisfaction with the Galatians. He is very upset and does not give thanks to them because they followed "a different gospel" that he did not preach. After he left Galatia, some Jewish Christians joined the community and taught that Gentiles should be circumcised to be Christian. They say that Gentile Christians also have to abide by Jewish laws. Against this different gospel, Paul argues that the law cannot be a condition for justification because it is God who justifies those who follow the Messiah Jesus and his faith (Gal 2:16, 21; 3:24). Throughout the letter, he argues that the law does not precede the promise or grace of God. Faith precedes the law because the former started earlier than the latter. Abraham has faith in God, and the law is given through Moses. But Paul does not reject the law; instead, he says, "For the whole law is summed up in a single commandment, 'You shall love your neighbor as yourself'" (Gal 5:14). The Galatians can be justified (meaning their good relationship with God) through Christ-like life and his faith. Their task is to fulfill "the law of Christ" (Gal 6:2). They are free when they participate in Jesus's faith. Among others, justification and freedom are among the most important themes of this letter.

Chapter Contents

1. The Occasion and Purpose of the Letter
2. Paul's Defense of His Gospel
3. Justification
4. Freedom

The Occasion and Purpose of the Letter

One of the biggest issues in the Galatian *ekklēsia* is Jewish Christians' push for circumcision for the Gentiles (Gal 2:12). In Antioch, Cephas used to eat with Gentiles. But when he received guests from James in Jerusalem, he chose to eat with Jewish brothers for fear of the circumcision faction. Seeing this, Paul was very upset because Cephas was craven and hypocritical. In other words, Cephas showed contempt for the Gentiles by choosing not to eat with them. Paul interpreted this act as a challenge to his gospel that God is impartial to all. So he says in Gal 2:14, "But when I saw that they were not acting consistently with the truth of the gospel, I said to Cephas before them all, 'If you, though a Jew, live like a Gentile and not like a Jew, how can you compel the Gentiles to live like Jews?'" With this issue of circumcision for the Gentile Christians, Paul defends the Gentile version of his gospel of faith.

Paul's Defense of His Gospel

Paul defends his gospel in several ways. First, one's right relationship with God is decided by faith, which is none other than faith in God. For Paul, God is faithful (cf. 1 Cor 1:9; 10:13; 2 Cor 1:18), and therefore, a person also must be faithful to him. In Jewish tradition and the Hebrew Bible, faith is about God. This faith begins with Abraham, who trusts God even before the law is given through Moses. So his argument is not the law first but the faith that fulfills the law. Keeping the law without faith will be blind. Paul says that he was blind when he had zeal for it: "You have heard, no doubt, of my earlier life in Judaism. I was violently persecuting the *ekklēsia* of God and was trying to destroy it. I advanced in Judaism beyond many among my people of the same age, for I was far more zealous for the traditions of my ancestors" (Gal 1:13–14). Because of this zeal for the law, he could not see the importance of God's love for all and that of faith. So he realizes that his love or zeal for the law actually prevented God's love to them.

Second, according to Paul, this faith also has to do with Jesus, who is the Messiah and Son of God. Jesus was faithful to God and fulfilled the law. Therefore, children of God must have Christ's faith (*pistis christou* as a subjective genitive). Based on this subjective genitive, Gal 2:16 can be translated as follows: "Yet we know that a person is justified not by the works of the law but through *Jesus Christ's faith*. And we have *come to participate in Christ Jesus's faith*, so that we might be justified by *Christ's faith*, and not by doing the works of the law because no one will be justified by the works of the law" (italics for emphasis). Having Christ's faith means to die with him and live in him.

Third, he also argues that God's grace or promise is the beginning or foundation of salvation; it is not the law or faith first. In this regard, his theology is thoroughly theocentric. It is God who called Abraham and made a covenant with him and his descendants. Then, Abraham must accept his grace and live by faith throughout his life. The law was given later through Moses in order to guide the children of God toward a good pasture. Therefore, the right order to keep for justification is God's grace, faith, and the law. While there is nothing wrong with the law, it cannot be a condition for justification. Since Abraham, faith has been working all the time down to Jesus and Paul himself. The law can be kept and fulfilled through the love of neighbor (cf. Gal 5:14). Jesus exemplified this love of neighbor through his faith.

Fourth, in his gospel, Christian freedom is important, but it does not mean that the Galatians are free to do anything. Rather, their freedom must be maintained "in Christ," which is a Christly manner. They are freed from slavery of human masters and must work for freedom of others because their freedom is not for themselves only (Gal 1:4; 5:1).

Fifth, "oneness" in Christ in Gal 3:28 should not be taken as the language of the sameness just like the imperial rhetoric of unity/concord (*homonoia*). "Oneness" does not mean that they are all the same, but it means that they are all equal before God; they are treated the same in terms of human rights and dignity.

Justification

Justification or righteousness is a complex term we need to tackle. If it is used for God, it refers to God's character or action. As we saw in Romans (chapter 18), Paul's fundamental claim is that God is righteous. In terms of his character, God is merciful, steadfast, and just. In terms of his action, God makes a covenant, protects his people, and guides them through discipline. So Micah tells them: "O mortal, what is good; and what does the LORD require of you but to do justice, and to love kindness, and to walk humbly with your God?" (Mic 6:8). Because God is righteous, the children of God have to live righteously (cf. Lev 20:26; Hab 2:4). As God is holy, his people must follow his holiness. Even in times of injustices, they have to live by their faith in God. Therefore, one can live righteously through faith, as Hab 2:4 says, "Look at the proud! Their spirit is not right in them, but *the righteous live by their faith*" (italics for emphasis). "Living by faith" is key to justification. In other words, in the Hebrew Bible as well as in Paul's letters, faith without living or work is incomplete or ineffective. Christ is the prime example of faith; he was faithful to God and demonstrated God's love in the world. Jesus lived righteously through his faith.

This above logic of faith and righteousness applies to the Galatians too. In Gal 2:16, Paul says that one is justified through Christ's faith (*pistis christou*), which is taken as a subjective genitive. His point is that a person can stand right before God through Jesus's faith. "Through Jesus's faith" means that one has to understand his work and follow his spirit, as Paul says, "and we have come to believe in (*eis*) Christ Jesus, so that we might be justified by Christ's faith, and not by doing the works of the law, because no one will be justified by the works of the law" (Gal 2:16). "To believe in (*eis*) Christ Jesus" must be different from "faith in Christ" (*pistis en christō*) in the sense that the former emphasizes faith's dynamic aspect. That is, Galatians must understand what Jesus did and participate in his faith. Only then may they be called righteous.

The above concept of "justification" differs from the forensic perspective of salvation in that God as a judge declares innocence to believers because of Jesus's substitutionary death for them. In Paul's undisputed letters, Jesus's death has to do with the demonstration of God's righteousness. Namely, his death is the result of what he proclaimed. Jesus was crucified because he preached a gospel that threatened the foundation of the Empire. In other words, one's justification is not by Jesus's death alone but through Christian participation in his faith that embodies God's presence in the world. One can live righteously by this faith, which advocates for the marginalized and the oppressed. Seen this way, the language of justification is not about one's legal status as in a court but about his/her ethical standing before God. Paul's point is not that one's justification was achieved already through Jesus but that he/she has to continue to live by the faith of Jesus. He states in Gal 2:20: "And it is no longer I who live, but it is Christ who lives in me. And the life I now live in the flesh I live *in the faith of* the Son of God, who loved me and gave himself for me" (Gal 2:20). Paul's point is that he wants to live by Jesus's faith.

Consider and discuss: Many churches and Christians believe that Paul's gospel is law-free because faith repeals or replaces the law. Because of this, there is a lack of Christian ethical mandate for improving human conditions in this world. But in fact, in Paul's view, the law is nothing wrong and it is fulfilled through Christ or neighborly love. Then how can you relate faith to the law in Paul's gospel?

Freedom

Christian freedom is often misunderstood. It does not mean that one is free from the law because only faith saves. In fact, Paul never says that faith replaces the law. Rather, the law is holy and good. The issue is not the law *per se* but person's misuse or zeal for it, resulting in blocking God's impartial love for all. In Galatia, Jewish Christians forced the circumcision law on to Gentile Christians. So Paul says, "For in Christ Jesus neither circumcision nor uncircumcision counts for anything; the only thing that counts is *faith working through love*" (Gal 5:6). He goes on to say: "For neither circumcision nor uncircumcision is anything; but a new creation is everything!" (Gal 6:15). The law must be fulfilled through the love of neighbor (Gal 5:14).

Christian freedom does not mean that Christians are free from death in the sense that they do not die because Jesus died their deaths. But in Paul's view, Christian freedom needs to die with Christ (cf. 2 Cor 5:14). Similarly, in Gal 1:4, he talks about the relation between Jesus's death and freedom: "who gave himself for our sins to set us free from the present evil age." As opposed to the traditional atonement theories, Paul does not say that Jesus's one-time perfect sacrifice is enough and necessary for salvation and freedom for Christians. "For our sins to set us free from the present evil age" does not mean that Jesus died instead of others, as in the forensic salvation perspective. In fact, "for our sins" can be a moral reason for which Jesus died. In other words, Jesus died because we did not die, in the sense that we were selfish. In this regard, Jesus's death is a moral sacrifice that challenges people to live through his faith. Therefore, Gal 1:4 can be understood alternatively: "Jesus gave himself because of our sins that we did not die, to set us free from the present evil age." This implies that we can be free from the evil age as long as we die to sin." So being free from the evil age can be possible when we deal with our sins through the example of Jesus's faith.

Paidagogos (Gal 3:24)

Paidagogos means variously: disciplinarian, custodian, or guardian, and it is often understood as repealing the law. This word appears in Gal 3:24 (also, 1 Cor 4:15). In Hellenistic culture, *paidagogos* is like a slave-guardian, who is responsible for children of the wealthy, and their primary job is to take these young students to school and to take care of them. With this view of the word, the law is compared to *paidagogos* until Christ came. That is, the law ended its function because Christ came. Many English Bibles follow the above interpretation: "Therefore the law was our disciplinarian until Christ came, so that we might be justified by faith" (NRSV); "So that the Law became our custodian until Christ so that we might be made righteous by faith" (CEB); "So the law was our guardian until Christ came that we might be justified by faith" (NIV).

However, *paidagogos* is understood positively in the Hebrew Bible in which the law serves as mother or nurse (Num 11:12). So the law can be perceived as a teacher who guides people to follow God's will. In Gal 3:24a, the law has been a good teacher until Christ came, but Jews did not follow it well. Here the problem is not the law *per se* but their crooked hearts. In 3:24b, the solution is implied: "so that we might be justified by faith." In the times of the law, Jews did not keep the law through faith. Now Christ showed God's righteousness through his faith. Therefore, the solution is to live by Jesus's faith (Gal 2:16); then the law will be fulfilled with the love of neighbor (Gal 5:14). Understood this way, the law is not replaced by Christ, but it is fulfilled through faith. Paul's point is not that faith in Christ made the law obsolete but that Christ fulfilled the law. Therefore, people have to follow his faith and fulfill the law by loving their neighbors (Gal 5:14).

Summary

1. Paul wrote Galatians to defend his gospel based on faith, against the so-called Judaizers (Jewish Christians) who forced Gentiles to be circumcised.

2. He defends his Gentile version of the gospel through faith. This "faith" was demonstrated by Jesus.

3. Galatians have to imitate Jesus's faith. What they need first is not to keep the law but live by faith.

4. Law also will be fulfilled through love. Otherwise, faith does not make the law obsolete; the law is fulfilled through the love of neighbor (Gal 5:14).

5. The concept of justification is ethical in that the Galatians are justified before God if they follow Christ's faith (Gal 2:16).

6. Christian freedom does not mean that one is free to do anything, but it means that Christians are bound to use it for others' freedom.

Further Reading

Braxton, Brad. *No Longer Slaves: Galatians and African American Experience.* Collegeville, MN: Liturgical, 2002.

Briggs, Sheila. "Galatians." In *Searching the Scriptures*. Vol. 2, *A Feminist Commentary*, edited by Elisabeth Schüssler Fiorenza, 218–36. New York: Crossroad, 1994.

Eisenbaum, Pamela. *Paul Was Not a Christian: The Original Message of a Misunderstood Apostle*. New York, NY: HarperOne, 2009.

Gaventa, Beverly. "The Maternity of Paul: An Exegetical Study of Galatians 4:19." In *The Conversation Continues: Studies in Paul and John in Honor of J. Louis Martyn*, edited by Robert T. Fortna and Beverly Gaventa, 189–210. Nashville, TN: Abingdon, 1990.

Hardin, Justin. *Galatians and the Imperial Cult: A Critical Analysis of the First-Century Social Context of Paul's Letter*. Tübingen: Mohr Siebeck, 2008.

Kahl, Brigitte. "No Longer Male: Masculinity Struggles Behind Galatians 3.28?" *Journal for the Study of the New Testament* 79 (2000) 34–49.

Kim, Yung Suk. *A Theological Introduction to Paul's Letters: Exploring a Threefold Theology of Paul*. Eugene, OR: Cascade, 2011.

Lopez, Davina. *The Apostle to the Conquered: Reimagining Paul's Mission*. Minneapolis, MN: Fortress, 2008.

Miguez, Néstor. "Galatians." In *Global Bible Commentary*, edited by Daniel Patte, 463–72. Nashville: Abingdon, 2008.

Osiek, Carolyn. "Galatians." In *Women's Bible Commentary: Revised Edition*, edited by Carol Newsom et al., 570–75. Louisville, KY: Westminster John Knox, 2012.

Parker, Angela. "One Womanist's Understanding of Paul's Problematic Self-Identity in Galatians." *Journal of Feminist Studies in Religion* 24.2 (2018) forthcoming.

Stendahl, Krister. "The Apostle Paul and the Introspective Conscience of the West." *Harvard Theological Review* 56 (1963) 199–215.

———. *Paul among Jews and Gentiles and Other Essays*. Minneapolis, MN: Fortress, 1976.

Tamez, Elsa. *The Amnesty of Grace: Justification by Faith from a Latin American Perspective*. Translated by Sharon H. Ringe. Nashville, TN: Abingdon, 1993.

Williams, Demetrius K. *An End to This Strife: The Politics of Gender in African American Churches*. Minneapolis: Fortress, 2004.

CHAPTER 21

Ephesians

I love the way Janie Crawford left her husbands / the one who wanted to change her into a mule / and the other who tried to interest her in being a queen. / A woman, unless she submits, / is neither a mule / nor a queen / though like a mule she may suffer / and like a queen pace the floor.

—Alice Walker[1]

The struggle, therefore, that now begins in the world is extremely complex, involving the historical role of Christianity in the realm of power—that is, politics—and in the realm of morals. In the realm of power, Christianity has operated with the unmitigated arrogance and cruelty—necessarily, since a religion ordinarily imposes on those who have discovered the true faith the spiritual duty of liberating the infidels. This particular true faith, moreover, is more deeply concerned about the soul than it is about the body, to which fact the flesh (and corpses of countless infidels) bears witness.

—James Baldwin[2]

Ephesians at a Glance

1. Ephesians was likely written by a disciple of Paul.
2. Ephesians is not an authentic Pauline text. Pauline authorship is disputed.

1. Walker, *In Search of Our Mothers' Gardens*, 7.
2. Baldwin, *Fire Next Time*, 45.

3. Ephesians was written in the last half of the first century CE or later.
4. The grammatical style and theological content of Ephesians differs from the seven authentic Pauline letters.
5. Ephesus, a Roman colony and capital of the province of Asia Minor, was a significant commercial center.
6. The Apostle Paul preached in Ephesus for about three years.
7. The author emphasizes salvation by grace and as a gift from God.
8. Ephesians concerns the incorporation of Gentile believers into God's plan of salvation.
9. Ephesians is one of several NT texts that contains the household codes and a spiritual gifts list.
10. The author views the believers as engaged in a spiritual battle with evil forces.

Introduction

THE LETTER TO THE Ephesians teaches God's free grace and salvation for believers and the inclusion of Gentiles through Jesus Christ within the ideological framework of dualism, predestination, spiritual warfare, and patriarchal order. According to the Acts of the Apostles, the Apostle Paul was not the first to preach the gospel of Jesus Christ in Ephesus (18:24). An eloquent Jewish man named Apollos, a native of Alexandria, Egypt, who knew the Scriptures very well, enthusiastically and boldly preached the gospel of Jesus in the synagogue in Ephesus (18:24–26). Despite all the accolades heaped upon Apollos, after hearing him preach in the synagogue, Priscilla and Aquila found it necessary to take him aside and teach him more accurately about the "Way of God." After Apollos leaves Ephesus, Paul arrives to find twelve disciples who had neither heard of the Holy Spirit nor been baptized in the name of the Lord Jesus (Acts 19:1–7). Paul preached in the synagogue in Ephesus for three months before he and the twelve disciples he anointed earlier were forced out by some opponents. He consequently preached for two years in the lecture Hall of Tyrannus where Paul claims all the Jewish and Greek residents of Asia heard the gospel (19:8–10; cf. 20:31). It was in Ephesus that books about powerful things or magic were collected and burned. Paul leaves Ephesus but not before causing an uproar by insulting the devotees of the great goddess Artemis when he asserted that gods made with human hands were not really gods (19:21–20:1). Eager to travel to Jerusalem, Paul does not return to Ephesus but sends for the elders of the *ekklēsia* there when he is in Miletus (20:16–38). Paul did not plant the *ekklēsia* in Ephesus, but he watered or nurtured it (1 Cor 3:6). It was among the Ephesian elders that Paul testified about the gospel of God's grace in order to build them up and give them an inheritance among the sanctified (20:24, 32); that imprisonments and persecutions await him (20:23); that the Holy Spirit has made them overseers to shepherd God's *ekklēsia* (20:28). These and other subjects are addressed in the letter to the Ephesians. Among Christians, Ephesians is most known for its emphasis on salvation by grace (2:8). Ephesians is structured like authentic Pauline letters with a salutation and blessing (chapter 1), the body of the letter (2:1—6:20) and a closing (6:21-24).

Chapter Contents

1. Salutation, Blessing, and Prayer Report
2. Saved by Grace through Jesus Christ
3. Inclusion of the Gentiles
4. Called Into One Body, Spirit, and Love (4:1—5:20)
5. Household Codes (5:21—6:9)
6. Clothe Yourselves for Spiritual Warfare

Salutation, Blessing, and Prayer Report

The author (hereafter called "Paul") identifies the Apostle Paul as the sender of the letter, reminding the addresses that Paul's apostleship is the will of God (1:1). God's will is a providential force in Ephesians (1:5, 9, 11). Different from most Pauline letters, Paul names no co-senders or associates in the salutation (cf. 1 Cor 1:1; 2 Cor 1:1; Gal 1:1–2). However, the closing implies that Paul is not alone. He mentions Tychicus as his dear brother and faithful minister whom he is sending to the Ephesians with a report of how Paul (and his co-laborers) are doing (6:21-22). The recipients of the letter are the holy ones (saints) that believe in Jesus Christ. Some of the best Greek manuscripts do not have the prepositional phrase "in Ephesus." It is possible that the letter was originally addressed to a general audience. Ephesians has a traditional greeting: "grace to you and peace from God our father and the Lord Jesus Christ" (Rom 1:1).

Verses 3–14 are like an ancient Jewish blessing (see 1 Kgs 8:15, 56; Ps 41:13). In the Greek, the blessing is an extended sentence consisting of many interconnected clauses. In the frequently occurring prepositional phrase "in whom," the relative pronoun "whom" primarily refers to Christ (1:7, 11, 13). The phrase "in Christ" is found in the blessing and throughout the letter (1:10, 12; 2:10, 13); God mediates God's blessings through or in Jesus Christ. The blessing addresses "God, the Father of our Lord Jesus Christ" (v. 3). God is the giver of every blessing; God gave the saints every spiritual blessing "in the heavenlies" (v. 3; 1:20; 2:6; 3:10; 6:12). The latter phrase is peculiar to Ephesians and may constitute seeds of later Gnostic thought along with other phrases like "made known to us the mystery of his will" (1:9) and "renewed in the spirit of your minds" (4:23).

Paul argues that through Christ Jesus, God pre-elected and adopted "us" (*hēmas*) to be God's children before God laid the foundation of the world, to be his holy ones and to be blameless (vv. 4, 5). This language can be read in various ways. Some interpret Paul's rhetoric as referring to predestination without free will and others argue that it signifies the foreknowledge of God and includes free will. Nothing happens unless it is within God's will. Everything functions within God's will for the "praise of [God's] glory" (vv. 6, 12, 14).

The love of God mediates God's gifts, blessings, and judgments. But Jesus's shed blood mediates redemption and forgiveness. God's grace makes it all possible. God lavishes abundant grace upon the saints with wisdom and intelligence, not capriciously (v. 8). God did not hide but revealed the mystery of God's will (v. 9; cf. 3:3, 4; Col 1:27–28). God's plan of salvation is brought together in Christ (v. 10; Col 1:20) and implemented according to God's will (v. 11). Both Paul and the Ephesians share in the experience of God's redemption and inheritance and the Spirit's seal (vv. 7, 11, 14; cf. 1 Thess 5:9; 2 Thess 2:14).

When Paul switches to the second person plural pronoun "you," he distances himself from the Ephesians, as perhaps the one who preached Jesus Christ to them: (a) "you heard the word of truth, the gospel of your salvation"; and (2) "after you believed, you were sealed with the Holy Spirit of promise" (v. 13). The blessing culminates with a refrain repeated throughout the blessing: "for the praise of [God's] glory" (v. 14).

Paul has heard about the faith and love of the Ephesians. He continually prays that God will give them a spirit of wisdom and revelation and that they might realize the hope of their calling, their shared inheritance, and the great power of God at work in Christ Jesus as the exalted one and head of the *ekklēsia* (1:15–23).

Saved by Grace through Jesus Christ

A significant theological claim in the body of the letter (2:1—6:20) is the claim that the Ephesians were saved by God's grace (vv. 5, 8). The Ephesians and Paul were naturally "children of wrath" (vv. 2, 3). All previously lived a life of transgression and sin. But God raised Jesus (an early Christian preaching; see Acts of the Apostles) and God raised "us," Paul declares, together with Christ (2:4). This joint action by God is salvation by grace. Deliverance or salvation comes from God's gracious action in Jesus Christ; it is the gift of God with no strings attached. It is an inheritance with no taxes, no stipulations, no required work or services to perform, and no limitations on the extent of "our" deliverance. But those saved by God's grace are expected to yield good works (v. 10). God's saving action is meant to benefit future generations and not just for the present (v. 7).

Inclusion of the Gentiles

For the first time Paul identifies his audience as "you Gentiles" (2:11–22), but, of course, Paul addresses them from the perspective of a Jewish man. He is also a prisoner for the sake of the Gentiles (3:1; 4:1). The Gentiles were once far but now are near (2:12–13, 17); they must not forget their past or previous relationship to the "circumcised ones"; they were "in the flesh," "without Christ" and foreigners, without a deliverer and a homeland, without hope and without God. But through Christ's blood they now fully participate in the promises, salvation, and citizenship of God (2:14, 15). Despite being uncircumcised, the Gentiles, through Christ, are now members of God's household or family (vv. 18–19). The mystery of God's plan was also revealed to the Gentiles and the Apostle Paul is the one through whom God revealed the "mystery of Christ" (3:1–13). Consequently, the Gentiles can also approach God with boldness and confidence; they participate in the body, communion, and inheritance. Paul offers a prayer for the Gentiles (3:14–21). God, as their Father, is "able to do superabundantly above anything we can ask or even conceive of . . . according to the power at work in us" (3:20).

Called into One Body, Spirit, and Love (4:1—5:20)

Paul continues by admonishing the Gentile Christians to live in a manner that is worthy of their calling (*klēsis*), interacting with one another in a spirit of love. The Gentiles are members of one body (the *ekklēsia*/assembly), empowered by one Spirit and have one purpose. Christ is the head of the body; through Christ, God mediates the gifts of grace. God's gifts allow the saints to function as apostles, prophets, evangelists, pastors, and teachers in the *ekklēsia*. The gifts should promote unity and mature behavior and thinking. The gifts also guard against deceptions. The Gentile Christians are both called to and called out; they are called into the body and called to abandon their old way of life, which includes abandoning those Gentiles still alienated from the life of God. It would seem that if God predestined the Gentile Christians to share in God's salvation and inheritance, to know the mysteries, and to be members of the body, then the Gentiles who do not believe (perhaps their relatives and other loved ones) are predestined to destruction and to be nonbelievers, sinners, and outsiders.

Consider and discuss: How might Paul's message to the Gentile Christians encourage readers to be exclusionary and encourage an "us versus them" attitude toward family and others who do not embrace Christianity or may embrace God through other religions? How might the language in Ephesians mask the complexities of life in the church and the reality of our imperfect humanity whether we are Christians or not?

Household Codes (5:21—6:9)

The household codes are the rules that govern the hierarchical relationship or lines of authority and power between a man and his wife; a father (or parents) or his/their children, and the father/master and his slaves. This structure mirrors that of the Greco-Roman household, prescribing an ideal household order from a primarily elite male perspective. Paul places the codes within a theological or Christological framework to encourage compliance within the household. Of course, women sometimes function as the head of their own households (see Luke 10:38–42; Acts 12:12; 16:15), but the ideal household is one in which the male is the head and everyone else submits to his authority. Wives are admonished to submit to and respect their husbands and slaves are to obey their masters with fear and trembling. Husbands/Fathers/Masters (one and the same) are to love, nourish and cherish their wives, not provoke their children to anger, and avoid speaking harshly to their slaves. The codes of conduct are set within the context of service to Christ, but the greater burden always lies with the subordinated members of the household and not with the husband/father/master. The household codes correlate with the expectations of the broader culture; neither Paul nor his disciples invented them.

Consider and discuss: How might these household codes contribute to violence in a household? Why do you think some readers reject some parts of the household codes (i.e., slaves obey your masters) but not others? How might adherence to these household codes negatively impact gender equality in society? In what ways do these ancient household codes not reflect some contemporary households?

Clothe Yourselves for Spiritual Warfare

Throughout Ephesians the theme of clothing oneself is used to encourage personal accountability and preventive behaviors, but in 6:10–20 we find it as an extended military metaphor. The saints must cloth themselves in the entire armor of God in order to protect themselves against the devil's (*diabolos*) schemes. The devil, it appears, has many lives and one would think is immortal. Their opponents are spiritual and not "flesh and blood." When the evil day arrives, the saints will be able to stand firm because they have taken every precaution to stand by clothing themselves with truth, justice/righteousness, the gospel of peace, faith, salvation, and God's word. These are symbolized by girded loins, body armor, shoes, shield, helmet, and sword. As God's ambassador in chains, Paul requests that the saints remain in constant prayer for themselves and for him as he continues to reveal the mystery of the gospel.

Consider and discuss: Why do you suppose Paul found the image of combat attire a suitable metaphor for the saints? How might emphasis on a spiritual opponent deflect from concrete, visible opponents and causes that Christians might be called to address?

Summary

1. God's will is mediated through Jesus Christ.
2. Salvation is the free gift of God's grace in Christ Jesus.
3. As children of God, Gentile Christians share in the same adoption, body, gifts, salvation, and inheritance with Jewish believers.

Further Reading

Bird, Jennifer G. "Ephesians." In *The Fortress Commentary on the Bible: The New Testament,* edited by Margaret Aymer, Cynthia Briggs Kittredge, and David A. Sánchez, 527–42. Minneapolis: Fortress, 2014.

———. "Ephesians." In *A Postcolonial Commentary on the New Testament Writings,* edited by R. S. Sugirtharajah and Fernando F. Segovia, 265–80. New York: T. & T. Clark, 2009.

MacDonald, Margaret Y. *Colossians and Ephesians.* Sacra Pagina 17. Collegeville, MN: Liturgical, 2000.

Martin, Clarice J. "The *Haustafeln* (Household Codes) in African American Biblical Interpretation: 'Free Slaves' and 'Subordinate Women.'" In *Stony the Road We Trod: African American Biblical Interpretation,* edited by Cain Hope Felder, 206–31. Minneapolis: Fortress, 1991.

Perkins, Pheme. *Ephesians.* Nashville: Abingdon, 1997.

Smith, Mitzi J. "Ephesians." In *True to Our Native Land: An African American Commentary of the New Testament,* edited by Brian Blount et al., 348–62. Minneapolis: Fortress, 2007.

Tanzer, Sarah J. "Ephesians." In *Searching the Scriptures: A Feminist Commentary.* Vol. 2, edited by Elisabeth Schüssler Fiorenza, 326–48. New York: Crossroad, 1998.

Yee, Tet-Lim N. *Jews, Gentiles and Ethnic Reconciliation: Paul's Jewish Identity and Ephesians.* Cambridge: Cambridge University Press, 2005.

CHAPTER 22

Colossians

The true measure of any society can be found in how it treats its most vulnerable members.

—Mahatma Gandhi

Colossians at a Glance

1. Colossians belongs to the Deutero-Pauline Letters.
2. The authorship of Paul is disputed.
3. It looks like Paul's authentic letters, but its writing style and theological views are different.
4. Colossians addresses false teachings in the *ekklēsia* such as Jewish mysticism and Gnosticism.
5. Household codes in the letter regulate relationships between spouses, between parents and children, and between masters and slaves.
6. Paul's egalitarian view of the community fades in the later *ekklēsia*.

Introduction

It is hard to date Colossians, but most probably it was written at least a generation after Paul's death. One consensus is that Colossians was written before Ephesians because there is a literary pattern that the latter depends on the former. Namely, most of the vocabulary in Ephesians comes from Colossians. In fact, these two letters are very similar to each other; for example, both have similar household codes (Col 3:18—4:1; Eph 5:21—6:9). The big difference between these two has more to do with their respective issues.

Chapter Contents

1. Authorship
2. The Author's Instructions
3. Theological Differences With Paul's Undisputed Letters

Authorship

Pauline authorship of Colossians is disputed because of its writing style and linguistic details. In Colossians, we see a long sentence (Col 1:3–8) and a redundant style of writing, which we do not see in Paul's undisputed letters: for example, "praying for you and asking" (Col 1:9; cf. 1:11, 23, 26; 3:16). There are also unusual expressions: "blood of his cross" (Col 1:20); "forgiveness of sins" (Col 1:14). These expressions are not found in Paul's undisputed letters.

The Author's Instructions

Colossians contains issues regarding Jewish mysticism: "Elemental spirits of the universe" (Col 2:8): following "principalities and powers" (Col 2:15); "worship of angels" (Col 2:18). In Gnostic or Jewish mysticism, self-abasement is promoted, as hinted in Col 2:23: "self-imposed piety, humility, and severe treatment of the body." In this mysticism, there is world-denying attitude, as seen in Col 2:21: "Do not handle, Do not taste, Do not touch." In the *ekklēsia*, some came from Jewish Gnosticism or Syncretistic form of Hellenistic Judaism and emphasizes religious piety and otherworldly spirituality. The author responds to the above issues by writing in the name of Paul and hopes to secure the congregation with the correct teaching about Jesus. The most important instruction to the *ekklēsia* is that Christ is more powerful than elemental spirits or any cosmic powers (Col 2:10, 15). More than that, "he is the image of the invisible God, the firstborn of all creation" (Col 1:15). He is the true ruler and creator: "for in him all things in heaven and on earth were created, things visible and invisible, whether thrones or dominions or rulers or powers—all things have been created through him and for him. He himself is before all things, and in him all things hold together (Col 1:16–17). He is also "the head of the body, the *ekklēsia*" (Col 2:18). The other important teaching to the *ekklēsia* is to live by household codes (Col 3:18—4:1). These codes counter Gnostic spirituality that denies this world.

Theological Differences with Paul's Undisputed Letters

There are theological differences between Colossians and Paul's undisputed letters. First, while Paul's eschatology is very imminent, Colossians does not emphasize the imminent apocalypse. Colossians has an emphasis on salvation for now and done already in Christ, as seen in Col 2:12–13: "When you were buried with him in baptism, you were also raised with him through faith in the power of God, who raised him from the dead. And when you were dead in trespasses and the uncircumcision of your flesh, God made you alive together with him, when he forgave us all our trespasses" (cf. Eph 2:5, 8). Paul's view of salvation is a future emphasis, as in Rom 5:10: "For if while we were enemies, we were reconciled to God through the death of his Son, much more surely, having been reconciled, will we be saved by his life."

Second, Christology in Colossians is very different from Paul's undisputed letters. In the former, we see high Christology in that Jesus is seen as God (cf. Col 1:15–18). But in the latter, Jesus has a role to play as the Son of God and the Messiah, who is also subordinate to God, as 1 Cor 15:28 implies, "When all things are subjected to him, then the Son himself will also be subjected to the one who put all things in subjection under him, so that God may be all in all."

Third, "the body of Christ" is used and understood differently. In Paul's undisputed letters, it is Christ's crucified body (cf. 1 Cor 11:23–26; Rom 7:4). Even if it is applied to the community, the concept of the body has more to do with a site of living or union. Thus, "the body of Christ" in 1 Cor 12:27 is read as Christic body. But in Colossians it is used as a metaphorical organism, as in Col 1:24: "for the sake of his body, that is, the *ekklēsia*." Moreover, in this later *ekklēsia*, the community is not egalitarian anymore. The head of the community is Christ (Col 1:18), and community members are structured hierarchically. In fact, in Paul's undisputed letters, he never uses "the body of Christ" with the *ekklēsia* side by side. Whenever he refers to the *ekklēsia*, he uses the form of the *ekklēsia* of God (1 Cor 1:2; 10:32; 11:22; 15:9; 2 Cor 1:1; Gal 1:13). For Paul, "the body of Christ" is primarily associated with Christ's real body and Christians' living of his body.

Summary

1. Colossians, Ephesians, and 2 Thessalonians belong to the Deutero-Pauline Letters.
2. Colossians is different from Paul's undisputed letters in terms of writing style and theological issues.
3. Thus, Pauline authorship is disputed.
4. Main issues include Jewish mysticism and otherworldly spirituality.
5. The author argues that Christ is everything and more powerful than other powers.
6. The letter also includes household codes and high Christology.

Further Reading

D'Angelo, Mary Rose. "Hebrews." In *Women's Bible Commentary: Twentieth-Anniversary Edition*, edited by Carol A. Newsom, Sharon H. Ringe and Jacqueline E. Lapsley, 608–12. Louisville: Westminster John Knox, 2012.

Elliott, Neil. "Good News to the Colonized?" In *Unsettling the Word: Biblical Experiments in Decolonization*, edited by Steve Heinrichs, 247–48. Manitoba, CN: CommonWord, 2018.

Johnson, E. Elizabeth. "Colossians." In *Women's Bible Commentary: Revised Edition*, edited by Carol Newsom et al., 585–87. Louisville, KY: Westminster John Knox, 2012.

Okure, Teresa. "Colossians." In *Global Bible Commentary*, edited by Daniel Patte, 490–99. Nashville, TN: Abingdon, 2004.

Standhartinger, Angela. "The Epistle to the Congregation in Colossae and the Invention of the 'Household Code.'" In *A Feminist Companion to the Deutero-Pauline Epistles*, edited by Amy-Jill Levine, 88–97. New York: Continuum, 2003.

CHAPTER 23

Philippians

> I emphasize that women were the primary recipients of the letter ... it is very likely that the followers of the Resurrected One in Philippi were mostly women and were led by women.
>
> —Elsa Tamez[1]

> If we are to have peace on earth, our loyalties must become ecumenical rather than sectional. Our loyalties must transcend our race, our tribe, our class, and our nation; and this means we must develop a world perspective.
>
> —Martin Luther King Jr.[2]

Philippians at a Glance

1. Paul wrote Philippians from prison to the Philippians in Philippi in eastern Macedonia.
2. The atmosphere of the letter reflects his last days in prison.
3. This is a composite letter, made up of possibly three letters: Letter A (4:10–20); Letter B (1:1—3:1; 4:21–23); Letter C (3:2—4:1).
4. Philippians is a warm letter that does not show a vast array of community issues.
5. Paul encourages the Philippians to stay strong in faith.

---

1. Tamez, *Philippians*, 6–7.
2. King, "Christmas Sermon on Peace," 70.

6. The hymn of Christ in 2:6–11 needs to be examined correctly in the literary context.

Introduction

PAUL WRITES PHILIPPIANS FROM prison (probably in Rome). Philippians is a composite document comprising at least three letters. Letter A (Phil 4:10–20) is about his thanksgiving for their financial support. Letter B (Phil 1:1—3:1; 4:21–23) is about his friendship and exhortations to the *ekklēsia*. Letter C (Phil 3:1—4:1) is about warnings against those who impose the circumcision of the Gentiles. Overall, Paul exhorts the Philippians to live like Christ and reminds them of the Christ hymn in Phil 2:6–11. He also urges them to maintain the unity of the *ekklēsia*. If this letter was written about 60 CE from Rome (cf. Phil 1:13; 4:22), it must contain his last-day thought about the gospel, mission, and eschatology.

Chapter Contents

1. The Context and Purpose of the Letter
2. Christ Hymn (2:6–11) and Christology

The Context and Purpose of the Letter

From prison, Paul writes a letter and renews his friendship with the Philippian *ekklēsia*. First, he shares joy with the Philippians because of their financial support and participation in his ministry: "I have been paid in full and have more than enough; I am fully satisfied, now that I have received from Epaphroditus the gifts you sent, a fragrant offering, a sacrifice acceptable and pleasing to God" (Phil 4:18). He is very content with his gospel mission despite his imprisonment and wants to visit them again (Phil 2:23–24).

Second, Paul exhorts them to "be of the same mind, having the same love, being in full accord and of one mind" (Phil 2:2). He continues: "Do nothing from selfish ambitions or conceit, but in humility regard others as better than yourselves" (Phil 2:3). In Phil 2:1–18, he encourages them to live according to Christ. For example, he encourages them to have the same mind rooted in Christ (Phil 2:5; 4:1–9) and cites a hymn of Christ to emphasize the importance of a humbling service toward others (Phil 2:6–11).

Third, Paul addresses false teachings about laws and circumcision (Phil 3:2–21) and admonishes the Philippians to move away from such teachings. In Phil 3:2, he gives warnings about some people who disrupt the congregation: "Beware of the dogs, beware of the evil workers, beware of those who mutilate the flesh!" According to Paul, what really matters is not the physical circumcision but the mind and heart that "worship in the Spirit of God" (Phil 3:3. cf. Rom 2:29). He lists his own life story where he could boast about the flesh (Phil 3:4-6): "Even though I, too, have reason for confidence in the flesh. If anyone else has reason to be confident in the flesh, I have more: circumcised on the eighth day, a member of the people of Israel, of the tribe of Benjamin, a Hebrew born of Hebrews; as to the law, a Pharisee; as to zeal, a persecutor of the *ekklēsia*; as to righteousness under the law, blameless." His concluding instruction to the *ekklēsia* is found in Phil 3:9: "And be found in him, not having a righteousness of my own that comes from the law, but one that comes through "faith of Christ," which is Jesus's faith. This verse echoes Gal 2:20 where Paul says a similar thing about Jesus's faith. The point is that the Philippians have to live by Jesus's faith, as Paul does the same.

Consider and discuss: Paul was imprisoned and sent a letter to the Philippians. Their relationship, based on the love of God, proved to be sound and helpful to both Paul and the Philippian *ekklēsia*. Paul was very encouraged by the fellowship of the *ekklēsia*. His soul was touched and did not give up hope in God. In the face of a prison nation, with a high incarceration among the minorities, in what way does this letter challenge Christians and the nation to rethink our view of the prison and inmates?

Christ Hymn (2:6–11) and Christology

Phil 2:6–11

Who, though he was in the form of God, did not regard equality with God as something to be exploited, but emptied himself, taking the form of a slave, being born in human likeness. And being found in human form, he humbled himself and became obedient to the point of death—even death on a cross. Therefore God also highly exalted him and gave him the name that is above every name, so that at the name of Jesus every knee should bend, in heaven and on earth and under the earth, and every tongue should confess that Jesus Christ is Lord, to the glory of God the Father.

Paul uses this early Christian hymn to encourage the Philippians to have the same mind that is in Christ (Phil 2:5). Because of this need, he emphasizes Christ's humbling work for humanity. In this hymn, Jesus was like God and took the appearance of a slave, experiencing all human fragility and weakness. He was obedient to the will of God, risking his life. Therefore, God highly exalted him. The point of this hymn is not that Jesus was God but that he was in the form of God (i.e., "to be like God") and gave himself for the world. Namely, God was seen, felt, and touched by humans through the marvelous life of Jesus. Jesus became Lord because of his faith and sacrifice. Thus, Paul is impressed with Jesus's life and faith, and he wants to live like and for him, as he says, "Yet whatever gains I had, these I have come to regard as loss because of Christ. More than that, I regard everything as loss because of the surpassing value of knowing Christ Jesus my Lord. For his sake I have suffered the loss of all things, and I regard them as rubbish, in order that I may gain Christ" (Phil 3:7–8).

Understood this way, *morphē* (3:6-7) should not be taken to mean Jesus's equality with God, as the NIV translates: "Who, being in very nature God." Rather, *morphē* means "form, outward appearance, shape."[3] So both "the form of God" (3:6) and "the form of a slave" (3:7) mean that Jesus was like God because he revealed God through his life. In a similar vein, Jesus was like a slave because he lived a miserable life like a slave.

Consider and discuss: There is another early Christian hymn in Col 1:15–20, which is very different from Phil 2:6–11. While the former clearly underscores high Christology, the latter is nuanced. In what way are these Christian hymns similar yet different?

Col 1:15–20

He is the image of the invisible God, the firstborn of all creation; for in him all things in heaven and on earth were created, things visible and invisible, whether thrones or dominions or rulers

---

3. Bauer, *Greek English Lexicon*, 659.

or powers—all things have been created through him and for him. He himself is before all things, and in him all things hold together. He is the head of the body, the *ekklēsia*; he is the beginning, the firstborn from the dead, so that he might come to have first place in everything. For in him all the fullness of God was pleased to dwell, and through him God was pleased to reconcile to himself all things, whether on earth or in heaven, by making peace through the blood of his cross.

Summary

1. Paul wrote Philippians from prison to the believers in Philippi in eastern Macedonia.

2. Philippians is a composite document, made up of probably three letters: Letter A (4:10–20); Letter B (1:1—3:1; 4:21–23); Letter C (3:2—4:1).

3. Philippians is a warm letter like 1 Thessalonians. Paul appreciates the Philippians' support for his ministry.

4. Paul warns about false teachings regarding Jewish laws and circumcision.

5. Paul reaffirms the gospel of Christ, based on faith.

6. Christology in Philippians is not the high Christology we see in Colossians.

Further Reading

Marchal, Joseph A. *The People Beside Paul*. Atlanta: Society of Biblical Literature Press, 2015.

———. *Philippians: An Introduction and Study Guide: Historical Problems, Hierarchical Visions, Hysterical Anxieties*. New York: T. & T. Clark, 2017.

———. "Slaves as Wo/men and Unmen: Reflecting Upon Euodia, Syntyche, and Epaphroditus in Philippi." In *The People Beside Paul*, edited by Joseph A. Marchal, 141–76. Atlanta: Society of Biblical Literature Press, 2015.

Stubbs, Monya. "Philippians." In *True to Our Native Land: An African American New Testament Commentary*, edited by Brian Blount et al., 363–79. Minneapolis, MN: Fortress, 2007.

Tamez, Elsa. *Philippians*. Wisdom Commentary. Collegeville, MN: Liturgical, 2017.
Williams, Demetrius K. "Philippians." In *Global Bible Commentary*, edited by Daniel Patte, 482–89. Nashville: Abingdon, 2004.
Works, Carla. "Philippians." In *Women's Bible Commentary: Revised Edition*, edited by Carol Newsom et al., 581–84. Louisville, KY: Westminster John Knox, 2012.

CHAPTER 24

Philemon

Oh, the abominations of slavery? Though Philemon be the proprietor, and Onesimus the slave, yet every case of slavery however lenient its afflictions and mitigated its atrocities, indicates an oppressor, the oppressed, and the oppression.

—Mrs. Zilpha Elaw (1986, 98)

Perhaps this is the reason he was separated from you for a while, so that you might have him back forever, no longer as a slave but more than a slave, a beloved brother.

—Phlm 15–16a, NRSV

Philemon at a Glance

1. Philemon is counted among the seven undisputed or authentic Pauline letters.
2. Philemon is dated from about the mid-50s to the early 60s CE.
3. Philemon is a letter written from prison.
4. Paul's self-identification as the "*prisoner* of Christ Jesus" is rare.
5. The location of Paul's imprisonment is unknown; possibilities include Ephesus, Caesarea Maritima, or Rome.
6. Philemon is the only Pauline letter that explicitly names a woman, Apphia, as an addressee.
7. Paul writes to appeal to Philemon to receive Onesimus back "as a brother and no longer as a slave."

8. Many scholars argue that Philemon concerns the return of a fugitive slave.
9. Philemon is the shortest extant Pauline letter.
10. Philemon was a significant text used by both pro-slavery and anti-slavery advocates in the American slavery debate.

Introduction

TRADITIONALLY, MOST SCHOLARS ASSERT that Philemon constitutes Paul's attempt to return the runaway slave, Onesimus, to his Christian slave master, Philemon. Thus, Paul intervenes in the protected relationship between an enslaver and his enslaved human property. Others have proposed that Onesimus was not a *fugitive* slave but perhaps (a) a slave that Philemon loaned to Paul for a set time, (b) served as Paul's apprentice, or (c) was Philemon's estranged brother. The primary basis on which scholars determine that Onesimus was a slave is the one occurrence of the Greek noun *doulos* (translated *slave*) at v. 16 where Paul asks Philemon to receive Onesimus "no longer as a slave [*doulos*] but as a brother." Of course, Paul often uses the slave metaphor to describe his own relationship to Jesus Christ or God (Rom 1:1; 1 Cor 9:19, 27; Gal 1:10). Whatever Onesimus's relationship to Philemon (and to Paul), Paul appeals to Philemon on the basis of love throughout the very brief letter in hopes of convincing him to receive Onesimus on Paul's terms and so that Paul does not have to pull rank on Philemon.

Both pro-slavery and anti-slavery advocates found the text sufficient to support their divergent views. If one presumes that Onesimus was a slave, one should read the letter in the context of ancient Roman slavery, particularly with regard to runaway slaves and manumission (emancipation). Concerning Philemon, Zilpha Elaw, a former enslaved African, stated that "slavery in every case, save those of parental government, criminal punishment, or the self-protecting detentions of justifiable war, if such can happen, involves a wrong, the deepest in wickedness of any included within the range of the second table (of the Law)."[1] Of course, Elaw did not foresee America's "New Jim Crow" laws and policies or its privatized prison nation through which we are witnessing the reinvention or recycling of slavery. Readers are encouraged to grapple with various pertinent issues that arise from a reading Philemon, in addition to the problem of enslavement, ancient and modern.

---

1. Elaw, "Memoirs of the Life," 98.

Chapter Contents

1. The Opening (vv. 1–7)
2. Love and Fictive Kinship Language
3. Paul's Appeal to Philemon
4. Paul's Complicity in the Invisibility and Silencing of Onesimus

The Opening (vv. 1–7)

One might expect that Paul would identify himself as a slave of Jesus Christ rather than as a prisoner if he is advocating for a slave. By using the plural possessive pronoun "our," Paul invites the named addressees (Philemon, Apphia, Archippus) to envision themselves as part of a larger community inclusive of Timothy, his coauthor, and himself. Timothy is not imprisoned with Paul, but Epaphras, Paul's fellow prisoner, also sends greetings (v. 23). Philemon is identified both as a dear friend and a coworker; other coworkers, Mark, Aristarchus, Demas and Luke, send greetings (v. 24).

Paul's use of the singular possessive second person pronoun "your" in reference to the *ekklēsia* (assembly) that convenes in Philemon's house affirms the latter's position as paterfamilias (father of the family) and master/lord (*kurios*) of the house and of its other occupants or subordinates. Philemon's status is not diminished; his religious leadership and social status coincide/overlap, maintaining the social hierarchy. Later, Philemon is not only a dear friend, but Paul's brother (v. 7). Their "sister" Apphia is a significant member of the house *ekklēsia*. Apphia is likely not Philemon's biological sister; she is probably a sister in ministry. Paul considers it necessary and prudent to mention her by name in relationship to the *ekklēsia* and his appeal on behalf of Onesimus.

Given three other explicit references to his incarceration in such a brief letter (vv. 9, 10, 13), Paul might be using his predicament to gain sympathy from Philemon or Paul's imprisonment has something to do with why Onesimus is with him in the first place. Although Onesimus is a name often given to male slaves, it remains a possibility that Onesimus was a freedman (former slave) or a free-born male and/or brother of Philemon. If Onesimus was a freedman or brother of Philemon and lived in his former slave owner/patron's or brother's home, Philemon would still be his *kurios* (lord/master).

After naming the addressees, Paul shifts to the first person singular pronoun "I." Paul highlights Philemon's virtues and uses them to convince him to receive Onesimus on Paul's terms. Paul is always praying for

Philemon because of reports of the love he has shown toward the saints. Paul mentions Philemon's faith toward the Lord Jesus, good deeds (love) as a result of effective faith, and their brotherhood (vv. 6–7). The receiving of Onesimus as a brother is the voluntary good deed that Paul hopes to convince Philemon to perform (v. 14).

Love and Fictive Kinship Language

Paul continues to appeal to Philemon on the basis of love rather than duty (vv. 8–9). Not only is Paul a prisoner of Christ Jesus, a subversive way of mitigating the power and authority of the Roman Empire over his life, but he is an old man (*presbyteros*). He is perhaps hoping to increase Philemon's sympathy toward him, soliciting more good deeds of love. While Philemon and the other leaders of the *ekklēsia* are brothers and sisters, demonstrating an equality among them, Onesimus is mentioned for the first time in the letter as Paul's child (*teknon*) (v. 10); Paul birthed (*gennaō*) or parented him while incarcerated. Paul asks Philemon to receive Onesimus as a brother. If Onesimus is a slave, the use of fictive kinship language will not alter his social subordination or the demeaning and inhumane relationship of the enslaved to his enslaver.

Consider and discuss: How do you think Apphia, as a woman or perhaps a mother who has experienced the pains of child birth and knows the risks, might respond to Paul's use of birthing language in relationship to Onesimus? Sometimes we are not conscious of the privileged positions from which we write, speak, teach, or preach, even when doing so metaphorically. In what ways might Paul's use of birthing language demonstrate appropriation of an experience that is foreign to his body and gender and demonstrate a position of privilege? Think of ways that we speak from a position of privilege without regard for those less privileged or impacted by what we have not experienced (e.g., incarcerated women who give birth in prison).

Paul's Appeal to Philemon

Paul describes Onesimus as previously useless but now useful. Slave masters expected their slaves to be useful or productive; a useless slave was a worthless slave. After all, a slave was a speaking tool, an instrument of labor, and the object of the enslaver's unmitigated pleasure, including sexual desires (v. 11). Alluding to the love he has for Onesimus as "my heart," Paul is reluctantly sending Onesimus back (v. 12), but hopes Philemon will receive him "no longer as a slave but more than a slave, as a beloved brother. . . . In the flesh and in the Lord" (v. 16)

Consider and discuss: Paul appeals to Philemon to welcome and receive Onesimus, in the language of hospitality and not of manumission. If Onesimus is Philemon's slave, Paul does not ask Philemon to set him free. Human trafficking or sex slavery is an epidemic in the USA and globally; even some Christians have been convicted of trafficking in humans. How would you read against the grain and perhaps "rewrite" this letter as an activist and abolitionist of modern-day slavery and sex trafficking?

Paul's Complicity in the Invisibility and Silencing of Onesimus

Paul does not disrupt the invisibility and silencing of Onesimus that results from being enslaved or subordinated. Onesimus is not a cowriter, even though the letter concerns his well-being and future; Philemon is written about and Paul speaks for him. Yet Onesimus may be present when Paul writes the letter, and he likely sent the letter with Onesimus (v. 12a). Onesimus is silenced. Onesimus is subordinated to all parties named as noted above. Philemon should comply with Paul's request because Paul is imprisoned, elderly (*presbyteros*), and his compliance would refresh Paul's heart (v. 20). Onesimus's feelings or desires are not revealed or considered. Nothing is said about the material or emotional impact on Onesimus's life. Even if Onesimus was Philemon's estranged brother, he would remain subordinated to Philemon as a member of his household and/or his house *ekklēsia*. Any honor that Philemon has within society is predicated on the shame or subordination of those of lower social status inside and outside of his household. Philemon benefits because he receives a "useful" Onesimus, will demonstrate that he is a man of good deeds and love by receiving Onesimus, and any expenses Philemon has incurred will be covered by Paul (v. 18).

Consider and discuss: In 2017 we have publicly witnessed the silencing of female Senators Elizabeth Warren, Kamala Harris, and Maxine Waters by their male colleagues in the US Senate. Out of such silencing we have derived hashtags #Resist, #IWillSpeak, and #ReclaimingMyTime. What are the ways in which society and religious institutions silence persons based on gender, race/ethnicity, sexuality, and/or social class? How are we complicit and how can we cease being complicit?

Summary

1. It is unclear whether or not Onesimus is a slave.
2. If Onesimus is a slave, one must read Philemon in the context of Roman slavery.
3. Paul appeals to Philemon on the basis of love and fictive kinship but does not advocate manumission if Onesimus is a slave.
4. Philemon can be a significant text for thinking critically about modern-day sex slavery and human trafficking.

Further Reading

Batten, Alicia J. "Philemon." In *Philippians, Colossians, Philemon*, edited by Mary Ann Beavis, 201–64. Wisdom Commentary 51. Collegeville, MN: Liturgical, 2017.

Brogdon, Lewis. *A Companion to Philemon*. Cascade Companions. Eugene, OR: Cascade, 2018.

Callahan, Allen Dwight. *The Embassy of Onesimus. The Letter of Paul to Philemon*. Valley Forge: Trinity, 1997.

Elaw, Zilpha. "Memoirs of the Life, Religious Experience, Ministerial Travels and Labors of Mrs. Zilpha Elaw." In *Sisters of the Spirit: Three Black Women's Autobiographies of the Nineteenth Century*, edited by William L. Andrews, 49–160. Bloomington: Indiana University Press, 1986.

Felder, Cain Hope. "The Letter to Philemon." In vol. 11 of *The New Interpreter's Bible*, edited by Leander Keck, 881–905. Nashville: Abingdon, 2005.

Jeal, Roy. *Exploring Philemon: Freedom, Brotherhood and Partnership in New Society*. Atlanta: SBL, 2015.

Johnson, Matthew V., James A. Noel, and Demetrius K. Williams, eds. *Onesimus Our Brother: Reading Religion, Race, and Culture in Philemon*. Minneapolis: Fortress, 2012.

Lewis, Lloyd A. "Philemon." In *True to Our Native Land: An African American New Testament Commentary*, edited by Brian Blount et al., 437–43. Minneapolis: Fortress, 2007.

Martin, Dale B. *Slavery as Salvation: The Metaphor of Slavery in Pauline Christianity*. New Haven: Yale University Press, 1990.

Punt, Jeremy. "Paul, Power and Philemon: 'Knowing Your Place': A Postcolonial Reading." In *Philemon in Perspective: Interpreting a Pauline Letter*, edited by D. Francois Tolmie, 223–50. Berlin: de Gruyter, 2010.

Smith, Mitzi J. "Philemon." In *Wesley One Volume Commentary of the Bible*. Indianapolis: Wesley Publishing House, forthcoming.

———. "Philemon." In *Women's Commentary of the Bible: Revised*, edited by Carol A. Newsom, Sharon H. Ringe, and Jacqueline E. Lapsley, 605–07. Louisville: Westminster John Knox, 2012.

CHAPTER 25

1–2 Thessalonians

Hope is being able to see that there is light despite all of the darkness.

—Desmond Tutu

1–2 Thessalonians at a Glance

1. First Thessalonians is the earliest letter by Paul (ca. 50 CE).
2. It was sent to the early Gentile converts at Thessalonica.
3. Second Thessalonians is among the Deutero-Pauline Letters, which means the authorship of Paul is disputed.
4. In 1 Thessalonians, Paul warns that the Lord will come back soon like a thief in the night. But in 2 Thessalonians, the author delays the Parousia by saying that there will be a sign before the Parousia (2 Thess 2:1–12).
5. First Thessalonians is a warm letter that reflects Paul's early Gentile mission. He established a business with manual work in order not to burden the Thessalonians while spreading the good news to them.
6. Paul's main teaching in 1 Thessalonians is that God of Jews is the true God and his Son Jesus is the Messiah who will come back soon to take them to glory.
7. In 2 Thessalonians, the author warns against those who claim that the Parousia happened already.

Introduction

FIRST THESSALONIANS WAS SENT to Paul's first Gentile *ekklēsia* in Thessalonica. This letter contains important information about his early mission strategy and teaching about God and Jesus. In general, this letter is very warm and does not reveal serious issues in the community. So he gives extended thanks for their faith and good work. However, there were some concerns about those who died before the Parousia. The main teaching of 1 Thessalonians is that Gentile converts should worship God through Jesus Christ and that the Lord will come back soon. He encourages them to stay in faith until the Lord comes back. By contrast, 2 Thessalonians raises a new issue that the Parousia is delayed unlike in 1 Thessalonians. The author says that there must be a sign before the Parousia. Otherwise, members of the *ekklēsia* must work hard until then. This implies that some people did not work, believing that the end was there with them already.

Chapter Contents

1. The Context of the Letter (1 and 2 Thessalonians)
2. Main Teachings of 1 Thessalonians
3. Main Teachings of 2 Thessalonians

The Context of the Letter (1 and 2 Thessalonians)

In Thessalonica, Paul worked hard to have Gentile converts while setting up a shop, working day and night. He left the city to preach the gospel elsewhere. Later, he sent Timothy to check on how the Thessalonians were doing. Timothy reported back to him, bringing the good news that the Thessalonians were doing well. So Paul gives extended thanks to them in 1 Thess 1–2. To those who are concerned about the resurrection of the dead, he confirms that there will be a Parousia and exhorts them to stay strong in faith. In 2 Thessalonians, the author deals with the enthusiasts who claim that the Parousia is already there and who do not work, and exhorts the Thessalonians to live worthy of God's calling.

Main Teachings of 1 Thessalonians

Paul sent Timothy to the Thessalonians after he left because he was anxious about their faith (1 Thess 3:2–5). But Timothy brought him the good news about their faith and love (1 Thess 3:6). So Paul gives much thanks in chapters 1–2 for their work of faith, love, and hope in Christ (1 Thess 1:3). He also reminds them of how much he cared for them for "the gospel of God in spite of great opposition" (1 Thess 2:2; cf. 2:8–9) "like a nurse tenderly caring for her own children" (1 Thess 2:7) and "a father with his children" (1 Thess 2:11). As the letter tells, the Thessalonians were strong in their faith in God and turned away from idols (1 Thess 1:9–10). Paul continues to instruct them to do the right thing by abstaining from fornication and controlling their own bodies in holiness and honor, "not with lustful passion, like the Gentiles who do not know God" (1 Thess 4:3–5).

Paul's main teaching is to assure the Thessalonians that there will be a day of transformation on the last day (1 Thess 4:13–18). He encourages them to have hope in God under any circumstances. He also reminds them that "the day of the Lord will come like a thief in the night" (1 Thess 5:2). Some people say that "there is peace and security" in the world (1 Thess 5:3). "Peace and security" echoes a Roman slogan like *Pax Romana* ("peace of Rome"). But this peace by Rome will collapse when the end comes. This Roman slogan is hollow and dangerous because people are ruled under this fake slogan of peace and security. But when the end comes, Roman peace and security will come to an end too. Thus, Paul asks the Thessalonians to live in the light as "children of light and children of the day," "not of the night or of darkness" (1 Thess 5:5). He believes that Rome will disappear eventually when the Lord comes back and asks his *ekklēsia* to live soberly until then. Until that Parousia, they must spread the good news of God to the world through Christ and show good works to others, proving that they are children of light. Paul encourages them to stand with God through faith, hope, and love: "But since we belong to the day, let us be sober, and put on the breastplate of faith and love, and for a helmet the hope of salvation" (1 Thess 5:8). He goes on to remind them of what to do in the *ekklēsia*: seeking to do good to one another and to all (1 Thess 5:15), rejoicing always (1 Thess 5:16), praying without ceasing (1 Thess 5:17), giving thanks in all circumstances (1 Thess 5:18), not quenching the Spirit (1 Thess 5:19), not despising the words of prophets (1 Thess 5:20), testing everything and holding fast to what is good (1 Thess 5:21), and abstaining from every form of evil (1 Thess 5:22).

Anti-Imperial Reading and 1 Thessalonians

Apparently, Paul was neither an abolitionist nor a political revolutionary. But that does not mean that he promoted slavery or that he was a dualist between the body and the soul, or between this world and the next world. His belief and actions are driven by the so-called "interim ethics" in the sense that the Lord will come back soon. So he believed that the slavery system or any form of evil in society will come to an end. But this does not mean that Christians have to wait for the Lord idly. Rather, they have to prove that they are children of light (1 Thess 5:5). Only in this limited sense does Paul's interim ethics have anti-imperial connotations because the Parousia will relativize all political powers. So he asks the Thessalonians to live a life of righteousness, away from the imperial propaganda that fills only the stomachs of the elites. This exhortation comes from his understanding that "the gospel of God" challenges Rome and its gospel with a slogan of peace and security (1 Thess 2:2, 8–9). "The gospel of God" (1 Thess 2:2, 8–9) is opposed to "the gospel of Rome," which promotes a slogan of peace and security. While Caesar brings peace and security through military might, Jesus does so through faith, hope, and love.

Consider and discuss: The Thessalonians worried about the death of some members in the *ekklēsia*. They were told that the Lord would come back before anyone in the *ekklēsia* died. But the reality was different. Some died and the resurrection did not happen. Paul encourages them to stay in the faith because God's victory will appear in the end. In light of the violence and death occurring in our time, how should we wait? What should we do in the interim? Is our only purpose as Christians or believers to wait for an end? When "good Christians" or "good people" die early or tragically, how can we comfort one another and maintain hope?

Main Teachings of 2 Thessalonians

The main teaching of 2 Thessalonians is twofold: encouraging the members of the *ekklēsia* to stay in their faith in the face of persecution; checking those who teach that the Parousia has already come (2 Thess 2:2–3). The author exhorts the members of the *ekklēsia* to keep their faith under any circumstances because God will keep them strong and repay their work. At the same time, the author warns against those who do not work: "For even when we were with you, we gave you this command: Anyone unwilling to work should not eat. For we hear that some of you are living in idleness, mere busybodies, not doing any work. Now such persons we command and exhort in the Lord Jesus Christ to do their work quietly and to earn their own living" (2 Thess 3:10–12).

Summary

1. First Thessalonians is Paul's earliest letter and the oldest one in the New Testament.
2. First Thessalonians is a warm letter that shows Paul's initial teaching and ministry among the Gentiles.
3. This letter contains early historical information about Paul's mission strategy and experience.
4. Paul tried to convert Gentiles to the God of Israel by preaching about his Son Jesus. His message was: 1) the Jewish God is the true God to whom they have to turn from idols; 2) Jesus is the Son of God who will return soon; and 3) therefore, they have to live the last days as the children of light.
5. Authorship of 2 Thessalonians is disputed because the author's apocalyptic view is very different from 1 Thessalonians.
6. Second Thessalonians deals with various issues such as persecutions and the mistaken view of the Parousia.

Further Reading

Ascough, R. S. "The Thessalonian Christian Community as a Professional Voluntary Association." *Journal of Biblical Literature* 119 (2000) 311–28.

Beavis, Mary. "2 Thessalonians." In *Women's Bible Commentary: Revised Edition*, edited by Carol Newsom et al., 592–94. Louisville: Westminster John Knox, 2012.

Koester, Helmut. "Imperial Ideology and Paul's Eschatology." In *Paul and Empire*, edited by Richard Horsley, 158–66. Harrisburg, PA: Trinity, 1997.

Míguez, Néstor. *The Practice of Hope: Ideology and Intention in 1 Thessalonians*. Minneapolis, MN: Fortress, 2012.

Smith, Abraham. *Comfort One Another: Reconstructing the Rhetoric and Audience of 1 Thessalonians*. Louisville, KY: Westminster John Knox, 1995.

Stubbs, Monya. "1 Thessalonians." In *Women's Bible Commentary*, edited by Carol Newsom et al., 588–91. Louisville, KY: Westminster John Knox, 2012.

Yeo, K. K. "1–2 Thessalonians." In *Global Bible Commentary*, edited by Daniel Patte, 500–507. Nashville: Abingdon, 2004.

CHAPTER 26

1–2 Timothy and Titus

Should the church be trying to erect a spiritual reign of terror over people by threatening earthly and eternal punishment on its own authority and commanding everything a person must believe and do to be saved? Should the church's word bring new tyranny and violent abuse to human souls?

—Dietrich Bonhoeffer[1]

1–2 Timothy and Titus at a Glance

1. First and Second Timothy and Titus are called "Pastoral Letters" or Pseudepigrapha.
2. Pseudepigrapha means writings written in somebody else's name.
3. Scholars believe that these three letters were not written by Paul because their writing style, vocabulary, and theological issues are very different from Paul's undisputed letters.
4. Two important issues dealt with in these letters are correct teaching and *ekklēsia* organization.
5. There are household codes and strict teachings about women.
6. First Tim 2:11–15 may be compared with 1 Cor 14:33b–36 because of their similarity.

---

1. Bonhoeffer, *Discipleship*, xxiii.

Introduction

THE PASTORAL LETTERS (1 Tim, 2 Tim, and Titus) reflect the nature of post-Pauline churches after Paul died. These churches have to deal with false teachings (1 Tim 1:3–11) that have to do with Gnosticism, asceticism (1 Tim 4:3; 6:20), and mystic experience (1 Tim 1:4: "myths and endless genealogies"). In response to these issues, the author (pastor) of these letters emphasizes the right teaching (1 Tim 2:1–15) and the right leadership of the *ekklēsia* (1 Tim 3:1–13).

Chapter Contents

1. Pastoral Letters as Pseudepigrapha
2. The Context of the Pastoral Letters
3. Main Teaching
4. Theological Differences with Paul's Undisputed Letters

Pastoral Letters as Pseudepigrapha

Pseudepigrapha means literature written in somebody else's name. Scholars believe that 1 Tim, 2 Tim, and Titus were not written by Paul for the following reasons. First, the vocabulary of these letters is very different from the authentic letters of Paul. About 30 percent of the words in the Pastoral Letters does not appear in Paul's undisputed letters, and many of these distinctive words appear in the second century CE. Moreover, some words have new meaning in these later letters. For example, faith means a set of teaching (1 Tim 1:19; 3:9; 4:1; 2 Tim 3:8; 4:7; Titus 1:13). But for Paul, it means trust or participation in God or Jesus. Righteousness means a person's morality (1 Tim 6:11; 2 Tim 2:22; 3:16; Titus 1:8). But for Paul, it means a person's right standing before God (cf. Gal 2:16). Second, Marcion omitted these pastoral letters from his canon (ca. 150 CE), which implies that he did not think that Paul wrote them. They are even placed in the appendix to the church's first canon. Third, there are theological differences between the Pastoral Letters and Paul's undisputed letters. Whereas Paul affirms women's leadership (1 Cor 11:5), the Pastoral Letters prohibit women's leadership in the *ekklēsia* (1 Tim 2:11–15). Whereas Paul discourages marriage because the end is near, the Pastoral Letters encourage it. Fourth, whereas Paul's undisputed letters do not have household codes, the Pastoral Letters require the *ekklēsia* to follow rigid household codes.

Pseudepigrapha

Pseudepigrapha means literature written in somebody else's name in ancient times. In other words, the real author's name is hidden. Why does this happen? First of all, in ancient culture, there is a tendency that students honor their deceased teacher by writing in the teacher's name. In this way, they think they continue their teacher's legacy. So Paul's students may have thought this way and wrote in his name. Second, if they write in their own names, their writings would not be well accepted because they are not famous like Paul. Since Paul is influential to many Christians across the board, his students had to write in his name. When they do so, they both continue and discontinue Paul's teaching and legacy. Dealing with the same kind of issues, their theological response is different from Paul's. The Pseudepigrapha is also found in Jewish literature long before Paul (Jewish Pseudepigrapha). In fact, Jews in the second century BCE and onward, struggling with their future status because of foreign domination, wrote literature under somebody else's name: names such as Abraham, Enoch, and Ezekiel.

Consider and discuss: Do you think Pseudepigrapha texts are forgeries? Why or why not? In modern culture, forgery or plagiarism is a serious issue and crime. But Pseudepigrapha is a literary product, rooted in the ancient culture where such writings were customarily accepted by the populace. How would you respond to these pastoral letters if they were not written by Paul?

The Context of the Pastoral Letters

False teachings in these pastoral letters include Jewish myths and ascetic lifestyles that prohibit marriage and certain foods (1 Tim 1:3–11; 4:3). Gnosticism emphasizes asceticism and teaches that people get to heaven through Jesus, the secret knowledge. It is also possible that some women with this view of Gnostic asceticism demanded radical equality with men in the *ekklēsia*. They may have followed Paul's egalitarian teaching that both women and men are equal before God, as in Gal 3:28. In this situation, the pastor wants to control the *ekklēsia* with the right teaching about Jesus from his perspective. This is how the *ekklēsia* becomes more conservative than before (1 Tim 2:11–15).

Consider and discuss: 1 Tim 2:11–15 is very similar to 1 Cor 14:33b–36 (an interpolation). Do you think 1 Cor 14:33b–36 came from 1 Tim 2:11–15? Why or why not? Compare two passages and discuss similarities and differences.

Main Teaching

To deal with false teachings, the pastor instructs the *ekklēsia* to have the same faith, which means to believe the same thing about Jesus; namely, faith means to believe something about Jesus. This is also a matter of *ekklēsia* doctrines (1 Tim 1:3–20; 2 Tim 2:14–26; Titus 1:10–16), which deals with who Jesus is and what he did. Some false teachers stress an ascetic lifestyle and argue that Christ has already returned. The pastor explains who these false teachers are and how the *ekklēsia* should respond. The answer is in 1 Tim 4:1–5:

> Now the Spirit expressly says that in later times some will renounce the faith by paying attention to deceitful spirits and teachings of demons, through the hypocrisy of liars whose consciences are seared with a hot iron. They forbid marriage and demand abstinence from foods, which God created to be received with thanksgiving by those who believe and know the truth. For everything created by God is good, and nothing is to be rejected, provided it is received with thanksgiving; for it is sanctified by God's word and by prayer.

To organize and run the *ekklēsia* well, the pastor elects *ekklēsia* offices such as bishops and deacons whose qualifications are stipulated in 1 Tim 3:1–13 (cf. Titus 1:5–9). Those qualifications are very strict and specific. One notable thing is that there is a condition that one must marry once. There are also other rules in the *ekklēsia*: respecting different ages (1 Tim 5:1–2); rules for widows (1 Tim 5:3–16); rules for elders (5:17–22). Likewise, the pastor wants to make sure that the *ekklēsia* is structured hierarchically with male leadership and adopts the social convention of gender hierarchy and master-slave relation. In this way, he wants the *ekklēsia* to survive and grow without pressures from the society (1 Tim 6:1–2; Titus 2:1–10).

Household Codes

Household codes regulate various social relations in the community: between parents and children; between spouses; between masters and slaves. These codes are not found in Paul's undisputed letters but only in the Deutero-Pauline Letters and Pastoral Letters: Col 3:18–4:1; Eph 5:21–6:9; Titus 2:1–10; cf. 1 Pet 2:18—3:7. While these household codes are less severe than the ones in society under the Roman Empire, one thing is clear: Paul's legacy about egalitarianism gave place to a socially conservative community. Below are the household codes found in the NT, which may be compared with one another.

Col 3:18—4:1	Eph 5:21—6:9	Titus 2:1–10	1 Pet 2:18—3:7
wives: be subject to your husbands, as is fitting in the Lord (3:18)	*wives:* be subject to your husbands, as you are to the Lord (5:22–24)	*older men:* be temperate, serious, prudent, sound in faith and love (2:2)	*wives:* accept husbands' authority; don't adorn yourselves outwardly (3:1–6)
husbands: love your wives and never treat them harshly (3:19)	*husbands:* love your wives, just as Christ loved the church (5:25–33)	*older women:* be reverent, not slander, teach and encourage younger women (2:3–5)	*husbands:* be considerate of your wives, paying honor to them (3:7)
children: obey your parents in everything (3:20)	*children:* obey your parents in the Lord, for this is right (6:1–3)	*younger women:* love their husbands and children, be self-controlled (2:4–5)]	x

Col 3:18—4:1	Eph 5:21—6:9	Titus 2:1-10	1 Pet 2:18—3:7
fathers: do not provoke your children, or they may lose heart (3:21)	***fathers:*** do not provoke you children to anger; bring them up in the Lord (6:4)	***younger men:*** be self-controlled, do good works, say nothing evil (2:6-8)	x
slaves: obey earthly masters in everything . . . fearing the Lord (3:22-25)	***slaves:*** obey your earthly masters, as you obey Christ (6:5-8)	***slaves:*** be submissive to their masters; not talk back, be faithful (2:9-10)	***slaves:*** accept masters' authority, even if you suffer; Christ also suffered (2:18-25)
masters: treat your slaves justly and fairly; you also have a Master in heaven (4:1)	***masters:*** stop threatening your slaves; you have the same Master in heaven (6:9)	x	x

Theological Differences With Paul's Undisputed Letters

There are many theological differences between Paul's undisputed letters and Pastoral Letters. First, the view of God is very different between them. In Paul's undisputed letters, he emphasizes God's initiative: God is steadfast, faithful, and righteous (Rom 1:16-17; 3:21-26). God is the source of life in Christ (1 Cor 1:30). God is the object of faith (1 Thess 1:8; Rom 3:30; 4:20; 5:1; 1 Cor 2:5). But in the Pastoral Letters, God is seen in abstract terms: "immortal, invisible, the only God" (1 Tim 1:17).

Second, there are Christological differences between Paul's undisputed letters and Pastoral Letters. In the former, Jesus's primary title is the Son of God who demonstrates God's righteousness in the world (Rom 3:21-26). The result is his crucifixion, which shows the power and wisdom of God (1 Cor 1:24-5). Christ is the foundation of the *ekklēsia* and he is an example of faith (*pistis christou*). But in the Pastoral Letters, Jesus is a mediator between God and humankind, and he is a ransom (1 Tim 2:5-6). He came to save sinners and finished the salvation business (1 Tim 1:15; 2 Tim 2:10).

Third, there are eschatological differences between Paul's undisputed letters and Pastoral Letters. Paul's eschatology is "already-but-not-yet" (cf. 1

Thess 5:1–11; 1 Cor 7:29–31). Though the Parousia has not come yet, Christians can expect a new time of God through the Spirit. The end will come shortly, but it is not yet. But in later churches after Paul, there is no urgency of waiting for the end. The pastor delays the Parousia by focusing on the present ministry and growth of the *ekklēsia*. Likewise, marriage and childbearing are very important to *ekklēsia* growth (1 Tim 2:15; 4:1–5).

Fourth, the view of faith is different between Paul's undisputed letters and the Pastoral Letters. Faith, according to Paul, is a word of commitment and action toward God's righteousness, which must be demonstrated in the world (Rom 1:16–17; 3:21–26). It also has to do with the imitation of Christ. Faith means to participate in Jesus's faith and death (Gal 2:16–20). In fact, God is the most faithful figure in Paul's view. Jesus is faithful to God; therefore, his followers must also be faithful to God. Paul's favorite phrase is *pistis christou* ("faith of Christ," a genitive case, for example, in Rom 3:21–22; Gal 2:16), which means that Jesus is faithful. More specifically, for Christians, to have faith means to die to sin and live to God (Rom 6:10–23). But in the Pastoral Letters, faith means a set of teachings ("faith as knowledge," 1 Tim 1:3–5; 4:6; 2 Tim 1:13). There is no sense of participating faith in God or in Christ. Likewise, Jesus becomes merely the object of faith (2 Tim 3:15): "faith in Christ" (*pistis en christo*).

Fifth, there are differences about women between Paul's undisputed letters and Pastoral Letters. Overall, Paul's view of women is very positive, though 1 Cor 11:2–16 is an ambiguous place to interpret. He has women coworkers (Phoebe and Prisca) and calls Junia (woman) to be among the prominent apostles (Rom 16:7). Women are free to participate in the Corinthian *ekklēsia*; they pray and prophesy (1 Cor 11:5). But in the Pastoral Letters, as in 1 Tim 2:11–15, women are not allowed to speak and teach in the *ekklēsia*. Even the law is used to support the subordination of women.

Sixth, there is a different view of marriage between Paul's undisputed letter and Pastoral Letters. Paul discourages marriage because of the imminent Parousia. Celibacy is preferred because a person can fully devote himself/herself to God (1 Cor 7:7–8, 36–38). Divorce is allowed conditionally if the unbelieving spouse wants. Spousal relations are interdependent (1 Cor 7). But in the Pastoral Letters, marriage is encouraged and younger widows are told to marry because the end is near (1 Tim 5:14).

Summary

1. Pastoral Letters (1 Tim, 2 Tim, and Titus) are considered Pseudepigrapha.

2. *Pseudepigrapha* are writings that attribute authorship to a known author that is not the actual author.
3. They contain household codes (Titus 2:1–10) and strict teachings about women (1 Tim 2:11–15).
4. The same author is believed to have written all three pastoral letters.
5. The author deals with false teachings and other matters about *ekklēsia* administration.
6. Overall, the post-Pauline churches become socially conservative and adopt the convention of society.

Further Reading

Bassler, Jouette. *1 Timothy, 2 Timothy, and Titus*. Nashville, TN: Abingdon, 1996.

Dewey, Joanna. "1 Timothy, 2 Timothy, and Titus." In *Women's Bible Commentary*, edited by Carol Newsom et al., 595–605. Louisville, KY: Westminster John Knox, 2012.

Maloney, Linda. "The Pastoral Epistles." In vol. 2 of *Searching the Scriptures: A Feminist Commentary*, edited by Elizabeth Schüssler Fiorenza, 361–80. New York: Crossroad, 1983.

Martin, Clarice J. "1–2 Timothy, Titus." In *True to Our Native Land. An African American Commentary on the New Testament*, edited by Brian Blount et al., 409–36. Minneapolis: Fortress, 2007.

———. "The *Haustafeln* (Household Codes) in African American Biblical Interpretation: 'Free Slaves' and 'Subordinate Women.'" In *Stony the Road We Trod: African American Biblical Interpretation*, edited by Cain Hope Felder, 206–31. Minneapolis: Fortress, 1991.

———. "'Somebody Done Hoo'dood the Hoodoo Man': Language, Power, Resistance and the Effective History of Pauline Texts in American slavery." In *Slavery in Text and Interpretation*, edited by Allen Callahan, Richard Horsley, and Abraham Smith, 203–33. Semeia Studies 83/84. Atlanta: Society of Biblical Literature, 1998.

Tamez, Elsa. *Struggles for Power in Early Christianity: A Study of 1 Timothy*. Translated by Gloria Kinsler. Maryknoll, NY: Orbis, 2007.

Thurston, Bonnie. "1 Timothy 5:13–16 and Leadership of Women in the Early Church." In *A Feminist Companion to the Deutero-Pauline Epistles*, edited by Amy-Jill Levine, 159–74. New York: Continuum, 2003.

Section IV

Catholic Texts

CHAPTER 27

Letter of James

I love the pure, peaceable, and impartial Christianity of Christ: I therefore hate the corrupt, slaveholding, women-whipping, cradle-plundering, partial and hypocritical Christianity of this land. Indeed, I can see no reason, but the most deceitful one, for calling the religion of this land Christianity.

—Frederick Douglass, Former Slave and Abolitionist[1]

But the wisdom from above is first pure, then peaceable, gentle, willing to yield, full of mercy and good fruits, without a trace of partiality and hypocrisy.

—James 3:17, NRSV

The richest whites have seventy-four times more wealth than the average white family. But among African Americans, the richest families have a staggering two hundred times more wealth than the average Black family.

—Keeanga-Yamahtta Taylor[2]

---

1. Douglass, *Narrative of the Life*, 363.
2. Taylor, *From #BlackLivesMatter to Black Liberation*, 7.

James at a Glance

1. James is a catholic or universal epistle written to no particular *ekklēsia* (church/assembly).
2. The date of James is uncertain (between mid-first century and early-second century CE).
3. An unknown Jewish author wrote James.
4. Place of origin is unknown, but it was likely written in the Jewish Diaspora.
5. Written in parenesis style, consisting of a list of moral imperatives or admonitions.
6. Members of the *ekklēsia* in the Diaspora are mostly the poor.
7. Poverty in James is the result of scandalous acts of oppression and exploitation.
8. Significant themes include suffering and endurance, temptation, wisdom, hypocrisy, wealth and poverty, faith and action.
9. James utilizes sixty-three *hapax legomena* (words appearing in no other NT text).
10. Martin Luther called James a "straw epistle" because of its imperative that faith without works is dead.

Introduction

JAMES IS ONE OF seven catholic (universal or general) epistles (with 1 and 2 Peter; 1, 2, 3 John and Jude). Authorship is ascribed to *James*; no other familial references are provided to further identify him. Perhaps this is strategic, adding to the universal appeal of the letter and leaving open the possibility that the author was James the brother of Jesus. James emerged as the leader of the Jerusalem Council that decided how the Gentiles would be incorporated into the Jesus movement (Acts 12:17; 15:1–31; Gal 1:19).

James is concerned with suffering and endurance/survival, socioeconomic oppression and exploitation, wisdom and teaching, and faith and action among the Diaspora believers. Diaspora refers to people who are displaced or exiled from their home or homelands. For people living in the Diaspora, the themes that James addresses would impact their lives differently from those who are not displaced but are at home. Some readers find comfort in James and others are disturbed by its content. In the sixteenth century, the Protestant Reformer Martin Luther (1483–1546) opposed the inclusion of James into the canon because it conflicted with his *sola fides* or by faith alone and not by works are we saved. However, the letter was accepted in the Alexandrian, Western, and Syrian churches in the third, fourth, and fifth centuries, respectively.

Contemporary readers night view James as a hodgepodge of ethical advice, somewhat like the Sermon on the Mount/Plain, but perhaps in the author's mind his teachings are interconnected. James shows familiarity with Hebrew Bible traditions and appears to know the Gospels of Matthew and Luke: the poor will possess the kingdom (2:5; Matt 5:3; Luke 6:20). Similar to Jesus's teachings in the Sermon on the Mount/Plain in the Gospels of Matthew and Luke, James admonishes his readers to follow the royal law that commands one to love others as one loves one's self—a significant imperative for displaced people that are often encouraged to value and love the oppressor more than one's self (2:9; Matt 22:39; Mark 12:31; Luke 10:27). And beneficial to both oppressed and oppressors is James's requirement that believers become doers and not just hearers of God's word (2:10; cf. Deut 22:6–7; Matt 5:19; Rev 1:3).

Chapter Contents

1. Salutation
2. Suffering and Endurance/Survival
3. Rich and Poor
4. Wisdom and Speech/Teaching
5. Faith and Action

Salutation

The author identifies himself metaphorically as a slave (*doulos*) of both God and the risen Christ (Messiah or anointed one) (1:1; cf. Phil 1:1; Rev 1:1). Perhaps by identifying himself as a slave the author aligns himself with the most vulnerable in the *ekklēsia*, namely the poor (*ptochos*), as opposed to rich exploiters of the poor. Yet, slaves, those generally occupying the lowest social position in a slave society like Rome, are not explicitly mentioned again. However, James does invoke *the law of liberty* (*aleutheria*) (1:25;

2:12), which might especially appeal to enslaved and/or colonized persons. Perhaps the poor are primarily slaves.

The letter is addressed to the Twelve tribes in the Diaspora. This reference to the Twelve tribes (also Abraham, Elijah, and Rahab, 2:22–25; 5:17) demonstrates an ancestral connection between the author's audience and the Hebrew children of the Hebrew Bible/OT. Jewish believers in the Diaspora are scattered or are living outside of Palestine or Judea. James refers to their assemblies as a synagogue and an *ekklēsia* (2:2; 5:14) where we know both Jews and Gentiles gathered and could signify houses and other indoor or outdoor spaces (cf. Acts 16:13–16).

Suffering and Endurance/Survival

Some womanist scholars have argued that God does not function as a liberator in every circumstance; sometimes God is a God of survival who helps the oppressed to persevere. James begins and ends the letter (1:2–4; 5:7–11) by making a connection between suffering and perseverance. Suffering and trials are tests of faith; faith produces perseverance. Perhaps perseverance is understood not as passive paralysis, but as action motivated by faith. How else might it result in lacking nothing? God does not test or tempt believers; desires and lusts tempt and sin results from yielding (1:12–16). Also, the conflicts and disputes within the assembly result from internal cravings, desiring what one does not possess but could possess if one asked God correctly (4:1–4). Those in the Diaspora should find joy in trials or oppression because it is simply one's faith being tested, but not by God. A tested faith yields perseverance. Is James saying that if the believers in the Diaspora can view their suffering as a test of faith (not by God), they will do all they can to survive or endure?

> **Consider and discuss:** How might James be understood as glorifying suffering or oppression? Considering our contemporary contexts, how do some people/groups find themselves in the Diaspora? When is such homelessness or displacement the result of oppression and a continued state of oppression? How is James's testimony about God as not being the source of trials and temptation different from other testimonies in the biblical text? Which do you prefer and how might our privilege inform our preferences?

Rich and Poor

James spends considerable time discussing the binary of rich and poor; no middle ground exists. That which is good news for the humble is not so for the rich. The humble brother should boast in his being exalted, but the rich in his being humbled and perishing (1:9–11). In the assembly, preference or bias is shown toward the wealthy. It seems that the poor *and* rich show favoritism toward the latter. Perhaps the poor have been complicit in their own oppression by also privileging the rich over themselves, engendering a kind of fear and fetish, and breaking the royal law of love. The rich oppress the poor outside of the assembly by dishonoring, suing, defrauding laborers of fair wages, and flaunting their wealth while neglecting the poor, including the orphans and widows (1:27; 2:6; 5:1–6). Any partiality is sin and constitutes a transgression of the law that admonishes believers to love one's neighbor as one's self (2:1–13). Simultaneously, James does not encourage a material or social reversal of fortunes or a redistribution of wealth, but a spiritual preference and future inheritance of the Kingdom for the poor (2:5).

Consider and discuss: What are evidences in our society and in our churches or religious institutions of the gap between the rich and the poor and a favoritism for the former? What are the causes of this gap? Who are the materially or socioeconomically poor in our societies? What can we do to dismantle poverty?

Wisdom and Speech/Teaching

James connects wisdom, faith, and hypocrisy; wisdom derives from God and is free for the asking (1:5–8). Hypocrisy is evidenced by a disconnectness between what we say or believe (through hearing/reading) and our behavior or conduct (1:19–27). We show wisdom when we are doers of God's word. Religion is being taught and modeled by those with loose tongues. They are all talk and show no care for the less fortunate, for the poor and/or widows and orphans. Their religion is a worthless one. Teachers of religion are held to a higher standard (3:1–12). Wisdom from God is pure, peaceful, gentle, flexible, merciful, and good fruit, demonstrating no trace of bias or hypocrisy (1:27; 3:13–18). James connects wisdom or the lack of wisdom with bitter envy, selfish ambition, disorder, and wickedness. As such, when the rich oppress and exploit the poor, they show lack of wisdom. When the poor show bias for the rich, they act unwisely.

Faith and Action

A thread running through all the above themes is faith. Faith allows one to persevere amidst suffering (which is imperative if the suffering will not be alleviated anytime soon); the poor should have faith in God's great reversal and their inheritance in the kingdom; faith will ask God for wisdom and receive it. Wisdom, as noted above, will engender and manifest itself as order (perhaps equality rather than disorder), justice (righteousness as opposed to wickedness), and love for others because of love of self (rather than selfish ambition and envy). Faith without works is dead (2:14–26). Abraham's faith in God led him to place his only son on the altar; Rahab's faith led her to conceal and give safe passage to the messengers who would destroy her city and people. James admonishes his readers to ask for, resist, care for, and do. He encourages his readers to pray, sing, praise, and anoint. Overwhelmingly his concern is for the poor, for whom faith without works is useless.

Consider and discuss: Binaries like good and bad, rich and poor, black and white, slave and free, male and female can cause us to neglect the liminal or in between spaces in which people find themselves and the complexity of life. How might the Diaspora be understood as liminal space? What or who gets ignored and/or silenced and what is the impact?

Summary

1. James is overwhelmingly concerned for the oppressed and displaced poor and their survival.
2. James understands wisdom as faith in action.
3. Through faith-action the displaced believers can survive, but they should know that God is not the author of temptation or their sufferings.

Further Reading

Aymer, Margaret P. *First Pure, Then Peaceable: Frederick Douglass, Darkness and the Epistle of James.* London: T. & T. Clark, 2007.

Byron, Gay L. "James." In *True to Our Native Land: An African American Commentary of the New Testament*, edited by Brian Blount et al., 461–75. Minneapolis: Fortress, 2007.

———. "James." In *Women's Commentary of the Bible: Revised and Updated*, edited by Carol A. Newsom, Sharon H. Ringe, and Jacqueline E. Lapsley, 613–15. Louisville: Westminster John Knox, 2012.

Coker, K. Jason. *James in Postcolonial Perspective: The Letter as Nativist Discourse.* Minneapolis: Fortress, 2015.

Hahn, Scott, and Curtis Mitch. *The Letter of St. James, the First and Second Letters of St. Peter and the Letter of St. Jude.* Ignatius Catholic Study Bible. 2nd ed. San Francisco: Ignatius, 2013.

Johnson, Luke Timothy. *The Letter of James.* Anchor Bible. New Haven: Yale University Press, 2005.

Levine, Amy-Jill, ed. *A Feminist Companion to the Catholic Epistles and Hebrews.* New York: T. & T. Clark, 2000.

Russaw, Kimberly. "Wisdom in the Garden. The Woman in Genesis 3 and Alice Walker's Sophia." In *I Found God in Me: A Womanist Biblical Hermeneutics Reader*, edited by Mitzi J. Smith, 223–35. Eugene, OR: Cascade, 2015.

Tamez, Elsa. *The Scandalous Message of James: Faith Without Works is Dead.* New York: Crossroad, 2002.

CHAPTER 28

Jude

In times of crisis, the wise build bridges, while the foolish build barriers. We must find a way to look after one another as if we were one single tribe

—T'Challa, from the movie *The Black Panther*

It was my good luck—perhaps—that I found myself in the church racket instead of some other, and surrendered to a spiritual seduction long before I came to any carnal knowledge. For when the pastor asked me, with that marvelous smile, "Whose little boy are you?" my heart replied at once, "Why yours."

—James Baldwin[1]

Jude at a Glance

1. Jude is one of the earliest writings of the NT.
2. Jude is a letter of exhortation or an exhortation in letter format.
3. Date and origin of the Jude is uncertain.
4. Jude was possibly written by Jude, the brother of Jesus.
5. Jude is addressed to the Beloved in God.
6. Jude is a one of the catholic or general epistles written to no specific assembly.
7. Jude quotes from the apocryphal text called 1 Enoch.

---

1. Baldwin, *Fire Next Time*, 29.

8. The author of 2 Peter used Jude as a source.
9. Jude is concerned with the infiltration of intruders in believing communities.
10. Verse 24 is a well-known doxology used often in Christian worship.

Introduction

JUDE WANTS HIS READERS to make it clear that they have one master, just as he is clear that Jesus Christ is his *despotēs* (slave master). But for some believers, it appears, such an expectation is unrealistic, constraining, and blind to context; they obviously do not see it the same way. Or perhaps, it is about how others are seen and defined. This brief twenty-five verse letter is best known for its benediction and perhaps for the writer's putative relationship to Jesus. It is plausible that Jude, the brother of Jesus, was the author as inscribed in v. 1. Jude, the brother of Jesus, was a significant leader and itinerant missionary in the Jesus movement in Palestine (1 Cor 9:5). Jude identifies himself as the slave (*doulos*) of Jesus Christ (his slave master, v. 5) and the brother of James (Jesus's other brother) (Mark 6:3). The former identification may function to signify the rigid authoritative relationship Jude has with Jesus Christ and therefore the relationship he proposes for his readers so as not to stumble (v. 24). The letter is addressed to the called, also known as God's beloved in the opening and throughout the letter (vv. 3, 17, 20). In a conventional greeting, Jude wishes mercy, peace, and love in abundance for his readers (v. 2); there is no concluding greeting. Mercy is a major theme of Jude's exhortation (vv. 21–23), despite the merciless and judgmental tone of the letter overall. Because the addressees are not specified by name or location, Jude is considered a general or universal (catholic) letter likely meant to reach a broad audience.

Chapter Contents

1. Reason for Writing: Dangerous Intruders
2. Reconstruction of Intruders
3. Exhortation
4. Benediction

Reason for Writing: Dangerous Intruders

It appears that although the recipients of Jude are safe, they are in danger of losing the faith because of the wicked influence of insiders that Jude would prefer be made outsiders. Jude writes to encourage them to contend (*epagōnizomai*) or struggle to maintain the faith entrusted to them (v. 3). Ungodly intruders have stealthily slipped in among them and as members of the community are using God's grace as an excuse to do whatever they please. The intruders deny that Jesus Christ is their only master (*kurios*) and lord (*despotēs*) (v. 4; *despotēs* most often refers to slave master, 1 Tim 6:1, 2; 2 Tim 2:21; Titus 2:9; 1 Pet 2:18; for Christ, 2:21; for God, Luke 2:29; Acts 4:24; Rev 6:10). Perhaps the intruders allow other persons, deities, and teachers to inform their lives and conduct in addition to the received gospel of Jesus.

Jude exhorts the beloved to remember what they already know: God destroyed the unbelievers that accompanied the Hebrews out of Egyptian bondage; the fallen angels that stepped out of order are confined in darkness until judgment day; and Sodom and Gomorrah and nearby cities were punished for engaging in sexual immorality (*ekporneuō*) and pursuing other flesh (*sarkos heteras*) (vv. 5–7; cf. Gen 14). Of course, not every NT writer describes the problem in Sodom and Gomorrah as sexual immorality (Matt 10:15; 11:23–24; Luke 10:12; 17:29). The reminder is a *caveat emptor* (let the buyer beware) so that the beloved do not stumble into or buy into the same destructive ideas and behaviors.

Reconstruction of Intruders

Jude refers to the intruders as "dreamers" (v. 8). They are not visionaries, but they are delusional in Jude's eyes and disloyal to Jesus Christ who should be their *despotes* too. They contaminate (*miainō*) flesh, reject (*atheteō*) lordship (*kurioteta*), and blaspheme the glorious ones (*doxas*). Jude compares the intruders' actions with the archangel Michael's. Even the archangel Michael did not blaspheme the devil (*diabolos*) when he contended (*diakrinomai*) with him about Moses's body; he simply rebuked him in the name of the Lord (v. 9; Exod 2:11–15). Perhaps Jude places the devil in the category of the glorious ones. The intruders are self-destructive, slandering what they do not understand (v. 10). The author further compares the intruders to Cain (who murdered his brother), Balaam, and Korah (Gen 4:1–16; Num 16:1–35; Deut 23:3–6). The intruders are a stain on their love feasts. A litany of metaphors signify the useless annoying presence of the intruders

(vv. 12–13). Quoting from 1 Enoch 1:9, Jude states that the intruders are the ungodly sinners that the prophet Enoch spoke about and that the Lord shall judge at his coming (v. 14b–15; cf. Gen 5:18–24). They are grumblers, like those who came out of Egypt and did not believe and that the Lord destroyed (vv. 5, 16). They indulge their own lusts and use bombastic speech and flattery to persuade the people to see things as they do (v. 16). Jude finally describes the intruders as divisive and fleshly or worldly, and they do not have the Spirit (v. 19). The intruders are constructed as other and in dualistic terms. The ungodly are not the beloved in God who are kept safe for Jesus Christ (v. 1b).

Consider and discuss: Often when we read texts like Jude, we see the opponents or adversaries constructed in them as enemies of God and thus as our enemies. It makes a difference who tells the story. How might we see the intruders as evidence of diverse believing communities that interpreted the Hebrew Scriptures and the words, life, and ministry of Jesus differently based on their own experiences and contexts? To what contemporary interreligious conflict might we compare Jude?

Consider and discuss: Perhaps the intruders are impulsive in their refusal to accept and willingness to slander what they do not understand. How can we see this scenario happening in households, in faith communities and in society today? When have you been the one accused of slandering that which you do not understand, or vice versa?

Exhortation

The beloved ones to whom Jude writes are also admonished to remember of apostles (v. 17). The rise of scoffers that indulge in their own ungodly lusts is to be expected in the last days (v. 18). The beloved must focus on building themselves up "on their most holy faith"; pray in the Holy Spirit; remain in God's love; anticipate Christ's mercy and show mercy on the wavering; and save those that they can (vv. 20–23). It is not clear that Jude has the intruders in mind when he exhorts the beloved to show mercy and to save those whom they can. The unwavering ones may be distinct from the ungodly intruders.

Benediction

The doxology or words of praise is well-known and used among contemporary Christians in worship. In it the writer acknowledges and praises God, "our Savior," for God's power to keep the beloved from stumbling and to cause them to stand faultless before God (v. 24). In the past, in the present, and in the future, glory, majesty, power, and authority belong to God who is their savior through Jesus Christ (v. 25).

Summary

1. The beloved in God are in danger of becoming like the ungodly.
2. Intruders have slipped in with a "perverted" understanding of God's grace.
3. God is powerful to keep God's beloved from succumbing to the ways of the intruders.

Further Reading

Bauckham, Richard. *Jude and the Relatives of Jesus in the Early Church.* Edinburgh: T. & T. Clark, 1990.

George, Larry. "Jude." In *True to Our Native Land: An African American Commentary of the New Testament*, edited by Brian Blount et al., 518–22. Minneapolis: Fortress, 2007.

Neyrey, Jerome H. *2 Peter, Jude.* Anchor Bible 37C. New York Doubleday, 1993.

Perkins, Pheme. "Jude." In *The Fortress Commentary on the Bible: The New Testament*, edited by Margaret Aymer et al., 711–14. Minneapolis: Fortress, 2014.

CHAPTER 29

1–3 John

Beyond Christology, the humanity of Jesus is what Christianity can offer today so that humanity may have a future...

—Jon Sobrino[1]

Any religion or philosophy which is not based on a respect for life is not a true religion or philosophy.

—Albert Schweitzer

1–3 John at a Glance

1. First, Second, and Third John are dated near the end of the first century CE.
2. The author may be one of the second-generation leaders in the Johannine community.
3. Given the style and language of these letters, the same author likely wrote all the letters of John.
4. First John is not a letter in format and content but a theological treatise that attacks Gnostic Christology.
5. Second and Third John are in letter format and deal with some local issues.
6. Overall, the themes of the Johannine epistles are similar to those in the Gospel of John.

---

1. Sobrino, *Christ the Liberator*, 291.

Introduction

ALTHOUGH THE JOHANNINE LETTERS are placed near the end of the New Testament, they should be read and studied together with the Gospel of John because they are all from the same community. Although we do not know who wrote these letters or when they were written, the consensus is that they were written in the later stage of the community's life. First John deals with a schism within the community and defends Jesus's humanity over against Gnostic Christology. Second John is addressed to the "elect lady" and deals with some false teaching, and 3 John is addressed to Gaius and deals with the issue of division in the community.

Chapter Contents

1. The Context of the Community
2. Comparing with the Fourth Gospel
3. Primary Teaching

The Context of the Community

It is very interesting to see schism within the Johannine community because members of this community experienced a split from the synagogue due to their faith in Jesus as the Messiah. In the later stage of community life, a new issue arises. Namely, a group of people left the community because they argued that Jesus did not come in the flesh, with a human body (1 John 2:18, 22; 4:3; 2 John 1:7). In other words, they denied Jesus's humanity, accepting Gnostic Christology. They are called the antichrist. In the Gnostic view, this material world is deemed as evil and transitory. Likewise, the body is a tomb of the soul, and the true hope of salvation must be spiritual only. But this view is not held in the Gospel of John, in which the world is loved by God (John 3:16). Moreover, in John, God sends Jesus to bring God's word to this world. Jesus sends his disciples into the world so that they continue the work of God. In his farewell prayer, Jesus prays to the Father, asking him not to take them out of the world but to protect them from the evil one (John 17:15).

Comparing with the Fourth Gospel

There are many thematic similarities between 1 John and the Fourth Gospel (John): light and darkness (1 John 1:5-7; 2:9-11; John 8:12; 12:46); abiding in Jesus (1 John 2:27-28; John 15:4, 6); the hostile world (1 John 3:13; John 15:18-19; 17:13-16); God's love of the world and sending of his Son (1 John 4:9; John 3:16); Jesus's laying down his life for others (1 John 3:16; John 10:11-18). There are also other similarities between them. First, the prologue is similar (1 John 4:1-3; John 1:1-18). Second, the role of the Spirit (1 John 4:1-3) is important as in the Fourth Gospel. Likewise, we find the Spirit of truth in 1 John 4:6, as in John 14-16. The difference is, however, that 1 John contrasts the Spirit of truth with the spirit of error (1 John 4:6). Third, Jesus's humanity is emphasized in 1 John 4:2 and John 1:14.

Primary Teaching

In 1 John, the author reminds the community of who Jesus is. He is sent by God to bring light and life to the world. Like the Johannine Prologue in John 1:1-18, 1 John 1:1-3 succinctly expresses the essence of good news to the community:

> We declare to you what was from the beginning, what we have heard, what we have seen with our eyes, what we have looked at and touched with our hands, concerning the word of life—this life was revealed, and we have seen it and testify to it, and declare to you the eternal life that was with the Father and was revealed to us—we declare to you what we have seen and heard so that you also may have fellowship with us; and truly our fellowship is with the Father and with his Son Jesus Christ.

Consider and discuss: Why do you think a group of members in the Johannine community believed in a Gnostic-type of Christ who is fully divine and not human at all? Perhaps early in the community there were possibilities of such a belief because the Johannine Prologue could be misunderstood easily in the way that Jesus may be seen as God. Especially, John 1:14 ("the Logos became flesh") could be read literally. How would you respond to this reasoning behind Gnostic Christology?

Summary

1. Scholars believe that the same author wrote all the letters of John.
2. The author comes from the second generation of the Johannine community.
3. Thus, there are a great deal of similarities between John's Gospel and these letters. For example, see similar themes of love, light, truth, joy, and testimony.
4. First John is not a letter but a theological sermon that deals with right teachings about God, Jesus Christ, and the world.
5. Second and Third John have letter forms and deal with local issues.
6. Gnostic Christology is one of the gravest issues in the later stage of the community.

Further Reading

Callahan, Allen Dwight. *A Love Supreme: A History of Johannine Tradition.* Minneapolis, MN: Fortress, 2005.

King, Karen L. *What Is Gnosticism?* Cambridge: Harvard University Press, 2005.

Lieu, Judith M. *The Theology of the Johannine Epistles.* Cambridge: Cambridge University Press, 1991.

O'Day, Gail. "1, 2, and 3 John." In *Women's Bible Commentary: Revised Edition*, edited by Carol Newsom et al., 622–24. Louisville, KY: Westminster John Knox, 2012.

Painter, John. *1, 2, and 3 John.* Collegeville, MN: Liturgical, 2002.

Rensberger, David. *1 John, 2 John, 3 John.* Nashville, TN: Abingdon, 1997.

Smith, D. Moody. *First, Second, and Third John.* Louisville, KY: Westminster John Knox, 1991.

Strecker, Georg. *The Johannine Letters: A Commentary on 1, 2, and 3 John.* Hermeneia. Minneapolis: Fortress, 1996.

CHAPTER 30

1 Peter

Rejoice! . . . even if now in this time you suffer.

—1 Pet 1:6

---

1 Peter at a Glance

1. First Peter is a catholic or general letter addressed to exiles in the Diaspora of North Asia Minor.
2. First Peter is written in the form of a baptismal homily (brief sermon).
3. The author is unknown, although some scholars propose that the Apostle Peter wrote it.
4. The author writes to encourage those living in the Diaspora to stand fast in the face of oppression.
5. First Peter contains a list of household codes.
6. The epistle was likely written in the late first century CE.
7. First Peter has no thanksgiving.
8. The author sends final greetings from a sister church in Babylon and his son Mark.
9. The author encourages unmitigated obedience to God and all human institutions.
10. The author believes that the final judgment begins with the house of God.

Introduction

THE AUTHOR KNOWS THAT the experience of exile can be an unbearable and depressing experience. If one can find reason to rejoice, one may very well do more than survive, for now and perhaps for the long haul. Twice in the opening blessing, 1 Peter admonishes the exiled and oppressed believers to rejoice (1:6, 8). Oppressors tend to assume that the oppressed rejoice because their sufferings are not so unbearable, that oppressed peoples have somehow adjusted to their afflictions, or that the oppressed are less than human (but superhuman when it comes to pain). But the oppressed often rejoice in order to persevere, to make it through and so as not to lose their minds, faith or hope. Rejoicing for the oppressed conjures hope. Most oppressed peoples have at some point in their lives experienced displacement and have been forcefully exiled into a strange and alien land or ushered into unimaginable conditions either by dominant oppressive governments, powers, institutions, and systems or by (un)natural disasters coupled with human indifference and/or cruelty.

Chapter Contents

1. Addressees
2. Reason for Writing: Even if You Suffer Now, Rejoice and Stand!

Addressees

First Peter is addressed to no particular *ekklēsia* exiled in the Diaspora of North Asia Minor (Pontus, Galatia, Cappadocia, Asia, Bithynia) (1:1–2). In other words, the addressees are not living in their homelands; they are in a strange or alien land. Their displacement does not make them aliens but estranged from the familiar. God chose and predestined them; the Spirit sanctified or set them apart, and called them to conduct themselves as holy and obedient people of God (1:15). The direct object of their obedience is Jesus Christ. They are called to be sprinkled (or baptized) with the blood of Jesus. It is presumed that they have already experienced a water baptism; it is stated that they received the Spirit's anointing. But the current situation calls for them to be baptized with Jesus's blood. Some traditions remain unbroken regardless of the circumstances of the audience; a conventional greeting follows the broad identification of the addressees: "May grace and peace be yours in abundance" (1:2c).

Reason for Writing: Even if You Suffer Now, Rejoice and Stand!

The greeting is followed by a blessing, tailor-made for the addressees who are suffering and being tested like imperishable gold in fire (1:3–12). The blessing is appropriate for a displaced people whose inheritance (of land, family, culture, and voice) has been taken or disrupted and who must now determine how to experience a new birth (spiritually, culturally, and materially?). God's great mercy has granted the dispersed exiles (spiritual) new birth and an imperishable inheritance to be revealed at the end; it is being protected in heaven by God's power. This is something to rejoice about. Jesus Christ, whom they have not seen, but love, is another reason for rejoicing "with an indescribable and glorious joy" (v. 8). First Peter's audience shares in Christ's sufferings; this is a source of joy (4:13). His sufferings were prophesied by the prophets and is beneficial for the readers. Through Christ they have become once again a people and a holy nation, even if they are physically displaced (2:9–10).

Consider and discuss: Some believers encourage the oppressed and displaced to be content with their displacement, economic poverty, and other forms of social or material oppression and to be satisfied instead with a mature spirituality and the promise of a future reward. Do you agree or disagree? Why or why not? How does 1 Peter support or not support such a view?

A major concern is that the exiles will not endure and that during their time of suffering their conduct will become ungodly or unholy. The author exhorts them to conduct themselves like God's chosen people, like royalty. They should conduct themselves in honorable ways so that even if they are maligned, their actions will demonstrate their godliness (2:12–15). The strict adherence to household codes that require persons of subordinate social status to submit to their superiors are reinforced, perhaps to avoid further oppression by the state. In 1 Peter, fear of God does not conflict with showing honor to the emperor or respect for all authoritative human institutions including slavery and marriage. The house of God mirrors the Roman patriarchal household and sociopolitical structure. Women (as the weaker human being) and slaves are to submit to their husbands/masters (2:13–15; 3:1–7). Perhaps the author attempts to mitigate and preempt any further or unnecessary suffering, not knowing himself how long the exiles will have to endure and learn to rejoice. Yet the author does assure the exiles that their oppressors will be held accountable in the judgment of God (4:5). The author's intent in writing this letter was to encourage the exiles in the Diaspora to stand firm in God's grace (5:12). To stand firm is to be humble before God, cast all cares upon God (and social superiors), demonstrate discipline in behavior, resist the roaring-lion tactics of the devil, and rejoice in the grace of God and promise of future restoration.

> **Consider and discuss:** Respectability politics expects oppressed and nonwhite minoritized peoples to live, behave, dress, and speak in ways that are above reproach or suspicion and argues that when they do so, they will never be subjected to abuse or oppression. What are the problems with this thinking and where might we see respectability politics operating in 1 Peter?

Summary

1. The exiled and dispersed are not alone in their suffering.
2. The exiled and dispersed are to behave themselves in ways that are above reproach.
3. The exiled and dispersed are to rejoice while they suffer.
4. God has promised a future restoration.

CHAPTER 31

2 Peter

2 Peter at a Glance

1. Second Peter is dated between 90 and 135 CE.
2. It is a general or catholic letter written to no particular geographical location or church.
3. Second Peter is dependent on the letter of Jude.
4. The author mentions the first letter he wrote (1 Peter).
5. Second Peter identifies Simon Peter, a slave and apostle of Jesus Christ as the author.
6. Second Peter claims to have been written prior to Peter's death.
7. The author assumes the role of a prophet predicting the future arrival of false prophets.
8. The author knows the letters of the Apostle Paul and classifies them as Scriptures.

Chapter Contents

1. The Audience
2. The Situation
3. The Solution

The Audience

IF THE AUTHOR IS writing to the same broad audience addressed in 1 Peter (3:1), then they are exiles in the Diaspora. However, the author does not identify the geographical location, he simply refers to his intended audience as receivers of a precious faith through God and Jesus Christ and as beloved (1:1; 3:1, 8). He perceives that his audience has become forgetful of the promises and goodness of God, which is evidenced by a lack of self-control and ungodly behavior; and they are in danger of stumbling away from the faith (1:4–10).

The Situation

The author writes to remind his audience that the prophets, who spoke by the will of God (and not with their own human interpretation), prophesied about false prophets and teachers (1:20–2:2). The author assumes the role of prophet, of course by the will of God, and prophesies that these same type of false prophets and teachers "will" appear among them. They are likely already among them and this is why he writes. The false prophets and teachers will malign the truth that they received from the apostles and will lure them into lustful, immoral, or wicked ways of living, exploiting them with deceptions (2:3, 13; 3:2). But they should remember that God has a day of judgment for which the ungodly will not be spared (2:9; 3:7). In support of his argument, the author recalls those who fell away or sinned that God did not spare: the angels that God cast into hell and deep darkness (cf. Jude 6); the people not saved with Noah; Sodom and Gomorrah; and those depraved by their own lusts and who despise authority so much that they boldly and willfully slander the "glorious ones" (2:4–16; cf. Jude 9). Although God refuses to save the ungodly, God will save the godly among them just like God saved Lot and Noah. False prophets/teachers are ridiculing them about the length of time that has passed without Christ returning. But a thousand years is like a day to God. What seems like a long time for humans is not for God. God is not slow to fulfill God's promises. That day is coming and will slip in like a burglar. And when it arrives, it will usher in cosmic destruction (3:9–12).

The Solution

The beloved of God are encouraged to keep waiting and to strive to be at peace with God and with the waiting. They are to live without blame and continually grow in God's grace (5:14–18).

Consider and discuss: Sometimes others are described or identified as false prophets because they are viewed as opponents or competitors and sometimes it is the accuser that lacks spiritual maturity and knowledge. How would one identify the false prophets of today? What is the difference between a false prophet or teacher and an imperfect, fallible human being with imperfect knowledge? How do we distinguish the two, and is it possible to do so? What is the connection between false prophets/teachers and complicity with injustice and oppression within and beyond the walls of the church?

Summary

1. False prophets and teachers are inevitable; expect them.
2. Continue to wait and God will fulfill God's promises in God's time.
3. Believers must continually grow in God's grace.

Further Reading for 1 and 2 Peter

Bartlett, David Lyon. *1 Peter*. Nashville: Abingdon, 1998.

Finger, Reta Halteman. "To Comfort the Afflicted: If We Read 1 Peter's Message to Immigrants, Exiles and Foreigners Only as a Metaphor, We Risk Missing the Point." *Sojourners Magazine* 42 (2013) 28–31.

George, Larry. "1 Peter." In *True to Our Native Land: An African American Commentary of the New Testament*, edited by Brian Blount et al., 476–87. Minneapolis: Fortress, 2007.

———. "2 Peter." In *True to Our Native Land: An African American Commentary of the New Testament*, edited by Brian Blount et al., 488–95. Minneapolis: Fortress, 2007.

González, Catherine Gunsalus. *1 & 2 Peter and Jude: A Theological Commentary on the Bible*. Louisville: Westminster John Knox, 2011.

Green, Joel B. *1 Peter*. New Horizons New Testament Commentary. Grand Rapids, MI: Eerdmans, 2007.

Horrell, David G. "Ethnicity, Empire and Early Christian Identity: Social-Scientific Perspectives on 1 Peter." In *Reading 1–2 Peter and Jude: A*

Resource for Students, edited by Eric F. Mason and Troy W. Martin, 135–49. Atlanta: Society of Biblical Literature, 2014.

Reeder, Caryn. "1 Peter 3:1–6: Biblical Authority and Battered Wives." *Bulletin for Biblical Research* 25 (2015) 519–39.

Smith, Shively T. J. *Strangers to Family: Diaspora and 1 Peter's Invention of God's Household*. Waco, TX: Baylor University Press, 2016.

Witherington, Ben, III. *Letters and Homilies for Hellenized Christians: A Socio-Rhetorical Commentary on 1–2 Peter*. Downers Grove, IL: InterVarsity, 2012.

Zeitlin, Irving M. *Jews: The Making of a Diaspora People*. Malden, MA: Polity, 2012.

CHAPTER 32

Hebrews

Written across our lives is a fatal flaw and within history runs an irrational and unpredictable vein. Like Abraham, we too sojourn in the land of promise, but so often we do not become "heirs with him in the same promise." Always our reach exceeds our grasp.

—Martin Luther King Jr.[1]

Since we are surrounded by so great a cloud of witnesses, let us also lay aside every weight and the sin that clings so closely, and let us run with perseverance the race that is set before us.

—Heb 12:1 NRSV

I believe that we have just got to keep some kind of faith that the people who want to make this country a good place to live can gain and influence politics in this country. I do have faith, as bad as the situation is now, for faith is the substance of things hoped for and evidence of things not seen.

—Fannie Lou Hamer, Civil Rights Activist[2]

Hebrews at a Glance

1. The genre of Hebrews is an extended sermon.
2. The author is an unknown preacher and he is likely Jewish.

1. King, *Strength to Love*, 88.
2. Hamer, "Sick and Tired of Being Sick and Tired," 171.

3. The writer is familiar with the Hebrew Bible traditions, especially the sacrificial system.
4. Hebrews was likely written between 60 and 96 CE.
5. Hebrews is possibly addressed to believers in Rome.
6. The preacher's Greek is some of the most refined in the NT.
7. The author demonstrates knowledge of Greek culture.
8. The audience is likely a mixture of Jews and Gentiles.
9. The preacher visualizes the prototype of the earthly sanctuary in heaven.
10. Jesus is the perfect High Priest and eternal intercessor.

Introduction

IF HEBREWS IS A sermon, the author is a preacher. Preachers speak in metaphorical language to help their audience visualize what is and what can be, to consider where they are and where or how they can be. Some preachers so desperately desire to reach their people, especially if some have already left the faith, that they resort to fire and brimstone messages. The preacher is not God, but he attempts to speak for God and to assist the people in developing and maintaining a relationship with God while nurturing and without losing his own. Although the actual author is unknown, scholars have proposed Apollos (the Alexandrian Jewish preacher), the Apostle Barnabas, Priscilla, Aquila, Philip, Timothy, Clement of Rome, or some other anonymous woman. Scholars no longer accept the traditional view that the Apostle Paul wrote the sermon.

Resembling an extended sermon rather than a letter, the author identified no sender or addressees, and it contains no greeting and prayer report, like we might find in a Pauline letter. The sermon begins with the words, "Although long ago God spoke in many and various ways to the ancestors by the prophets, in these last days he spoke to us by the son" (1:1–2). The fact that the author sees himself preaching in these last days might explain some of the harsh rhetoric, given the urgency of now. Hebrews is an exhortation about the ways that God "spoke" through his son. The heart of the sermon is the ongoing intercessory ministry of Jesus.

The preacher is not meticulous with regard to noting his references and/or sources like a contemporary preacher might be. Like a preacher or like a bishop, he quotes Scripture using various quotation formulas and sometimes none at all. He asserts that "someone has testified somewhere," "the one who said," "it is said," "it is attested," "the Holy Spirit also testifies," or "we know the one who said" (2:6; 3:7, 15; 5:5; 7:17, 21; 10:15, 30). Every now and then he names a source like David (4:7). He must know his mixed audience well, and they him. And they both know the Scriptures and Greek.

Chapter Contents

1. The Audience and Their Context
2. Jesus is God's Ultimate Agent
3. High Priestly Ministry of Jesus
4. Exemplars of Faith

The Audience and Their Context

From our reading of Hebrews, we might reconstruct an identity of the author's perception of his audience. The audience and the writer share common Hebrew ancestors, but they could be both Jewish and Gentile believers that are holy partners in their high calling (1:1; 3:1). They are at risk of allowing unbelief to turn them away from God; perhaps because they are not as attentive to Jesus's proclamation as they should be (3:12). The writer admonishes them to exhort each other while it is today (3:13). After all, these are the last days. The audience is also at risk of missing out on the eternal "rest" through disobedience. They must hold fast their confession; approach the throne of grace boldly so that they might obtain help and mercy in their time of need (4:14–16; 10:22–23). The preacher's audience is described as deficient in their ability to understand, stuck on foundational beliefs and unable to advance toward perfection (5:11–12; 6:1–2). They need to be reminded of God's promises and the exemplars that preceded them and thus are exhorted to become "imitators of those who through faith and patience inherit the promises" (6:12). Perhaps some of them do not attend the community assembly and need to be reminded to love one another and do good deeds (10:24–25). The preacher perceives that some are willingly engaged in sin after having been exposed to the truth, and for them there is no more sacrifice for sin (10:26). In previous days, because of having been enlightened in the truth, they endured sufferings rather than commit sin (10:32). They are exhorted not to abandon their confidence, but learn to endure so that they might receive the promise (10:35–36). Endure trials as a form of discipline, he exhorts (12:7). It seems that the audience is experiencing some kind of suffering, oppression, or persecution, and are perhaps losing faith and falling apart. Some scholars have argued that the context might be persecution during the reign of the Roman Emperor Nero in 66–68 CE. But it is difficult to know the exact context.

The preacher's audience is in danger of crossing a line of no return. The preacher evokes some tough love when he asserts that "it is impossible to restore again to repentance those who have once been enlightened, have tasted the heavenly gift, and have shared in the Holy Spirit, and have tasted the goodness of the word of God and the powers of the age to come, and then have fallen away since on their own they are crucifying again the Son of God and are holding him up to contempt" (6:4–6). The preacher wants his audience to endure whatever persecution and sufferings they are experiencing with their faith intact and without sin or without falling away.

Discuss and consider: How might the author be like a "fire and brimstone" preacher? What is the impact of "fire and brimstone" preaching on people's lives? What are some contemporary examples of this type of preaching?

Jesus is God's Ultimate Agent

Jesus is described early in the sermon as God's ultimate agent and example of faith. Jesus, God's son, is God's prophet in "the last days"; he is heir, creative agent, and sustainer of all things; reflects God's glory; and bears the exact image of God (1:2–3, 10). Jesus purified their sins and assumed his position at God's right hand. As God's begotten son, Jesus is superior to the angels; the angels worship him. Jesus loved justice and hated wickedness; he is God's ultimate anointed one (1:4–14). Yet, for a short period (during his incarnation) Jesus was inferior to the angels, but God crowned Jesus Christ with glory and honor because he endured suffering and death so that his people would not have to (2:8–9–10). Those saved by Jesus's suffering and death share the same Father; they are Jesus's siblings (2:11). Jesus came to help Abraham's descendants, the human family, and for this reason it was necessary for Jesus to become like his siblings, human in every respect. Because Jesus did not yield to temptation and sin when he was tested by his sufferings, he is the perfect one to assist those who are now being tested in these last days so that they too might overcome (2:16–18). This experience qualifies Jesus to be the perfect high priest.

High Priestly Ministry of Jesus

Jesus is identified as "the apostle and high priest of our confession" (3:1). He is the high priest of high priests, the ultimate high priest appointed by God. Jesus, as noted above, was like human beings in every way and yet without sin. He is the merciful, faithful, holy, and blameless high priest, like Melchizedek. Melchizedek (meaning in Hebrew "his righteous/just king" or "king of righteousness/justice) is the name of the King of Salem (ancient name for Jerusalem), priest of God Most High who appeared out of nowhere. He served Abram bread and wine and blessed him in God's name. Abram responded by giving his tithe (a tenth of everything) to King Melchizedek (Gen 14:18–20; Ps 110:4). In Hebrews, Jesus fulfills the prophetic word in Ps 110:4 and is made a priest forever like Melchizedek. Jesus is high priest by the power of an indestructible life (7:16). Unlike other human high priests, Jesus atones for sins only once for all and does not have to offer sacrifices for his own sins; he is sinless. Jesus's priesthood transcends those of human, earthly priests; he lives eternally to make intercession for humanity in the heavenly temple (7:25). Through the promises of God, Jesus is the mediator of a better, more perfect covenant (8:1–6).

Consider and discuss: We often describe Eve and Adam's behavior in the Garden of Eden as sin, even though the biblical text does not explicitly name it as sin (Gen 2–3). Their environment or context was exponentially more pristine than the one Jesus entered, and they had face-to-face contact with God and yet they made decisions that we often describe using terms like "disobedience" and "sin." Is it possible to be a human being, raised by other imperfect human beings, surrounded by imperfect human beings, in an imperfect world and yet not commit a sin? Elaborate. Perhaps the author has particular behaviors in mind that he or she considers sin?

Exemplars of Faith

What is at stake for the preacher's audience is a loss of faith and eternal rest. Obviously, Jesus is the perfect example of faith under fire. But should the preacher's audience not be convinced that Jesus Christ was really like them, other exemplars have lived who were not perfect like Jesus, and they demonstrated faith. Chapter 11 begins with a definition of faith as "the assurance of things hoped for, the conviction of things not seen" (11:1). Jesus ever lives making intercession for the believers; this they must know by faith and hold as a source of hope, because they cannot see into the heavenly sanctuary. The preacher provides a catalog of human siblings from long ago who walked by faith, not being able to see the promise: Abel and Enoch pleased God—Abel with his sacrifice and Enoch in the way he lived—but each died without knowing how much they pleased God. The preacher drops another dose of tough love: "without faith it is not possible to please God" (11:6)! It is problematic to approach God without belief that God exists and that God will reward those who seek God. People and things responded in faith to the call of God. Noah, Abraham, Isaac, Jacob, Joseph, Moses, the Hebrew children passing through the Red Sea, the walls of Jericho, Rahab, and many others acted by faith. These and others constitute a "great cloud of witnesses" or exemplars (12:1). Readers familiar with the stories of the hall of faith'ers know they were not perfect, that they did not demonstrate faith in every situation. For example, Abraham and Sarah used the young Egyptian slave Hagar's body as a surrogate, a sexual object, and an incubator to produce an heir for Abraham when their faith in God's promises wavered and dissipated for a period of time (Gen 16:1–15). Yet their names are listed in the hall of faith. Isaac, following in his father's footsteps, lied as his father had previously done and asserted that his wife was not his wife but his sister, exposing her to potential sexual violence or rape. They made their wives sexually available to another man to save themselves (Gen 20:1–7; 26:6–10). Some women are eclipsed or erased from the tradition in Hebrews. The significant role of Pharaoh's daughter and Moses's sister Miriam in saving Moses are minimized or absent (11:24–26). Barak is named as a conqueror of kingdoms and yet Deborah, the judge and prophet without whom Barak refused to go to battle is missing from the list. And Jael who put the final nail, so to speak, in the coffin of the enemy king in that battle is not memorialized in the preacher's hall of faith either (11:32–33). Perhaps the patriarchal bias speaks to the gender of the preacher.

Consider and discuss: Faith, especially under trying circumstances, is more complex than many religious people permit. Considering the lives of the persons listed in Heb 11 who are cited as paragons of exemplary faith, how might we think of faith in more complex ways that allow for human imperfection and frailty?

Summary

1. Some believers have fallen away from the faith under trying circumstances.
2. The preacher is trying to minimize the damage and encourage his audience to remain faithful.
3. The believers have unrestricted, unmitigated access to the intercessory ministry of Jesus.
4. Jesus is the perfect high priest and intercessor because as a human being he maintained his faith and did not sin when tested with sufferings.
5. The human exemplars who were inducted into the hall of faith were not perfect.
6. Faith is not to be equated with perfection and women's faith is taken for granted.

Further Reading

Attridge, Harold W. *The Epistle to the Hebrews.* Hermeneia. Philadelphia: Fortress, 1989.

D'Angelo, Mary Rose. "Hebrews." In *Women's Bible Commentary: Twentieth-Anniversary Edition,* edited by Carol A. Newsom, Sharon H. Ringe, and Jacqueline E. Lapsley, 608–12. Louisville: Westminster John Knox, 2012.

deSilva, David A. "Hebrews." In *The Fortress Commentary of the Bible: The New Testament,* edited by Margaret Aymer et al., 625–53 . Minneapolis: Fortress, 2014.

———. *Perseverance in Gratitude: A Socio-Rhetorical Commentary on Epistle "to the Hebrews."* Grand Rapids: Eerdmans, 2000.

Eisenbaum, Pamela. "Father and Son: The Christology of Hebrews in Patrilineal Perspective." In *A Feminist Companion to the Catholic Epistles and Hebrews*, edited by Amy-Jill Levine and Maria Mayo Robbins, 127–46. London: T. & T. Clark, 2004.

Lloyd-Jones, Martyn. *A Merciful and Faithful High Priest: Studies in the Book of Hebrews*. Wheaton, IL: Crossway, 2017.

Massey, James Earl. "Hebrews." In *True to Our Native Land: An African American Commentary on the Bible*, edited by Brian Blount et al., 444–60. Minneapolis: Fortress, 2007.

Section V

The Apocalypse of John/The Book of Revelation

CHAPTER 33

Contemporary and Ancient Apocalyptic Texts and Their Significance

CONTEMPORARY APOCALYPTIC AND POST-APOCALYPTIC films and television shows can help readers understand and recognize some characteristics of Jewish and Early Christian apocalyptic literature (e.g., *2 Enoch*, *4 Ezra* [*2 Esdras*], *2 Baruch*, *3 Baruch*, *Apocalypse of Abraham*, *Apocalypse of Moses*, the book of Daniel, the book of Revelation, the *Apocalypse of Peter*, *Apocalypse of Paul*, and the *Ascension of Isaiah*. Revelation is the only NT text explicitly identified as an Apocalypse).[1] The context of the 2001 film *Apocalypse Now: Redux* by Francis Ford Coppola is the Vietnam War in 1968. The US president was Lyndon B. Johnson. One of the main protagonists, Captain Willard (Martin Sheen), is sent on a mission to assassinate a rogue American Colonel named Kurtz (Marlon Brando) who succumbed to the horrors of war and is considered a military threat. Kurtz, who seems confused as to who the real enemy is, has indiscriminately slaughtered both Americans and native Cambodians. Kurtz has no troops under his command, except the natives and an equally confused American journalist, when Willard arrives. The temple where Kurtz is living sits at the end of the river. Having survived the hazardous journey up the river, Willard arrives to find a bloody scene of dead bodies strewn on the ground, left where they were slain, and decapitated bodies and heads hanging from tree limbs. Kurtz imprisons Willard and reads to him from a book in the temple before releasing him. Kurtz submits to his fate and allows Willard to execute him with a sword, leaving a bloody scene in the temple. When Willard emerges from the temple, all the natives who once worshipped Kurtz fall down in obeisance to Willard as if he is a god. Willard, the military's avenging angel, is no saint sent on a mission to eradicate an evil that did not exist in himself and in other military leaders fighting in the Vietnam War. Like the dragon

---

1. We also find an apocalyptic worldview or apocalyptic discourse in the following NT texts: Mark 13; Matt 24; Luke 21; and 1 Cor 15.

in Revelation, Kurtz was viewed by his superiors as a "fallen angel" but so was Willard. Humanity is more complex than sacred texts often allow, and sometimes complexity is present but readers refuse to see it. Darkness or evil is resident or can emerge in any human being when triggered by an experience like the Vietnam War.

Contemporary apocalyptic and post-apocalyptic films and television shows center around conflict, often among human beings or between human beings and destructive and/or predatory alien forces. The conflict ends in a final decisive battle and the possibility of renewal for the victors or conquerors.[2] Apocalyptic literature can develop among and/or for oppressed, marginalized, and/or colonized peoples subjected to perceived, real, and/or anticipated injustice and oppression. Prophets/seers receive revelations; they are sometimes wise persons made wise by the Divine who communicate the revelations they received. Apocalyptic texts, like many of the biblical texts, are pseudonymous; the person to whom authorship is ascribed was not the actual author (e.g., Moses did not write the Pentateuch or the *Apocalypse of Moses*). While texts identified as apocalyptic literature share common features, they can also have unique or distinctive features, content, function, and form. Form, content, and purpose may change with and through time and circumstances. With this in mind, some characteristics of Jewish and early Christian apocalyptic literature include the following:

1. A human being, often a prophet or seer, receives visions, dreams, or revelations from God. The revelation is mediated through a divine being such as an angel or messenger. The literary framework of the revelation is a narrative or story. In other words, the revelation is presented in the form of a written report about interconnected sequential visions.

2. In divinely mediated visions and dreams, the visionary or dreamer is escorted and transported on journeys to heaven(s), Jerusalem, Hades, hell, the Temple, under the altar. John, the author of Revelation/Apocalypse was shown souls or people who had been slaughtered, crying out to God from under the alter (Rev 9:6). In the second century CE Ethiopic *Apocalypse of Peter* (a text that originated in Egypt) Peter is shown hell as a very gloomy place of destruction. Visionary scenes often consist of symbolic and strange hybrid human-like beasts and

---

2. Some film and television titles include *The Birth of a Nation* (same title for 1915 rise of the KKK; 2017 Nat Turner's revolt), *Apocalypse Now, Apocalypse Now Redux, Book of Eli, Walking Dead, Blade Runner, The Hunger Games, Dawn of the Dead, The Postman, The Book of Revelation, Planet of the Apes, Dream Warrior, Independence Day,* and *Zombie Apocalypse*.

other images. In the second century CE *Ascension of Isaiah*, Isaiah is shown a world hidden from all human beings; he is taken on a journey, ascending to six heavens and above.

3. Extensive revelations about the unfolding of history and succession of kingdoms are characteristic of Jewish apocalyptic literature like *Enoch* and *Daniel*. Although apocalyptic prophesies were written after the fact, they characterize history as predetermined by God.

4. Heavenly scenes reveal the glory of God and the throne of God, the presence of Jesus Christ, and angels and other heavenly beings worshipping and singing the praises of God.

5. Some apocalyptic literature anticipates salvation or redemption from the present evil conditions and/or powers on a final or last day when a final judgment occurs (eschatologically). Sometimes the final judgment is preceded by or includes a general resurrection and a specific resurrection of the dead. At the judgment, books (of life and death) are opened. The wicked and the godly are judged and rewarded or punished, respectively.

6. It discloses otherworldly or transcendent realities that are temporal and spatial. It concerns the temporal in that it anticipates an end time, the culmination of time, and significant events take place according to time (e.g., the thousand-year period or millennium in Rev 20:4–10). It is spatial in that other worlds, Hades, hell, a new earth, and heavens are revealed or anticipated. Significant events like worship, judgment, and destruction occur in those spaces.

7. Signs in the heavens (e.g., darkening or melting of the sun, falling stars and blood-red moon, earthquakes, lightning, and thunder) and on earth (e.g., proliferation of wars, persecution, and erosion of religious liberties) demonstrate that the end of the present age is imminent. Signs occur prior to the final judgment. Other signs include plagues unleashed upon the earth similar to those that inflicted the Egyptians during the Exodus event.

8. It is often written to/for a community perceived to be in distress, crises, or perhaps noncompliant. It provides an interpretation or diagnosis of the present situation and may encourage perseverance, faith, and hope. Certain ethical behaviors or resistance may be prescribed. Apocalyptic literature functions differently depending on the situation from which the literature arises and wishes to address.

9. And it can envision the creation of another reality beyond and more favorable or just than the current reality. A reversal of circumstances and restoration of fortunes is envisioned following the final and decisive battle between opposing forces. Present evils are criticized and a better future is promised.

In his *Confessions of Nat Turner*, former African slave and leader of the 1831 slave revolt in Southampton County, Virginia, Nat Turner saw himself as God's prophet. Turner understood his calling as God's prophet and his apocalyptic visions as products of or interconnected with wisdom that God gave him. Turner stated that the Spirit appeared before him, directed him regarding earthly things, and sent him back to his master from whom he had fled. Once returned, Turner had visions and dreams (revelations from God) involving war between black and white spirits, a darkened sun, loud thunder, and figures of men in the heavens. As a result of his visions, Turner imagined that the great eschatological (final) day of judgement would take the form of a slave revolt that he would lead. Turner's 1831 slave revolt resulted in the slaughter of men, women, and children in the city of Jerusalem.[3] Turner testified that he learned to read and write but does not recall ever learning the alphabet.[4] African slaves in the American South were prohibited from learning to read or write. When they did learn to read, they often did so surreptitiously and illicitly. In the rare occasions that enslavers permitted, their lessons were circumscribed. In both cases, the Bible was their primary, if not only, text. Turner likely read the Apocalypse/Revelation. In Revelation, the wicked are punished in the final day of judgement and the New Jerusalem descends to earth. In Turner's *Confessions*, wisdom, prophetic, and apocalyptic traditions collide and are intertwined as perhaps with some Jewish and early Christian apocalyptic literature. And God is understood to be in control of everything.

Further Reading

Carey, Greg, and L. Gregory Bloomquist, eds. *Vision and Persuasion: Rhetorical Dimensions of Apocalyptic Discourse*. St. Louis, MO: Chalice, 1999.

Collins, Adela Yarbro. "Apocalypse Now: The State of Apocalyptic Studies Near the End of the First Decade of the Twenty-first Century." *Harvard Theological Review* 104 (2011) 447–57.

---

3. Turner, "Confessions of Nat Turner," 249–53.
4. Turner, "Confessions of Nat Turner," 250.

———. *Cosmology and Eschatology in Jewish and Christian Apocalypticism*. Leiden: Brill, 2000.

Collins, John J., ed. *Apocalypse: The Morphology of a Genre*. Semeia Studies 14. Atlanta: Scholars, 1979.

Cook, David. *Contemporary Muslim Apocalyptic Literature*. Religion and Politics Series. Syracuse: Syracuse University Press, 2005.

Filiu, Jean-Pierre. *Apocalypse in Islam*. Berkeley: University of California Press, 2011.

Fletcher-Louis, Crispin. "Jewish Apocalypticism." In *Handbook for the Study of the Historical Jesus*, edited by Tom Holmén and Stanley E. Porter, 1582. Leiden: Brill, 2009.

Gross, Matthew Barrett, and Mel Gilles. *The Last Myth: What the Rise of Apocalyptic Thinking Tells Us About America*. New York: Prometheus, 2012.

Gurr, Barbara. *Race, Gender, and Sexuality in Post-Apocalyptic TV and Film*. New York: Palgrave Macmillan, 2015.

Hanson, Paul. *The Dawn of Apocalyptic: The Historical and Sociological Roots of Jewish Apocalyptic Eschatology*. Philadelphia: Fortress, 1979.

Himmelfarb, Martha. *Ascent to Heaven in Jewish and Christian Apocalypses*. New York: Oxford University Press, 1993.

Keller, Catherine. *Apocalypse Now and Then: A Feminist Guide to the End of the World*. Boston: Beacon, 1996.

Kiel, Micah D., and Barbara Rossing. *Apocalyptic Ecology: The Book of Revelation, the Earth and the Future*. Collegeville, MN: Liturgical, 2017.

McCown, C. C. "Hebrew and Egyptian Apocalyptic Literature." *Harvard Theological Review* 18 (1925) 357–411.

Rehill, Annie. *The Apocalypse Is Everywhere: A Popular History of America's Favorite Nightmare*. Santa Barbara, CA: ABC-CLIO, 2010.

Schneemelcher, Wilhelm, ed. *New Testament Apocrypha*. Louisville: Westminster John Knox, 1989.

Taylor, Richard A. *Interpreting Apocalyptic Literature: An Exegetical Handbook*. Grand Rapids, MI: Kregel Academic, 2016.

Turner, Nat. "The Confessions of Nat Turner, the Leader of the Late Insurrections in South Hampton, VA." In *Slave Narratives*, edited by William L. Andrews and Henry Louis Gates Jr., 241–66. New York: Library of America, 2000.

CHAPTER 34

Apocalypse of John/Book of Revelation

> And about this time, I had a vision—and I saw white spirits and black spirits engaged in battle, and the sun was darkened—the thunder rolled in the Heavens, and blood flowed in streams.... The great day of judgment was at hand.
>
> —Nat Turner, enslaved African and Slave Revolt Leader[1]

> Justice is not a natural part of the lifecycle of the United States, nor is it a product of evolution; it is always the outcome of struggle.
>
> —Keeanga-Yamahtta Taylor[2]

Apocalypse of John at a Glance

1. The book is self-identified as an Apocalypse or Revelation and a prophecy.
2. Visions are revealed to the scribe/author named John, the prophet/seer of God, while he is on the island of Patmos in Asia.
3. Some scholars identify the Apocalypse/Revelation as nonviolent resistance literature.
4. Revelation contains both prophetic (visionary) and apocalyptic elements within the framework of a pastoral letter addressed to seven churches.

1. Turner, "Confessions of Nat Turner," 252.
2. Taylor, *From #BlackLivesMatter to Black Liberation*, 5

5. Revelation is generally believed to have been written sometime between 69 CE and 96 CE.
6. The socio-historical context is imperial persecution and/or the demands of the Roman imperial cult.
7. The Apocalypse contains a number of literary forms, including letters, hymns, vision/eyewitness reports, beatitudes/blessings, woe/judgment oracles, and exhortation.
8. John constructs a particular imaginative experience using symbolism and rhetoric through which he hopes to create a worldview and impact behavior.
9. The primary subjects of the visions are God, who sits enthroned in heaven, and Jesus Christ as the Lamb of God.
10. Scholars identify the beast (empowered by the dragon/Satan), the nemesis of God and the Lamb, as symbolic of Rome.

Introduction

READING IS AN ACT of decoding, of determining and/or knowing what each letter means, what letters mean when they form words, what individual words can mean alone and in connection with other words, and so on. Decoding words that construct visual images is complicated and requires that readers develop and use poetic (symbolic abstract) imagination. And when the text in which images are linguistically constructed (with language) and its historical context are foreign and ancient, the decoding task is further complicated. Revelation is somewhat like a sci-fi film drawing readers into strange, unfamiliar, and horrifying images. Contemporary apocalyptic films captivate us by combining what is familiar to us with what is novel, strange, symbolic, and frightening. The more foreign an image or symbol is to our everyday experience and culture, the more difficult to decode. John, of course, constructed his epistle using symbolism that was culturally accessible and decodable by his audiences (members of the seven churches—Ephesus, Smyrna, Pergamum, Thyatira, Sardis, Philadelphia, and Laodicea). Modern readers must attempt to access the cultural knowledge that John shared with his audience. But we, as modern readers, can never fully or precisely bridge the gap that time and culture impose. Yet some modern interpreters claim to reinterpret or decode Revelation with precision, making one-to-one correlations between the symbolic universe John constructs and our contemporary political and religious contexts. Others have proposed allegorical readings of Revelation, drawing direct spiritual correlations between the symbolism of the ancient text and the faith lives of modern believers. Of course, any access to historical information about the first-century context in which John wrote helps modern readers shed light on the potential meaning of Revelation. In addition to historical context, modern scholars attempt to access Revelation's meaning by analyzing the language or rhetoric of the text. Such scholars ask, of what was John attempting to convince his readers and how does he do so? Through Revelation, John attempts to raise his readers' consciousness about their own behaviors and relationships in the world and with the dominant powers of the world; to shape the world view and perceptions of his ancient readers; to construct an alternative understanding or decoding of the world and events impacting his ancient readers; and to persuade toward a particular course of action or behaviors.

Revelation is explicitly identified as "the revelation [Greek: *apokalypsis*] of Jesus Christ" that God gave to him so that he might show God's slaves (Greek: *douloi*) future events (1:1–3). The phrase "the revelation of Jesus Christ" may mean that the revelation derives from and/or is about Jesus as Messiah (anointed of God). The text constitutes one extensive revelation channeled through many visions. God's revelation is mediated through God's angel, not directly from the Christ (as the Apostle Paul claimed for himself in Galatians) to God's slave (*doulos*) John so he might be a witness (Greek: *martyria*) about everything he saw concerning God's word *and* testimony (*martyria*) of Jesus Christ. A martyr in the Apocalypse/Revelation is an eyewitness who shares that which he saw or was shown to him by a divine being or messenger (angel); his objective is not to die but to testify. However, he might die as a result of his testimony. The testimony should raise readers' consciousness and motivate them to become uncompromising doers of God's word and/or conquerors (2:7, 11, 26, 28; 3:5, 12, 21; 5:1; 6:2; 12:11; 13:7).

The vision reports are generally introduced with the phrase or formula *and I saw* (Greek: *kai eidon*) or less often as *and he showed me* (Greek: *kai edeiksen moi*). A blessing is pronounced upon the one who reads the prophecy aloud and those who both hear and keep it (1:3). In their secret assemblies in the hush/brush harbors in the deep darkness of the woods amidst the beasts of fields, enslaved Africans prayed out loud to ensure that God would hear them. In the Apocalypse, witnessing, hearing, and doing are crucial because of the nearness of time (*kairos*); temporality or time and timeliness are significant in Revelation. Events occur in time, they mark time, and in the end, time ends and starts anew.

Many regard chapters 12–14 as signifying a mythical time or story of the beginning of things, as a retrospective look at where it all started and why the Apocalypse/Revelation is necessary. In chapter 12 a pregnant woman clothed with the sun is about to give birth to the Messiah. The Satan, disguised as a dragon, awaited the child's debut into the world but was outwitted when the child was received in the heavens. Subsequently, war breaks out between the archangel Michael and the Satan (God's nemesis or adversary), and the latter is defeated and exiled to the earth. The dragon makes war with the woman's first born *and* all the rest of her children (12:4, 17). On earth, the dragon/the Satan empowers the beast and it wages war with the churches of God. John is chosen to receive the revelation and to communicate it by letter to the seven churches in Asia Minor, in the midst of the war. John takes his readers through a series of visions with him; the final one is a panoramic view of the new heavens and earth and the descent of the New Jerusalem on earth. The Apocalypse closes with John's signature, a final blessing, a warning to anyone tempted to alter the testimony of the book, and reassurance that Jesus Christ will return. The overall message is that God sees and knows everything; God is in control and God has a plan.

Chapter Contents

1. Historical and Rhetorical Context
2. The Seven Churches of Asia Minor
3. Apocalyptic Visions: Of God, the Lamb, Worship, the Dragon, the Beasts, and the Women
4. Justice, Judgment, and Transformation

Historical and Rhetorical Context

The simplest answer as to why John writes is that the Spirit directed him to do so (1:11, 19). In his inaugural vision John is shown seven stars being held in the right hand of one like the child of a human being (son of man) while he walks among the seven golden lampstands; the seven stars are revealed to be the angels of the seven churches represented by the lampstands (1:20). The prophet is told to write both what is shown to him and what shall take place. Thus, his visions recall the past, interpret the present, and reveal the future.

Similar to Paul's letter to the Galatians, John begins by claiming special revelation from God and by pronouncing a blessing upon those who read the letter aloud (to their people in their assemblies) and upon the hearers and doers of the prophecy (1:1–3). The seven churches need to be reminded and/or informed that they are at risk of being conquered and not conquerors of the challenges they face as colonized subjects of the Roman Empire. Kingdom loyalty and obedience is demonstrated by the object and quality of one's worship. Significantly, John and those whom he admonishes to conquer or overcome are slaves (*douloi*) of God; equally noteworthy is the fact that virtually no kingdom has been built or maintained without slave labor. The text is set in the middle to late first century CE when Rome, a slave society, ruled the then known world. John wrote from the Island of Patmos in Asia between about 69 CE and 96 CE, which encompasses the period known as the Flavian dynasty (the imperial reign of Vespasian and his two sons Titus and Domitian). Of course, the second Jewish temple was destroyed during that time in 70 CE. We have no evidence that Rome exiled John to the island. Perhaps this was a self-imposed exile so that he might receive a much-needed pastoral word from God. Some scholars argue that John wrote during a time of widespread persecution against Christians; others believe that they endured sporadic persecution; and still others assert no persecution of Christians occurred during this time. Many scholars believed that emperor worship or the promulgation of the imperial cult constituted a significant problem for members of the Jesus movement. Perhaps John and some members of the seven churches considered the required participation in the imperial cult to be a form of religious persecution and encouraged them to compromise their faith. It is possible for an ancient author to speak of persecution generally and not have in mind widespread persecution but persecution of a segment of an expanding community. The Acts of the Apostles states that the *ekklēsia* was persecuted by Paul and yet it seems that he pursued only the Hellenists who fled into the Diaspora. The Twelve apostles and others like the prophet Agabus remained in Jerusalem and evidently were not subjected to the same level of persecution, if any at all (Acts 8:1–3; 11:27–28; 21:9–10). Regardless, John identifies himself as one who shares in their persecution, whatever that might entail (Rev 1:9).

One way that colonized subjects and citizens of the Roman Empire demonstrated piety and/or allegiance to Rome was through participation in the imperial cult. The justice and worship of God and testimony of Jesus as God's Messiah conflicted with expectations of the empire. In Rome, "patriotism" and religious piety interconnected, with the latter demonstrating the former and the former reenacted in the latter. The imperial cult was political; through worship and ritual the people acknowledged and embodied the dominance, power, and omnipresence of Rome and its emperors and empresses, living and dead. Under the Republic, Julius Caesar (100–45 BCE) was officially divinized or acknowledged as a god by the Roman state upon his death. The first Roman emperor Augustus (Octavian) reigned from 31 BCE to 14 CE; after his death he was deified (*divus*), as were subsequent Roman emperors (and some emperors' wives). The first manifestation of the imperial cult or emperor worship was when Augustus permitted the Greek cities of Asia Minor to set up temples to him. The imperial cult functioned to unify the Empire and was practiced by the army scattered through the empire and by individuals in various Roman provinces where imperial cult or worship centers were established, such as at Pergamum in Asia Minor.

The Emperor Domitian (81–96 CE) demanded that the people recognize him as "Lord (*Dominus*) and God (*Deus*)" and participate in his cult *during* his lifetime. Participation in the imperial cult could be economically and socially lucrative for persons in the Roman provinces like Asia Minor where the seven churches were located. Persons skilled as artisans and other trades benefited financially from providing items for the imperial cult. In the Acts of the Apostles a local silversmith in Ephesus (one of the seven churches) named Demetrius, who made and sold silver shrines of the great goddess Artemis, became enraged and incited the people against the Apostle Paul because he arrived preaching that gods made with human hands were not gods. Demetrius reminded the Ephesians that their livelihood and wealth relied on the business that the Roman imperial cult generated (Acts 19:23–41). Some people could barter for position and money in exchange for public demonstrations of devotion to the imperial cult.

It is possible that empresses, who were sometimes the priestesses to the imperial cult of their dead emperor husbands, served as models for the function of priestesses elsewhere in the empire. The first priestesses served from the death of Augustus and they include Livia (priestess of deified Augustus), Antonia Minor (grandmother of Caligula made priestess of the deified Augustus), and Agrippina the Younger (priestess of deified Claudius); the latter may have been the last. But beginning with the deification of Drusilla, the Emperor Caligula's sister, in 38 CE, imperial women became the object of worship, but never to the same extent as imperial males. Livia was deified by Claudius in 42 CE; Claudia, Nero's daughter with Poppaea, who died when she was under four months old, was deified in the first century CE. Temples and statues were erected to both deified women and men. Priests and priestesses served the imperial cults of both men and women. Some towns within the Roman Empire elected to worship imperial women who were never officially deified at Rome; local cities and towns were permitted some leeway in terms of how they would participate in the imperial cult. Literary evidence for Rome cannot be regarded as a precise model for the cult in local towns. Thus,

John's critique of each of the seven churches is particular to their distinct, if proximate, locations, and with some overlap.

Both priestesses and priests (not necessarily married to one another) officiated in the imperial cult. Priests and priestesses officiating in the imperial cult wore golden crowns bearing the images or busts (heads) of the emperor(s)/empress(es) and other male and female imperial family members, particularly, it seems, in Asia Minor. Emperors wore golden crowns adorned with images of gods like Jupiter, Juno, and Minerva. The emperors were made sacramentally present through the priests and priestesses of the imperial cult who wore the image of the emperor in their golden crowns. The imperial cult could include the celebration of the emperor's birthdays, birthdays of the emperor's wife and relatives, the day of the emperor's ascension to the throne, an annual day of vows of well-being for the emperor. Imperial images were believed to have supernatural powers. After one nation conquered another nation, the conquered nation was faced with reality that their god(s) proved less powerful in war than the gods of the victors. This acknowledgement of dominance and of being conquered was demonstrated in worship.

Consider and discuss: In 2016, Colin Kaepernick, a National Football League professional football player, refused to stand for the national anthem (the "Star-Spangled Banner") during official games as a public form of protest of police brutality against nonwhite minoritized peoples and other forms of systemic racism in the USA. Some of Kaepernick's fellow American citizens, primarily white (but not exclusively), vehemently disagreed with the manner of his protest. Some disagreed with his decision to "take the knee" (kneel rather than stand) calling his actions unpatriotic and/or disrespectful to veterans, misrepresenting or failing to understand the reasons for his protest. How are expectations of allegiance to country or patriotism similar or different from Rome's expectations of its citizens and colonized persons under the empire? What is nationalism? How are nationalism and imperialism similar or different? What expressions of loyalty might empire or nation impose on individuals or groups that might conflict with what it means to show loyalty to God and to demonstrate God's love and justice?

Revelation shows what it looks like and means to continually worship God or to worship the beast and its image. The churches cannot worship both; any compromise is unacceptable and is not a characteristic of a conqueror or overcomer. The Roman Empire, on the other hand, allowed for its subjects to demonstrate loyalty and piety toward the empire *and* toward one's own cultural and/or personal deities. In the Apocalypse, believers are a kingdom of kings and priests signifying the interconnected reality of the political and the religious and the religious and the political both in heaven and on earth (1:6; 5:10). But readers are not to worry because God's dominion is eternal (1:6). John is both a co-sufferer with the churches and a subject of God's kingdom. The churches face a number of challenges and their loyalty to God is threatened by those who claim to be Jews but who belong to the synagogue of Satan (2:9–10; 3:9), their proximity to Satan's throne (2:13; 2:24), failure to remember what they learned and heard from God (3:3), the trappings of wealth (3:9,17), and the prevalence of false teachings and prophetesses and prophets like Jezebel, Balaam, and Nicolaitans, who encourage fornication and indulgence in food sacrificed to idols (2:2, 14–15, 20). Historically, the marriage of Jezebel and King Ahab of Israel was perhaps a political union. In their union, worship and politics interconnected and became problematic. Jezebel was blamed for Ahab's worship of Baal and other evil deeds. Jezebel's plot to have Naboth killed so that Ahab could take his property was unforgivable; and she has been forever made a symbol of idolatry, false prophesy, evil, treachery, and prostitution (cf. 1 Kgs 16:30–33; 22:1–25; 2 Sam 11–12).

The churches must conquer or be conquered, but some have already been slaughtered (perhaps refusing to participate in emperor worship) because of their loyalty to the word of God and their testimony of Jesus; their blood cries out from under the altar, "how long?" (6:9–10). Others face the same fate (6:11). Believers are compelled to worship demons and human-made idols of gold, silver, bronze, stone, and wood (9:20–21). The inhabitants of the land are forced to worship the beasts of the earth (13:8, 12); their refusal or compliance has both spiritual and socioeconomic consequences (13:16)

Consider and discuss: In what ways can a focus on religious persecution encourage contemporary Christians and members of other religions to ignore the ways in which we ourselves might be complicit in oppression or injustices?

The Seven Churches of Asia Minor

John uses a conventional greeting for his letters to the churches: "Grace to you and peace." The greeting consists of themes found in the letters and the Apocalypse as a whole: the pre-existence and eternal existence of God, God's throne, kings of the earth, Jesus Christ as the faithful witness and ruler of earthly kings, Seven spirits, God's liberated people as a kingdom and priests, the eternal glory and dominion of God, and the Parousia (1:4–8). Next, John identifies himself using the first-person singular "I" and recalls his inaugural vision in which he is commanded to write to the seven churches (1:9–20). In the Spirit on the "Lord's day," John hears a voice in a vision that instructs him to write what he sees in a book (*biblion*) and send the book to the seven churches. The voice, loud as a trumpet and like the sound of many waters, belongs to a human being or child of a human (son of man); he wears a long robe with a golden sash, has a white luminous head and hair, eyes like fire, feet with bronze, from his mouth protrudes a two-edged sword, holds seven stars in his right hand, and stands among seven golden lampstands. John prostrates himself in worship before the human being who identified himself as the risen, living, eternal Christ who holds the keys of Death and Hades. The child of a human decodes the symbol of the seven stars and lampstands; they are the angels of the seven churches and the seven churches, respectively. John's description of the child of a human being resembles but is not identical with the figure in Daniel's vision (Dan 7:9–13). The risen Christ is the author of the letters and John is his scribe.

The seven churches—Ephesus, Smyrna, Pergamum, Thyatira, Sardis, Philadelphia, and Laodicea—were located in close proximity to one another in Asia Minor (modern-day Turkey), which was a providence of the Roman Empire. Laodicea was named after the sister-wife of Antiochus II, Laodice, and it was refounded in the third century BCE. When the Romans assumed control of Laodicea incorporating it into the province of Asia, it was developed into a wealthy and significant city. It was so wealthy that when it suffered damage from earthquakes, the Laodiceans rebuilt their city without assistance from imperial or local rulers. Laodicea was a banking center and globally known for the primary source of its wealth, its black glossy wool. A significant Jewish population lived in the city. Laodicea was also known for its famous medical school. John accuses Laodicea of being neither hot nor cold, but lukewarm. Laodicea, Ephesus, Smyrna, Sardis, and Philadelphia were located on a significant trade road and were busy and ambitious commercial centers that demonstrated their loyalty to the Empire. Laodicea is the most important of the seven. In the region of the seven churches, the council of the province (*Koinon*) was chiefly responsible for maintaining the worship of the emperor. The Laodiceans were introduced to the imperial cult quite early and participated in the *Koinon*. Ancient coins (numismatic artifacts) show that several friendship treaties were brokered between Laodicea and nearby cities like Smyrna, Pergamum, and Ephesus. Numismatic evidence from the Roman period also shows that the Egyptian goddess Isis and the composite god Serapis were worshiped in that region, as well as Helios, Demeter, Zeus Laodicenus, Asclepius (a healing deity), Artemis the huntress, and the Ephesian Artemis. The Ephesians boasted of being the "temple-keeper of the great Artemis and of the statue that fell from heaven" (Acts 19:35). Pergamum, a seat of Roman administration in Asia, hosted a great temple to Zeus, boasted of many pagan temples, and was the first Asia Minor municipality to build a temple deifying an emperor. In Thyatira, cultic propaganda declared the Roman emperor the incarnation of Apollo and thus a son of Zeus. Philadelphia and Smyrna are the only churches not condemned in the Apocalypse.

In most of the seven letters John uses the same identifying language to describe the author as used to characterize the child of a human (Jesus Christ) in the inaugural vision: For Ephesus, he is the one "who holds the seven stars in his right hand and walks among the seven golden lampstands" (2:1); For Smyrna, "the first and the last, who was dead and came to life" (2:8); for Pergamum, "he who has the sharp two-edge sword" (2:12); for Thyatira, "the son of God, who has eyes like a flame of fire and whose feet are like burnished bronze" (2:18); for Sardis, "he who has the seven spirits of God and the seven stars" (3:1); for Philadelphia, "the holy one, the true one, who has the key of David, who opens and no one will shut, who shuts and no one opens" (3:7); and for Laodicea, "the Amen, the faithful and true witness, the origin of God's creation" (3:14). Each identification of the Divine is followed by the same epistemological introductory formula "I know." The Divine sees or knows everything they have done or not done and the challenges they face. Each letter ends with the refrain, "Let any who has an ear listen to what the Spirit is saying to the churches"; and each includes a conditional promise of a future reward to the church that conquers or prevails (over the beast and its image). The general structure of the letters is as follows: (a) A formulaic "I know your works (your affliction for Sardis; where you live, for Smyrna) ..."; (b) a statement of an issue he has with the church and sometimes a call to remembrance; (c) a call for repentance and promise of destruction if they refuse to do what they hear; (d) a commendation; and (e) the refrain and promise. Most of the seven churches are revealed to have shown endurance in the face of evil doers, affliction, slander, impotency, the presence of Satan's throne and the synagogue of Satan, false prophets (teachings of Balaam, the

Nicolaitans, and the prophetess Jezebel), and murdered witnesses. In the ways that they are faithful, they are admonished to hold fast. In the ways that they have failed or lost their first love, they are called to repent. But all are encouraged to be conquerors.

Apocalyptic Visions: Of God, the Lamb, Worship, the Dragon, the Beasts, and the Women

Every tongue, tribe, and nation were indebted to Caesar for the peace and salvation they enjoyed, according to Roman imperial rhetoric. But every tongue, nation, tribe, and created being will worship God and the slaughtered lamb (5:13–14; 7:9). In chapters 4 and 5, John is shown an open door to the heavenly throne room where four living creatures that surround the throne and the twenty-four white-robed elders wearing their gold crowns worship God continuously singing: "Holy, Holy, Holy, is the Lord God, the Almighty, who was and is and is to come" (4:8). God is worthy of honor, glory, and gratitude as the creator of all things. In God's right hand John sees a scroll sealed with seven seals that no one in heaven or on earth was worthy to open, except the slaughtered lamb (the lion of the tribe of Judah, the Root of David), the risen Christ (5:5). He is worthy because of the many ethnically and culturally diverse people whom he ransomed with his blood to establish a kingdom and a priesthood (5:10). Myriad angels join the heavenly chorus singing the lamb's praises: he is worthy to receive power, wealth, wisdom, might, honor, glory, and blessing belonging to the lamb (5:11–12; cf. 7:9–11). Rome possessed, valued, desired, and conquered for power, wealth, wisdom, might, honor, glory, and blessing, but it is not worthy.

Revelation repeatedly exhorts readers to worship God and sing God's praises. Revelation contains nine hymns, seven of which are call and response (antiphonal). The final amen response comes from the four living creatures and the elders who surround the heavenly throne (5:13–14). From the first to the last vision the readers are shown and encouraged to worship God and the lamb as is done in the heavenly throne room. In the last vision John is shown the river of life flowing from the throne of God and of the Lamb where God's servants will worship God in the New Jerusalem (22:1–7).

In chapters 6–8, the Lamb opens the seven seals on the scroll that John saw in God's right hand. The first through fifth seals unleash havoc upon the earth. The sixth seal ushers in the great day of wrath unleashing a catastrophic earthquake and cosmic events including falling stars, the blackening of the sun, and the moon turning blood red. So terrible is that day that earthly kings, the rich and powerful, slave and free would rather be buried under the rubble than face God's wrath (6:12–17). The breaking of the seventh seal is disrupted with another vision involving the sealing of a symbolic 144,000 from among the metaphorical twelve tribes of Israel who are the slaves (*douloi*) of God that received the seal of God in their foreheads (7:1–8). Perhaps this 144,000 from the twelve tribes represent the dispersed in Asia Minor (cf. Jas 1:1). In chapter 14 the 144,000 are further described as an elite group who never succumbed to the seductions of Rome, the great whore. The 144,000 are male virgins who did not defile themselves with women; the Father's name is tattooed in their foreheads.

During this pause in the opening of the last seal, John also sees an innumerable multitude that have endured great tribulation (*thlipsis*) standing before God's throne rendering unceasing worship (7:9–17). In chapter 8 the lamb opens the final and seventh seal of the scroll, initiating time-out in heaven (8:1). This silence is accentuated by the presence of seven angels with trumpets they do not blow until another angel has burned incense on the altar mingled with the prayers of the saints ascending before God (8:2–5). The seven angels break the silence with the successive blowing of their trumpets unleashing catastrophe, cosmic disasters, and plague-like events that parallel the breaking of the scrolls (8:6–20). After the sixth trumpet is blown, we find two disruptions in the narrative, two intervening visions (10:1–11; 11:1–14). When the seventh trumpet sounds, a curtain is drawn back revealing the throne room scene and loud voices declare a great reversal; the kingdom of the world becomes the eternal kingdom of God and the Messiah. And the heavenly temple is opened as the twenty-four elders resume their worship before the throne.

Consider and discuss: As a colonized man living under the dominance of the Roman Empire, in what ways does John demonstrate a hybrid existence? In other words, are there ways in which Revelation re-inscribes or imitates the values and ways of empire while discouraging participation in the Empire and its ways? In what ways does John depict God and the New Jerusalem behaving similar to imperial Rome?

The Woman, the Dragon, the Beast, and the Lamb

As noted, chapter 12 is a flashback to precipitating events; it is a myth of origins. The scene opens in heaven with the presentation of a pregnant woman in the throes of painful child birth. The nameless woman in labor dons a crown of twelve stars, but she has no clothing or shoes. The sun is her covering (reminiscent of Eve), and she stands on the moon. Some argue that she symbolizes the Virgin Mary and others assert that she represents God's church. The woman in labor represents a great sign, but another portent appears on the scene (cf. Isa 7:10–14; 9:6). The great ten-horned, seven-headed dragon wearing seven crowns wages war against the woman in her most vulnerable state, intent on destroying her child. Already the dragon (later identified as the ancient serpent, the Devil, Satan, and the deceiver of the world) has cast a third of the stars or angels in heaven to the earth with the swipe of its tail. When the male child is born, he is taken from his mother and given to God. God prepared a sanctuary for the child's mother in the wilderness where she has fled to be nourished for 1,260 days. The child and his mother are protected from the dragon. But war breaks out in heaven between the archangel Michael and his army and the great red dragon and his troops ending with the defeat and exile of the dragon and his angels to the earth (see Dan 10:13; 12:1; Jude 9). War in heaven is depicted in no other Jewish or early Christian apocalyptic literature (cf. Isa 14:12–21; 2 Enoch 29:4–5). Heaven's victory is celebrated by a solo. However, the dragon's wrath was not extinguished; he pursued the child's mother into the wilderness (cf. the story of Hagar, Gen 16). Unable to capture the woman and her child or to inundate her with water, the dragon wages war with her other children who hear and keep God's word and the testimony of Jesus.

In chapter 13, readers are introduced to two beasts, one arising from the sea and the other from the earth but both deriving their authority, power, and throne from the dragon. The first beast arising out of the sea resembles the dragon in that it has ten horns upon seven heads but its ten crowns are worn on its horns (and not its heads). The beast amazes the cosmos, luring it to worship the dragon as the mightiest power on the earth; its power and authority is limited to forty-two months during which time it waged war against the saints, conquering them. For a time, every tribe, people, language, and nation on the earth whose names did not appear in the book of life worshipped the dragon through the beast. The second two-horned lamb-like beast speaks like a dragon, a deceiver, and an adversary of God. The second beast's impact is spiritual, physical, and economical. Those who refuse to worship the beast or to be branded with its mark are killed and prohibited from buying and selling.

APOCALYPSE OF JOHN/BOOK OF REVELATION

Justice, Judgment, and Transformation

In chapter 14, the scene moves to a vision of 144,000, the male virgins who refused to be seduced by the whore Babylon (Rome). As conquerors, they refused to worship Rome. While readers may be sure that God does not exclude women from being among the faithful conquerors that resist the authority and power of empire and who demonstrate loyalty to God and to the Lamb, the text is another matter. The redeemed 144,000 sing a new song that only they could learn, perhaps based on their unique experience and testimonies of resistance and of overcoming. While the 144,000 are the first fruits of the harvest, they are not the only harvest. They are human and yet without deceit and blameless. The vision of the male virgins is followed by the vision of three angels, each with their own pronouncement: The first issues a call for everyone on earth to fear, glorify, and worship God as creator of all things; the hour of justice/judgment has arrived. The second announces the fall of Babylon or the great Rome, feminized as a woman who caused all nations to commit fornication with her. The third angel announces the wrath and judgment of God upon those who worshipped the beast. Another three angels emerge from the temple and the altar and participate in the harvesting of the earth when the one like a child of humanity with a sickle in his hand appears seated on a cloud.

Consider and discuss: Where do you see gender stereotypes in the narrative? What are the implications of those stereotypes? Where do you see simplistic polarities (e.g., good and evil)? What are the implications of such polarities? How do we reinscribe these polarities in our theologies?

In chapters 15–16 seven plagues are poured out upon the earth, followed by judgment of the great whore Babylon. In chapter 15 angels with seven plagues constitute the last and great sign in the heavens, manifesting and culminating with the wrath of God. Prior to the seven plagues, John saw a multitude of those who had conquered the beast and the image and the number of its name standing on a sea of glass with harps and singing the song of Moses and the Lamb. The song of Moses recalls the plagues God poured out upon Egypt before God liberated the Hebrew slaves (Exod 7–11). The plagues parallel those poured out on Egypt during the Exodus event. The seven angels with the plagues emerge from the heavenly temple. They received their seven bowls full of God's wrath from the four living creatures; there is no access to the temple until the culmination of the plagues. In chapter 16 at the signal of the loud voice, seven plagues inflict the earth. The first plague is painful sores on the worshippers of the beast and its image. The second plague contaminates the sea with blood and every living creature in it dies. The third plague turns the other bodies of water into blood as retributive justice for the blood of the saints and prophets; the third angel sings a hymn of justice and the altar responds, the altar under which the blood of the saints cried for justice. The plague is a scorching sun so hot that its victims curse God. The fifth plague plunges the throne and kingdom of the beast into darkness. The sixth plague dries up the river Euphrates to clear a path for the kings of the east in preparation for the great and final battle of Harmagedon (Hebrew). This NT *hapax legomenon* (occurring only once) refers to the place of a symbolic war that will culminate in God's sovereignty. With the seventh angel, the voice from the temple announces that "it is done," producing lightning, thunder, earthquakes, and hail that destroy the great city Babylon and other cities of the nations. The plagues impact all aspects of the created order: the land, the waters, and all living things on land and in the waters, the atmospheric elements. Sins of injustice, hate, and oppression in all forms impact all of creation—humanity and the natural environment. The plagues are God's just response to idolatry and persecution.

Consider and discuss: In recent years, we have experienced an increase in natural disasters and scientists have warned about the impact of global warming. What is global warming? (If you do not know, do your research.) How do we abuse the earth and its resources in ways that might contribute to global warming?

Fallen Babylon and Fallen Woman

In chapters 18–19, the woman held responsible for the seducing of Babylon (Rome) is shown in the wilderness sitting on the beast (the Roman Empire). She is decked in purple (the color of royalty and wealth) and scarlet (often associated with prostitution and sin). She is depicted as a high class prostitute lavishly adorned with gold and pearls and holds a cup full of abominations and impurities. Another angel descends from heaven to earth and announces the fall of "Babylon the Great." At the news of her destruction, the angelic choir and the four living beasts and twenty-four elders break out in a Hallelujah chorus praising God for his just and true judgments against the great whore that corrupted the earth. The marriage of the Lamb, Jesus Christ, and his redeemed bride is announced. Upon seeing the Lamb, John prostrates himself before the Lamb to worship him, but the Lamb forbids it because like John he is a slave of God. "Worship God!" the Lamb insists.

Consider and discuss: In the Apocalypse, Jesus is portrayed as encouraging readers to worship God and not himself. How do contemporary Christian churches worship Jesus rather than God? How might the way in which we see Jesus in relation to God impact how we relate to other religions and religious people?

Chapters 19–20 continue with a vision of the imprisonment of the dragon (serpent/Satan) in a bottomless pit where he is constrained with a huge chain for a thousand-year period during which time he is unable to further deceive the nations. During this period, judgment begins in heaven and the books of life and death are opened. The resurrected ones who were slaughtered when they refused to worship the beast and its image sit in judgment with Christ during the millennium while Satan is detained. At the end of the thousand years, Satan will be released to make his final attempt to deceive the nations. The final battle occurs at Gog and Magog, where Satan attempts to conquer the saints and the heavenly city (see Ezek 38–39). In the battle, the Devil and his army are forced to join the beast and its image in the lake of fire; they are consumed. In chapter 21 the New Jerusalem, the holy city, descends from heaven where God is enthroned. A loud voice announces how God does not give up on being among and with human beings; God obliterates all pain and death and makes all things new. The saints who were not deceived by the Satan, the beasts, and false prophets and whose names were written in the Lamb's book of life inherit the new earth and heaven; all others inherit the second death signified by the lake of fire. One of seven angels gives John an up-close and detailed view of the new holy city and the bride. The city contains no temple; God and the Lamb are the temple. The city receives its light and warmth from God and the Lamb; there is no sun or moon. Nations and kings still exist bringing their glory into the city and guided by God's light and the lamb.

In the final chapter 22, the angel continues showing John around the holy city. The river of life flows from the throne of God and the Lamb, the therapeutic tree of life bearing twelve varieties of fruit is for the continual health of humanity. God and the throne of the Lamb will be located in the midst of the city. The inhabitants will see God's face, unlike Moses in Hebrew Bible tradition (Exod 33:20; Deut 4:12). The names of God and the Lamb are stamped in the forehead of the citizens of the city, perhaps demonstrating their obvious loyalty to the Divine. The angels complete the visionary tour by assuring John of the veracity and credibility of the words of the visions and of what will shortly occur. The visions close, reiterating a blessing upon those who do what they have heard: "See I am coming soon. Blessed is the one who keeps the words of the prophecy of this book" (22:7). The closing and final benediction of the book (*biblion*) ends with John's "signature" as the one who heard and saw the visions and words of the Revelation and his overwhelming response to worship the angel who mediated the revelation. Just as the Lamb prohibited John from worshipping him, directing him instead to worship God, so does the angel (22:9). The angel directs John to leave the book unsealed because the prophecy is imminent. The people have been judged and the Alpha and Omega will return soon with reward and punishment. A final blessing is pronounced upon the faithful who are clothed in white robes. Jesus also signs the letter as the one who sent the angel with the testimony for the seven churches (22:16). Since the inclusion of the book of Revelation in the authoritative canon remained contested and uncertain until the fourth century CE, it is ironic that it closes the NT canon with a caveat for anyone who should revise the prophecy contained in it.

Summary

1. God speaks to God's prophet John through visions and communicates God's message using apocalyptic symbols.
2. Despite the challenges of Empire and false prophecies, God's people can be overcomers.
3. God sees and hears and speaks in times of trouble to God's people.
4. Even though God is enthroned in heaven, God has eyes and ears on earth.
5. The goal of witnessing about God and Jesus is not death but death can be the consequence.
6. Gender and other biases of the seer and his context leave their imprint on his testimony.
7. Chapters 12–14 constitute a myth of origins.
8. God demonstrates that God is in control and God is more powerful than the most powerful empire on earth.

Further Reading

Blount, Brian K. *Can I Get a Witness? Reading Revelation through African American Culture*. Louisville: Westminster John Knox, 2005.

———. *Revelation: A Commentary*. Louisville: Westminster John Knox, 2009.

Boesak, Allan A. *Comfort and Protest: The Apocalypse from a South African Perspective*. Philadelphia: Westminster, 1987.

Darden, Lynne St. Clair. *Scripturalizing Revelation: An African American Postcolonial Reading of Empire*. Atlanta: Society of Biblical Literature, 2015.

deSilva, David A. *Seeing Things John's Way: The Rhetoric of the Book of Revelation*. Louisville: Westminster John Knox, 2009.

Fiorenza, Elisabeth Schüssler. *The Book of Revelation: Justice and Judgment*. 2nd ed. Minneapolis: Fortress, 1998.

González, Catherine Gunsalus, and Justo L. González. *The Book of Revelation*. WBComp. Louisville: Westminster John Knox, 1997.

Huber, Lynn. "Unveiling the Bride: Revelation 19:1–9 and Roman Social Discourse." In *A Feminist Companion to the Apocalypse of John*, edited by Amy-Jill Levine, 159–79. FCNTECW 13. London: Bloomsbury, 2010.

Kearsley, R. "Women and Public Life in Imperial Asia Minor: Hellenistic Tradition and Augustan Ideology." *Ancient West and East* 4 (2005) 98–121.

Martin, Clarice J. "Polishing an Unclouded Mirror. A Womanist Reading of Rev 18:13." In *From Every People And Nation: The Book of Revelation in Intercultural Perspective*, edited by David Rhoads, 82–109. Minneapolis: Fortress, 2005.

Moss, Candida. *The Myth of Persecution: How Early Christians Invented the Story of Martyrdom*. New York: Harper One, 2013.

Pagels, Elaine. *Revelation: Visions, Prophecy and Politics in the Book of Revelation*. New York: Penguin, 2013.

Pippin, Tina. *Death and Desire: The Rhetoric of Gender in the Apocalypse of John*. LCBI. Louisville: Westminster John Knox, 1992.

———. "Eros and the End: Reading for Gender in the Apocalypse of John." *Semeia* 59 (1991) 193–210.

———. "Revelation/Apocalypse of John." *Women's Commentary of the Bible: Revised and Updated*, edited by Carol A. Newsom, Sharon H.

Ringe, and Jacqueline E. Lapsley, 627–32. Louisville: Westminster John Knox, 2012.

Rossing, Barbara R. *The Choice Between Two Cities. Whore, Bride, and Empire in the Apocalypse*. Harvard Theological Studies. Harrisburg, PA: Trinity, 2009.

Ruiz, Jean-Pierre. "Politics of Praise: A Reading of Revelation 19:1–10." In *SBL Seminary Papers*, 374–94. Atlanta: Scholars, 1997.

Sánchez, David Arthur. *From Patmos to Barrio: Subverting Imperial Myths*. Minneapolis: Fortress, 2008.

Sechrest, Love. "Antitypes, Stereotypes, and Antetypes: Jezebel, the Sun Woman, and Contemporary Black Women." In *Womanist Interpretations of the Bible: Expanding the Discourse*, edited by Gay L. Byron and Vanessa Lovelace, 113–38. Atlanta: Society of Biblical Literature Press, 2016.

Slater, Thomas. *Revelation as Civil Disobedience: Witness Not Warriors in John's Apocalypse*. Nashville: Abingdon, 2018.

Smith, Mitzi J. "Fashioning Our Own Souls. A Womanist Reading of the Virgin-Whore Binary in Matthew and Revelation." In *I Found God in Me: A Womanist Biblical Hermeneutics Reader*, edited by Mitzi J. Smith, 158–82. Eugene, OR: Cascade, 2015.

Smith, Shanell T. *The Woman Babylon and the Marks of Empire: Reading Revelation with a Postcolonial Womanist Hermeneutics of Ambiveilance*. Minneapolis: Fortress, 2014.

Bibliography

Adewale, Olubiyi Adeniyi. "An Afro-Sociological Application of the Parable of the Rich Man and Lazarus." *Black Theology* 4 (2006) 27–43.
Adichie, Chimamanda Ngozi. "The Danger of a Single Story." TED Talk, 2009. https://youtu.be/D9Ihs241zeg.
Aland, Kurt, and Barbara Aland. *The Text of the New Testament: An Introduction to the Critical Editions and to the Theory and Practice of Modern Textual Criticism.* 2nd ed. Grand Rapids, MI: Eerdmans, 1995.
American Bible Society. *The Gospel according to Luke in Gullah Sea Island Creole with Marginal Text of the King James Version.* New York: American Bible Society, 1995.
An, Choi Hee, and Katheryn Pfisterer Darr, eds. *Engaging the Bible: Critical Readings from Contemporary Women.* Minneapolis: Augsburg Fortress, 2006.
Andrews, William L., and Henry Louis Gates, editors: *Slave Narratives.* New York: Library of America, 2000.
Ascough, R. S. "The Thessalonian Christian Community as a Professional Voluntary Association." *Journal of Biblical Literature* 119 (2000) 311–28.
Aslan, Reza. *Zealot. The Life and Times of Jesus of Nazareth.* New York: Random House, 2013.
Attridge, Harold W. *The Epistle to the Hebrews.* Hermeneia. Philadelphia: Fortress, 1989.
Aymer, Margaret P. *First Pure, Then Peaceable: Frederick Douglass, Darkness and the Epistle of James.* London: T. & T. Clark, 2007.
———. "Outrageous, Audacious, Courageous, Willful: Reading the Enslaved Girl of Acts 12." In *Womanist Interpretations of the Bible: Expanding the Discourse*, edited by Gay L. Byron and Vanessa Lovelace, 265–90. Semeia Studies. Atlanta: Society of Biblical Literature, 2016.
Badiou, Alain. *Saint Paul: The Foundation of Universalism.* Translated by Ray Brassier. Stanford: Stanford University Press, 2003.
Bailey, Randall C. "That's Why They Didn't Call the Book Hadassah! The Interse(ct)/(x)ionality of Race/Ethnicity, Gender, and Sexuality in the Book of Esther." In *They Were All Together in One Place? Toward Minority Biblical Criticism*, edited by Randall C. Bailey, Tat-Siong Benny Liew and Fernando F. Segovia, 227–50. Semeia Studies 57. Atlanta: Society of Biblical Literature, 2009.
Bailey, Randall, et al. "African and African Diasporan Hermeneutics." In *The Africana Bible*, edited by Hugh R. Page Jr., 19–24. Minneapolis: Fortress, 2010.
Bailey, Randall, and Jacquelyn Grant, eds. *The Recovery of Black Presence. An Interdisciplinary Exploration.* Nashville: Abingdon, 1995.

Bailey, Randall C., Tat-Siong Benny Liew and Fernando F. Segovia, editors. *They Were All Together in One Place? Toward Minority Biblical Criticism.* SemeiaSt 57. Atlanta: Society of Biblical Literature, 2009.

Baldwin, James. *The Fire Next Time.* New York: Vintage, 1991.

———. *I Am Not Your Negro.* New York: Vintage, 2017.

Bantam, Brian. *Redeeming Mulatto. A Theology of Race and Christian Hybridity.* Waco, TX: Baylor University Press, 2010.

Barlow, Maude and Tony Clarke. "Water Privatization." *Global Policy Forum.* Polaris Institute, Jan 2004. https://www.globalpolicy.org/component/content/article/209/43398.html.

Barrett, C. K. *The New Testament Background: Selected Documents.* New York: HarperOne, 1995.

Bartlett, David Lyon. *1 Peter.* Nashville: Abingdon, 1998.

Bassler, Jouette. "1 Corinthians." In *Women's Bible Commentary: Revised Edition*, edited by Carol Newsom et al., 557–65. Louisville, KY: Westminster John Knox, 2012.

———. *1 Timothy, 2 Timothy, and Titus.* Nashville, TN: Abingdon, 1996.

———. *Navigating Paul: An Introduction to Key Theological Concepts.* Louisville, KY: Westminster John Knox, 2006.

Batten, Alicia J. "Philemon." In *Philippians, Colossians, Philemon*, edited by Mary Ann Beavis, 201–64. Wisdom Commentary 51. Collegeville, MN: Liturgical, 2017.

Bauckham, Richard. *Jude and the Relatives of Jesus in the Early Church.* Edinburgh: T. & T. Clark, 1990.

Bauer, Walter. *A Greek English Lexicon of the New Testament.* Chicago: University of Chicago Press, 2001.

Beaton, Richard. "Messiah and Justice: A Key to Matthew's Use of Isaiah 42:1–4?" *Journal for the Study of the New Testament* 75 (1999) 5–23.

Beavis, Mary. "2 Thessalonians." In *Women's Bible Commentary: Revised Edition*, edited by Carol Newsom et al., 592–94. Louisville: Westminster John Knox, 2012.

Bell, Sinclair, and Teresa Ramsby, eds. *Free at Last! The Impact of Freed Slaves on the Roman Empire.* London: Bloomsbury, 2012.

Bird, Jennifer G. "Ephesians." In *The Fortress Commentary on the Bible: The New Testament*, edited by Margaret Aymer, Cynthia Briggs Kittredge, and David A. Sánchez, 527–42. Minneapolis: Fortress, 2014.

———. "Ephesians." In *A Postcolonial Commentary on the New Testament Writings*, edited by R. S. Sugirtharajah and Fernando F. Segovia, 265–80. New York: T. & T. Clark, 2009.

———. *Permission Granted: Take the Bible into Your Own Hands.* Louisville: Westminster John Knox, 2015.

Blount, Brian K. *Can I Get a Witness? Reading Revelation through African American Culture.* Louisville: Westminster John Knox, 2005.

———. *Cultural Interpretation: Reorienting the New Testament.* Minneapolis: Fortress, 1995.

———. *Go Preach! Mark's Kingdom Message and the Black Church Today.* Maryknoll, NY: Orbis, 1998.

———. *Revelation: A Commentary.* Louisville: Westminster John Knox, 2009.

———. *Then the Whisper Put on Flesh: New Testament Ethics in an African American Context.* Nashville: Abingdon, 2001.

Boesak, Allan A. *Comfort and Protest: The Apocalypse from a South African Perspective*. Philadelphia: Westminster, 1987.
Bonhoeffer, Dietrich. *The Cost of Discipleship*. New York: Touchstone, 1995.
———. *Discipleship*. Minneapolis, MN: Fortress, 2015.
———. *Ethics*. Minneapolis, MN: Fortress, 2009.
Bonz, Marianne Palmer. *The Past as Legacy: Luke-Acts and Ancient Epic*. Minneapolis: Fortress, 2000.
Borg, Marcus. *Jesus: The Life, Teachings, and Relevance of a Religious Revolutionary*. New York: HarperOne, 2015.
Bose, Christine E. "Intersectionality and Global Gender Inequality." *Gender and Society* 26 (2012) 67–72.
Bovon, François. *The Last Days of Jesus*. Louisville: Westminster/John Knox, 2006.
———. *Luke 1: A Commentary on the Gospel of Luke 1:1—9:50*. Hermeneia. Minneapolis: Fortress, 2002.
———. *Luke 2: A Commentary on the Gospel of Luke 9:51—19:27*. Hermeneia. Minneapolis: Fortress, 2013.
———. *Luke 3: A Commentary on the Gospel of Luke 19:28—24:53*. Hermeneia. Minneapolis: Fortress, 2012.
———. *New Testament and Christian Apocrypha*. Edited by Glenn E. Snyder. Grand Rapids, MI: Baker, 2011.
Bradley, Keith R. *Slavery and Rebellion in the Roman World, 140 B.C.–70 B.C.* Bloomington: Indiana University Press, 1989.
———. *Slavery and Society at Rome*. Cambridge: Cambridge University Press, 1994.
Braxton, Brad. *No Longer Slaves: Galatians and African American Experience*. Collegeville, MN: Liturgical, 2002.
Brettler, Marc Zvi. "Biblical Authority: A Jewish Pluralistic View." In *Engaging Biblical Authority: Perspectives on the Bible as Scripture*, edited by William P. Brown, 1–9. Louisville: Westminster/John Knox, 2007.
Briggs, Sheila. "Galatians." In *Searching the Scriptures*. Vol. 2, *A Feminist Commentary*, edited by Elisabeth Schüssler Fiorenza, 218–36. New York: Crossroad, 1994.
Brock, Ann Graham. *Mary Magdalene, the First Apostle: The Struggle for Authority*. Harvard Theological Studies 51. Cambridge: Harvard Divinity School, 2003.
Brock, Rita Nakashima. "Dusting the Bible on the Floor: A Hermeneutics of Wisdom." In *Searching the Scriptures*. Vol. 1, *A Feminist Introduction*, edited by Elisabeth Schüssler Fiorenza, 64–75. New York: Crossroad, 1997.
Brogdon, Lewis. *A Companion to Philemon*. Cascade Companions. Eugene, OR: Cascade, 2018.
Brooten, Bernadette J. "Enslaved Women in Basil of Caesarea's Canonical Letters: An Intersectional Analysis." In *Doing Gender—Doing Religion: Fallstudien zur Intersektionalität im frühen Judentum, Christentum und Islam*, edited by Ute E. Eisen et al., 325–55. Tübingen: Mohr Siebeck, 2013.
———. "Junia—Outstanding among the Apostles (Romans 16:7)." In *Women Priests: A Catholic Commentary on the Vatican Declaration*, edited by J. Leonard and Arlene Swidler, 141–44. New York: Paulist, 1977.
———. *Women Leaders in the Ancient Synagogue*. Providence, RI: Brown Judaic Studies, 1982.

Brown, Michael Joseph. "The Gospel of Matthew." In *True to Our Native Land. An African American Commentary of the New Testament*, edited by Brian Blount et al., 85–120. Minneapolis: Fortress, 2007.

———. "Hearing the Master's Voice." In *Engaging Biblical Authority: Perspectives on the Bible as Scripture*, edited by William P. Brown, 10–17. Louisville: Westminster/John Knox, 2007.

———. *The Lord's Prayer Through North African Eyes: A Window into Early Christianity*. New York: T. & T. Clark, 2004.

Brueggemann, Walter, William C. Placher, and Brian K. Blount. *Struggling with Scripture*. Louisville: Westminster/John Knox, 2002.

Bryant, K. Edwin. *Paul and the Rise of the Slave: Death and Resurrection of the Oppressed in the Epistle to the Romans*. Boston, MA: Brill, 2016.

Byrne, Brendan. *The Hospital of God: A Reading of Luke's Gospel*. Collegeville, MN: Liturgical, 2000.

Byron, Gay L. "Black Collectors and Keepers of Tradition: Resources for a Womanist Biblical Ethic of (Re)Interpretation." In *Womanist Interpretations of the Bible: Expanding the Discourse*. Edited by Gay L. Byron and Vanessa Lovelace, 187–208. Atlanta: Society of Biblical Literature, 2016.

———. "James." In *True to Our Native Land: An African American Commentary of the New Testament*, edited by Brian Blount et al., 461–75. Minneapolis: Fortress, 2007.

———. "James." In *Women's Commentary of the Bible: Revised and Updated*, edited by Carol A. Newsom, Sharon H. Ringe, and Jacqueline E. Lapsley, 613–15. Louisville: Westminster John Knox, 2012.

———. *Symbolic Blackness and Ethnic Difference in Early Christian Literature*. New York: Routledge, 2002.

Byron, Gay L., and Vanessa Lovelace. *Womanist Interpretations of the Bible: Expanding the Discourse*. Atlanta: Society of Biblical Literature, 2016.

Callahan, Allen Dwight. *The Embassy of Onesimus. The Letter of Paul to Philemon*. Valley Forge: Trinity, 1997.

———. "John." In *True to Our Native Land: An African American New Testament Commentary*, edited by Brian Blount et al., 186–212. Minneapolis, MN: Fortress, 2007.

———. *A Love Supreme: A History of Johannine Tradition*. Minneapolis, MN: Fortress, 2005.

———. "A Note on 1 Corinthians 7.21." *Journal of Interdenominational Theological Center* 17 (Fall 1989–Spring 1990) 110–14.

———. *The Talking Book: African American and the Bible*. New Haven: Yale University Press, 2006.

Calpine, Teresa J. *Women, Work and Leadership in Acts*. Tübingen: Mohr Siebeck, 2014.

Cannon, Katie G. "The Biblical Mainstay of Liberation." In *Engaging Biblical Authority: Perspectives on the Bible as Scripture*, edited by William P. Brown, 18–28. Louisville: Westminster/John Knox, 2007.

Cannon, Katie, Emilie Townes, and Angela Sims, eds. *Womanist Theological Ethics: A Reader*. Louisville, KY: Westminster John Knox, 2011.

Carbado, Devon W. "Colorblind Intersectionality." *Signs* 38 (2013) 811–45.

Card, Michael. *Mark: The Gospel of Passion*. Downers Grove, IL: InterVarsity, 2012.

Cardoza-Orlandi, Carlos F. "'Lámpara es a mis pies tu plalabra': Biblical Authority at the Crossroads." In *Engaging Biblical Authority: Perspectives on the Bible as Scripture*, edited by William P. Brown, 27–35. Louisville: Westminster/John Knox, 2007.

Carey, Greg. *Sinners: Jesus and His Earliest Followers*. Waco, TX: Baylor University Press, 2009.

Carey, Greg, and L. Gregory Bloomquist, eds. *Vision and Persuasion: Rhetorical Dimensions of Apocalyptic Discourse*. St. Louis, MO: Chalice, 1999.

Carroll, M. Daniel. *Christians at the Border: Immigration, the Church and the Bible*. 2nd ed. Grand Rapids, MI: Brazos, 2013.

Cartlidge, David R., and David L. Dugan. *Documents and Images for the Study of the Gospels*. 3rd ed. Minneapolis: Fortress, 2015.

Charles, Ronald. *Paul and the Politics of Diaspora*. Minneapolis, MN: Fortress, 2014.

Choi, Jin Young. *Postcolonial Discipleship of Embodiment: An Asian and Asian American Feminist Reading of the Gospel of Mark*. New York: Palgrave Macmillan, 2015.

Chun, Jennifer Jihye, George Lipsitz, and Young Shin. "Intersectionality as a Social Movement Strategy: Asian Immigrant Women Advocates." *Signs* 38 (2013) 917–40.

Coker, K. Jason. *James in Postcolonial Perspective: The Letter as Nativist Discourse*. Minneapolis: Fortress, 2015.

Collins, A. J., and John Collins. *King and Messiah as Son of God: Divine, Human, and Angelic Messianic Figures in Biblical and Related Literature*. Grand Rapids, MI: Eerdmans, 2008.

Collins, Adela Yarbro. "Apocalypse Now: The State of Apocalyptic Studies Near the End of the First Decade of the Twenty-first Century." *Harvard Theological Review* 104 (2011) 447–57.

———. *Cosmology and Eschatology in Jewish and Christian Apocalypticism*. Leiden: Brill, 2000.

Collins, John J., ed. *Apocalypse: The Morphology of a Genre*. Semeia Studies 14. Atlanta: Scholars, 1979.

———. *The Scepter and the Star: The Messiahs of the Dead Sea Scrolls and Other Ancient Literature*. New York: Doubleday, 1995.

Collins, Patricia Hill. *Black Feminist Thought: Knowledge, Consciousness, and the Politics of Empowerment*. 2nd ed. New York: Routledge, 1991.

———. "It's All in the Family: Intersections of Gender, Race, and Nation." *Hypatia* 13 (1998) 62–82.

Collins, Patricia Hill, and Sirma Bilge. *Intersectionality*. Malden, MA: Polity, 2016.

Columella, Lucius Junius Moderatus. *De Re Rustica: IV on Agriculture*. Translated by Harrison Boyd Ash. Loeb Classical Library 361. Cambridge: Harvard University Press, 1977.

Cone, James. *The Cross and the Lynching Tree*. Maryknoll, NY: Orbis, 2013.

Cook, David. *Contemporary Muslim Apocalyptic Literature*. Religion and Politics Series. Syracuse: Syracuse University Press, 2005.

Copeland, M. Shawn. *Enfleshing Freedom: Body, Race and Being*. Minneapolis: Fortress, 2009.

Countryman, William. "Reading Scripture—and Rereading It." *Anglican Theological Review* 86 (2004) 573–84.

Crenshaw, Kimberlé. "Demarginalizing the Intersection of Race and Sex: A Black Feminist Critique of Antidiscrimination Doctrine, Feminist Theory, and Antiracist Politics." *University of Chicago Legal Forum*, 1989: 139–67.

———. "Mapping the Margins: Intersectionality, Identity Politics, and Violence against Women of Color." *Stanford Law Review* 43 (1991) 1241–99.

Crenshaw, Sumi Cho, and Leslie McCall. "Toward a Field of Intersectionality Studies: Theory, Applications, and Praxis." *Signs: Journal of Women in Culture and Society* 38 (2013) 785–810.

Crossan, Dominic. *The Historical Jesus: The Life of a Mediterranean Jewish Peasant*. San Francisco: Harper Collins, 1991.

Crowder, Stephanie Buckhanon. "Gospel of Luke." In *True to Our Native Land: An African American New Testament Commentary*, edited by Brian L. Blount et al., 158–85. Minneapolis: Fortress, 2007.

———. *When Momma Speaks: The Bible and Motherhood from a Womanist Perspective*. Louisville, KY: Westminster John Knox, 2016.

Culpepper, Alan. *The Gospel and Letters of John*. Nashville, TN: Abingdon, 1998.

D'Angelo, Mary Rose. "Colossians." In *Searching the Scriptures: A Feminist Commentary*, vol. 2, edited by Elizabeth Schüssler Fiorenza, 313–24. New York: Crossroad, 1983.

———. "Hebrews." In *Women's Bible Commentary: Twentieth-Anniversary Edition*, edited by Carol A. Newsom, Sharon H. Ringe, and Jacqueline E. Lapsley, 608–12. Louisville: Westminster John Knox, 2012.

Darden, Lynne St. Clair. *Scripturalizing Revelation: An African American Postcolonial Reading of Empire*. Atlanta: Society of Biblical Literature, 2015.

Davies, W. D. *Paul and Rabbinic Judaism: Some Rabbinic Elements in Pauline Theology*. Philadelphia: Fortress, 1965.

Davis, Kathy. "Intersectionality as Buzzword: A Sociology of Science Perspective on What Makes a Feminist Theory Successful." *Feminist Theory* 9 (2008) 67–83

Day, Linda, and Carolyn Pressler, eds. *Engaging the Bible in a Gendered World. An Introduction to Feminist Biblical Interpretation in Honor of Katharine Doob Sakenfeld*. Louisville: Westminster/John Knox, 2006.

De la Torre, Miguel. *Reading the Bible from the Margins*. Maryknoll, NY: Orbis, 2002.

deSilva, David A. "Hebrews." In *The Fortress Commentary of the Bible: The New Testament*, edited by Margaret Aymer et al., 625–53. Minneapolis: Fortress, 2014.

———. *Perseverance in Gratitude: A Socio-Rhetorical Commentary on Epistle "to the Hebrews."* Grand Rapids: Eerdmans, 2000.

———. *Seeing Things John's Way: The Rhetoric of the Book of Revelation*. Louisville: Westminster John Knox, 2009.

Dewey, Joanna. "1 Timothy, 2 Timothy, and Titus." In *Women's Bible Commentary*, edited by Carol Newsom et al., 595–605. Louisville, KY: Westminster John Knox, 2012.

———. "Mark." In *Searching the Scriptures*. Vol. 2, *A Feminist Commentary*, edited by Elizabeth Schüssler Fiorenza, 470–509. New York: Crossroad, 1994.

Dhamoon, Rita Kaur. "Considerations on Mainstreaming Intersectionality." *Political Research Quarterly* 64 (2011) 230–43.

Dickerson, Febbie. "Acts 9:36–43: The Many Faces of Tabitha, a Womanist Reading." In *I Found God in Me: A Womanist Biblical Hermeneutics Reader*, edited by Mitzi J. Smith, 297–312. Eugene, OR: Cascade, 2015.

———. *The Widow and the Judge: A Womanist Investigation of Jesus' Parable*. Womanist Readings in Scripture Series. Edited by Mitzi Smith and Gay Byron. Lanham, MD: Fortress/Lexington, forthcoming.

Douglass, Frederick. *Narrative of the Life of Frederick Douglass, An American Slave. Written by* Himself. Boston: Anti-Slavery Office, 1845. In *Slave Narratives*, edited by William L. Andrews and Henry Louis Gates, 267–368. New York: Library of America, 2000.

Dube, Musa W. *Postcolonial Feminist Interpretation of the Bible*. St. Louis: Chalice, 2000.

DuBois, Page. *Slavery, Antiquity and its Legacy*. New York: Oxford University Press, 2009.

———. *Truth and Torture*. New York: Routledge, 1991.

Ehrman, Bart, and Bruce Metzger. *The Text of the New Testament: Its Transmission, Corruption, and Restoration*. New York: Oxford University Press, 2005.

Eisenbaum, Pamela. "Father and Son: The Christology of Hebrews in Patrilineal Perspective." In *A Feminist Companion to the Catholic Epistles and Hebrews*, edited by Amy-Jill Levine and Maria Mayo Robbins, 127–46. London: T. & T. Clark, 2004.

———. *Paul Was Not a Christian: The Original Message of a Misunderstood Apostle*. New York, NY: HarperOne, 2009.

Ekblad, Eugene Robert, Jr. *Reading the Bible with the Damned*. Louisville: Westminster John Knox, 2005.

Elaw, Zilpha. "Memoirs of the Life, Religious Experience, Ministerial Travels and Labors of Mrs. Zilpha Elaw." In *Sisters of the Spirit: Three Black Women's Autobiographies of the Nineteenth Century*, edited by William L. Andrews, 49–160. Bloomington: Indiana University Press, 1986.

Elliott, Neil. *The Arrogance of Nations: Reading Romans in the Shadow of Empire*. Minneapolis, MN: Fortress, 2008.

———. "Good News to the Colonized?" In *Unsettling the Word: Biblical Experiments in Decolonization*, edited by Steve Heinrichs, 247–48. Manitoba, Canada: CommonWord, 2018.

Elliott, Neil, and Mark Reasoner, eds. *Documents and Images for the Study of Paul*. Minneapolis, MN: Fortress, 2011.

Epp, Eldon Jay. *Junia: The First Woman Apostle*. Minneapolis, MN: Fortress, 2005.

Evans, Craig A. *Fabricating Jesus. How Modern Scholars Distort the Gospels*. Downers Grove, IL: InterVarsity, 2006.

Fagan, Brian. *Elixir: A History of Water and Humankind*. New York: Bloomsbury, 2011.

Felder, Cain Hope. "The Letter to Philemon." In vol. 11 of *The New Interpreter's Bible*, edited by Leander Keck, 881–905. Nashville: Abingdon, 2005.

———. *Troubling Biblical Waters. Race, Class and Family*. Maryknoll, NY: Orbis, 1993.

———, ed. *Stony the Road We Trod: African American Biblical Interpretation*. Minneapolis: Fortress, 1991.

Fiensy, David A. *Insights from Archaeology*. Reading the Bible in the 21st Century. Minneapolis, Fortress, 2017.

Filiu, Jean-Pierre. *Apocalypse in Islam*. Berkeley: University of California Press, 2011.

Finger, Reta Halteman. "To Comfort the Afflicted: If We Read 1 Peter's Message to Immigrants, Exiles and Foreigners Only as a Metaphor, We Risk Missing the Point." *Sojourners Magazine* 42 (2013) 28–31.

Fitzmyer, Joseph A. *The Acts of the Apostles*. Anchor Bible 31. New York: Doubleday 1998.

Fletcher-Louis, Crispin. "Jewish Apocalypticism." In *Handbook for the Study of the Historical Jesus*, edited by Tom Holmén and Stanley E. Porter, 1582. Leiden: Brill, 2009.

France, R. T. *The Gospel of Mark*. Grand Rapids, MI: Eerdmans, 2014.

———. *The Gospel of Matthew*. Grand Rapids, MI: Eerdmans, 2007.

Freire, Paulo. *Pedagogy of the Oppressed*. New York: Continuum, 1997.

Gafney, Wil. "Reading the Hebrew Bible Responsibly." In *The Africana Bible*, edited by Hugh R. Page Jr., 45–51. Minneapolis: Fortress, 2010.

Garnsey, Peter. *Ideas of Slavery from Aristotle to Augustine*. Cambridge: Cambridge University Press, 1996.

Gaventa, Beverly. *Acts*. Abingdon New Testament Commentaries. Nashville: Abingdon, 2003.

———. "The Maternity of Paul: An Exegetical Study of Galatians 4:19." In *The Conversation Continues: Studies in Paul and John in Honor of J. Louis Martyn*, edited by Robert T. Fortna and Beverly Gaventa, 189–210. Nashville, TN: Abingdon, 1990.

———. *Our Mother Saint Paul*. Louisville, KY: Westminster John Knox, 2007.

George, Larry. "1 Peter." In *True to Our Native Land: An African American Commentary of the New Testament*, edited by Brian Blount et al., 476–87. Minneapolis: Fortress, 2007.

———. "2 Peter." In *True to Our Native Land: An African American Commentary of the New Testament*, edited by Brian Blount et al., 488–95. Minneapolis: Fortress, 2007.

———. "Jude." In *True to Our Native Land: An African American Commentary of the New Testament*, edited by Brian Blount et al., 518–22. Minneapolis: Fortress, 2007.

Georgi, Dieter. *Remembering the Poor: The History of Paul's Collection for Jerusalem*. Nashville, TN: Abingdon, 1992.

Glancy, Jennifer A. *Slavery in Early Christianity*. Minneapolis: Fortress, 2006.

Gomes, Peter J. *The Good Book: Reading the Bible with Mind and Heart*. New York: William Morrow, 1996.

González, Catherine Gunsalus. *1 & 2 Peter and Jude: A Theological Commentary on the Bible*. Louisville: Westminster John Knox, 2011.

González, Catherine Gunsalus, and Justo L. González. *The Book of Revelation*. WBComp. Louisville: Westminster John Knox, 1997.

González, Justo L. *Acts: The Gospel of the Spirit*. Maryknoll, NY: Orbis, 2001.

———. *The Story Luke Tells: Luke's Unique Witness to the Gospel*. Grand Rapids, MI: Eerdmans, 2015.

Green, Bridgett A. "'Nobody's Free until Everybody's Free': Exploring Gender and Class Injustice in a Story about Children (Luke 18: 15–17)." In *Womanist Interpretations of the Bible: Expanding the Discourse*, edited by Gay L. Byron and Vanessa Lovelace, 291–310. Semeia Studies 85. Atlanta: Society of Biblical Literature, 2016.

Green, Joel B. *Conversion in Luke-Acts: Divine Action, Human Cognition and the People of God*. Grand Rapids, MI: Baker Academic, 2015.

———. *1 Peter*. New Horizons New Testament Commentary. Grand Rapids, MI: Eerdmans, 2007.

———. *The Gospel of Luke*. The New International Commentary on the New Testament. Grand Rapids, MI: Eerdmans, 1997.

———. *Seized by Truth. Reading the Bible as Scripture*. Nashville: Abingdon, 2007.

———, ed. *Hearing the New Testament: Strategies for Interpretation.* 2nd ed. Grand Rapids, MI: Eerdmans, 2010.
Gross, Matthew Barrett, and Mel Gilles. *The Last Myth: What the Rise of Apocalyptic Thinking Tells Us About America.* New York: Prometheus, 2012.
Guillaumont, A., et al., trans. *The Gospel According to Thomas.* Leiden: Brill, 1959.
Gupta, Nijay K. "Teach Us, Mary: The Authority of Women Teachers in the Church in Light of the Magnificat (Luke 1:46–55)." *Pricilla Papers* 29 (2015) 11–14.
Gurr, Barbara. *Race, Gender, and Sexuality in Post-Apocalyptic TV and Film.* New York: Palgrave Macmillan, 2015.
Hahn, Scott, and Curtis Mitch. *The Letter of St. James, the First and Second Letters of St. Peter and the Letter of St. Jude.* Ignatius Catholic Study Bible. 2nd ed. San Francisco: Ignatius, 2013.
Hamer, Fannie Lou. "Sick and Tired of Being Sick and Tired." In *Can I Get a Witness? Prophetic Religious Voices of African American Women: An Anthology*, edited by Marcia Y. Riggs, 170–82. Maryknoll, NY: Orbis, 1991.
Hanson, Paul. *The Dawn of Apocalyptic: The Historical and Sociological Roots of Jewish Apocalyptic Eschatology.* Philadelphia: Fortress, 1979.
Hardin, Justin. *Galatians and the Imperial Cult: A Critical Analysis of the First-Century Social Context of Paul's Letter.* Tübingen: Mohr Siebeck, 2008.
Harrill, Albert J. *Manumission of Slaves in Early Christianity.* Tübingen: Mohr Siebeck, 1998.
———. "Paul and Slavery: The Problem of 1 Corinthians 7.21." *Biblical Research* 39 (1994) 5–28.
———. *Slaves in the New Testament: Literary, Social and Moral Dimensions.* Minneapolis: Fortress, 2009.
Harrington, Daniel J. *Interpreting the New Testament: A Practical Guide.* Collegeville, MN: Liturgical, 1979.
Hawk, L. Daniel. *Joshua in 3-D. A Commentary on Biblical Conquest and Manifest Destiny.* Eugene, OR: Cascade, 2010.
Hayes, John H., and Carl R. Holladay. *Biblical Exegesis: A Beginner's Handbook.* 3rd ed. Louisville: Westminster/John Knox, 2007.
Heinrichs, Steve, editor. *Unsettling the Word: Biblical Experiments in Decolonization.* Manitoba, Canada: CommonWord, 2018.
Hendricks, Obery M., Jr. *The Politics of Jesus: Rediscovering the True Revolutionary Nature of Jesus's Teachings and How They Have Been Corrupted.* New York: Three Leaves, 2006.
———. *The Universe Bends Toward Justice: Radical Reflections on the Bible, the Church, and the Body Politic.* Maryknoll, NY: Orbis, 2011.
Hengel, Martin. *Judaism and Hellenism: Studies in Their Encounter in Palestine during the Early Hellenistic Period.* Eugene, OR: Wipf and Stock, 2003.
Herzog, William R. II. *Parables as Subversive Speech. Jesus as Pedagogue of the Oppressed.* Louisville: Westminster/John Knox, 1994.
Hildago, Jacqueline. *Revelation in Aztlán: Scriptures, Utopias, and the Chicano Movement.* New York: Palgrave Macmillan, 2016.
Himmelfarb, Martha. *Ascent to Heaven in Jewish and Christian Apocalypses.* New York: Oxford University Press, 1993.
hooks, bell. *Ain't I a Woman: Black Women and Feminism.* Boston: South End, 1981.
———. *Feminist Theory from Martin to Center.* Boston: South End, 1984.

Horrell, David G. "Ethnicity, Empire and Early Christian Identity: Social-Scientific Perspectives on 1 Peter." In *Reading 1–2 Peter and Jude: A Resource for Students*, edited by Eric F. Mason and Troy W. Martin, 135–49. Atlanta: Society of Biblical Literature, 2014.

Horsley, Richard. *1 Corinthians*. Abingdon, TN: Abingdon, 1998.

———. *Jesus and the Powers: Conflict, Covenant and the Hope of the Poor*. Minneapolis: Fortress, 2011.

Hoyt, Thomas L., Jr. "Romans." In *True to Our Native Land: An African American Commentary of the New Testament*, edited by Brian Blount et al., 249–75. Minneapolis: Fortress, 2007.

Huber, Lynn. "Unveiling the Bride: Revelation 19:1–9 and Roman Social Discourse." In *A Feminist Companion to the Apocalypse of John*, edited by Amy-Jill Levine, 159–79. FCNTECW 13. London: Bloomsbury, 2010.

Hudson-Weems, Clenora. *Africana Womanism: Reclaiming Ourselves*. Troy, MI: Bedford, 1993.

Hurston, Zora Neale. *The Sanctified Church*. Berkeley: Turtle Island, 1981.

Hylen, Susan. *Imperfect Believers: Ambiguous Characters in the Gospel of John*. Louisville, KY: Westminster John Knox, 2009.

Ibita, Ma. Marilou. "A Conversation with the Story of the Lord's Supper in 1 Corinthians 11:17–34." In *1 and 2 Corinthians: Texts @ Contexts*, edited by Yung Suk Kim, 97–114. Minneapolis: Fortress, 2013.

Isasi-Diaz, Ada María. "Kin-dom of God." In *In Our Own Voices: Latino/a Renditions of Theology*, edited by Ada María Isasi-Diaz, 171–89. Maryknoll, NY : Orbis, 2010.

———. "*La Palabra de Dios en Nosotras*—The Word of God in Us." In *Searching the Scriptures*. Vol. 1, *A Feminist Introduction*, edited by Elisabeth Schussler Fiorenza, 86–97. New York: Crossroad, 1997.

Janssen, Claudia. "Bodily Resurrection (1 Cor 15)? The Discourse of Resurrection in Karl Barth, Rudolf Bultmann, Dorothee Soelle and Contemporary Theology." *Journal for the Study of the New Testament* 79 (2000) 61–78.

Jarvis, Cynthia A., and E. Elizabeth Johnson, eds. *Feasting on the Gospels: A Feasting on the Word Commentary*. Vol. 1, *Matthew, Chapters 1–13*. Louisville: Westminster John Knox, 2013.

Jeal, Roy. *Exploring Philemon: Freedom, Brotherhood and Partnership in New Society*. Atlanta: SBL, 2015.

Jennings, William James. *Acts*. A Theological Commentary on the Bible. Louisville: Westminster/John Knox, 2017.

Jewett, Robert. *Romans*. Hermeneia Commentary. Minneapolis, MN: Fortress, 2007.

Johnson, E. Elizabeth. "Colossians." In *Women's Bible Commentary: Revised Edition*, edited by Carol Newsom et al., 585–87. Louisville, KY: Westminster John Knox, 2012.

Johnson, Luke Timothy. *The Letter of James*. Anchor Bible. New Haven: Yale University Press, 2005.

———. *Reading Romans: A Literary and Theological Commentary*. Reading the New Testament. Macon, GA: Smyth & Helwys, 2013.

Johnson, Matthew V., James A. Noel, and Demetrius K. Williams, eds. *Onesimus Our Brother: Reading Religion, Race, and Culture in Philemon*. Minneapolis: Fortress, 2012.

Jones, Rich, and Damian Robinson. "Water, Wealth, and Social Status at Pompeii: The House of the Vestals in the First Century." *American Journal of Archaeology* 109 (2005) 695–710.

Josephus. *Jewish Wars.*

Joshel, Sandra R., and Lauren Hackworth Petersen. *The Material Life of Roman Slaves.* New York: Cambridge University Press, 2016.

Kahl, Brigitte. "No Longer Male: Masculinity Struggles Behind Galatians 3.28?" *Journal for the Study of the New Testament* 79 (2000) 34–49.

Kartzow, Marianne Bjelland. "'Asking the Other Question': An Intersectional Approach to Galatians 3:28 and the Colossian Household Codes." *Biblical Interpretation* 18 (2010) 364–89.

Kearsley, R. "Women and Public Life in Imperial Asia Minor: Hellenistic Tradition and Augustan Ideology." *Ancient West and East* 4 (2005) 98–121.

Keller, Catherine. *Apocalypse Now and Then: A Feminist Guide to the End of the World.* Boston: Beacon, 1996.

Kiel, Micah D., and Barbara Rossing. *Apocalyptic Ecology: The Book of Revelation, the Earth and the Future.* Collegeville, MN: Liturgical, 2017.

Kim, Chan-Hie. "Reading the Cornelius Story from an Asian Immigrant Perspective." In *Reading from This Place: Social Location and Biblical Interpretation in the United States*, edited by Fernando F. Segovia and Mary Ann Tolbert, 165–74. Minneapolis: Fortress, 1995.

Kim, Grace Ji-Sun. *Embracing the Other: Transformative Spirit of Love.* Grand Rapids, MI: Eerdmans, 2015.

Kim, Yung Suk. *Biblical Interpretation: Theory, Process, and Criteria.* Eugene, OR: Pickwick, 2013.

———. *Christ's Body in Corinth: The Politics of a Metaphor.* Minneapolis, MN: Fortress, 2008.

———. "'Imitators' (*Mimetai*) in 1 Cor. 4:16 and 11:1: A New Reading of Threefold Embodiment." *Horizons in Biblical Theology* 33 (2011) 147–70.

———. *Messiah in Weakness. A Portrait of Jesus from the Perspective of the Dispossessed.* Eugene, OR: Cascade, 2016.

———. *Resurrecting Jesus: The Renewal of New Testament Theology.* Eugene, OR: Cascade, 2015.

———. *A Theological Introduction to Paul's Letters: Exploring a Threefold Theology of Paul.* Eugene, OR: Cascade, 2011.

———. *A Transformative Reading of the Bible: Explorations in Holistic Human Transformation.* Eugene, OR: Cascade, 2013.

———. *Truth, Testimony, and Transformation: A New Study of the "I Am" Sayings of Jesus in the Fourth Gospel.* Eugene, OR: Cascade, 2014.

Kim, Yung Suk, and Jin-ho Kim, eds. *Reading Minjung Theology in the Twenty-First Century: Selected Writings by Ahn Byung-Mu and Modern Critical Responses.* Eugene, OR: Pickwick, 2013.

King, Karen L. *The Gospel of Mary of Magdala.* Jesus and the First Woman Apostle. Santa Rosa, CA: Polebridge, 2003.

———. *What Is Gnosticism?* Cambridge: Harvard University Press, 2005.

King, Martin Luther, Jr. "A Christmas Sermon on Peace." In *The Trumpet of Conscience*, 70. New York: Harper and Row, 1968.

———. *Strength to Love.* Philadelphia: Fortress, 1963.

———. *Where Do We Go From Here: Chaos or Community?* Boston: Beacon, 2010.

Kinukawa, Hisako. "The Miracle Story of the Bent-Over Woman (Luke 13:10–17): An Interaction-Centered Interpretation." In *Transformative Encounters: Jesus and Women Reviewed*, edited by R. Kitzberger, 292–314. Leiden: E. J. Brill, 2000.

Klauck, Hans. *The Religious Context of Early Christianity: A Guide to Graeco-Roman Religions*. Minneapolis, MN: Fortress, 2003.

Klein, Robert H. *The Synoptic Problem: An Introduction*. Valley Forge, PA: InterVarsity, 1988.

Koester, Helmut. *History, Culture and Religion of the Hellenistic Age*. 2nd ed. Berlin: Gruyter, 1995.

———. *History and Literature of Early Christianity: Introduction to the New Testament*. Berlin: Gruyter, 1987.

———. "Imperial Ideology and Paul's Eschatology." In *Paul and Empire*, edited by Richard Horsley, 158–66. Harrisburg, PA: Trinity Press International, 1997.

Kysar, Robert. *John the Maverick Gospel*. Louisville, KY: Westminster John Knox, 2007.

Lefkowitz, Mary, and Maureen Fant, eds. *Women's Life in Greece and Rome: A Source Book in Translation*. Baltimore, MD: Johns Hopkins University Press, 2016.

Lettsome, Raquel S. "The Gospel of Mark." In *The New Testament: Fortress Commentary on the Bible*, edited by Margaret Aymer, Cynthia Briggs Kittredge, and David A. Sánchez, 173–215. Minneapolis, Fortress, 2014.

Levine, Amy-Jill. *A Feminist Companion to John*. Vol. 1. New York: Sheffield, 2003.

———. "Gospel of Matthew." In *Women's Bible Commentary: Twentieth-Anniversary Edition*, edited by Carol A. Newsom, Sharon H. Ringer, and Jacqueline E. Lapsley, 465–77. Louisville: Westminster/John Knox, 2012.

———. *The Misunderstood Jew: The Church and the Scandal of the Jewish Jesus*. New York: HarperOne, 2006.

———. *Short Stories by Jesus: The Enigmatic Parables of a Controversial Rabbi*. New York: HarperOne, 2015.

———, ed. *A Feminist Companion to the Acts of the Apostles*. Cleveland: Pilgrim, 2004.

———, ed. *A Feminist Companion to the Catholic Epistles and Hebrews*. New York: T. & T. Clark, 2000.

———, ed. *A Feminist Companion to the Gospel of Mark*. Sheffield, England: Sheffield, 2001.

Lewis, Lloyd A. "Philemon." In *True to Our Native Land: An African American New Testament Commentary*, edited by Brian Blount et al., 437–43. Minneapolis: Fortress, 2007.

Lieu, Judith M. *The Theology of the Johannine Epistles*. Cambridge: Cambridge University Press, 1991.

Liew, Benny Tat-Siong. "Haunting Silence: Trauma, Failed Orality and Mark's Messianic Secret." In *Psychoanalytic Meditations between Marxist and Postcolonial Readings of the Bible*, edited by Benny Tat-Siong Liew and Erin Runions, 99–128. Semeia Studies. Atlanta: Society of Biblical Literature, 2016.

———. "Margins and (Cutting-) Edges: On the (Il)Legitimacy and Intersections of Race, Ethnicity, and (Post)Colonialism." In *Postcolonial Biblical Criticism. Interdisciplinary Intersections*, edited by Stephen D. Moore and Fernando F. Segovia, 114–65. New York: T. & T. Clark, 2007.

———. *Politics of Parousia. Reading Mark Inter(Con)Textually*. New York: Brill, 1999.

Lloyd-Jones, Martyn. *A Merciful and Faithful High Priest: Studies in the Book of Hebrews.* Wheaton, IL: Crossway, 2017.

Long, A. A. *Hellenistic Philosophy: Stoics, Epicureans, Sceptics.* Los Angeles, CA: University of California Press, 1986.

Lopez, Davina. *The Apostle to the Conquered: Reimagining Paul's Mission.* Minneapolis, MN: Fortress, 2008.

Luz, Ulrich. *Matthew 1–7: A Commentary.* Hermeneia. Minneapolis: Fortress, 2007.

———. *Matthew 8–20: A Commentary.* Hermeneia. Minneapolis: Fortress, 2001.

———. *Matthew 21–28: A Commentary.* Hermeneia. Minneapolis: Fortress, 2005

MacDonald, Margaret Y. *Colossians and Ephesians.* Sacra Pagina 17. Collegeville, MN: Liturgical, 2000.

Maloney, Linda. "The Pastoral Epistles." In vol. 2 of *Searching the Scriptures: A Feminist Commentary*, edited by Elizabeth Schüssler Fiorenza, 361–80. New York: Crossroad, 1983.

Marchal, Joseph A. "Difficult Intersections and Messy Coalitions (But in a Good Way)." *Journal of Feminist Studies in Religion* 30 (2014) 158–61.

———. *The People Beside Paul.* Atlanta: Society of Biblical Literature Press, 2015.

———. *Philippians: An Introduction and Study Guide: Historical Problems, Hierarchical Visions, Hysterical Anxieties.* New York: T. & T. Clark, 2017.

———. "Slaves as Wo/men and Unmen: Reflecting Upon Euodia, Syntyche, and Epaphroditus in Philippi." In *The People Beside Paul*, edited by Joseph A. Marchal, 141–76. Atlanta: Society of Biblical Literature Press, 2015.

Martin, Clarice J. "1–2 Timothy, Titus." In *True to Our Native Land. An African American Commentary on the New Testament*, edited by Brian Blount et al., 409–36. Minneapolis: Fortress, 2007.

———. "Acts of the Apostles." In *Searching the Scriptures. Vol. 2, A Feminist Commentary*, edited by Elisabeth Schüssler Fiorenza, 763–99. New York: Crossroad, 1994.

———. "A Chamberlain's Journey and the Challenge of Interpretation of Liberation." *Semeia* 47 (1989) 105–35.

———. "The Eyes Have It: Slaves in the Communities of Christ Believers." In *Christian Origins*, edited by Richard Horsley, 221–39. Minneapolis: Fortress, 2010.

———. "The *Haustafeln* (Household Codes) in African American Biblical Interpretation: 'Free Slaves' and 'Subordinate Women.'" In *Stony the Road We Trod: African American Biblical Interpretation*, edited by Cain Hope Felder, 206–31. Minneapolis: Fortress, 1991.

———. "Polishing an Unclouded Mirror. A Womanist Reading of Rev 18:13." In *From Every People And Nation: The Book of Revelation in Intercultural Perspective*, edited by David Rhoads, 82–109. Minneapolis: Fortress, 2005.

———. "The Rhetorical Function of Commercial Language in Paul's Letter to Philemon (verse 18)." In *Persuasive Artistry: Studies in New Testament Rhetoric in Honor of George A Kennedy*, edited by Duane Frederick Watson and George Alexander Kennedy, 321–37. Journal for the Study of the Old Testament, Supplemental Series 50. Sheffield: Sheffield Academic, 1991.

———. "'Somebody Done Hoo'dood the Hoodoo Man': Language, Power, Resistance and the Effective History of Pauline Texts in American slavery." In *Slavery in Text and Interpretation*, edited by Allen Callahan, Richard Horsley, and Abraham Smith, 203–33. Semeia Studies 83/84. Atlanta: Society of Biblical Literature, 1998.

Martin, Dale B. *The Corinthian Body.* New Haven: Yale University Press, 1995.

———. *Sex and the Single Savior: Gender and Sexuality in Biblical Interpretation.* Louisville, KY: Westminster John Knox, 2006.

———. *Slavery as Salvation: The Metaphor of Slavery in Pauline Christianity.* New Haven: Yale University Press, 1990.

Martyn, J. Louis. *History and Theology in the Fourth Gospel.* Louisville, KY: Westminster John Knox, 1968.

Massey, James Earl. "Hebrews." In *True to Our Native Land: An African American Commentary on the Bible,* edited by Brian Blount et al., 444–60. Minneapolis: Fortress, 2007.

Matthews, Shelley, and Benny Tat-Siong Liew. *The Acts of The Apostles: An Introduction and Study Guide: Taming the Tongues of Fire.* New York: T. & T. Clark, 2017.

McCown, C. C. "Hebrew and Egyptian Apocalyptic Literature." *Harvard Theological Review* 18 (1925) 357–411.

McKenna, Megan. *Luke: The Book of Blessings and Woes.* Hyde Park, NY: New City, 2009.

Meggitt, Justin. *Paul, Poverty, and Survival.* Edinburgh: T. & T. Clark, 1998.

Menéndez-Antuña, Luis. "Male-Bonding, Female Vanishing: Representing Gendered Authority in Luke 23:26—24:53." *Early Christianity* 4 (2013) 490–506.

Metzger, Bruce. *A Textual Commentary on the Greek New Testament.* 2nd revised ed. Peabody, MA: Hendrickson Publishers, 2005.

Meyer, Marvin W., ed. *The Ancient Mysteries: A Sourcebook of Sacred Texts.* Philadelphia, PA: University of Pennsylvania Press, 1999.

———, ed. *The Nag Hammadi Scriptures: The Revised and Updated Translation of Sacred Gnostic Texts.* New York: HarperOne, 2009.

Miguez, Néstor. "Galatians." In *Global Bible Commentary,* edited by Daniel Patte, 463–72. Nashville: Abingdon, 2008.

———. *The Practice of Hope: Ideology and Intention in 1 Thessalonians.* Minneapolis, MN: Fortress, 2012.

Mills, Kay. *This Little Light of Mine: The Life of Fannie Lou Hamer.* New York: Plume, 1994.

Moss, Candida. *The Myth of Persecution: How Early Christians Invented the Story of Martydom.* New York: Harper One, 2013.

Moxnes, Halvor. "Identity in Jesus' Galilee—From Ethnicity to Locative Intersectionality." *Biblical Interpretation* 18 (2010) 390–416.

Myers, Ched. *Binding the Strong Man: A Political Reading of Mark's Story.* Maryknoll, NY: Orbis, 2008.

Nadella, Raj. *Dialogue Not Dogma: Many Voices in the Gospel of Luke.* New York: T. & T. Clark, 2011.

Nash, Jennifer C. "Re-Thinking Intersectionality." *Feminist Review* 89 (2008) 1–15.

Newheart, Michael. *'My Name is Legion': The Story and Soul of the Gerasene Demoniac.* Collegeville, MN: Liturgical, 2004.

———. *Word and Soul: A Psychological, Literary, and Cultural Reading of the Fourth Gospel.* Collegeville, MN: Liturgical, 2001.

Neyrey, Jerome H. *2 Peter, Jude.* Anchor Bible 37C. New York Doubleday, 1993.

———. "Lost in Translation: Did it Matter if Christians 'Thanked' God or 'Gave God Glory'?" *Catholic Biblical Quarterly* 71 (2009) 1–23.

O'Day, Gail. "1, 2, and 3 John." In *Women's Bible Commentary: Revised Edition,* edited by Carol Newsom et al., 622–24. Louisville, KY: Westminster John Knox, 2012.

———. "The Gospel of John." In *Women's Bible Commentary: Revised Edition*, edited by Carol Newsom et al., 517–30. Louisville, KY: Westminster John Knox, 2012.
Odell-Scott, David. *Paul's Critique of Theocracy: A Theocracy in 1 Corinthians and Galatians*. New York: T. & T. Clark, 2009.
Okure, Teresa. "Colossians." In *Global Bible Commentary*, edited by Daniel Patte, 490–99. Nashville, TN: Abingdon, 2004.
Osiek, Carolyn. "Galatians." In *Women's Bible Commentary: Revised Edition*, edited by Carol Newsom et al., 570–75. Louisville, KY: Westminster John Knox, 2012.
Osman, Ahmed. *Out of Egypt: The Roots of Christianity Revealed*. London: Arrow, 1999.
Pae, Keun-Joo Christine. "Minjung Theology and Global Peacemaking." In *Reading Minjung Theology in the Twenty-first Century*, edited by Yung Suk Kim and Jin-Ho Kim, 164–83. Eugene, OR: Pickwick, 2013.
Pagels, Elaine. "Paul and Women: A Response to Recent Discussion." *Journal of the American Academy of Religion* 40 (1972) 538–49.
———. *Revelation: Visions, Prophecy and Politics in the Book of Revelation*. New York: Penguin, 2013.
Painter, John. *1, 2, and 3 John*. Collegeville, MN: Liturgical, 2002.
Pallares, Jose Cardenas. *Poor Man Called Jesus: Reflections on the Gospel of Mark*. Maryknoll, NY: Orbis, 1986.
Park, Kyung-mi. "John." In *Global Bible Commentary*, edited by Daniel Patte, 401–11. Nashville, TN: Abingdon, 2004.
Parker, Angela. "One Womanist's Understanding of Paul's Problematic Self-Identity in Galatians." *Journal of Feminist Studies in Religion* 34.2 (2018) forthcoming.
Pathrapankal, Joseph. "1 Corinthians." In *Global Bible Commentary*, edited by Daniel Patte, 444–50. Abingdon, TN: Abingdon, 2004.
Patte, Daniel. *Ethics of Biblical Interpretation: A Reevaluation*. Louisville, KY: Westminster John Knox Press, 1995.
———. "Romans." In *Global Bible Commentary*, edited by Daniel Patte, 429–43. Nashville, TN: Abingdon, 2005.
Patterson, Orlando. *Slavery and Social Death: A Comparative Study*. Cambridge: Harvard University Press, 1982.
Perkins, Pheme. *Ephesians*. Nashville: Abingdon, 1997.
———. "Jude." In *The Fortress Commentary on the Bible: The New Testament*, edited by Margaret Aymer et al., 711–14. Minneapolis: Fortress, 2014.
Perrin, Norman. *Jesus and the Language of the Kingdom*. Philadelphia: Fortress, 1976.
Perry, Peter S. *Insights from Performance Criticism*. Minneapolis: Fortress, 2016.
Pervo, Richard I. *Acts of the Apostles*. Hermeneia. Minneapolis: Fortress, 2009.
Phanon, Yuri. "Is She a Sinful Woman or a Forgiving Woman? An Exegesis of Luke 7:36–50." *Asian Journal of Pentecostal Studies* 19 (2016) 59–84.
Pippin, Tina. *Death and Desire: The Rhetoric of Gender in the Apocalypse of John*. LCBI. Louisville: Westminster John Knox, 1992.
———. "Eros and the End: Reading for Gender in the Apocalypse of John." *Semeia* 59 (1991) 193–210.
———. "Revelation/Apocalypse of John." *Women's Commentary of the Bible: Revised and Updated*, edited by Carol A. Newsom, Sharon H. Ringe, and Jacqueline E. Lapsley, 627–32. Louisville: Westminster John Knox, 2012.
Powell, Mark Allan. *Jesus as a Figure in History: How Modern Historians View the Man from Galilee*. Louisville: Westminster John Knox, 1998.

———. "Jesus and the Pathetic Wicked: Re-visiting Sanders's View of Jesus' Friendship with Sinners." *Journal for the Study of the Historical Jesus* 23 (2015) 188–208.

———. *What Is Narrative Criticism?* Minneapolis: Fortress, 1990.

Powery, Emerson. "Mark." *True to Our Native Land: An African American New Testament Commentary*, edited by Brian K. Blount et al., 121–57. Minneapolis: Fortress, 2007.

Punt, Jeremy. "Identity and Human Dignity amid Power and Liminality in 1 Corinthians 7:17–24." In *1 and 2 Corinthians: Texts @ Contexts*, edited by Yung Suk Kim, 9–30. Minneapolis: Fortress, 2013.

———. "Paul, Power and Philemon: 'Knowing Your Place': A Postcolonial Reading." In *Philemon in Perspective: Interpreting a Pauline Letter*, edited by D. Francois Tolmie, 223–50. Berlin: de Gruyter, 2010.

Reeder, Caryn. "1 Peter 3:1–6: Biblical Authority and Battered Wives." *Bulletin for Biblical Research* 25 (2015) 519–39.

Rehill, Annie. *The Apocalypse Is Everywhere: A Popular History of America's Favorite Nightmare*. Santa Barbara, CA: ABC-CLIO, 2010.

Reid, Barbara. *The Gospel According to Matthew*. Vol. 1. New Collegeville Bible Commentary. Collegeville, MN: Liturgical, 2005.

———. "The Gospel of Luke: Friend or Foe of Women Proclaimers of the Word?" *Catholic Biblical Quarterly* 78 (2016) 1–23.

Reimer, Ivoni Richter. *Women in the Acts of the Apostles: A Feminist Liberation Perspective*. Minneapolis: Fortress, 1995.

Rensberger, David. *1 John, 2 John, 3 John*. Nashville, TN: Abingdon, 1997.

Rhoads, David, David Esterline, and Jae Won Lee, eds. *Luke-Acts and Empire: Essays in Honor of Robert L. Brawley*. Princeton Theological Monograph Series 151. Eugene, OR: Pickwick, 2011.

Rhoads, David, Joanna Dewey, and Donald Michie. *Mark as Story: An Introduction to the Narrative of a Gospel*. 3rd ed. Minneapolis: Fortress, 2012.

Richards, E. Randolph, and Brandon J. O'Brien. *Misreading Scripture with Western Eyes: Removing Cultural Blinders to Better Understand the Bible*. Downers Grove, IL: Intervarsity, 2012.

Rieger, Joerg. "Reclaiming People Power." In *Unsettling the Word: Biblical Experiments in Decolonization*. edited by Steven Heinrichs, 208–9. Manitoba, Canada: CommonWord, 2018.

Riggs, Marcia Y. *Can I Get a Witness? Prophetic Religious Voices of African American Women: An Anthology*. Maryknoll, NY: Orbis, 1997.

Rivera-Rodríguez, Luis. "Toward a Diaspora Hermeneutics (Hispanic North America)." In *Character Ethics and the Old Testament: Moral Dimensions of Scripture*, edited by M. Daniel Carroll R., and Jacqueline Laosley, 169–89. Louisville: Westminster John Knox, 2007.

Robinson, James M. *Jesus According to the Earliest Witness*. Minneapolis: Fortress, 2007.

Robinson, James M., John S. Kloppenborg, and Paul Hoffmann, eds. *The Sayings Gospel Q in Greek and English with Parallels from the Gospels of Mark and Thomas*. English and Greek ed. Minneapolis: Fortress, 2002.

Roetzel, Calvin. *2 Corinthians*. Abingdon, TN: Abingdon, 2007.

Rossing, Barbara R. *The Choice Between Two Cities. Whore, Bride, and Empire in the Apocalypse*. Harvard Theological Studies. Harrisburg, PA: Trinity, 2009.

Ruiz, Jean-Pierre. "Politics of Praise: A Reading of Revelation 19:1–10." In *SBL Seminary Papers*, 374–94. Atlanta: Scholars, 1997.

Russaw, Kimberly. "Wisdom in the Garden. The Woman in Genesis 3 and Alice Walker's Sophia." In *I Found God in Me: A Womanist Biblical Hermeneutics Reader*, edited by Mitzi J. Smith, 223–35. Eugene, OR: Cascade, 2015.

Salazar, María del Carmen. "A Humanizing Pedagogy: Reinventing the Principles and Practice of Education as a Journey Toward Liberation." *Review of Research in Education* 37 (2013) 121–48.

Salzman, James. *Drinking Water: A History*. New York: Overlook Duckworth, 2012.

Sánchez, David Arthur. "Ambivalence, Mimicry, and the *Ochlos* in the Gospel of Mark." In *Reading Minjung Theology in the Twenty-First Century*, edited by Yung Suk Kim and Jin-Ho Kim, 134–47. Eugene, OR: Pickwick, 2013.

———. *From Patmos to Barrio. Subverting Imperial Myths*. Minneapolis: Fortress, 2008.

Sanders, Boykin. "1 Corinthians." In *True to Our Native Land: An African American New Testament Commentary*, edited by Brian Blount et al., 276–306. Minneapolis, MN: Fortress, 2007.

Sanders, E. P. *Judaism: Practice and Belief, 63 BCE–66 CE*. Minneapolis, MN: Fortress, 2016.

———. *Paul: The Apostle's Life, Letters, and Thought*. Minneapolis, MN: Fortress, 2015.

———. *Paul and Palestinian Judaism: A Comparison of Patterns of Religion*. Philadelphia, PA: Fortress, 1977.

Schneemelcher, Wilhelm, ed. *New Testament Apocrypha*. Louisville: Westminster John Knox, 1989.

Schneiders, Sandra. *Written That You May Believe: Encountering Jesus in the Fourth Gospel*. New York: Crossroad, 2003.

Schüssler Fiorenza, Elisabeth. *The Book of Revelation: Justice and Judgment*. 2nd ed. Minneapolis: Fortress, 1998.

———. "Defending the Center, Trivializing the Margins." 29–48 in *Reading the Bible in the Global Village: Helsinki*. Atlanta: Society of Biblical Literature, 2000.

———. "The Ethics of Biblical Interpretation: Decentering Biblical Scholarship." *Journal of Biblical Literature* 107 (1988) 3–17.

———. *In Memory of Her: A Feminist Theological Reconstruction of Christian Origins*. New York: Crossroad, 1994.

———. "Introduction: Exploring the Intersections of Race, Gender, Status and Ethnicity in Early Christian Studies." In *Prejudice and Christian Beginnings: Investigating Race, Gender, and Ethnicity in Early Christian Studies*, edited by Laura Nasrallah and Elisabeth Schüssler Fiorenza, 1–23. Minneapolis: Fortress, 2009.

———. *Jesus and the Politics of Interpretation*. New York: Continuum, 2000.

———. *Jesus: Miriam's Child, Sophia's Prophet. Critical Issues in Feminist Christology*. New York: T. & T. Clark, 2015.

———. *Rhetoric and Ethic: The Politics of Biblical Studies*. Minneapolis: Augsburg Fortress, 1999.

Sechrest, Love. "Antitypes, Stereotypes, and Antetypes: Jezebel, the Sun Woman, and Contemporary Black Women." In *Womanist Interpretations of the Bible: Expanding the Discourse*, edited by Gay L. Byron and Vanessa Lovelace, 113–38. Atlanta: Society of Biblical Literature Press, 2016.

———. *A Former Jew: Paul and the Dialectics of Race*. New York: T. & T. Clark, 2010.

———. "Identity and the Embodiment of Privilege in Corinth." In *1 and 2 Corinthians: Texts @ Contexts*, edited by Yung Suk Kim, 9–30. Minneapolis: Fortress, 2013.

Segovia, Fernando F. *Decolonizing Biblical Studies. A View from the Margins*. Maryknoll, NY: Orbis, 2000.

Segovia, Fernando F., and Mary Ann Tolbert, eds. *Teaching the Bible: The Discourses and Politics of Biblical Pedagogy*. Minneapolis: Fortress, 2009.

Segovia, Fernando F., and R. S. Sugirtharajah. *A Postcolonial Commentary on the New Testament Writings*. New York: T. & T. Clark, 2009.

Segovia, Fernando F., and Stephen D. Moore. *Postcolonial Biblical Criticism: Interdisciplinary Intersections*. New York: T. & T. Clark, 2007.

Sell, Nancy A. "The Magnificat as a Model for Ministry: Proclaiming Justice, Shifting Paradigms, Transforming lives." *Liturgical Ministry* 10 (2001) 31–40.

Shaner, Katherine A. *Enslaved Leadership in Early Christianity*. New York: Oxford University, Press, 2018.

Sharp, Carolyn J. *Wrestling the Word: The Hebrew Scriptures and the Christian Believer*. Louisville: Westminster John Knox, 2010.

Skinner, Matthew L. *Intrusive God, Disruptive Gospel: Encountering the Divine in the Book of Acts*. Grand Rapids, MI: Brazos, 2015.

Slater, Thomas. *Afrocentric Interpretations of Jesus and the Gospel Tradition: Things Black Scholars See that White Scholars Overlook*. New York: Edwin Mellen, 2015.

———. *Revelation as Civil Disobedience: Witness Not Warriors in John's Apocalypse*. Nashville: Abingdon, 2018.

———. "Son of Man." In vol. 2 of *Oxford Encyclopedia of the Bible and Theology*, edited by Samuel Balentine, 316–21. New York: Oxford University Press, 2015.

Smith, Abraham. *Comfort One Another: Reconstructing the Rhetoric and Audience of 1 Thessalonians*. Louisville, KY: Westminster John Knox, 1995.

Smith, Barbara. "Racism and Women's Studies." In *But Some of Us Are Brave*, edited by Gloria T. Hull, et al., 48–51. Old Westbury, NY; Feminist, 1982.

Smith, D. Moody. *First, Second, and Third John*. Louisville, KY: Westminster/John Knox, 1991.

Smith, Mitzi J. "Chloe, a Freedwoman in Corinth (1 Cor 1:10): A Womanist Reconstruction." In *After the Corinthian Women Prophets: Rhetoric, Power, and Possibilities*, edited by Joseph Marchal. Semeia Studies. Forthcoming.

———. *The Construction of the Other in the Acts of the Apostles: Charismatics, the Jews, and Women*. Princeton Theological Monograph Series 154. Eugene, OR: Pickwick, 2011.

———. "*Dis*-membering, Sexual Violence, and Confinement: A Womanist Intersectional Reading of the Story of the Levite's Wife (Judges 19)." In *Insights from African American Interpretation*, series edited by Mark Alan Powell, 99–122. Minneapolis: Fortress, 2017.

———. "Ephesians." In *True to Our Native Land: An African American Commentary of the New Testament*, edited by Brian Blount et al., 348–62. Minneapolis: Fortress, 2007.

———. "Epistemologies, Pedagogies, and the Subordinated Other: Luke's Parallel Construction of the Ethiopian Eunuch and the Alexandrian Apollos." In *Womanist Sass and Talk Back: Social (In)justice, Intersectionality, and Biblical Interpretation*, 46–69. Eugene, OR: Cascade, 2018.

———. "Fashioning Our Own Souls. A Womanist Reading of the Virgin-Whore Binary in Matthew and Revelation." In *I Found God in Me: A Womanist Biblical Hermeneutics Reader,* edited by Mitzi J. Smith, 158–82. Eugene, OR: Cascade, 2015.

———. *Insights from African American Interpretation*. Minneapolis: Fortress, 2017.

———. "'Love Never Fails': Rereading 1 Cor 13 with a Womanist Hermeneutic of Love's Struggle." In *Theologies of Failure,* edited by Roberto Sirvent and Duncan Reyburn. Eugene, OR: Cascade, forthcoming.

———. "Philemon." In *Wesley One Volume Commentary of the Bible*. Indianapolis: Wesley Publishing House, forthcoming.

———. "Philemon." In *Women's Commentary of the Bible: Revised*, edited by Carol A. Newsom, Sharon H. Ringe, and Jacqueline E. Lapsley, 605–07. Louisville: Westminster John Knox, 2012.

———. "Slavery in the Early Church." In *True to Our Native Land: An African American Commentary of the New Testament*, edited by Brian Blount et al., 11–22. Minneapolis: Fortress, 2007.

———. "Slavery, Torture, Systemic Oppression, and Kingdom Rhetoric: A Womanist Reading of Matt 25:1–13." *Insights from African American Biblical Interpretation,* edited by Mark Alan Powell, 77–97. Eugene, OR: Cascade, 2017.

———. "Water is a Human Right, but It *Ain't* Free: A Womanist Reading of John 4:1–42." In *Womanist Sass and Talk Back: Social (In)justice, Intersectionality, and Biblical Interpretation*. Eugene, OR: Cascade, 2018.

———. *Womanist Sass and Talk Back. Social (In)Justice, Intersectionality, and Biblical Interpretation*. Eugene, OR: Cascade, 2018.

———, ed. *I Found God in Me: A Womanist Biblical Interpretation Reader*. Eugene, OR: Cascade, 2015.

Smith, Mitzi J., and Lalitha Jayachitra, eds. *Teaching All Nations: Interrogating the Matthean Great Commission*. Minneapolis: Fortress, 2014.

Smith, Shanell T. *The Woman Babylon and the Marks of Empire: Reading Revelation with a Postcolonial Womanist Hermeneutics of Ambiveilance*. Minneapolis: Fortress, 2014.

Smith, Shively T. J. *Strangers to Family: Diaspora and 1 Peter's Invention of God's Household*. Waco, TX: Baylor University Press, 2016.

Sobrino, Jon. *Christ the Liberator: A View from the Victims*. Maryknoll, NY: Orbis, 2001.

Solon, Pablo. "UN Declares Water as Human Right." *ClimateandCapitalism*, July 28, 2010. http://climateandcapitalism.com/2010/07/28/un-declares-water-a-human-right/.

Soulen, Richard N. *Sacred Scripture: A Short History of Interpretation*. Louisville: Westminster/John Knox, 2009.

Spencer, F. Scott. *Salty Wives, Spirited Mothers, and Savvy Widows: Capable Women of Purpose and Persistence in Luke's Gospel*. Grand Rapids, MI: Eerdmans, 2012.

Sri, Edward, and Curtis Mitch. *The Gospel of Matthew*. Catholic Commentary on Sacred Scripture. Grand Rapids, MI: Baker Academic, 2010.

Standhartinger, Angela. "The Epistle to the Congregation in Colossae and the Invention of the 'Household Code.'" In *A Feminist Companion to the Deutero-Pauline Epistles*, edited by Amy-Jill Levine, 88–97. New York: Continuum, 2003.

St. Clair, Raquel. *Call and Consequences. A Womanist Reading of Mark*. Minneapolis: Fortress, 2008.

Stendahl, Krister. "The Apostle Paul and the Introspective Conscience of the West." *Harvard Theological Review* 56 (1963) 199–215.

———. *Paul among Jews and Gentiles and Other Essays*. Minneapolis, MN: Fortress, 1976.

Stevenson, Bryan. *Just Mercy: A Story of Justice and Redemption*. New York: Penguin, 2014.

Strecker, Georg. *The Johannine Letters: A Commentary on 1, 2, and 3 John*. Hermeneia. Minneapolis: Fortress, 1996.

Stubbs, Monya. "1 Thessalonians." In *Women's Bible Commentary*, edited by Carol Newsom et al., 588–91. Louisville, KY: Westminster John Knox, 2012.

———. *Indebted Love: Paul's Subjection Language in Romans*. Eugene, OR: Wipf and Stock, 2013.

———. "Philippians." In *True to Our Native Land: An African American New Testament Commentary*, edited by Brian Blount et al., 363–79. Minneapolis, MN: Fortress, 2007.

Sugirtharajah, R. S. "Critics, Tools, and the Global Arena." In *Reading the Bible in the Global Village: Helsinki*, edited by Elisabeth Schüssler Fiorenza, R. S. Sugirtharajah, Krister Stendahl and James Barr, 59–60. Atlanta: Society of Biblical Literature, 2000.

———. *The Postcolonial Bible*. Sheffield: Sheffield, 1998.

———. *The Postcolonial Biblical Reader*. Malden, MA: Blackwell, 2006.

———. ed. *Voices from the Margin: Interpreting the Bible in the Third World*. Maryknoll, NY: Orbis, 1997.

Sultana, Farhana and Alex Loftus. *Right to Water: Politics, Governance, and Social Struggles*. New York: Routledge, 2012.

Tacitus. "Calgacus' Address to the Caledonians." *The Agricola and The Germania*. London: Penguin, 1970.

Tamez, Elsa. *The Amnesty of Grace: Justification by Faith from a Latin American Perspective*. Translated by Sharon H. Ringe. Nashville, TN: Abingdon, 1993.

———.*Philippians*. Wisdom Commentary. Collegeville, MN: Liturgical, 2017.

———. *The Scandalous Message of James: Faith Without Works is Dead*. New York: Crossroad, 2002.

———. *Struggles for Power in Early Christianity: A Study of 1 Timothy*. Translated by Gloria Kinsler. Maryknoll, NY: Orbis, 2007.

Tanzer, Sarah J. "Ephesians." In *Searching the Scriptures: A Feminist Commentary*. Vol. 2, edited by Elisabeth Schüssler Fiorenza, 326–48. New York: Crossroad, 1998.

Taylor, Keeanga-Yamahtta. *From #BlackLivesMatter to Black Liberation*. Chicago: Haymarket, 2016.

Taylor, Richard A. *Interpreting Apocalyptic Literature: An Exegetical Handbook*. Grand Rapids, MI: Kregel Academic, 2016.

Thurman, Howard. *Jesus and the Disinherited*. Boston: Beacon, 1976.

Thurston, Bonnie. "1 Timothy 5:13–16 and Leadership of Women in the Early Church." In *A Feminist Companion to the Deutero-Pauline Epistles*, edited by Amy-Jill Levine, 159–74. New York: Continuum, 2003.

Tiffany, Frederick C., and Sharon H. Ringe. *Biblical Interpretation: A Roadmap*. Nashville: Abingdon, 1996.

Trible, Phyllis. "Authority of the Bible." In *The New Interpreter's Study Bible*, edited by Walter Harrelson, 2248–54. Nashville, TN: Abingdon, 2003.

Turner, Nat. "The Confessions of Nat Turner, the Leader of the Late Insurrections in South Hampton, VA." In *Slave Narratives*, edited by William L. Andrews and Henry Louis Gates Jr., 241–66. New York: Library of America, 2000.

Upkong, Justin. "Luke." In *Global Bible Commentary*, edited by Daniel Patte, 385–94. Nashville: Abingdon, 2004.

———. "Parable of the Shrewd Manager (Luke 16:1–13). An Essay in Inculturation Biblical Hermeneutic." *Semeia* 73 (1996) 189–210.

Vakayil, Prema. *Women Shall Prophesy (Joel 2:28): Anna, the Prophetess (Lk. 2:36–38), A Study in Luke's Biblical Perspective*. Bangalore: Asian Trading Corporation, 2007.

Vanderkam, James. *An Introduction to Early Judaism*. Grand Rapids, MI: Eerdmans, 2000.

Walker, Alice. *In Search of Our Mothers' Gardens. Womanist Prose*. San Diego: Harcourt Brace, 1983.

Water for All Campaign. "Top 10 Reasons to Oppose Water Privatization." *Water for All Campaign to keep Water as Public Trust*. http://www.citizen.org/documents/top10-reasonstoopposewaterprivatization.pdf.

Weems, Renita. *Just a Sister Away*. West Bloomfield, MI: Warner, 2005.

———. "Reading *Her Way* through the Struggle: African American Women and the Bible." In *Stony the Road we Trod. African American Biblical Interpretation*, edited by Cain Hope Felder, 57–77. Minneapolis: Augsburg Fortress, 1991.

———. *Showing Mary: How Women Can Share Prayers, Wisdom and the Blessings of God*. New York: Warner, 2005.

Welborn, Laurence. "Paul and Pain: Paul's Emotional Therapy in 2 Corinthians 1.1–2.13; 7.5–16 in the Context of Ancient Psychagogic Literature." *New Testament Studies* 57 (2011) 547–70.

———. *Paul, the Fool of Christ: A Study of 1 Corinthians 1–4 in the Comic-Philosophic Tradition*. New York: T. & T. Clark, 2009.

———. *Paul's Summons to Messianic Life*. New York: Columbia University Press, 2015.

———. "That There May Be Equality: The Contexts and Consequences of a Pauline Ideal." *New Testament Studies* 59 (2013) 73–90.

Westphal, Merold. *Whose Community? Which Interpretation? Philosophical Hermeneutics for the Church*. Grand Rapids, MI: Baker Academic, 2009.

Williams, Demetrius K. "The Acts of the Apostles." *In True to Our Native Land. An African American Commentary of the New Testament*, edited by Brian Blount et al., 213–48. Minneapolis: Fortress, 2007.

———. *An End to This Strife: The Politics of Gender in African American Churches*. Minneapolis: Fortress, 2004.

———. "Philippians." In *Global Bible Commentary*, edited by Daniel Patte, 482–89. Nashville: Abingdon, 2004.

———. "'Upon All Flesh': Acts 2, African Americans, and Intersectional Realities." In *They Were All Together in One Place? Toward Minority Biblical Criticism*, edited by Randall C. Bailey, Tat-Siong Benny Liew and Fernando F. Segovia, 289–310. Semeia Studies 57. Atlanta: Society of Biblical Literature, 2009.

Wimbush, Vincent L. "Knowing Ex-centrics/Ex-centric Knowing." In *Mis-Reading America. Scriptures and Difference*, edited by Vincent L. Wimbush, 1–22. New York: Oxford University Press, 2013.

———, ed. *African Americans and the Bible: Sacred Texts and Social Textures*. New York: Continuum, 2003.

———, ed. *MisReading America: Scriptures and Difference*. New York: Oxford University Press, 2013.
Wingeier-Rayo, Philip. "Jesus as Migrant: A Biblical Understanding of Immigration as a Cross-Cultural Model for Ministry." *Apuntes* 35 (2015): 19–32.
Winkler, Inga T. *The Human Right to Water: Significance, Legal Status and Implications for Water Allocation*. Oxford: Hart, 2014.
Wire, Antoinette Clark. *The Corinthian Women Prophets: A Reconstruction through Paul's Rhetoric*. Minneapolis, MN: Fortress, 1990.
Witherington, Ben, III. *Letters and Homilies for Hellenized Christians: A Socio-Rhetorical Commentary on 1–2 Peter*. Downers Grove, IL: InterVarsity, 2012.
Works, Carla. "Philippians." In *Women's Bible Commentary: Revised Edition*, edited by Carol Newsom et al., 581–84. Louisville, KY: Westminster John Knox, 2012.
Wright, N. T. *The Last Word: Beyond the Bible Wars to a New Understanding of the Authority of Scripture*. New York: HarperSanFrancisco, 2005.
Yamasaki, Gary. *Insights from Filmmaking for Analyzing Biblical Narrative*. Minneapolis: Fortress, 2016.
Yang, Seung Ai. "The Word of Creative Love, Peace, and Justice." In *Engaging Biblical Authority. Perspectives on the Bible as Scripture*, edited by William P. Brown, 132–40. Louisville: Westminster/John Knox, 2007.
Yee, Tet-Lim N. *Jews, Gentiles and Ethnic Reconciliation: Paul's Jewish Identity and Ephesians*. Cambridge: Cambridge University Press, 2005.
Yeo, K. K. "1–2 Thessalonians." In *Global Bible Commentary*, edited by Daniel Patte, 500–507. Nashville: Abingdon, 2004.
———. "Pauline Theological Counseling of Love in the Language of the Zhuangzi." In *1 and 2 Corinthians: Texts @ Contexts*, edited by Yung Suk Kim, 117–28. Minneapolis: Fortress, 2013.
———, ed. *Navigating Romans through Cultures: Challenging Readings by Charting a New Course*. New York: T. & T. Clark, 2004.
Yorke, Gosnell. "Bible Translation in Africa: An Afrocentric Perspective." *BT* 51 (2000): 114–23.
———. "Bible Translation in Anglophone Africa and her Diaspora. A Postcolonialist Agenda. *BTh* 2 (2004): 153–66.
Zeitlin, Irving M. *Jews: The Making of a Diaspora People*. Malden, MA: Polity, 2012.
Zong, Jie and Jeanne Batalova, "Frequently Requested Statistics on Immigrants and Immigration in the United States." March 8, 2017. https://www.migrationpolicy.org/article/frequently-requested-statistics-immigrants-and-immigration-united-states.

www.ingramcontent.com/pod-product-compliance
Lightning Source LLC
Chambersburg PA
CBHW020606300426
44113CB00007B/525